SETTLERS

The Mythology of the White Proletariat
from Mayflower to Modern

J. Sakai

PMPRESS KERSPLEBEDEB

2014

Settlers: The Mythology of the White Proletariat from Mayflower to Modern, by J. Sakai

Originally published under the title "Mythology of the White Proletariat: A Short Course in Understanding Babylon" in 1983, this 4th edition published in 2014 contains the original text (only lightly edited to standardize spellings, punctuation, etc.) as well as two appendices, "Cash & Genocide" (originally published in *Crossroad* in April 1989) and an interview with Ernesto Aguilar conducted on June 17, 2003, and originally aired on the Latino-culture program *Sexto Sol* on KPFT radio in Houston, Texas.

copyright J. Sakai, 2014
this edition copyright Kersplebedeb
Second Printing
ISBN: 978-1-62963-037-3
Library of Congress Control Number: 2014908057

Kersplebedeb Publishing and Distribution
CP 63560
CCCP Van Horne
Montreal, Quebec
Canada H3W 3H8
www.kersplebedeb.com
www.leftwingbooks.net

PM Press
P.O. Box 23912
Oakland, CA 94623
www.pmpress.org

Layout by Kersplebedeb
Cover Design by John Yates

Printed in the USA by the Employee Owners of
Thomson-Shore in Dexter, Michigan
www.thomsonshore.com

SETTLERS

THE MYTHOLOGY OF
THE WHITE PROLETARIAT

FROM MAYFLOWER
TO MODERN

by J. Sakai

For those who made this book a reality

James Yaki Sayles
i had never had
an editor before. So it was with real "shock and awe"
that i read his first
long kite to me, with over two hundred changes
and corrections that he wanted made.

David Saxner
When i took the Greyhound to
Chicago to see the book in final form,
"DS" was still cutting up type in long
strips and pasting it down alongside the pictures
he had found.
Day after day, in those pre-computer times,
"DS" had laid out the book into physical pages for
the printer.
His prison artist side and his
dedication to the struggle
were in the first printing of this work.

To all the comrads of Kamp 7

CONTENTS

Author's Note

In the Fall 1961, i found myself with other militant Sit-In veterans in the reborn Oakland chapter of Congress of Racial Equality, picketing a major store which had refused to hire New Afrikans. Even in the Bay Area that was the custom and law back then. It had started years earlier for me in high school in L.A.'s 1950s San Fernando Valley, where as the lone uneducated leftist i had tried unsuccessfully to sell copies of the socialist labor party newspaper (the only one i could get) every week to my classmates. At the same time was working as an Asian houseboy for the family of a Jewish used car dealer (stereotypes abound for a reason). Was fired for taking a night off for my own high school graduation. The wife lost it and screamed, "People like you don't need graduations!" A month later was living in a different state to find a job and avoid the "colored" military draft. And active as the novice food drive coordinator in a long, bitter, ugly hospital workers' strike, whose main public demand was pay raises up to the federal minimum wage (we lost badly).

Have been through a thousand campaigns and movement groups since then, and can't believe i've been so dumb so often. In 1975, while mostly active doing Afrikan liberation movement support with radical exiles from various countries, i started writing a historical investigation into the puzzling class politics of euro-amerikan workers. Which i naively thought would only be a quick movement paper. Eight years later what became re-titled as *Settlers* was finished. Even then i didn't believe there was any audience for it, and planned to only photocopy fifty copies of my typed draft for internal education in the underground black liberation army coordinating committee. Comrades with more sense than myself insisted that we publish it as a book if only for the liberation movement. Over the years, we took it through three editions, but finally it's time to hand it on to new publishers. Remember only, i wrote this with my life.

J. Sakai, 2014

The minority puts a dogmatic view in place of the critical, and an idealist one in place of the materialist. They regard mere discontent, instead of real conditions, as the driving wheel of revolution. Whereas we tell the workers: You have to go through 15, 20, 50 years of civil wars and national struggles, not only in order to change conditions but also to change yourselves and make yourselves capable of political rule; you, on the contrary, say: "We must come to power immediately, or else we may as well go to sleep." Whilst we make a special point of directing the German workers' attention to the undeveloped state of the German proletariat, you flatter the national feeling and the status-prejudice of the German artisans in the crudest possible way—which, admittedly, is more popular. Just as the word "people" has been made holy by the democrats, so the word "proletariat" has been made holy by you.

Karl Marx, on the 1850 split in the German Communist League

INTRODUCTION

One day a friend introduced me to a young New Afrikan brother who was selling things on the sidewalk outside a large office building. When our talk turned to this book, the young brother looked up proudly and said: "I already know *everything* about the White Man, and he knows *nothing* about me." As we were talking away I couldn't help thinking how many people had the same thought. Because they know that the white man is completely racist and treacherous, they wrongly assume that they know all about his society. This is really the point that this book begins from.

In, fact, the 1960s breakthrough of "ethnic studies programs" at universities has been dialectically turned around and used against us. We are getting imperialist-sponsored and imperialist-financed "Asian studies," "Black studies," "Puerto Rican studies," "Indian studies," "ethnic studies" pushed back down our throats. Some of the most prominent Third World intellectuals in the U.S. Empire are getting paid good salaries by the imperialists to teach us our histories. Why?

U.S. imperialism would rather that all Third World people in their Empire remain totally blank and ignorant about themselves, their nations, their cultures, their pasts, about each other, about everything except going to work in the morning. *But that day is over.*

So instead they oppose enlightenment by giving in to it in form, but not in essence. Like ju-jitsu, our original demand that our separate and unique histories be uncovered and recognized is now being used to throw us off our ideological balance. The imperialists promote watered-down and distorted versions of our pasts as oppressed Third World nations and peoples.

3

The imperialists even concede that their standard "U.S. history" is a white history, and is supposedly *incomplete* unless the long-suppressed Third World histories are *added* to it. Why?

The key to the puzzle is that Theirstory (imperialist Euro-Amerikan mis-history) is not incomplete; it isn't true at all. Theirstory also includes the standard class analysis of Amerika that is put forward into our hands by the Euro-Amerikan Left. Theirstory keeps saying, over and over: *"You folks, just think about your own history; don't bother analyzing white society, just accept what we tell you about it."*

In other words, it's as if British liberals and "socialists" had told Afrikan anti-colonial revolutionaries in Ghana or Kenya to just study their own "traditions"—but not to study the British Empire. Theirstory is not incomplete at all. It's a series of complete lies, an ideological worldview cleverly designed to further imperialist domination of the oppressed.

This work throws the light of historical materialism on Babylon itself. For so long the oppressed have been the objects of investigation by Euro-imperialist sociology, anthropology, psychology, etc.—all to further pacifying and controlling us (anthropology, for example, had its origins as an intelligence service for European colonialization of the world). Now it is time to scientifically examine the oppressor society.

The final point we must make is that this document—while it deals with *aspects* of our history within the U.S. Empire—is nothing like a history of Asians here. Nor is it a history of Indian nations, the Afrikan Nation, Aztlán, or other Third World nations or peoples. While we discuss Third World struggles and movements, this is not a critical examination of these political developments. This is a reconnaissance into enemy territory.

I

THE HEART OF WHITENESS

1. The Land is the Basis of Nationhood

The key to understanding Amerika is to see that it was a chain of European settler colonies that expanded into a settler empire. To go back and understand the lives and consciousness of the early English settlers is to see the embryo of today's Amerikan Empire. This is the larger picture that allows us to finally relate the class conflicts of settler Euro-Amerikans to the world struggle.

The mythology of the white masses holds that those early settlers were the poor of England, convicts and workers, who came to North Amerika in search of "freedom" or "a better way of life." Factually, that's all nonsense. The celebrated Pilgrims of Plymouth Rock, for example, didn't even come from England (although they were English). They had years before emigrated as a religious colony to Holland, where they had lived in peace for over a decade. But in Holland these predominately middle class people had to work as hired labor for others. This was too hard for them, so they came to North Amerika in search of less work and more money. At first, according to the rules of their faith, they farmed the land in common and shared equally. Soon their greed led them into fighting with each other, slacking off at assigned tasks, etc., until the colony's leaders had to give in to the settlers' desires and divide up the stolen land (giving "to every family a parcel of land").[1]

This is typical of the English invasion forces. A study of roughly 10,000 settlers who left Bristol from 1654–85 shows that **less than 15% were proletarian**. Most were youth from the lower-middle classes; Gentlemen & Professionals 1%; Yeomen & Husbandmen 48%; Artisans & Tradesmen 29%.[2] The typical age was 22–24 years. In other words, the sons and daughters of the middle class, with experience at agriculture and craft skills, were the ones who thought they had a practical chance in Amerika.

What made North Amerika so desirable to these people? Land. Euro-Amerikan liberals and radicals have rarely dealt with the Land question; we could say that they don't have to deal with it, since their people already have all the land. What lured Europeans to leave their homes and cross the Atlantic was the chance to share in conquering Indian land. At that time there was a crisis in England over land ownership and tenancy due to the rise of capitalism. One scholar of the early invasion comments on this:

> "Land hunger was rife among all classes. Wealthy clothiers, drapers, and merchants who had done well and wished to set themselves up in land were avidly watching the market, ready to pay almost any price for what was offered. Even prosperous yeomen often could not get the land they desired for their younger sons ... It is commonplace to say that land was the greatest inducement the New World had to offer; but it is difficult to overestimate its psychological importance to people in whose minds land had always been identified with security, success and the good things of life."[3]

It was these "younger sons," despairing of owning land in their own country, who were willing to gamble on the colonies. The brutal Enclosure Acts and the ending of many hereditary tenancies acted as a further push in the same direction. These were the principal reasons given on the Emigration Lists of 1773–76 for settling in Amerika.[4] So that participating in the settler invasion of North Amerika was a relatively easy way out of the desperate class struggle in England for those seeking a privileged life.*

Then, too, many English farmers and artisans couldn't face the prospect of being forced down into the position of wage labor. Traditionally, hired laborers were considered so low in English society that they ranked far below mere failures, and were considered degraded outcasts. Many English (including the "Levellers," the anti-capitalist revolutionary outbreak of the 17th century) thought wage laborers should lose their civil rights and English citizenship. Public opinion was so strong on this that the early English textile factories were filled with Irish and Welsh immigrants, children from the poorhouses and single women. So jumping the ocean in search of land was not some mundane career decision of comparing dollars and cents to these Englishmen—it was a desperate venture for continued status and self-respect.[5]

The various colonies competed with each other in offering inducements to new settlers. In the South the "headright" system gave each new settler 50 acres for transporting themselves from England. Eventually Pennsylvania and the Carolinas offered even more land per settler as a lure. And land was "dirt cheap" for Europeans.

---

* It is hard for us to imagine how chaotic and difficult English life was in that transitional period. The coming of capitalism had smashed all the traditional securities and values of feudal England, and financed its beginnings with the most savage reduction of the general living standard. During the course of the sixteenth century wages in the building trades went down by over half, while the price of firewood, wheat, and other necessities soared by five times. By encouraging this outflow the British ruling class both furthered their Empire and eased opposition at home to their increasing concentration of wealth and power. And the new settlers, lusting for individual land and property, were willing to endure hardships and uncertainties for this prized goal. They were even more willing to kill for it.

In Virginia ten shillings bought a tract of one hundred acres; in Pennsylvania the best land sold per acre at what a carpenter would earn in a day. When new communities of invaders were started on the edges of conquered areas, the settlers simply divided up the land. For example, when Wallington, Conn. was founded in 1670 each settler family got between 238–476 acres. This amount was not unusual, since colonial Amerika was an orgy of land-grabbing. In fact, much of the land at first wasn't even purchased or rented—it was simply taken over and settled. As much as two-thirds of the tilled land in Pennsylvania during the 1700s was occupied by white squatters, protected by settler solidarity.[6]

So central was the possession of land in the personal plans of the English settlers that throughout the colonial period there was a shortage of skilled labor. Richard Morris's study of labor in colonial Amerika concluded: *"In the main, the ultimate economic objective of colonial workmen was security through agriculture rather than industry ... As soon as a workman had accumulated a small amount of money he could, and in many cases did, take up a tract of land and settle on it as a farmer."*[7]

Where land was not available, settlers refused to come. Period. This is why the British West Indies, with their favorable climate, were less attractive to these settlers than wintry New England. As early as 1665 a member of the Barbados Assembly complained, noting that the limited space of that island had already been divided up: "Now we can get few English servants, having no lands to give them at the end of their time, which formerly was their main allurement." And British servants, their terms up, would leave the Indies by the thousands for Amerika.[8]

It was this alone that drew so many Europeans to colonial North Amerika: the dream in the settler mind of each man becoming a petty lord of his own land. Thus, the tradition of individualism and egalitarianism in Amerika was rooted in the poisoned concept of equal privileges for a new nation of European conquerors.

2. The Foundations of Settler Life

The life of European settlers—and the class structure of their society—was abnormal because it was dependent upon a foundation of conquest, genocide, and enslavement. The myth of the self-sufficient, white settler family "clearing the wilderness" and supporting themselves through their own initiative and hard labor, is a propaganda fabrication. **It is the absolute characteristic of settler society to be parasitic**, dependent upon the super-exploitation of oppressed peoples for its style of life. Never has Euro-Amerikan society completely supported itself. This is the decisive factor in the consciousness of all classes and strata of white society from 1600 to now.

Settler society was raised up, above the level of backward Old Europe, by a foundation of conquest. This conquest was a miracle drug for a Europe convulsed with the reaction of decaying feudalism and deadly capitalism. Shot into the veins of the Spanish feudal nation, for instance, the miracle drug of "New World" conquest gave Spain the momentary power to overrun North Africa, Holland, and Italy before her historical instant waned. For the English settlers, this conquest made real the bourgeois vision of building a whole new European society. Like many such "fixes," for Euro-Amerikans this conquest was addicting; it was habit-forming and rapidly indispensable, not only culturally, but in the mechanism of an oppressor society whose lifeblood was new conquest. We will examine this later, in the relationship of settlerism to imperialism. For now, it is enough to see that this conquest is a material fact of great magnitude, an economic and social event as important as the emergence of the factory system or the exploitation of petroleum in the Middle East.

We stress the obvious here, because the Euro-Amerikan settlers have always made light of their invasion and occupation (although the conquered territory is the precondition for their whole society). Traditionally, European settler societies throw off the propaganda smokescreen that they didn't really conquer and dispossess other nations—they claim with false modesty that they merely moved into vacant territory! So the early English settlers depicted Amerika as empty—"a howling wilderness," "unsettled," "sparsely populated"—just waiting with a "VACANT" sign on the door for the first lucky civilization to walk in and claim it. Theodore Roosevelt wrote defensively in 1900: "...the settler and pioneer have at bottom had justice on their side; this great continent could not have been kept as nothing but a game preserve for squalid savages."[9]

It is telling that this lie is precisely the same lie put forward by the white "Afrikaner" settlers, who claim that South Africa was literally totally uninhabited by any Afrikans when they arrived from Europe. To universal derision, these European settlers claim to be the *only* rightful, historic inhabitants of South Afrika. Or we can hear similar defenses put forward by the European settlers of Israel, who claim that much of the Palestinian land and buildings they occupy are rightfully theirs, since the Arabs allegedly decided to voluntarily abandon it all during the 1948–49 war. Are these kind of tales any less preposterous when put forward by Euro-Amerikan settlers?

Amerika was "spacious" and "sparsely populated" only because the European invaders destroyed whole civilizations and killed off millions of Native Amerikans to get the land and profits they wanted. We all know that when the English arrived in Virginia, for example, they encountered an urban, village-dwelling society far more skilled than they in the arts of medicine, agriculture, fishing—and government.*[10] This civilization was reflected in a chain of three hundred Indian nations and peoples stretched from the Arctic Circle to the tip of South America, many of whom had highly developed societies. There was, in fact, a greater population in these Indian nations in 1492 than in all of Western Europe. Recent scholarly estimates indicate that at the time of Columbus there were 100 million Indians in the Hemisphere: ten million in North America, twenty-five million in Central Mexico, with an additional sixty-five million elsewhere in Central and Southern America.[11]

These numbers have long been concealed, since they give rise to the logical question of what happened to this great mass of people. The European invaders—Spanish, Dutch, English, Portuguese, and

---

* The first government of the new USA, that of the Articles of Confederation, was totally unlike any in autocratic Europe, and had been influenced by the government of the Six-Nation Iroquois Confederation.

French—simply killed off millions and millions to safeguard their conquest of the land and provide the disposable slave labor they needed to launch their "New World." Conservative Western historical estimates show that the Spanish "reduced" the Indian population of their colonies from some 50 million to only 4 million by the end of the 17th century.[12]

And from the 10 million Indians that once inhabited North Amerika, after four centuries of settler invasion and rule there were in 1900 perhaps 200,000–300,000 surviving descendants in the USA.[13] That was the very substantial down-payment towards the continuing blood price that Third World nations have to pay to sustain the Euro-Amerikan way of life.

So when we hear that the settlers "pushed out the Indians" or "forced the Indians to leave their traditional hunting grounds," we know that these are just code-phrases to refer politely to the most barbaric genocide imaginable. It could well be the greatest crime in all of human history. Only here the Adolf Eichmanns and Heinrich Himmlers had names like Benjamin Franklin and Andrew Jackson.

The point is that genocide was not an accident, not an "excess," not the unintended side-effect of virile European growth. **Genocide was the necessary and deliberate act of the capitalists and their settler shock-troops.** The "Final Solution" to the "Indian Problem" was so widely expected by whites that it was openly spoken of as

MASSACRE OF THE ST. FRANCIS INDIANS.

a commonplace thing. At the turn of the century a newspaper as "respectable" as the *New York Times* could editorially threaten that those peoples who opposed the new world capitalist order would "be extinguished like the North American Indian."[14] Only a relative handful of Indians survived the time of the great extermination campaigns. You see, the land wasn't "empty" after all—and for Amerika to exist the settlers had to deliberately *make* the land "empty."

The second aspect of Colonial Amerika's foundation was, of course, slavery. It is hardly necessary to repeat here the well-known history of that exploitation. What is necessary is to underline how universally European capitalist life was dependent upon slavery, and how **this exploitation dictated the very structure of Euro-Amerikan society.**

The mythology of the white masses pretends that while the evil planter and the London merchant grew fat on the profits of the slave labor, the "poor white" of the South, the Northern small farmer, and white worker were all uninvolved in slavery and benefited not at all from it. The mythology suggests that slavery even *lowered* the living standard of the white masses by supposedly holding down wages and monopolizing vast tracts of farmland. Thus, it is alleged, slavery was not in the interests of the white masses.*

Yet Karl Marx observed: "Cause slavery to disappear and you will have wiped America off the map of nations."[15] Marx was writing during the zenith of the cotton economy of the mid-1800s, but this most basic fact is true from the bare beginnings of European settlement in Amerika. Without slave labor there would have been no Amerika. It is as simple as that. Long before the cotton economy of the South flourished, for example, Afrikan slaves literally built the City of New York. Their work alone enabled the original Dutch settlers to be fed and sheltered while pursuing their drinking, gambling, fur-trading, and other non-laboring activities. Afrikans were not only much of early New York's farmers, carpenters, and blacksmiths, but also comprised much of the City's guards.

---

* Similar arguments relative to today are advanced by the "Don't-Divide-The-Working-Class" revisionists, who want to convince us that the Euro-Amerikan masses are "victims of imperialism" just like us.

The Dutch settlers were so dependent on Afrikan labor for the basics of life that their Governor finally had to grant some Afrikan slaves both freedom and land in return for their continued food production. The Afrikan-owned land on Manhattan included what is now known as Greenwich Village, Astor Place, and Herald Square. Later, the English settlers would pass laws against Afrikan land ownership, and take these tracts from the free Afrikans. Manhattan was thus twice stolen from oppressed peoples.[16]

Indian slavery was also important in supporting the settler invasion beachhead on the "New World." From New England (where the pious Pilgrims called them "servants") to South Carolina, the forced labor of Indian slaves was essential to the very survival of the young

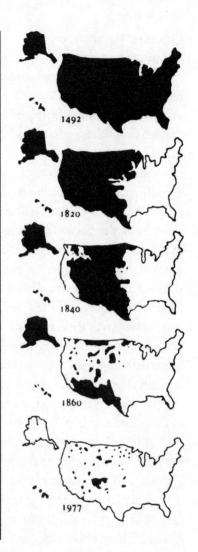

INDIAN LANDS WITHIN UNITED STATES

IN 1492, 541 INDIAN NATIONS—APPROXIMATELY 10 MILLION PEOPLE— LIVED IN WHAT IS NOW THE UNITED STATES. THE U.S. GOVERNMENT RATIFIED 371 TREATIES WITH THESE INDIAN NATIONS BETWEEN 1776 AND 1871. CHIEF RED CLOUD OF THE LAKOTA SAID: "THEY MADE MANY PROMISES TO US, BUT THEY ONLY KEPT ONE: THEY PROMISED TO TAKE OUR LAND, AND THEY TOOK IT." THE MODERN AMERICAN INDIAN MOVEMENT HAS SOUGHT TO RESTORE THE INDIAN LAND BASE BY DEMANDING THAT THE UNITED STATES HONOR ITS TREATY OBLIGATIONS WITH THE INDIAN NATIONS.

Colonies. In fact, the profits from the Indian slave trade were the economic mainstay of the settler invasion of the Carolinas. In 1708 the English settlements in the Carolinas had a population of 1,400 Indian slaves and 2,900 Afrikan slaves to 5,300 Europeans. Indian slaves were common throughout the Colonies—in 1730 the settlers of Kingston, Rhode Island had 223 Indian slaves (as well as 333 Afrikan slaves). As late as 1740 we know that some 14,000 Indian slaves labored in the plantations of South Carolina.[17]

The recorded number of Indian slaves within Colonial English settlements was only a small indication of the larger picture, since most Indian slaves were sold to Jamaica, Barbados, and other West Indian colonies. One reason for the depopulation of the once numerous Indian peoples of the Southern Colonies was the unrestrained ravages of the slave trade. In the first five decades of the English settlement of the Carolinas, it appears that the **main cash export item was Indian slaves.** Armed expeditions, made up largely of Indian puppet soldiers already addicted to rum and other capitalist consumer goods, scoured the countryside for Indians to capture and sell. The total sold away is unknown, but large. We do know that in just six years after 1704, some 12,000 Indian slaves were sold out of Charleston to the West Indies.[18]

Additional uncounted thousands of Indian slaves were exported from the other settlements of the Middle and New England Colonies. Indian slaves in large numbers were very difficult to deal with, since the settlers were trying to hold them on terrain that was more theirs than the invaders. Usually, the minimum precaution would be to in effect swap Indian slaves around, with New England using slaves from Southern Colonies—and vice-versa. In most cases the slave catchers killed almost all the adult Indian men as too dangerous to keep around, only saving the women and children for sale.[19]

But by 1715 the "divers conspiracies, insurrections…" of rebellious Indian slaves had reached the point where all the New England Colonies barred any further imports of Indian slaves.[20] The Pilgrims of New England had seen that the most profitable and safe use of their Indian slaves was to sell them abroad. Indeed, the wife and nine-year-old son of "King Philip," the great leader of the 1675

Indian uprising, were sold into West Indian captivity (as was even then customary with many captured Indians).

Thus, the early settlers were not just the passive beneficiaries of a far off Afrikan slave trade—they bankrolled their settlements in part with the profits of their own eager explorations into Native slave trading. The point is that White Amerika has never been self-sufficient, has never completely supported itself. Indian slavery died out, and was gradually lost in the great river of Afrikan slavery, only because the settlers finally decided to exterminate the heavily de-populated Indian nations altogether.

The essence is not the individual ownership of slaves, but rather the fact that world capitalism in general and Euro-Amerikan capitalism in specific had forged a slave-based economy in which all settlers gained and took part. Historian Samuel Eliot Morison, in his study of *The European Discovery of America*, notes that after repeated failures the Europeans learned that North Amerikan settler colonies were not self-sufficient; to survive they needed large capital infusions and the benefits of sustained trade with Father Europe.[21] But why should the British aristocracy and capitalists invest in small family farms—and how great a trade is possible when what the set-tlers themselves produced was largely the very raw materials and foodstuffs they themselves needed? Slavery throughout the "New World" answered these questions. It was the unpaid, expropriated la-bor of millions of Indian and Afrikan captive slaves that created the surpluses on which the settler economy floated and Atlantic trade flourished.

So all sections of white settler society—even the artisan, work-er, and farmer—were totally dependent upon Afrikan slave labor: the fisherman whose low-grade, "refuse fish" was dried and sold as slave meal in the Indies; the New York farmer who found his market for surpluses in the Southern plantations; the forester whose timber was used by shipyard workers rapidly turning out slave ships; the clerk in the New York City export house checking bales of tobacco awaiting shipment to London; the master cooper in the Boston rum distillery; the young Virginia overseer building up his "stake" to try and start his own plantation; the immigrant German farmer renting a team of five slaves to get his farm started; and on and on. While the cream of the profits went to the planter and merchant capitalists, the entire settler economy was raised up on a foundation of slave labor, slave products, and the slave trade.

Nor was it just slavery within the Thirteen Colonies alone that was essential. The commerce and industry of these Euro-Amerikan settlers was interdependent with their fellow slave-owning capitalists of the West Indies, Central and Southern America. Massachusetts alone, in 1774, distilled 2.7 million gallons of rum—distilled from the molasses of the West Indies slave plantations.[22] Two of the largest industries in Amerika were shipbuilding and shipping, both creatures of the slave trade. Commerce with the slave colonies of not only England, but also Holland, Spain, and France, was vital to the young Amerikan economy. Eric Williams, Walter Rodney, and others have shown how European capitalism as a whole literally capitalized itself for industrialization and World Empire out of Afrikan slavery. It is important to see that all classes of Euro-Amerikan settlers were equally involved in building a new bourgeois nation on the back of the Afrikan colonial proletariat.

By the time of the settler War of Independence, the Afrikan nation made up over 20% of the non-Indian population—one Afrikan colonial subject for every four settlers. Afrikan slaves, although heavily concentrated in the plantation colonies, were still represented throughout the settler territories. Their proportion in the non-Indian population ranged from 2–3% in upper New England to 8% in Rhode Island, to 14% in New York, and to 41% and 60% respectively in Virginia and South Carolina.[23] While they mainly labored as the agricultural proletariat, Afrikan labor played a crucial role in all the major trades and industries of the times. The colonized Afrikan nation, much more than the new Euro-Amerikan settler nation, was a complete nation—that is, possessing among its people a complete range of applied sciences, practical crafts, and productive labor. Both that colonized nation and the Indian nations were self-sufficient and economically whole, while the Euro-Amerikan invasion society was parasitic. While the class structure of the new Afrikan nation was still in a formative stage, distinct classes were visible within it well before the U.S. War of Independence.

In Virginia, it appears that an overwhelming majority of the skilled workers—carpenters, ship pilots, coopers, blacksmiths, etc.—were Afrikans. Nor was it just nonmarket production for direct use on the plantation; Afrikan artisans produced for the commercial market, and were often hired out by their masters. For example, we know that George Washington was not only a planter but also what would today be called a contractor—building structures for other planters with his gang of Afrikan slave carpenters (the profits were split between "The Father of Our Country" and his slave overseer).[24] The Afrikan presence in commerce and industry was widespread and all-pervasive, as one labor historian has summarized:

> "Some of the Africans who were brought to America in chains
> were skilled in woodcarving, weaving, construction, and
> other crafts. In the South, Black slaves were not only field
> hands; many developed a variety of skills that were needed
> on a nearly self-sufficient plantation. Because skilled labor of
> whatever color was in great demand, slaves were often hired
> out to masters who owned shops by the day, month, or year
> for a stipulated amount. Some were hired out to shipmasters,
> serving as pilots and managers of ferries. Others were used in
> the maritime trades as shipcaulkers, longshoremen, and sail-
> makers. A large number of slaves were employed in Northern
> cities as house servants, sailors, sailmakers, and carpenters.
> New York had a higher proportion of skilled slaves than any
> other Colony—coopers, tailors, bakers, tanners, goldsmiths,
> cabinetmakers, shoemakers, and glaziers. Both in Charleston
> and in the Northern cities, many artisans utilized slave labor
> extensively."[25]

Afrikans were the landless, propertyless, permanent workers of the U.S. Empire. They were not just slaves—the Afrikan nation as a whole served as a proletariat for the Euro-Amerikan oppressor nation. This Afrikan colony supported on its shoulders the building of a Euro-Amerikan society more "prosperous," more "egalitarian," and yes, more "democratic" than any in semi-feudal Old Europe. The Jeffersonian vision of Amerika as a pastoral European democracy was rooted in the national life of small, independent white land-owners. Such a society had no place for a proletariat within its ranks—yet, in the age of capitalism, could not do without the labor of such a class. Amerika imported a proletariat from Afrika, a pro-letariat permanently chained in an internal colony, laboring for the benefit of all settlers. Afrikan workers might be individually owned, like tools and draft animals, by some settlers and not others, but in their colonial subjugation they were as a whole owned by the entire Euro-Amerikan nation.

3. Euro-Amerikan Social Structure

When we point out that Amerika was the most completely bourgeois nation in world history, we mean a four-fold reality: (1) Amerika had no feudal or communal past, but was constructed from the ground up according to the nightmare vision of the bourgeoisie. (2) Amerika began its national life as an oppressor nation, as a colonizer of op-pressed peoples. (3) Amerika not only has a capitalist ruling class, but all classes and strata of Euro-Amerikans are bourgeoisified, with a preoccupation for petty privileges and property ownership the normal guiding star of the white masses. (4) Amerika is so decadent that it has no proletariat of its own, but must exist parasitically on the colonial proletariat of oppressed nations and national minorities. Truly, a Babylon "whose life was death."

The settler masses of Colonial Amerika had a situation totally unlike their cousins back in Old Europe. For the privileges of con-quest produced a nonproletarian society of settlers. The large major-ity of settlers were of the property-owning middle classes (insofar as classes had yet become visible in the new society): tradesmen, self-employed artisans, and land-owning farmers. Every European who wanted to could own land. Every white settler could be a property owner. No wonder immigration to the "New World" (newly con-quered, newly enslaved) was so popular in Old Europe. No wonder life in Amerika was spoken of almost as a fable by the masses of Old Europe. Young Amerika was capitalism's real-life Disneyland.

The Euro-Amerikan class structure at the time of the 1775 War of Independence was revealing:

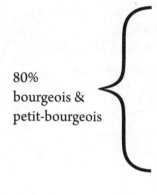

80%
bourgeois &
petit-bourgeois

10% Capitalists: Great Planters, large merchants, etc.

20% Large farmers, professionals, tradesmen & other upper-middle elements

40% Small land-owning farmers

10% Artisans: blacksmiths, coopers, carpenters, shipwrights, etc.

15% Temporary workers, usually soon moving upwards into the ranks of the small farmers

5% Laborers[26]

Not only was the bourgeois class itself quite large, but some **70% of the total population of settlers were in the various propertied middle classes.** The overwhelming majority were landowners, including many of the artisans and tradesmen, and an even larger portion of the Euro-Amerikans were self-employed or preparing to be. The small "poor" element of lumpen and permanent laborers was only 5% of the settler population, and without influence or cohesion in such a propertied society. We can see why Virginia's Gov. Fauquier complained in 1759, while bemoaning his inability to attract settler recruits for the militia: *"Every man in this colony has land, and none but Negroes are laborers."* (U.S. imperialism still has this same problem of white military recruitment today.)[27]

The plantation areas, which were obviously the most dominated by a small elite owning a disproportionate share of the wealth, showed no lesser degree of general settler privilege and unification. South Carolina was the State with the highest degree of large plantation centralization; yet there, too, no settler working class development was evident. The South Carolina settler class structure shows only an intensification of the same bourgeois features evident at the national level:

86%
bourgeois &
petit-bourgeois

3% Great Planter elite
      (above 1,000 acres landholding)
15% Planters (500–999 acres)
8% Merchants & shop owners
5% Professionals
42% Middle & small farmers
      (under 500 acres)
10% Artisans

14% Laborers
      (majority only temporary)

When we speak of the small, land-owning farmer as the largest single element in settler society, it is important to see what this means. An example is Rebecca Royston of Calvert County, Maryland, who died in 1740 with an estate worth £81 (which places her well in the middle of the small-medium farmers). That sum represented the value of 200 acres of farmland, 31 head of cattle, 15 of sheep, 29 pigs, 1,463 lbs. of tobacco stored for market, 5 feather beds, 2 old guns, assorted furniture, tools and kitchen utensils, and the contract of an 8-year-old indentured child servant. No wealth, no luxury, but a life with some small property, food, shelter, and a cash crop for market.[28] Certainly a far reach upwards from the bitter, bare existence of the colonial Afrikan proletariat (or, for that matter, the British or French proletariat of the period).

Although there were Euro-Amerikan craftsmen and workers they never coalesced into a proletariat because they were too privileged and transitory in condition. It is important to grasp firmly that the mere presence of settler craftsmen and workers doesn't automatically mean that they were a conscious class. With their extra-proletarian living standard and their future in the propertied middle classes, most settler workmen had no reason to develop a proletarian consciousness. Further, the rapid turnover of settlers in these strata left no material basis for the formation of a class.

We can see this more clearly when we examine the details of work and wages. Rather than the mass-production factory, the Colonial-era workshop was a setting for the highly-skilled, piece-by-piece, hand production of a few craftsmen. Even a shipyard customarily only employed five to ten artisans and workers of all types, total. The workshop was a business owned and managed by the Master artisan, who might employ in his workshop one or two journeymen artisans and several apprentices, servants or slaves.[29] It is easy to grasp how, in small settler communities, social and class lines were blurred and still unformed. For example, most of the settler artisans were also small farmers who grew some or all of their own food.

While some artisans never advanced, others were already becoming small capitalists, since the historic extension of the craft workshop was capitalist manufacture. The most famous Colonial-era settler artisan, Paul Revere, was not only a silversmith and an artist-engraver, but also a dentist and the small capitalist operator of a copper foundry. In the Colonial era the majority of Euro-Amerikan artisans and wage laborers eventually bought farmland and/or business property and rose into the middle strata.

The special and non-proletarian character of settler artisans and workers (which has been so conveniently forgotten about by today's Euro-Amerikan radicals) was well-known a century ago by Europeans such as Marx and Engels. In 1859 Marx wrote of "... *the United States of North America, where, though classes already exist, they have not yet become fixed, but continually change and interchange their elements in constant flux...* "[30] What Marx saw in this class fluidity was the ultimate privilege of settler society—the privilege of having no proletariat at all. He later pointed out: "*Hence the relatively high standard of wages in the United States. Capital may there try its utmost. It cannot prevent the labor market from being continuously emptied by the continuous conversion of wages laborers into independent, self-sustaining peasants. The position of wages laborer is for a very large part of the American people but a probational state, which they are sure to leave within a shorter or longer term.*"[31] And Marx was writing not about a momentary or temporary phase, but about basic conditions that were true for well over two centuries in Amerika.

Those settlers never had it so good! And those Europeans who chose or were forced to work for wages got the highest wages in the capitalist world. The very highest. Tom Paine, the revolutionary propagandist, boasted that in Amerika a "common laborer" made as much money as an English shopkeeper![32] We know that George Washington had to pay his white journeyman carpenter £40 per year, plus 400 lbs. of meat, 20 bushels of corn, and the use of a house and vegetable garden. Journeymen tailors in Virginia earned £26–32 per year, plus meals, lodging, laundry service, and drink.[33]

In general, it's commonly agreed that Euro-Amerikan workers earned at least *twice* what their British kinfolk made—some reports say the earnings gap was *five or six times* what Swedish or Danish workers earned.[34] Even a whole century later, the difference was still so large that Marx commented:

> *"Now, all of you know that the average wages of the American agricultural laborer amount to more than double that of the English agricultural laborer, although the prices of agricultural produce are lower in the United States than in the United Kingdom..."*[35]

It was only possible for settler society to afford this best-paid, most bourgeoisified white workforce because they had also obtained the least-paid, most proletarian Afrikan colony to support it.

Many of those settler laborers were indentured servants, who had signed on to do some years of unpaid labor (usually four) for a master in return for passage across the Atlantic. It is thought that as many as half of all the pre-1776 Europeans in Amerika went through this temporarily unfree status. Some settler historians dwell on this phenomenon, comparing it to Afrikan slavery in an attempt to obscure the rock of national oppression at the base of Amerika. Harsh as the time of indenture might be, these settlers would be free—and Afrikan slaves would not. More to the national difference between oppressor and oppressed, white indentured servants could look hopefully toward the possibility of not only being free, but of themselves becoming landowners and slavemasters.

For this initiation, this "dues" to join the oppressor nation, was a rite of passage into settler citizenship. For example, as early as 1629 almost one member out of six of Virginia's House of Burgesses was a former indentured servant. Much of Pennsylvania's prosperous German farming community originally emigrated that way.[36] Christopher Hill, the British Marxist historian, directly relates the European willingness to enter servitude to the desire for land ownership, describing it as "a temporary phase through which one worked one's way to freedom and land-ownership."[37]

This is important because it was only this bottom layer of settler society that had the potential of proletarian class consciousness. In the early decades of Virginia's tobacco industry, gangs of white indentured servants worked the fields side-by-side with Afrikan and Indian slaves, whom in the 1600s they greatly outnumbered. This was an unstable situation, and one of the results was a number of joint servant-slave escapes, strikes, and conspiracies. A danger to the planter elite was evident, particularly since white servants constituted a respectable proportion of the settler population in the two tobacco colonies—accounting for 16% in Virginia in 1681 and 10% in Maryland in 1707.[38]

The political crisis waned as the period of bound white plantation labor ended. First, the greater and more profitable river of Afrikan labor was tapped to the fullest, and then the flow of British indentured servants slacked off. The number of new European servants entering Virginia fell from 1,500–2,000 annually in the 1670s to but 91 in 1715.[39] However, the important change was not in numbers but in social role.

Historian Richard Morris, in his study of Colonial-era labor, says of European indentured servants on the plantations: "...but with the advent of Negro slavery they were gradually supplanted as field workers and were principally retained as overseers, foremen or herdsmen."[40] In other words, even the very lowest layer of white society was lifted out of the proletariat by the privileges of belonging to the oppressor nation.

Once these poor whites were raised off the fields and given the chance to help boss and police captive Afrikans, their rebellious days were over. The importance of this experience is that it shows the material basis for the lack of class consciousness by early Euro-Amerikan workers, and how their political consciousness was direct-ly related to how much they shared in the privileges of the larger set-tler society. Further, the capitalists proved to their satisfaction that dissent and rebelliousness within the settler ranks could be quelled by *increasing* the colonial exploitation of other nations and peoples.

II

STRUGGLES & ALLIANCES

The popular political struggles of settler Amerika—the most important being the 1775–83 War of Independence—gave us the first experience of alliances between Euro-Amerikan dissenters and oppressed peoples. What was most basic in these alliances was their purely tactical nature. Not unity, but the momentary convergence of the fundamentally differing interests of some oppressors and some of the oppressed. After all, the national division between settler citizens of emerging Amerika and their colonial Afrikan subjects was enormous—while the distance between the interests of Indian nations and that of the settler nation built on their destruction was hardly any less. While tactical alliances would bridge this chasm, it is important to recognize how calculated and temporary these joint efforts were.

We emphasize this because it is necessary to refute the settler propaganda that Colonial Amerika was built out of a history of struggles "for representative government," "democratic struggles" or "class struggles," in which common whites and Afrikans joined together. No one, we note, has yet summoned up the audacity to maintain that the Indians too wished to fight and die for settler "democracy." Yet that same claim is advanced for Afrikan prisoners (slaves), as though they either had more common interests with their slavemasters, or were more brainwashed. To examine the actual conflicts and conditions under which alliances were reached totally rips apart these lies.

A clear case is Bacon's Rebellion, one of the two major settler uprisings prior to the War of Independence. In this rebellion an insurgent army literally seized state power in the Virginia Colony in 1676. They defeated the loyalist forces of the Crown, set the capital city on fire, and forced the Governor to flee. Euro-Amerikans of all classes as well as Afrikan slaves took part in the fighting, the latter making up much of the hard core of the rebellion's forces at the war's end.

Herbert Aptheker, the Communist Party USA's expert on Afrikans, has no hesitation in pointing to this rebellion as a wonderful, heroic example for all of us. He clearly loves this case of an early, anti-capitalist uprising where "whites and Blacks" joined hands:

> "...But, the outstanding example of popular uprising, prior
> to the American Revolution itself, is Bacon's Rebellion
> of 1676 ... a harbinger of the greater rebellion that was to
> follow it by exactly a century. The Virginia uprising was
> directed against the economic subordination and exploita-
> tion of the colony by the English rulers, and against the
> tyrannical and corrupt administrative practices in the
> colony which were instituted for the purpose of enforcing
> that subordination. Hence, the effort, led by the young
> planter, Nathaniel Bacon, was multi-class, encompassing
> in its ranks slaves, indentured servants, free farmers and
> many planters; it was one in which women were, as an
> anti-Baconite contemporary noted, 'great encouragers and
> assisters' and it was one in which demands for political
> reform along democratic lines formed a central feature of
> the movement."[1]

It makes you wonder how a planter came to be leading such an advanced political movement? Aptheker is not the only Euro-Amerikan radical to point out the important example in this uprising. To use one other case: In 1974 a paper dealing with this was presented at a New Haven meeting of the "New Left" Union of Radical Political Economists (URPE). It was considered important enough to be published in the Cambridge journal *Radical America*, and then to be reprinted as a pamphlet by the New England Free Press. In this paper Theodore W. Allen says of early Virginia politics:

> "...The decisive encounter of the people against the bourgeoi-sie occurred during Bacon's Rebellion, which began in April, 1676 as a difference between the elite and sub-elite planters over 'Indian policy', but which in September became a civil war against the Anglo-American ruling class. ... The tran-scendent importance of this record is that there, in colonial Virginia, one hundred and twenty-nine years before William Lloyd Garrison was born, the armed working class, black and white, fought side by side for the abolition of slavery."[2]

Aptheker and Allen, as two brother settler radicals, clearly agree with each other that Bacon's Rebellion was an important revolutionary event. But in Allen's account we suddenly find, without explanation, that a dispute over "Indian policy" between some planters trans-formed itself into an armed struggle by united white and Afrikan workers to end slavery! That is a hard story to follow. Particularly since Bacon's Rebellion is a cherished event in Southern white his-tory, and Bacon himself a notable figure. There is, in fact, an impos-ing "Memorial Tablet" of marble and bronze in the Virginia State Capitol, in the House of Delegates, which singles out Bacon as *"A Great Patriot Leader of the Virginia People."*[3] So even Virginia's seg-regationist white politicians agreed with Aptheker and Allen about this "democratic" rebellion. This truly is a unity we should not forget.

Behind the rhetoric, the real events of Bacon's Rebellion have the sordid and shabby character we are so familiar with in Euro-Amerikan politics. It is, however, highly instructive for us. The story begins in the summer of 1675. The settlers of Virginia Colony were angry and tense, for the alarms of "King Philip's Rebellion"—the famed Indian struggle—had spread South from Massachusetts. Further, the Colony was in an economic Depression due to both low tobacco prices and a severe drought (which had cut crop yields down by as much as three-quarters).[4]

One of the leading planters on the Colony's frontier was Nathaniel Bacon, Jr., the newest member of the Colony's elite. Bacon

had emigrated just the year before, swiftly purchasing two plantations on the James River. He and his partner, William Byrd (founder
of the infamous Virginia planter family), had also obtained commissions from Governor Berkeley to engage in the lucrative Indian fur
trade. All this was not difficult for Bacon, for he came from a wealthy
English family—and was cousin to both Governor Berkeley's wife
and to Nathaniel Bacon, Sr. (a leading planter who was a member of
Virginia's Council of State).

In the Spring of that year, 1675, Governor Berkeley honored
young Bacon by giving him an appointment to the Council of State.
As events were to prove, Bacon's elite lifestyle and rapid political rise
did but throw more fuel on the fires of his arrogance and unlimited
ambition.

In July of 1675 war broke out between the settlers and the
Susquehannock Indians. As usual, the war was started by settler
harassment of Indians, climaxing in a militia raid which mistakenly
crossed the border into Maryland—and mistakenly attacked the
Susquehannock, who were allied to the settlers. The Susquehannock
resisted, and repelled the Virginians' attack. Angry that the Indians
had dared to resist their bullying intrusion, the Virginia militia returned in August with reinforcements from the Maryland militia.
This new settler army of 1,100 men surrounded the Susquehannock
fort. Five Susquehannock leaders were lured out under pretense of a
parley and then executed.

Late one night all the besieged Susquehannock—men, wom-
en, and children—silently emptied out their town and slipped away.
On their way out they corrected five settler sentries. From then
on the Susquehannock took to guerrilla warfare, traveling in small
bands and ambushing isolated settlers. Nathaniel Bacon, Jr. was an
avid "hawk," whose lust for persecuting Indians grew even greater
when Indian guerrillas killed one of his slave overseers. To Bacon
that was one injury too many.

At that time the Virginia settlers had become polarized over
"Indian policy," with Bacon leading the pro-war faction against
Governor Berkeley. Established English policy, which Governor
Berkeley followed, called for temporary alliances with Indian na-
tions and temporary restraints on settler expansionism. This was

> ... in short what wee did in that
> short time and poor condition wee were in was
> to destroy the King of the Susquahannocks and
> the King of Oconogee [i.e. Occaneechee] and
> the Manakin King with a 100 men, besides what
> [was?] unknown to us. The King's daughter wee
> took Prisonner with some others and could
> have brought more, But in the heat of the Fight
> wee regarded not the advantage of the Prisoners
> nor any plunder, but burn't and destroid all.
> And what we reckon most materiall is That
> wee have left all nations of Indians [where wee
> have bin] ingaged in a civill warre amongst
> themselves, soe that with great ease wee hope to
> manadge this advantage to their utter Ruine and
> destruction.
>
> *from Nathaniel Bacon's report on the 1676*
> *expedition against the Indians*

---

not due to any Royal humanitarianism, but was a recognition of overall strategic realities by the English rulers. The Indian nations held, if only for a historical moment, the balance of power in North America between the rival British, French, and Spanish Empires. Too much aggression against Indian territories by English settlers could drive the Indians into allying with the French. It is also true that temporary peace with nearby Indians accomplished three additional ends: The very profitable fur trade was uninterrupted; Indians could be played off against each other, with some spying and fighting for the settlers; Indian pledges could be gotten to return runaway Afrikan slaves (although few were ever returned). So under the peace treaty of 1646 (after Indian defeats in the 1644–46 war), nineteen Indian tribes in Virginia accepted the authority of the British Crown. These subject Indians had to abide by settler law, and were either passive or active allies in settler wars with Indians further West.

By the time Bacon's overseer was corrected by the no-longer friendly Susquehannock, the political dispute between Bacon and Governor Berkeley had boiled over into the public view. Earlier, Bacon and Byrd had secretly suggested to Governor Berkeley that they be given a monopoly on the Indian fur trade.[5] Corrupt as the planters were, this move was so crudely self-serving that it was doomed to rejection. Berkeley dismissed their greedy proposal. Then, Bacon was wiped out of the fur trade altogether. In March 1676 the Virginia Assembly, reacting to rumors that some traders were illegally selling guns to the Indians, permanently suspended all the existing traders and authorized commissioning a wholesale replacement by new traders. Bacon was outraged, his pride and pocketbook stung, his anger and ambition unleashed.

The dispute between Bacon and Governor Berkeley was very clear-cut. Both favored war against the formerly-allied Susquehannock. Both favored warring on any Indians opposing settler domination. But Berkeley believed in the usefulness of keeping some Indian subjects—as he said: *"I would have preservd those Indians that I knew were hourely at our mercy to have beene our spies and intelligence to find out the more bloudy Ennimies."* Bacon disagreed, scorning all this as too meek, too soft, almost treasonous; he believed in wiping out *all* Indians, including allied and subject Indians. As he put it in his "Manifesto": *"Our Design"* was *"to ruin and extirpate all Indians in General."* Thus did Bacon's Rebellion define its main program. This was a classic settler liberal-conservative debate, which still echoes into our own times, like that between Robert F. Kennedy vs. George Wallace, OEO vs. KKK, CIA vs. FBI, and so on.

Bacon had been denied a militia officer's commission by Gov. Berkeley on the grounds that he refused to follow British policy. But

RIGHT: "BACON DEMANDING HIS COMMISSION" FROM GOVERNOR BERKELEY, FROM THE 1904 BOOK *MAKERS OF VIRGINIA HISTORY*.

in May, 1676, Bacon refused to be blocked by Gov. Berkeley any longer. He had become a charismatic leader among the frontier settlers, and he and his neighbors were determined to reach a "Final Solution" to their Indian problem. This was an increasingly popular program among the settler masses, since it also promised to end their economic Depression by a new round of looting Indian lands and goods. Nothing raises more enthusiasm among Euro-Amerikan settlers than attacking people of color—they embrace it as something between a team sport and a national religion. Thus did the Rebellion win over the settler masses.

In May 1676, word came to the settlers on the frontier from their Occaneeche Indian allies that a band of Susquehannock had camped near the Occaneeche fort on the Roanoke River. Bacon and his friends formed a vigilante group, against government orders, and promptly rode off to begin their war against all Indians. **This marks the beginning of Bacon's Rebellion.**

When Bacon and his men arrived at the Occaneeche fort they were exhausted, out of food, and clearly in no shape to fight. The fawning Occaneeche treated the settlers to a festive dinner. They even proposed that Bacon's force should rest while the Occaneeche would defeat the Susquehannock for them. Naturally, Bacon agreed. Using treachery the Occaneeche overran the Susquehannock, killing some thirty of them. The surviving prisoners were either publicly executed or given to Bacon as slaves.

But this did not end the battle, for Bacon and his vigilante band had really come to kill and enslave all the Indians. The Occaneeche were rumored to have a store of beaver furs worth some £1,000. At least some of Bacon's men later confessed "that the great designe was to gett the beaver..." In any case, Bacon demanded that the Occaneeche give him all the loot from the Susquehannock camp plus additional friendly Indians as slaves. Even at that, the servile Occaneeche leader tried to temporize, offering to give him hostages. Suddenly Bacon's force assaulted the unprepared Occaneeche. Most of the Indians inside the fort were killed, although they did stand off the settler assault. The surprised Occaneeche outside their fort were helpless, however. As Bacon proudly reported, his heroic settler comrades *"fell upon the men, woemen and children without, disarmed*

and destroid them all..." Bacon's Rebellion had won its first important victory, and he and his men marched homeward, loaded with
loot and new slaves, as heroes.

Bacon was now the most popular figure in the Virginia Colony,
famed and respected as an Indian killer. Berkeley's refusal to grant
him a military commission meant nothing, for Bacon was acclaimed
as "The People's General." He, much more than any Governor or
Councilor, commanded the loyalty of the settler masses. Nor did
he find any trouble attracting armed volunteers to do his bidding.
Wiping out and looting all the Indians around was a program many
whites could relate to, particularly since Governor Berkeley, under
popular pressure, had forced the subject Indians to turn in their
muskets and disarm. Killing disarmed oppressed people is much
more satisfying to Euro-Amerikans than having to face armed foes.
In fact, as one historian pointed out: *"Bacon and his men did not kill
a single enemy Indian but contented themselves with frightening away,
killing, or enslaving most of the friendly neighboring Indians, and taking
their beaver and land as spoils."*

Now Bacon was on the offensive against Governor Berkeley
and his clique as well. Over and over he publicly damned Berkeley
as a traitor to settlers. Bacon was swinging from his heels, aiming
at nothing less than state power. His big gun against the Governor
was the charge that Berkeley was a secret "friend" to the Indians. No
charge could have been more damaging. As we all know, when Euro-
Amerikans really get serious about fighting each other the most vicious accusation they can hurl at one another is that of "nigger-lover"
or "Indian-lover" or some such.

Bacon charged that the Governor was literally a traitor who
had secretly sold the Indians guns so that they could attack the
settlers. We can see the parallels to the 1960s, when white liberals
were widely charged with giving Third World militants money, legal aid, and even weapons so that they could kill whites. Berkeley,
charged Bacon, had so intimidated the settlers "that no man dare to
destroy the Indians ... until I adventured to cutt the knott, which
made the people in generall look upon mee as the countries friend."
Bacon's wife, whose ardent support for the Rebellion led some of
today's Euro-Amerikan radicals to see feminist stirrings in it, cried

"Thanks bee to God" that her husband "did destroy a great many of the Indians..."[6] Killing, enslaving, and robbing was the exact central concern of this movement—**which Euro-Amerikans tell us is an example of how we should unite with them!** There's a message there for those who wish to pick it up.

Bacon had been proscribed as a lawbreaker and rebel, but he still easily won election to the Assembly which was to meet on June 5, 1676. He typically chose to ensure his control of the Henrico County elections by capturing the site with his vigilantes. Even though Bacon was for repealing the 1670 Assembly decision denying propertyless freemen voting rights, these votes and assemblies were just window-dressing to his dictatorial ambitions.

On June 7, 1676, the Rebellion suffered its first reverse. Bacon was captured as he and fifty of his armed band tried to slip into Jamestown, the capital of Virginia Colony. Then began a dizzying series of maneuvers, coups, and countercoups. Preferring shame to execution, Bacon begged Gov. Berkeley's pardon on bended knee in front of the crowded Assembly. He was quickly pardoned—and even restored to his position on the Council of State. Young Bacon just as quickly fled Jamestown, returning on June 23, 1676, with over 500 armed supporters. He easily captured the capital, Governor and all. But now he in turn had to release Gov. Berkeley and his loyal supporters, for they invoked their settlers' right to return home to defend their plantations and women against the Indians.

It was at that point that we find white indentured servants entering the scene. Without an army, with almost all of the planters turned against him, an exiled Gov. Berkeley outbids Bacon for support. Berkeley promises freedom to white indentured servants of the Baconites, if they will desert their masters and take arms with the loyalist forces of the Crown. He also authorizes looting, with every white servant sharing in the confiscated estates of the Baconites. Aided by the lucky recapture of three armed ships, Gov. Berkeley soon rebuilt his military forces.

On Sept. 7, 1676, the loyalists arrived at Jamestown. Governor Berkeley shrewdly offered a general pardon to all rebel settlers except Bacon and his two chief lieutenants. Although they still commanded the fortified capital, Bacon's men abandoned their positions in immediate flight, without any pretense of battle. Most eagerly took up Berkeley's offer of pardon.

Now it was Bacon's turn to find himself virtually armyless, deserted by many of his followers. It appears as though a good number of settlers rallied to and deserted from the various sides depending on how the tide of fortune was running. They had an opportunistic regard for their immediate gain as the main contour in their minds. Just one month before, Bacon had been confidently sketching out how sister rebellions could easily be ignited in Maryland and South Carolina, and how if London refused their demands then an independent nation could be formed. This, incidentally, is why Jefferson and the other 1776 patriots considered Bacon one of the first architects of the United States.[7] But now his situation was perilous.

In his extreme need, refusing to swallow the bitter dose of either compromise or defeat, Bacon followed Gov. Berkeley's example—but did him one better. Bacon recruited not only the white servants of his opponents, but also their Afrikan slaves. Hundreds of new recruits flocked to his army. On Sept. 19, 1676, Baconite forces recaptured Jamestown. Once again there was no battle. Berkeley's forces deserted him as swiftly as Bacon's had, and the fortified capital was abandoned. Bacon, ever the master psychologist, had skillfully barricaded his besieging ramparts with the bodies of both his new Indian slaves and the captured wives of loyalists. That night he triumphantly ordered Jamestown put to the torch, and the fires that consumed the capital were dramatic evidence that he was once again master of Virginia.

But then Bacon died suddenly from an unexpected illness. His successor as "General" of the Rebellion lost heart, and made a secret deal with the Crown to disarm the rebel forces. The last die-hards were some 80 Afrikan slaves and 20 white servants, who refused to surrender to a fate they knew all too well. They were tricked into coming aboard a ship, taken out to the middle of the river, and forced to disarm at cannonpoint. As quickly as it had begun, Bacon's Rebellion was over.

Out of the debris of this chaotic dispute we can pick out the central facts. First, that there was no democratic political program or movement whatsoever. Bacon's Rebellion was a popular movement,

representing a clear majority of the settlers, to resolve serious economic and social problems by stepping up the exploitation of oppressed peoples. Far from being "democratic," it was more nearly
fascistic. Bacon was the diseased mind of the most reactionary faction of the planters, and in his ambitious schemes the fact that a few
more freemen or ex-slaves had paper voting rights meant little. Far
from fighting to abolish slavery, the Rebellion actually hoped to add
to the number of slaves by Indian conquest.

And, finally, there was no "Black and White unity" at all.
Needing fighting bodies, Bacon at the very end offered a deal to his
opponents' slaves. He paid in the only coin that was meaningful—a
promise of freedom for them if he won. Those Afrikans who signed
up in his army didn't love him, trust him, view him as their leader, or
anything of the kind. They were tactically exploiting a contradiction
in the oppressor ranks, maneuvering for their freedom. It is interesting to note that those Indians who did give themselves up to unity
with the oppressors, becoming the settlers' lackeys and allies, were
not protected by it, but were destroyed.

We can also see here the contradiction of "democratic" reforms within the context of settler capitalism. Much has been made
of the reforms of "Bacon's Assembly" (the June 1676 session of
the Virginia Assembly, which was so named because of its newly
elected majority of Baconites and their sympathizers). Always singled out for praise by Euro-Amerikan historians was "Act VII" of
the Assembly, which restored voting rights to propertyless freemen.
The most eminent Euro-Amerikan radical labor historian, Philip S.
Foner, has written how:

> "...the rebellion ... gained a number of democratic rights for
> the people. The statute preventing propertyless freemen from
> electing members to the House of Burgesses was repealed.
> Freeholders and freemen of every parish gained the right to
> elect the vestries of the church. None of these democratic
> reforms remained after the revolt was crushed, yet their
> memories lived on. Bacon was truly the 'Torchbearer of the
> Revolution', and for generations after any leader of the com-
> mon people was called a 'Baconist.'"[8]

It is easy to see how contemptible these pseudo-Marxist, white supremacist lies are. When we examine the *entire* work of that legislature of planter reforms, we find that the first three acts passed *all involved furthering the genocidal war against the Indians.* Act III legalized the settler seizure of Indian lands, previously guaranteed by treaty, "deserted" by Indians fleeing from Bacon's attacks. How meaningful is a "democratic" extension of voting rights amidst the savage expansion of a capitalist society based on genocide and enslavement? Would voting rights for white ranchers have been the "democratic" answer at Wounded Knee? Or "free speech" for prison guards the answer at Attica?

The truth is that Euro-Amerikans view these bourgeois-democratic measures as historic gains because to them they are. But not to us. The inner content, the essence of these reforms was the consolidation of a new settler nation. Part of this process was granting full citizenship in the settler society to all strata and classes of Euro-Amerikans; as such, these struggles were widespread in Colonial Amerika, and far more important to settlers than mere wage disputes.

The early English settlers of Virginia Colony, for example, were forced to import German, Polish, and Armenian craftsmen to their invasion beachhead, in order to produce the glass beads used in the fur trade (as well as pitch used in shipbuilding, etc.). Since these "foreign" craftsmen were not English, they were considered subjects and not members of the Colony. So in 1619 those European artisans went on strike, quickly winning full citizenship rights—"as free as any inhabitant there whatsoever."[9]

Similar struggles took place throughout the Colonial Era, in both North and South. In 1689 Leisler's Rebellion (led by a German immigrant merchant) in New York found the settler democrats ousting the British garrison from Albany, and holding the State capital for several years. The New York State Assembly has its origins in the settler legislature granted by the Crown as a concession after the revolt had been ended. The Roosevelt family first got into settler politics as supporters of Leisler.[10]

We need to see the dialectical unity of democracy and oppression in developing settler Amerika. The winning of citizenship rights by poorer settlers or non-Anglo-Saxon Europeans is democratic in form. The enrollment of the white masses into new, mass instruments of repression—such as the formation of the infamous Slave Patrols in Virginia in 1727—is obviously anti-democratic and reactionary. Yet these opposites in form are, in their essence, united as aspects of creating the new citizenry of Babylon. This is why our relationship to "democratic" struggles among the settlers has not been one of simple unity.

This was fully proven in practice once again by the 1776 War of Independence, a war in which most of the Indian and Afrikan peoples opposed settler nationhood and the consolidation of Amerika. In fact, the majority of oppressed people gladly allied themselves to the British forces in hopes of crushing the settlers.

This clash, between an Old European Empire and the emerging Euro-Amerikan Empire, was inevitable decades before actual fighting came. The decisive point came when British capitalism decided to clip the wings of the new Euro-Amerikan bourgeoisie—they restricted emigration, hampered industry and trade, and pursued a long-range plan to confine the settler population to a controllable strip of territory along the Atlantic seacoast. They proposed, for their own imperial needs, that the infant Amerika be permanently stunted. After all, the European conquest of just the Eastern shores of North America had already produced, by the time of Independence, a population almost one-third as large as that

APPROXIMATE FRONTIER LINE
OF THE COLONIES IN 1774

of England and Ireland. They feared that unchecked, the Colonial tail might someday wag the imperial dog (as indeed it has).

While some patriots, such as Samuel Adams, had for many years been certain of the need for settler independence from England, the settler bourgeoisie was, in the main, conservative and uncertain about actual war. **It was the land question that in the end proved decisive in swaying the doubtful among the settler elite.**

By first the Proclamation Act of 1763 and then the Quebec Act of 1773, the British capitalists kept trying to reserve for themselves alone the great stretches of Indian land West of the Alleghenies. This was ruinous to the settler bourgeoisie, who were suffering from the first major Depression in Amerikan history. Then as now, real estate speculation was a mania, a profitable obsession to the Euro-Amerikan patriots. Ben Franklin, the Whartons and other Philadelphia notables tried to obtain vast acreages for speculation. George Washington, together with the Lees and Fitzhughs, formed the Mississippi Company, which tried to get 2.5 million acres for sale to new settlers. Heavily in debt to British merchant-bankers, the settler bourgeoisie had hoped to reap great rewards from seizing new Indian lands as far West as the Mississippi River.[11]

The British Quebec Act of 1773, however, attached all the Amerikan Midwest to British Canada. The Thirteen Colonies were to be frozen out of the continental land grab, with their British cousins doing all the looting. And as for the Southern planter bourgeoisie, they were faced with literal bankruptcy as a class without the profits of new conquests and the expansion of the slave system. It was this one issue that drove them, at the end, into the camp of rebellion.[12]

Historian Richard G. Wade, analyzing the relation of frontier issues to the War of Independence, says of British restrictions on settler land-grabbing: "… settlers hungered to get across the mountains and resented any efforts to stop them. The Revolution was fought in part to free the frontier from this confinement."[13]

Like Bacon's Rebellion, the "liberty" that the Amerikan Revolutionists of the 1770s fought for was in large part the freedom to conquer new Indian lands and profit from the commerce of the slave trade, without any restrictions or limitations. In other words, the bourgeois "freedom" to oppress and exploit others. The successful future of the settler capitalists demanded the scope of independent nationhood.

But as the first flush of settler enthusiasm faded into the unhappy realization of how grim and bloody this war would be, the settler "sunshine soldiers" faded from the ranks to go home and stay home. Almost one-third of the Continental Army deserted at Valley Forge. So enlistment bribes were widely offered to get recruits. New York State offered new enlistments 400 acres each of Indian land. Virginia offered an enlistment bonus of an Afrikan slave (guaranteed to be not younger than age ten) and 100 acres of Indian land. In South Carolina, Gen. Sumter used a share-the-loot scheme, whereby each settler volunteer would get an Afrikan captured from Tory estates. Even these extraordinarily generous offers failed to spark any sacrificial enthusiasm among the settler masses.[14]

It was Afrikans who greeted the war with great enthusiasm. But while the settler slavemasters sought "democracy" through wresting their nationhood away from England, their slaves sought liberation by overthrowing Amerika or escaping from it. Far from being either patriotic Amerikan subjects or passively enslaved neutrals, the Afrikan masses threw themselves daringly and passionately into the jaws of war on an unprecedented scale—that is, into their own war, *against slave Amerika and for freedom.*

The British, short of troops and laborers, decided to use both the Indian nations and the Afrikan slaves to help bring down the settler rebels. This was nothing unique; the French had extensively used Indian military alliances and the British extensively used Afrikan slave recruits in their 1756–63 war over North America (called "The French & Indian War" in settler history books). But the Euro-Amerikan settlers, sitting on the dynamite of a restive, nationally oppressed Afrikan population, were terrified—and outraged.

This was the final proof to many settlers of King George III's evil tyranny. An English gentlewoman traveling in the Colonies wrote that popular settler indignation was so great that it stood to unite Rebels and Tories again.[15] Tom Paine, in his revolutionary pamphlet *Common Sense*, raged against "...that barbarous and hellish power which hath stirred up Indians and Negroes to destroy us."[16] But oppressed peoples saw this war as a wonderful contradiction to be exploited in the ranks of the European capitalists.

Lord Dunmore was Royal Governor of Virginia in name, but ruler over so little that he had to reside aboard a British warship anchored offshore. Urgently needing reinforcements for his outnumbered command, on Nov. 5, 1775, he issued a proclamation that any slaves enlisting in his forces would be freed. Sir Henry Clinton, commander of British forces in North America, later issued an even broader offer:

> "I do most strictly forbid any Person to sell or claim Right over any Negroe, the property of a Rebel, who may claim refuge in any part of this Army; And I do promise to every Negroe who shall desert the Rebel Standard, full security to follow within these Lines, any Occupation which he shall think proper."[17]

Could any horn have called more clearly? By the thousands upon thousands, Afrikans struggled to reach British lines. One historian of the Exodus has said: *"The British move was countered by the Americans, who exercised closer vigilance over their slaves, removed the able-bodied to interior places far from the scene of the war, and threatened with dire punishment all who sought to join the enemy. To Negroes attempting to flee to the British the alternatives 'Liberty or Death' took on an almost literal meaning. Nevertheless, by land and sea they made their way to the British forces."[18]*

The war was a disruption to Slave Amerika, a chaotic gap in the European capitalist ranks to be hit hard. Afrikans seized the time—not by the tens or hundreds, but by the many thousands. Amerika shook with the tremors of their movement. The signers of the Declaration of Independence were bitter about their personal losses: Thomas Jefferson lost many of his slaves; Virginia's Governor Benjamin Harrison lost thirty of "my finest slaves"; William Lee lost sixty-five slaves, and said two of his neighbors "lost every slave they had in the world"; South Carolina's Arthur Middleton lost fifty slaves.[19]

Afrikans were writing their own "Declaration of Independence" by escaping. Many settler patriots tried to appeal to the British forces to exercise European solidarity and expel the Rebel slaves. George

Washington had to denounce his own brother for bringing food to
the British troops, in a vain effort to coax them into returning the
Washington family slaves.[20] Yes, the settler patriots were definitely
upset to see some real freedom get loosed upon the land.

To this day no one really knows how many slaves freed themselves during the war. Georgia settlers were said to have lost over
10,000 slaves, while the number of Afrikan escaped prisoners in
South Carolina and Virginia was thought to total well over 50,000.
Many, in the disruption of war, passed themselves off as freemen and
relocated in other territories, fled to British Florida and Canada, or
took refuge in Maroon communities or with the Indian nations. It
has been estimated that 100,000 Afrikan prisoners—some 20% of
the slave population—freed themselves during the war.[21]

The thousands of rebellious Afrikans sustained the British war
machinery. After all, if the price of refuge from the slavemaster was
helping the British throw down the settlers, it was not such a dis-
tasteful task. Lord Dunmore had an "Ethiopian Regiment" of ex-
slaves (who went into battle with the motto "Liberty to Slaves" sewn
on their jackets) who helped the British capture and burn Norfolk,
Va. on New Year's Day, 1776.[22] That must have been sweet, indeed.
Everywhere, Afrikans appeared with the British units as soldiers,
porters, road-builders, guides, and intelligence agents. Washington
declared that unless the slave escapes could be halted the British
Army would inexorably grow "like a snowball in rolling."[23]

It was only under this threat—not only of defeat, but defeat in part by masses of armed ex-slaves—that the settlers hurriedly reversed their gears and started recruiting Afrikans into the
Continental U.S. Army. The whole contradiction of arming slaves
and asking them to defend their slavemasters was apparent to many.
Fearing this disruption of the concentration camp culture of the
plantations—and fearing even more the dangers of arming masses
of Afrikans—many settlers preferred to lose to their British kith and
kin rather than tamper with slavery. But that choice was no longer
fully theirs to make, as the genie was part-way out of the bottle.

On Dec. 31, 1775, Gen. Washington ordered the enlistment of
Afrikans into the Continental Army, with the promise of freedom at
the end of the war. Many settlers sent their slaves into the army to

take their place. One Hessian mercenary officer with the British said: "The Negro can take the field instead of the master; and therefore, no regiment is to be seen in which there are not Negroes in abundance..." Over 5,000 Afrikans served in the Patriot military, making up a large proportion of the most experienced troops (settlers usually served for only short enlistments—90 days duty being the most common term—while slaves served until the war's end or death).[24]

For oppressed peoples the price of the war was paid in blood. Afrikan casualties were heavy (one-half of the Afrikans who served with the British in Virginia died in an epidemic).[25] And the Indian nations allied to the Crown suffered greatly as the tide of battle turned against their side. The same was true of many Afrikans captured in British defeats. Some were sold to the West Indies and others were executed. A similar heavy fate fell on those recaptured while making their way to British lines. The settler mass community organizations, such as the infamous "Committees of Correspondence" in New York and Massachusetts, played the same role up North that the Slave Patrols played in the South, of checking and arresting rebellious Afrikans.[26]

Even those who had allied with the victorious settlers did not necessarily find themselves winning anything. Many Afrikans were disarmed and put back into chains at the war's end, despite solemn settler promises. John Hancock, President of the Continental Congress, may have presented Afrikan U.S. troops with a banner—which praised them as "The Bucks of America"—but that didn't help Afrikans such as Captain Mark Starlin. He was the first Afrikan captain in the Amerikan naval forces, and had won many honors for his near-suicidal night raids on the British fleet (which is why the settlers let him and his all-Afrikan crew sail alone). But as soon as the war ended, his master simply reclaimed him. Starlin spent the rest of his life as a slave. He, ironically enough, is known to historians as an exceptionally dedicated "patriot," super-loyal to the new settler nation.[27]

What was primary for the Afrikan masses was a strategic relationship with the British Empire against settler Amerika. To use an Old European power against the Euro-Amerikan settlers—who were the nearest and most immediate enemy—was just common sense to many. **65,000 Afrikans joined the British forces—over ten for every one enlisted in the Continental U.S. ranks.**[28] As Lenin said in discussing the national question: *"The masses vote with their feet."* And in this case they voted against Amerika.

Secondarily, on an individual level Afrikans served with various forces in return for release from slavery. There was no real "political unity" or larger allegiance involved, just a quid pro quo. On the European sides as well, obviously. If the British and Patriot sides could have pursued their conflict without freeing any slaves or disrupting the slave system, they each gladly would have done so. Just as the slave enlistments in Bacon's Rebellion demonstrated only the temporary and tactical nature of alliances between oppressed and oppressor forces, so the alignment of forces in the settler War of Independence only proved that **the national patriotic struggle of Euro-Amerikans was opposite to the basic interests and political desires of the oppressed.**

Even in the ruins of British defeat, the soundness of this viewpoint was borne out in practice. While the jubilant Patriots watched the defeated British army evacuate New York City in 1783, some 4,000 Afrikans swarmed aboard the departing ships to escape Amerika. Another 4,000 Afrikans escaped with the British from Savannah, 6,000 from Charleston, and 5,000 escaped aboard British ships prior to the surrender.[29] Did these brothers and sisters "lose" the war—compared to those still in chains on the plantations?

Others chose neither to leave nor submit. All during the war Indian and Afrikan guerrillas struck at the settlers. In one case, three hundred Afrikan ex-slaves fought an extended guerrilla campaign against the planters in both Georgia and South Carolina. Originally allied to the British forces, they continued their independent campaign long after the British defeat. They were not overcome until 1786, when their secret fort at Bear Creek was discovered and overwhelmed. This was but one front in the true democratic struggle against Amerika.

THE CONTRADICTIONS
OF NATION & CLASS

1. Crisis Within the Slave System

The slave system had served Amerika well, but as the settler nation matured what once was a foundation stone increasingly became a drag on the growth of the new Euro-Amerikan Empire. The slave system, once essential to the life of white society, now became worse than an anachronism; it became a growing threat to the well-being of settler life. While the settler masses and their bourgeois leaders still intended to exploit the oppressed to the fullest extent, increasingly they came to believe that *one specific form* of exploitation—Afrikan slavery—had to be shattered.

Nothing is gained without a price. As "natural" and "Heaven-sent" as the great production of Afrikan slave labor seemed to the planters, this wealth was bought at the cost of mounting danger to settlers as a whole. For the slave system imported and concentrated a vast, enemy army of oppressed right in the sinews of white society. This was the fatal contradiction in the "Slave Power" so clearly seen by early settler critics of slavery. Benjamin Franklin, for example, not only gave up slave-owning himself, but in 1755 wrote that slavery should be banned and only Europeans permitted to live in North America.[1] Twenty years later, as the Articles of

Confederation were being debated, South Carolina's Lynch stated that since Afrikans were property they shouldn't be taxed any more than sheep were. Franklin acidly replied: "Sheep will never make insurrection!"[2]

Thomas Jefferson of Virginia probably personified this contradiction more visibly than any other settler. He is well-known in settler history books as the liberal planter who constantly told his friends how he agonized over the immorality of slavery. He is usually depicted as an exceptional human being of great compassion and much intellect. What was pushing and pressuring his capitalist mind was the contradiction between his greed for the easy life of the slave-master, and his fear for the safety of his settler nation.[3]

He knew that successful revolution against settler rule was a possibility, and that in a land governed by ex-slaves the fate of the former slave-masters would be hard. As he put it: *"... a revolution of the wheel of fortune, an exchange of situation is among possible events..."* That is why, as U.S. President in 1791, he viewed the great Haitian Revolution led by Toussaint L'Ouverture as a monstrous danger. His Administration quickly appropriated relief funds to subsidize the French planters fleeing that island.

Jefferson's agile mind came up with a theoretical solution to their "Negro problem"—gradual genocide. He estimated that returning all slaves to Afrika would cost Amerika $900 million in lost capital and transportation expenses—a sum 45 times the annual export earnings of the settler economy at the time! This was an impossible cost, one that would have bankrupted not only the planters but the entire settler society as well.

President Jefferson's solution to this dilemma was to take all Afrikan children away from their parents for compact shipment to the West Indies and Afrika, while keeping the adults enslaved to support the Amerikan economy for the rest of their lives.* This would theoretically generate the necessary profits to prop up the capitalist economy, while still moving towards an all-white Amerika. Jefferson mused: *"... the old stock would die off in the ordinary course of nature ...*

---

* Although Jefferson never admitted it, most of these children would probably never survive.

until its final disappearance." The President thought this Hitlerian fantasy both "practicable" and "blessed."

It is easy to understand why this fantastic plan never became reality: the oppressor will never willingly remove his claws from the oppressed so long as there are still more profits to be wrung from them. Jefferson himself actively bought more and more slaves to maintain his pseudo-Grecian lifestyle. As President he signed the 1808 bill allegedly banning the importation of new slaves in part, we suspect, because this only raised the price he could obtain from his slave-breeding business.

Jefferson gloated over the increase in his wealth from the birth of new slaves: "...I consider the labor of a breeding woman as no object, and that a child raised every two years is of more profit than the crop of the best laboring man." It sums matters up to note that President Jefferson, who believed that the planters should restrict and then wipe out entirely the Afrikan colony, ended his days owning more slaves than he started with.[4]

The Northern States had slowly begun abolishing slavery as early as Vermont in 1777, in the hopes that the numbers of Afrikans could be kept down. It was also widely believed by settlers that in small numbers the "child-like" ex-slaves could be kept docile and easily ruled. The explosive growth of the number of Afrikans held prisoner within the slave system, and the resultant eruptions of Afrikan struggles in all spheres of life, blew this settler illusion away.

The Haitian Revolution of 1791 marked a decisive point in the politics of both settler and slave. The news from Santo Domingo that Afrikan prisoners had risen and successfully set up a new nation electrified the entire Western Hemisphere. When it became undeniably true that Afrikan people's armies, under the leadership of a 50-year-old former field hand, had in protracted war out-maneuvered and out-fought the professional armies of the Old European Powers, the relevancy of the lesson to Amerika was intense. Intense.

The effect of Haiti's great victory was felt immediately. Haitian slaves forcibly evacuated from that island with their French masters helped spread the word that Revolution and Independence were possible. The new Haitian Republic proudly offered citizenship to any Indians and Afrikans who wanted it, and thousands of free

LEFT: TOUSSAINT L'OUVERTURE; RIGHT: IN HAITI, "REVENGE TAKEN BY
THE BLACK ARMY FOR THE CRUELTIES PRACTISED ... BY THE FRENCH."

Afrikans emigrated. This great breakthrough stimulated rebellion
and the vision of national liberation among the oppressed, while
hardening the resolve of settler society to defend their hegemony
with the most violent and naked terror.

The Virginia insurrection led by Gabriel some nine years later,
in which thousands of Afrikans were involved, as well as that of Nat
Turner in 1831, caused discussions within the Virginia legislature
on ending slavery. The 1831 uprising, in which sixty settlers died,
so terrified them that public rallies were held in Western Virginia
to demand an all-white Virginia. Virginia's Governor Floyd publicly
endorsed the total removal of all Afrikans out of the State.[5] If such
proposals could be entertained in the heartland of the slave system,
we can imagine how popular that must have been among settlers in
the Northern States.

The problem facing the settlers was not limited to potential
uprisings on the plantations. Everywhere Afrikan prisoners were
pressing beyond the colonial boundaries set for them. The situation became more acute as the developing capitalist economy
created trends of urbanization and industrialization. In the early
1800s the Afrikan population of many cities was rising faster than

that of Euro-Amerikans. In 1820 Afrikans comprised at least 25% of the total population of Washington, Louisville, Baltimore, and St. Louis; at least 50% of the total population in New Orleans, Richmond, Mobile, and Savannah. The percentage of whites own-ing slaves was higher in the cities than it was in the countryside. *In cities such as Louisville, Charleston, and Richmond, some 65–75% of all Euro-Amerikan families owned Afrikan slaves.* And the commerce and industry of these cities brought together and educated masses of Afrikan colonial proletarians—in the textile mills, mines, iron-works, docks, railroads, tobacco factories, and so on.[6]

In such concentrations, Afrikans bent and often broke the bars surrounding them. Increasingly, more and more slaves were no longer under tight control. Illegal grog shops (white-owned, of course) and informal clubs flourished on the back streets. Restrictions on even the daily movements of many slaves faltered in the urban crowds.

Contemporary white travelers often wrote of how alarmed they were when visiting Southern cities at the large numbers of Afrikans on the streets. One historian writes of New Orleans: "It was not unusual for slaves to gather on street corners at night, for example, where they challenged whites to attempt to pass ... nor was it safe to accost them, as many went armed with knives and pistols in flagrant defiance of all the precautions of the Black Code."[7] A Louisville newspaper editorial complained in 1835 that "Negroes scarcely re-alize the fact that they are slaves ... insolent, intractable..."[8]

It was natural in these urban concentrations that slave escapes (prison breaks) became increasingly common. The Afrikan com-munities in the cities were also human forests, partially opaque to the eye of the settler, in which escapees from the plantations quietly sought refuge. During one 16 month period in the 1850s the New Orleans settler police arrested 982 "runaway slaves"—*a number equal to approximately 7% of the city's slave population.* In 1837 the Baltimore settler police arrested almost 300 Afrikans as proven or suspected escapees—a number equal to over 9% of that city's slave population.[9]

And, of course, these are just those who were caught. Many others evaded the settler law enforcement apparatus. Frederick

Douglass, we remember, had been a carpenter and shipyard worker in Baltimore before escaping Northward to pursue his agitation. At least 100,000 slaves did escape to the North and Canada during these years.

Nor should it be forgotten that some of the largest armed insurrections and conspiracies of the period involved the urban proletariat. The Gabriel uprising of 1800 was based on the Richmond proletariat (Gabriel himself was a blacksmith, and most of his lieutenants were other skilled workers). So many Afrikans were involved in that planned uprising that one Southern newspaper declared that prosecutions had to be halted lest it bankrupt the Richmond capitalists by causing "the annihilation of the Blacks in this part of the country."[10]

The Charleston conspiracy of 1822, led by Denmark Vesey (a free carpenter), was an organization of urban proletarians—stevedores, millers, lumberyard workers, blacksmiths, etc. Similarly, the great conspiracy of 1856 was organized among coal mine, mill, and factory workers across Kentucky and Tennessee. In its failure, some 65 Afrikans were killed at Senator Bell's iron works alone. It was particularly alarming to the settlers that those Afrikans who had been given the advantages of urban living, and who had skilled positions, just used their relative mobility to strike at the colonial system all the more effectively.[11]

From among the ranks of free Afrikans outside the South came courageous organizers, who moved through the South like guerrillas leading their brethren to freedom. And not just a few exceptional leaders, such as Harriet Tubman; in 1860 we know that five hundred Underground organizers went into the South from Canada alone. On the plantations the Afrikan masses resisted in a conscious, political culture. A letter from a Charleston, SC plantation owner in 1844 tells how all the slaves in the area secretly celebrated every August 1st—the anniversary of the end of slavery in the British West Indies.[12]

Abolishing slavery was the commonly proposed answer to this increasing instability in the colonial system. The settler bourgeoisie, however, which had immense capital tied up in slaves, could hardly be expected to take such a step willingly. One immediate response in the 1830s was to break up the Afrikan communities in the cities. In the wake of the Vesey conspiracy, for instance, the Charleston City Council urged that the number of male Afrikans in the city "be greatly diminished."[13] And they were.

Throughout the South much of the Afrikan population was gradually shipped back to the plantations, declining year after year until the Civil War. In New Orleans the drop was from 50% to 15% of the city population; in St. Louis from 25% to only 2% of the city population.[14] The needs of the new industrial economy were far less important to the bourgeoisie than breaking up the dangerous concentrations of oppressed, and regaining a safe, Euro-Amerikan physical domination over the key urban centers.

One Northern writer traveling through the South noted in 1859 that the Afrikans had been learning too much in the cities: *"This has alarmed their masters, and they are sending them off, as fast as possible, to the plantations where, as in a tomb, no sight or sound of knowledge can reach them."*[15] In addition to the physical restrictions, the mass terror, etc. that we all know were imposed, it is important to see that settler Amerika reacted to the growing consciousness of Afrikans by attempting to isolate and physically break up the oppressed communities. It is a measure of how strongly the threat of Revolution was rising in the Afrikan nation that the settlers had to restructure their society in response. The relative backwardness of the Southern economy was an expression of the living contradictions of the slave system.

2. Slavery vs. Settlerism

Slavery had become an obstacle to both the continued growth of settler society and the interests of the Euro-Amerikan bourgeoisie. It was not that slavery was unprofitable itself. It was, worker for worker, much more profitable than white wage-labor. Afrikan slaves in industry cost the capitalists less than one-third the wages of white workingmen. Even when slaves were rented from another capitalist, the savings in the factory or mine were still considerable. For example, in the 1830s almost one third of the workers at the U.S. Navy shipyard at Norfolk were Afrikans, rented at only two-thirds the cost of white wage-labor.[16]

But the Amerikan capitalists needed to greatly expand their labor force. While the planters believed that importing new millions of Afrikan slaves would most profitably meet this need, it was clear that this would only add fuel to the fires of the already insurrectionary Afrikan colony. Profit had to be seen not in the squeezing of a few more dollars on a short-term, individual basis, but in terms of the needs of an entire Empire and its future. And it was not just the demand for labor alone that outmoded the slave system.

Capitalism needed giant armies of settlers, waves and waves of new European shock-troops to help conquer and hold new territory, to develop it for the bourgeoisie, and garrison it against the oppressed. The Mississippi Valley, the Plains, the Northern territories of Mexico, the Pacific West—a whole continent of land and resources awaited, that could only be held by millions of loyal settlers. After Haiti, it was increasingly obvious that a "thin, white line" of a few soldiers, administrators, and planters could not safely hold down whole oppressed nations. Only the weight of masses of oppressors could provide the Euro-Amerikan bourgeoisie with the Empire they desired. This was a fundamental element in the antagonistic, but symbiotic, relationship of the white masses to their rulers.

The slave system had committed the fatal sin of restricting the white population, while massing great numbers of Afrikans. In the 1860 Census we can see the disparity of the settler populations of North and South. Excluding the border States of Delaware and Maryland, the slave States had a median population density of a bare 18 whites per sq. mile. The most heavily populated slave State—Kentucky—had a population of only 31 whites per sq. mile. In sharp contrast, Northern States such as Ohio, New Jersey, and Massachusetts had populations of 59, 81, and 158 whites per sq. mile respectively.[17] This disparity was not only large, but was qualitatively significant for the future of the Euro-Amerikan Empire.

It is no surprise that the planter bourgeoisie viewed society far differently than did the New York banker or Massachusetts mill

owner. The thought of an Amerika crowded with millions and millions of poverty-stricken European laborers, all sharing citizenship
with their mansion-dwelling brothers, horrified the planter elite.
They viewed themselves as the founders of a future Amerika that
would become a great civilization akin to Greece and Rome, a Slave
Empire led by the necessarily small elite of aristocratic slave-owners.

These retrogressive dreams had definite shape in plans for expansion of the "Slave Power" far beyond the South. After all, if the
Spanish Empire had used armies of Indian slaves to mine the gold,
silver, and copper of Peru and Mexico, why could not the Southern
planter bourgeoisie colonize the great minefields of New Mexico,
Utah, Colorado, and California, with millions of Afrikan helots
sending the great mineral wealth of the West back to Richmond
and New Orleans? These superprofits might finance a new World
Empire, just as they once did for semi-feudal Spain.

Why could not the plantation system be extended—not just
to Texas, but to swallow up the West, Mexico, Cuba, and Central
America? If masses of Afrikans already sweated so profitably in the
factories, mills, and mines of Birmingham and Richmond, why
couldn't the industrial process be an integral part of a new Slave
Empire that would bestride the world (as Rome once did Europe
and North Afrika)?

The planter capitalists who tantalized themselves with these
bloody dreams had little use for great numbers of penniless European
immigrants piling up on their doorstep. While Northerners saw the
increasing dangers of a slave economy, with its mounting, captive
armies of Afrikans, the planters saw the same dangers in importing
a white proletariat. The creation of such an underclass would inevitably, they thought, divide white society, since the privileged life of
settlerism could only stretch so far. Or in other words, too many
whites meant an inevitable squabble over dividing up the loot.

In 1836 Thomas R. Dew of William & Mary College warned
his Northern cousins that importing Europeans who were meant
to stay poor could only lead to class war: "Between the rich and
the poor, the capitalist and the laborer ... When these things shall
come—when the millions, who are always under the pressure of
poverty, and sometimes on the verge of starvation, shall form your

numerical majority, (as is the case now in the old countries of the world) and universal suffrage shall throw the political power into their lands, can you expect that they will regard as sacred the tenure by which you hold your property?"[18]

These were prophetic words, but in any case the deadlock between these two factions of the settler bourgeoisie meant that both sides carried out their separate policies during the first half of the 1800s. While the merchant and industrial capitalists of the North recruited the dispossessed of Europe, the Southern planters fought to expand the "Slave Power." Edmund Ruffin the famous Virginia planter, smugly boasted that: "One of the greatest benefits of the institution of African slavery to the Southern States is its effect in keeping away from our territory, and directing to the North and Northwest, the hordes of immigrants now flowing from Europe."[19] Such is the blindness of doomed classes.

THE FINEST FARMING LANDS

WHEAT — CORN — COTTON — FRUITS & VEGETABLES

EQUAL TO ANY IN THE WORLD!!!
MAY BE PROCURED
At FROM $8 to $12 PER ACRE.
Near Markets, Schools, Railroads, Churches, and all the blessings of Civilization.
1,200,000 Acres, in Farms of 40, 80, 120, 160 Acres and upwards, in ILLINOIS, the Garden State of America.

The Illinois Central Railroad Company offer, ON LONG CREDIT, the beautiful and fertile PRAIRIE LANDS lying along the whole line of their Railroad, 700 MILES IN LENGTH, upon the most Favorable Terms, for enabling Farmers, Manufacturers, Mechanics, and Workingmen to make for themselves and their families a competency, and a HOME they can call THEIR OWN, as will appear from the following statements:

IV

SETTLER TRADE UNIONISM

1. The Rise of White Labor

Settler Amerika got the reinforcements it needed to advance into Empire from the great European immigration of the 19th century. Between 1830–1860 some 4.5 million Europeans (two-thirds of them Irish and German) arrived to help the settler beachhead on the Eastern shore push outward.[1] The impact of these reinforcements on the tide of battle can be guessed from the fact that they numbered more than the total settler population of 1800. At a time when the young settler nation was dangerously dependent on the rebellious Afrikan colony in the South, and on the continental battleground greatly outnumbered by the various Indian, Mexican, and Afrikan nations, these new legions of Europeans played a decisive role.

The fact that this flood of new Europeans also helped create contradictions within the settler ranks has led to honest confusions. Some comrades mistakenly believe that a white proletariat was born, whose trade union and socialist activities placed it in the historic position of a primary force for revolution (and thus our eventual ally). The key is to see what was *dominant* in the material life and political consciousness of this new labor stratum, then and now.

The earlier settler society of the English colonies was relatively "fluid" and still unformed in terms of class structure. After all, the original ruling class of Amerika was back in England, and even the

large Virginia planter capitalists were seen by the English aristocracy as mere middle-men between them and the Afrikan proletarians
who actually created the wealth. To them George Washington was
just an overpaid foreman. And while there were great differences in
wealth and power, there was a shared privilege among settlers. Few
were exploited in the scientific socialist sense of being a wage-slave
of capital; in fact, wage labor for another man was looked down
upon by whites as a mark of failure (and still is by many). Up until
the mid-1800s settler society then was characterized by the unequal
but general opportunities for land ownership and the extraordinary
fluidity of personal fortunes by Old European standards.

This era of early settlerism rapidly drew to a close as Amerikan
capitalism matured. Good Indian land and cheap Afrikan slaves became more and more difficult for ordinary settlers to obtain. In the
South the ranks of the planters began tightening, concentrating as
capital itself was. One historian writes:

> "During the earlier decades when the lower South was being
> settled, farmers stood every chance of becoming planters.
> Until late in the fifties [1850s –ed.] most planters or their
> fathers before them started life as yeomen, occasionally with a
> few slaves, but generally without any hands except their own.
> The heyday of these poor people lasted as long as land and
> slaves were cheap, enabling them to realize their ambition to
> be planters and slaveowners as so many succeeded in doing ...
> But the day of the farmer began to wane rapidly after 1850. If
> he had not already obtained good land, it became doubtful
> he could ever improve his fortunes. All the fertile soil that
> was not under cultivation was generally held by speculators at
> mounting prices."[2]

While in the cities of the North, the small, local business of the independent master craftsman (shoemaker, blacksmith, cooper, etc.)
was giving way step by step to the large merchant, with his regional
business and his capitalist workshop/factory. This was the inevitable casualty list of industrialism. At the beginning of the 1800s it
was still true that *every* ambitious, young Euro-Amerikan apprentice

worker could expect to eventually become a master, owning his own little business (and often his own slaves). There is no exaggeration in saying this. We know, for example, that in the Philadelphia of the 1820s craft masters actually outnumbered their employees by 3 to 2—and that various tradesmen, masters, and professionals were an absolute majority of the Euro-Amerikan male population.[3]

But by 1860 the number of journeymen workers compared to masters had tripled, and a majority of Euro-Amerikan men were now wage-earners.[4] Working for a master or merchant was no longer just a temporary stepping-stone to becoming an independent landowner or shopkeeper. This new white workforce for the first time had little prospect of advancing beyond wage-slavery. Unemployment and wage-slashing were common phenomena, and an increasing class strife and discontent entered the world of the settlers.

In this scene the new millions of immigrant European workers, many with Old European experiences of class struggle, furnished the final element in the hardening of a settler class structure. The political development was very rapid once the nodal point was reached: From artisan guilds to craft associations to local unions. National unions and labor journals soon appeared. And in the workers' movements the championing of various socialist and even Marxist ideas was widespread and popular, particularly since these immigrant masses were salted with radical political exiles (Marx, in the Inaugural Address to the 1st International in 1864, says: "...crushed by the iron hand of force, the most advanced sons of labor fled in despair to the transatlantic Republic...")

All this was but the *outward form* of proletarian class consciousness, made all the more convincing because those white workers subjectively believed that they were proletarians—"the exploited," "the creators all wealth," "the sons of toil," etc. etc. In actuality this was clearly untrue. While there were many exploited and poverty-stricken immigrant proletarians, these new Euro-Amerikan workers *as a whole were a privileged labor stratum.* As a labor aristocracy it had, instead of a proletarian, revolutionary consciousness, a *petit-bourgeois consciousness that was unable to rise above reformism.*

This period is important for us to analyze, because here for the first time we start to see the modern political form of the

Euro-Amerikan masses emerge. Here, at the very start of industrial capitalism, are trade unions, labor electoral campaigns, "Marxist" organizations, nation-wide struggles by white workers against the capitalists, major proposals for "White and Negro" labor alliance.

What we find is that this new class of white workers was indeed angry and militant, but so completely dominated by petit-bourgeois consciousness that they always ended up as the pawns of various bourgeois political factions. Because they clung to and hungered after the petty privileges derived from the loot of Empire, they *as a stratum* became rabid and reactionary supporters of conquest and the annexation of oppressed nations. The "trade union unity" deemed so important by Euro-Amerikan radicals (then and now) kept falling apart and was doomed to failure. Not because white workers were racist (although they were), but because this alleged "trade union unity" was just a ruse to divide, confuse, and stall the oppressed until new genocidal attacks could be launched against us, and completely drive us out of their way.

This new stratum, far from possessing a revolutionary potential, was unable to even take part in the *democratic* struggles of the 19th century. When we go back and trace the Euro-Amerikan workers' movements from their early stages in the pre-industrial period up thru the end of the 19th century, this point is very striking.

In the 1820s–30s, before white workers had even developed into a class, they still played a major role in the political struggles of "Jacksonian Democracy." At that time the "United States" was a classic bourgeois democracy—that is, direct "democracy" for a handful of capitalists. Even among settlers, high property qualifications, residency laws, and sex discrimination limited the vote to a very small minority. So popular movements, based among angry small farmers and urban workingmen, arose in State after State to strike down these limitations—and thus force settler government to better share the spoils of Empire.

In New York State, for example, one liberal landmark was the "Reform Convention" of 1821, where the supporters of Martin Van Buren swept away the high property qualifications that had previously barred white workingmen from voting. This was a significant victory for them. Historian Leon Litwack has pointed out that the

1821 Convention "has come to symbolize the expanded democracy which made possible the triumph of Andrew Jackson seven years later." Van Buren became the hero of the white workers, and was later to follow Jackson into the White House.[5]

Did this national trend "for the extension and not the restriction of popular rights" (to quote the voting rights committee of the Convention) involve the unity of Euro-Amerikan and Afrikan workers? No. In fact, the free Afrikan communities in the North **opposed these reform movements** of the settler masses. The reason is easy to grasp: Everywhere in the North, the pre–Civil War popular struggles to enlarge the political powers of the settler masses also had the program of taking away civil rights from Afrikans. These movements had the public aim of driving all Afrikans out of the North. The 1821 New York "Reform Convention" gave all white workingmen the vote, while simultaneously *raising* property qualifications for Afrikan men so high that it effectively disenfranchised the entire community. By 1835 it was estimated that only 75 Afrikans out of 15,000 in that State had voting rights.[6]

This unconcealed attack on Afrikans was in point of fact a compromise, with Van Buren restraining the white majority which hated even the few, remaining shreds of civil rights left for well-to-do Afrikans. Van Buren paid for this in his later years, when opposing politicians (such as Abraham Lincoln) attacked him for letting any Afrikans vote at all. For that matter, this new, expanded settler electorate in New York turned down bills to let Afrikans vote for many years thereafter. In the 1860 elections while Lincoln and the GOP were winning New York by a 32,000 vote majority, only 1,600 votes supported a bill for Afrikan suffrage. Frederick Douglass pointed out that civil rights for Afrikans was supported by "neither Republicans nor abolitionists."[7]

These earlier popular movements of settler workingmen found significant expression in the Presidency of Andrew Jackson, the central figure of "Jacksonian Democracy." This phrase is used by historians to designate the rabble-rousing, anti-elite reformism he helped introduce into settler politics. His role in the early political stirrings of the white workers was so large that even today some Euro-Amerikan "Communist" labor historians proudly refer to *"the national struggle for economic and political democracy led by Andrew Jackson."*[8]

Jackson did indeed lead a "national struggle" to enrich not only his own class (the planter bourgeoisie) but his entire settler nation of oppressors. He stood at a critical point in the great expansion into Empire. During his two administrations he personally led the campaigns to abolish the National Bank (which was seen by many settlers as protecting the monopolistic power of the very few top capitalists and their British and French backers) and to ensure settler prosperity by annexing new territory into the Empire. In both he was successful.

The boom in slave cotton and the parallel rise in immigrant European labor was tied to the removal of the Indian nations from the land. After all, the expensive growth of railroads, canals, mills, and workshops was only possible with economic expansion—an expansion that could only come from the literal expansion of Amerika through new conquests. And the fruits of new conquests were very popular with settlers of all strata, North and South. The much-needed expansion of cash export crops (primarily cotton) and trade was being blocked as the settler land areas ran up against the Indian–U.S. Empire borders. In particular, the so-called "Five Civilized Nations" (Creeks, Cherokees, Choctaws, Chickasaws, and Seminoles), Indian nations that had already been recognized as sovereign territorial entities in U.S. treaties, held much of the South: Northern Georgia, Western North Carolina, Southern Tennessee, much of Alabama, and two-thirds of Mississippi.[9]

The settlers were particularly upset that the Indian nations of the Old Southwest showed no signs of collapsing, "dying out" or trading away their land. All had developed stable and effective agricultural economies, with considerable trade. Euro-Amerikans, if anything, thought that they were too successful. The Cherokee, who had chosen a path of adopting many Western societal forms, had a national life more stable and prosperous than that of the Euro-Amerikan settlers who eventually occupied those Appalachian regions after they were forced out. A Presbyterian Church report in 1826 records that the Cherokee nation had: 7,600 houses, 762 looms, 1,488 spinning wheels, 10 sawmills, 31 grain mills, 62 blacksmith shops, 18 schools, 70,000 head of livestock, a weekly newspaper in their own

THE TRAIL OF TEARS, PAINTED BY ROBERT LINDNEUX IN 1942.
(WOOLAROC MUSEUM, BARTLESVILLE, OKLAHOMA)

language, and numerous libraries with "thousands of good books."
The Cherokee national government had a two-house legislature and
a supreme court.[10]

Under the leadership of President Jackson, the U.S. government ended even its limited recognition of Indian sovereignty, and
openly encouraged land speculators and local settlers to start seizing
Indian land at gunpoint. A U.S. Supreme Court ruling upholding
Cherokee sovereignty vs. the State of Georgia was publicly ridiculed
by Jackson, who refused to enforce it. In 1830 Jackson finally got
Congress to pass the Removal Act, which authorized him to use
the army to totally relocate or exterminate all Indians east of the
Mississippi River. The whole Eastern half of this continent was now
to be completely cleared of Indians, every square inch given over to
the needs of European settlers. In magnitude this was as sweeping
as Hitler's grand design to render continental Europe free of Jews.
Under Jackson's direction, the U.S. Army committed genocide on an
impressive scale. The Cherokee nation, for instance, was dismantled,
with **one-third of the Cherokee population dying in the winter of
1838** (from disease, famine, exposure, and gunfire as the U.S. Army
marched them away at bayonet point on "The Trail of Tears").[11]

So the man who led the settlers' "national struggle for economic and political democracy" was not only a bourgeois politician, but
in fact an apostle of annexation and genocide. The president of "The
Trail of Tears" was a stereotype frontiersman—a fact which made
him popular with poorer whites. After throwing away his inheritance
on drinking and gambling, the young Jackson moved to the frontier
(at that time Nashville, Tenn.) to "find his fortune." That's a common
phrase in the settler history books, which only conceals the reality
that the only "fortune" on the frontier was from genocide. Jackson
eventually became quite wealthy through speculating in Indian land
(like Washington, Franklin, and other settlers before him) and owning a cotton plantation with over one hundred Afrikan slaves. The
leader of "Jacksonian Democracy" had a clear, practical appreciation
of how profitable genocide could be for settlers.

First as a land speculator then as a slavemaster, and finally as
General and then President, Jackson literally spent the whole of his
adult life *personally* involved in genocide. During the Creek War of
1813–14 Jackson and his fellow frontiersmen slaughtered hundreds
of unarmed women and children—afterwards skinning the bodies to make souvenirs.*[12] Naturally, Jackson had a vicious hatred of
Indians and Afrikans. He spent the majority of his years in public
office pressing military campaigns against the Seminole in Florida,
who had earned special enmity by sheltering escaped Afrikans. U.S.
military campaigns in Florida against first the Spanish and then the
Seminole, were in large part motivated by the need to eliminate this
land base for independent Afrikan regroupment.

The Seminole Wars that went on for over 30 years began when
Jackson was an army officer and ended after he had retired from the
White House—though he still sent Washington angry letters of
advice on the war from his retirement. They were as much Afrikan
wars as Indian wars, for the escaped Afrikans had formed liberated
Afrikan communities as a semi-autonomous part of the sheltering
Seminole Nation.[13]

---

* While some of Hitler's Death Camp officers are said to have made lampshades
out of the skins of murdered Jews, the practicalities of frontier life led Jackson
and his men to make bridle reins out of their victims' skins.

The first attacks on these Afrikan-Seminole took place in 1812–14, when Georgia vigilantes invaded to enslave the valuable Afrikans. Afrikan forces wiped out almost all of the invaders (including the commanding Georgia major and a U.S. General). Two years later, in 1816, U.S. naval gunboats successfully attacked the Afrikan Ft. Appalachicola on the Atlantic Coast; two hundred defenders were killed when a lucky shot touched off the Afrikan ammunition stores. The next year, in 1817, army troops under Jackson's command invaded Florida in the First Seminole War. The Afrikans and Seminoles evaded Jackson's troops and permanently withdrew deeper into Central Florida.

The decisive Second Seminole War began in 1835 when the Seminole Nation, under the leadership of the great Osceola, refused to submit to U.S. removal to Oklahoma. A key disagreement was that the settlers insisted on their right to separate the Seminole from their Afrikan co-citizens, who would then be reenslaved and put on the auction block. When the Seminole refused, Jackson angrily ordered the Army to go in and "eat (Osceola) and his few." Fighting a classic guerrilla war, 2,000 Seminole and 1,000 Afrikan fighters inflicted terrible casualties on the invading U.S. Army. Even capturing Osceola in a false truce couldn't give the settlers victory.

Finally, U.S. Commanding General Thomas Jesup conceded that none of the Afrikans would be reenslaved, but all could relocate to Oklahoma as part of the Seminole Nation. With this most of the Seminole and Afrikan forces surrendered and left Florida.* Those who refused to submit simply retreated deeper into the Everglades and kept ambushing any settlers who dared to follow. In 1843 the U.S. gave up trying to root the remaining Seminole guerrillas out of the swamps.

The settlers lost some 1,600 soldiers killed and additional thousands wounded or disabled through disease. The war—which Gen. Jesup labeled "a Negro, not an Indian, war"—cost the U.S. some $30 million. That was *eighty times* what President Jackson had promised Congress he would spend in getting rid of *all* Indians East of the

---

* Even in the Oklahoma Territory, repeated outbreaks of guerrilla campaigns by Afrikan-Seminole forces were reported as late as 1842.

Mississippi. By the time he left office, Jackson was infuriated that
the Seminole and Afrikans were resisting the armed might of the
Empire year after year. He urged that the Army concentrate on finding and killing all the enemy women, in order to put a final, biologi-
cal end to this stubborn Nation. He boasted that he had used this
strategy quite successfully in his own campaigns against Indians.[14]

Time and again Jackson made it clear that he favored a "Final
Solution" of total genocide for all Indians. In his second State of
the Union Address, Jackson reassured his fellow settlers that they
should not feel guilty when they "tread on the graves of extinct nations," since the wiping out of all Indian life was just as "natural" as
the passing of generations! Could anyone miss the point? After
years and decades soaked in aggression and killing, could any Euro-
Amerikan *not know* what Jackson stood for? Yet he was the chosen
hero of the Euro-Amerikan workers of that day.

While Hitler never won an election in his life—and had to use
the armed power of the state to violently crush the German workers and their organizations—Jackson was swept into power by the
votes of Euro-Amerikan workmen and small farmers. His jingois-
tic expansionism was popular with all sectors of settler society, in
particular with those who planned to use Indian land to help solve
settler economic troubles. Northern workers praised him for his

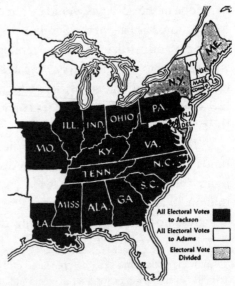

Sweep of the
national democracy.
The electoral vote
in 1828.

All Electoral Votes
to Jackson

All Electoral Votes
to Adams

Electoral Vote
Divided

opposition to the old colonial elite of the Federalist Party, his stand on the National Bank, and his famous "Equal Protection Doctrine." The latter piously declaimed that government's duty was not to favor the rich, but through taxation and other measures to give aid "alike on the high and low, the rich and the poor..." of settler society.[15]

Jackson was the historic founder of today's Democratic Party; not only in organization, but in first welding together the electoral coalition of Southern planters and Northern "ethnic" workers. He was the first President to claim that he was born in a log cabin, of lowly circumstances. This "redneck" posture, enhanced by his bloody military adventures, was very popular with the mass of small slave-owners in his native South—and with Northern workers as well! Detailed voting studies confirm that in both the 1828 and 1832 elections, Jackson received the overwhelming majority of the votes of immigrant Irish and German workers in the North.[16] White workmen joined his Democratic Party as a new crusade for equality among settlers. In the New York mayoral election of 1834, organized white labor marched in groups to the polls singing:

> "Mechanics, cartmen, laborers
> Must form a close connection,
> And show the rich Aristocrats,
> Their powers at this election...

> "Yankee Doodle, smoke 'em out
> The Proud, the banking faction.
> None but such as Hartford Feds
> Oppose the poor and Jackson..."[17]

Underneath the surface appearance of militant popular reform, of workers taking on the wealthy, these movements were only attempts to more equally distribute the loot and privileges of Empire among its *citizens*. That's why the oppressed colonial *subjects* of the Empire had no place in these movements.

The line between oppressors and oppressed was unmistakably drawn. Afrikan and Indian alike opposed this "Jacksonian Democracy." The English visitor Edward Abdy remarked that he "never knew a man of color that was not an anti-Jackson man."[18] On their side, the white workingmen of the 1830s knowingly embraced the architects of genocide as their heroes and leaders. Far from *joining* the democratic struggles around the rights of the oppressed, the white workers were firmly committed to *crushing* them.

Even as they were gradually being pressed downward by the emerging juggernaut of industrial capitalism—faced with wage cuts, increasing speed-up of machine-powered production, individual craft production disappearing in the regimented workshop, etc.—those Euro-Amerikan workers saw their hope for salvation in non-proletarian special privileges and a desperate clinging to petit-bourgeois status. At a time when the brute labor of the Empire primarily rested on the backs of the unpaid, captured Afrikan proletariat, the white workers of the 1830s were only concerned with winning the Ten-Hour Day for themselves. In the 1840s as the Empire annexed the Northern 40% of Mexico and by savage invasion reduced truncated Mexico to a semi-colony, the only issue to the white workingmen's movement was how large would their share of the looting be? It is one thing to be bribed by the bourgeoisie, and still another to demand, organize, argue, and beg to be bribed.

The dominant political slogan of the white workers movement of the 1840s was *"Vote Yourself A Farm."* This expressed the widespread view that it was each settler's *right* to have cheap land to farm, and that the ideal lifestyle was the old Colonial-era model of the self-employed craftsmen who also possessed the security of being part-time farmers. The white labor movement, most particularly the influential newspaper, *Working Man's Advocate* of New York, called for new legislation under which the Empire would guarantee cheap tracts of Indian and Mexican land to all European settlers (and impoverished workmen in particular).*[19] The white workers literally demanded their traditional settler right to be petit-bourgeois—"little bourgeois," petty imitators who would annex their small, individual plots each time the real bourgeoisie annexed another oppressed nation. It should be clear that the backwardness of white labor is not a matter of "racism," of "mistaken ideas," of "being tricked by the

---

* The Homestead Act of 1851 was one result of this campaign.

capitalists" (all idealistic instead of materialist formulations); rather, it is a class question and a national question.

This stratum came into being with its feet on top of the proletariat and its head straining up into the petit-bourgeoisie. It's startling how narrow and petty its concerns were in an age when the destiny of peoples and nations was being decided, when the settler Empire was trying to take into its hands the power to decree death to whole nations. We keep coming back to genocide, the inescapable center of settler politics in the 19th century. So to fully grasp the politics of emerging white labor, we must penetrate to the connection between their class viewpoint and genocide.

2. The Popular Appeal of Genocide

By 1840 most of the Indian nations of the East had been swept away, slaughtered or relocated. By 1850 the Empire had consolidated its grip on the Pacific Coast, overrunning and occupying Northern Mexico. The Empire had succeeded in bringing the continent under its control. These victories produced that famous "opportunity" that the new waves of European immigrants were coming for. But these changes also brought to a nodal point the contradictions within the fragmented settler bourgeoisie, between planter and mercantile/industrial capital—contradictions which were reflected in all facets of settler society. The tremendous economic expansion of the conquests was a catalyst.

The ripping open of the "New South" to extend the plantation system meant a great rise of Afrikan slaves on the Western frontier. These new cotton areas became primarily Afrikan in population. And the ambitious planter bourgeoisie started seeding slave labor enterprises far outward, as tentacles of the "Slave Power." So at a salt mine in Illinois, a gold mine in California, a plantation in Missouri, aggressive planters appeared with their "moveable factories" of Afrikan slaves. Southern adventurers even briefly seized Nicaragua in 1856 in a premature attempt to annex all of Central Amerika to the "Slave Power."

If the clearing away of the Indian nations had unlocked the door to the spread of the slave system, so too it had given an opportunity to the settler opponents of the planters. And their vision was not of a reborn Greek slaveocracy, but of a brand-new European Empire, relentlessly modern, constructed to the most advanced bourgeois principles with the resources of an entire continent united under its command. This new Empire would not only dwarf any power in Old Europe in size, but would be secured through the power of a vast, occupying army of millions of loyal settlers. This bourgeois vision could hardly be considered crackpot, since 20th century Amerika is in large part the realization of it, but the vision was of an all-European Amerika, an all-white continent.

We can only understand the deep passions of the slavery dispute, the flaring gunfights in Missouri and "Bloody Kansas" between pro-slavery and anti-slavery settlers, and lastly the grinding, monumental Civil War of 1861–1865, as the final play of this greatest contradiction in the settler ranks. It was not freedom for Afrikans that motivated them. No, the reverse. It was their own futures, their own fortunes. Gov. Morton of Ohio called on his fellows to realize their true interests: "We are all personally interested in this question, not indirectly and remotely as in a mere political abstraction—but directly, pecuniarily, and selfishly. *If we do not exclude slavery from the Territories, it will exclude us.*"

To millions of Euro-Amerikans in the North, the slave system had to be halted because it filled the land with masses of Afrikans instead of masses of settlers. To be precise: In the 19th century a consensus emerged among the majority of Euro-Amerikans that just as the Indian nations before them, the dangerous Afrikan colony had to be at first contained and then totally eliminated, so that the land could be filled by the loyal settler citizens of the Empire.

This was a strategic view endorsed by the majority of Euro-Amerikans. It was an explicit vision that required genocide. How natural for a new Empire of conquerors believing that they had, like gods, totally removed from the earth one family of oppressed nations, to think nothing of wiping out another. The start was to confine Afrikans to the South, to drive them out of the "Free" States in the North. Indeed, in the political language of 19th century settler politics, the word "Free" also served as a code-phrase that meant "non-Afrikan."

The movement to confine Afrikans to the Slave South took both governmental and popular forms. Four frontier States—Illinois, Indiana, Iowa, and Oregon—passed "immigration" clauses in their constitutions which barred Afrikans as "aliens" from entering the State.[20] It's interesting that the concept of Afrikans as foreign "immigrants"—a concept which tacitly admits separate Afrikan nationality—keeps coming to the surface over and over. Legal measures to force Afrikans out by denying them the vote, the right to own land, use public facilities, practice many professions and crafts, etc. were passed in many areas of the North at the urging of the white mobs. White labor not only refused to defend the democratic rights of Afrikans, but played a major role in these new assaults.

Periodic waves of mass terror also were used everywhere against Afrikan communities in the North. The Abolitionist press records 209 violent mob attacks in the North between 1830–1849. These violent assaults were not the uncontrolled outpouring of blind racism, as often suggested. Rather, they were carefully organized offensives to achieve definite goals. These mobs were usually led by members of the local ruling class (merchants, judges, military officers, bankers, etc.), and made up of settlers from all strata of society.[21] The three most common goals were: (1) To reverse some local advance in Afrikan organization, education or employment; (2) To destroy the local Abolitionist movement; (3) To reduce the Afrikan

"Hanging a Negro in Clarkson Street"

population. In almost every case the mobs, representing both the local ruling class and popular settler opinion, were successful. In almost no cases did any significant number of Euro-Amerikans interfere with the mobs, save to "restore order" or to nobly protect a few lives *after* the violence had gained its ends.

But to most settlers in the North these attacks were just temporary measures. To them the heart of the matter was the slave system. They thought that without the powerful self-interest of the planters to "protect" Afrikans, that Afrikans as a whole would swiftly vanish from this continent. Today it may sound fantastic that those 19th century Euro-Amerikans expected to totally wipe out the Afrikan population. Back then it was taken as gospel truth by most settlers that in a "Free" society, where Afrikans would be faced with "competition" (their phrases) from whites, they as inferiors must perish. The comparison was usually made to the Indians—who "died out" as white farmers took their land, as whole villages were wiped out in unprovoked massacres, as hunger and disease overtook them, as they became debilitated with addiction to alcohol, as the survivors were simply driven off to concentration camps at gunpoint. Weren't free Afrikans losing their jobs already? And weren't there literally millions of new European farmers eager to take the farmland that Afrikans had lived on and developed?

Nor was it just the right-wingers that looked forward to getting rid of "The Negro Problem" (as all whites referred to it). All tendencies of the Abolitionists contained not only those who defended the human rights of Afrikans, but also those who publicly or privately agreed that Afrikans must go. Gamaliel Bailey, editor of the major abolitionist journal *National Era*, promised his white readers that after slavery was ended all Afrikans would leave the U.S. The North's most prominent theologian, Rev. Horace Bushnell, wrote in 1839 that emancipation would be "one bright spot" to console Afrikans, who were "doomed to spin their brutish existence downward into extinction..." That extinction, he told his followers, was only Divine Will, and all for the good. Rev. Theodore Parker was one of the leading spokesmen of radical abolitionism, one who helped finance John Brown's uprising at Harper's Ferry, and who afterwards defended him from the pulpit. Yet even Parker believed in an all-white

Amerika; he firmly believed that: *"The strong replaces the weak. Thus, the white man kills out the red man and the black man. When slavery is abolished the African population will decline in the United States, and die out of the South as out of Northampton and Lexington."*[22]

While many settlers tried to hide their genocidal longings behind the fictions of "natural law" or "Divine Will," others were more honest in saying that it would happen because Euro-Amerikans were determined to make it happen. Thus, even during the Civil War, the House of Representatives issued a report on emancipation that strongly declared: "…the highest interests of the white race, whether Anglo-Saxon, Celt, or Scandinavian, require that the whole country should be held and occupied by these races alone." In other words, they saw no contradiction between emancipation and genocide. The leading economist George M. Weston wrote in 1857 that: "When the white artisans and farmers want the room which the African occupies, they will not take it by rude force, but by gentle and gradual and peaceful processes. The Negro will disappear, perhaps to regions more congenial to him, perhaps to regions where his labor can be more useful, perhaps by some process of colonization we may yet devise; *but at all events he will disappear."*[23]

National political movements were formed by settlers to bring this day about. The Colonization movement, embodied in the American Colonization Society, organized hundreds of local chapters to press for national legislation whereby Afrikans would be removed to new colonies in Afrika, the West Indies or Central America. U.S. Presidents from Monroe in 1817 to Lincoln in 1860 endorsed the society, and the semi-colony of Liberia was started as a trial. Much larger was the Free Soil Party, which fought to reserve the new territories and States of the West for Europeans only. This was the main forerunner of the Republican Party of 1854, the first settler political party whose platform was the defeat of the "Slave Power."

The Republican Party itself strongly reflected this ideology of an all-white Amerika. Although most of its leaders supported limited civil rights for Afrikans, they did so only in the context of the temporary need for Empire to treat its subjects humanely. Sen. William Seward of New York was the leading Republican spokesman before the Civil War (during which he served as Lincoln's Secretary of State). In his famous Detroit speech during the 1860 campaign, he said: *"The great fact is now fully realized that the African race here is a foreign and feeble element, like the Indian incapable of assimilation..."* Both would, he promised his fellow settlers, *"altogether disappear."* Lincoln himself said over and over again during his entire political career that all Afrikans would eventually have to disappear from North America. The theme of Afrikan genocide runs like a dark thread, now hidden and now visible in the violent weaving of the future, throughout settler political thought of that day.

It should be remembered that while most Northern settlers opposed Afrikan slavery for these reasons by the 1860s, even after the Civil War settlers promoted Indian, Mexicano, and Chinese en-slavement when it was useful to colonize the Southwest and West. One settler account of the Apache–U.S. wars in the Southwest re-veals the use of slavery as a tool of genocide:

> "More than anything else, it was probably the incessant kid-napping and enslavement of their women and children that gave Apaches their mad-dog enmity toward the whites ... It was officially estimated that 2,000 Indian slaves were held by the white people of New Mexico and Arizona in 1866, after 20 years of American rule—unofficial estimates placed the figure several times higher ... 'Get them back for us,' Apaches begged an Army officer in 1871, referring to 29 children just stolen by citizens of Arizona; 'our little boys will grow up slaves, and our little girls, as soon as they are large enough, will be diseased prostitutes, to get money for whoever owns them...' Prostitution of captured Apache girls, of which much mention is made in the 1860s and 1870s, seemed to trouble the Apaches exceedingly."[24]

So that at the same time that the U.S. was supposedly ending slavery and "Emancipating" Afrikans, the U.S. Empire was using slavery of the most barbaric kind in order to genocidally destroy the Apache. It was colonial rule and genocide that were primary.

3. White Labor Against the Oppressed

The great democratic issues of that time could only grow out of this intense, seething nexus of Empire and colony, of oppressor nation and oppressed nations. Nothing took place that was not a factor on the battleground of Empire and oppressed. Nothing. Everyone was caught up in the war, however dimly they understood their own position. The new millions of immigrant European workers were desperately needed by the Empire. By 1860 half of the populations of New York, Chicago, Pittsburgh, and St. Louis were new immigrant Europeans. These reinforcements were immediately useful in new offensives against the Indian, Afrikan, and Mexicano peoples. While the settler economy was still absolutely dependent upon the forced labor of the Afrikan proletariat (cotton alone accounted for almost 60% of U.S. export earnings in 1860), the new reinforcements provided the means to reverse the dangerous concentrations of Afrikans in the metropolitan centers.

Frederick Douglass said in 1855: "Every hour sees us elbowed out of some employment to make room perhaps for some newly arrived immigrants, whose hunger and color are thought to give them a title to especial favor. White men are becoming house-servants, cooks and stewards, common laborers and flunkeys to our gentry…" The Philadelphia newspaper *Colored American* said as early as 1838 that free Afrikans "have ceased to be hackney coachmen and draymen,* and they are now almost displaced as stevedores. They are rapidly losing their places as barbers and servants." In New York City Afrikans were the majority of the house-servants in 1830, but by 1850 Irish house-servants outnumbered the entire Afrikan population there.[25] The Empire was swiftly moving to replace the rebellious and dangerous Afrikan proletariat by more submissive and loyal Europeans.

Even in the Deep South, urban Afrikan proletarians were increasingly replaced by loyal European immigrants. In New Orleans the draymen were all Afrikan in 1830, but by 1840 were all Irish.[26] One historian points out: "Occupational exclusion of Blacks actually began before the Civil War. In an unpublished study, Weinbaum has demonstrated conclusively such exclusion and decline [of skilled Afrikan workers –ed.] for Rochester, New York, Blacks between 1840 and 1860. My own work shows a similar decline in Charleston, SC, between 1850 and 1860. And these trends continued in Southern cities during Reconstruction. A crucial story has yet to be told. The 1870 New Orleans city directory, Woodward pointed out, listed 3,460 Black carpenters, cigarmakers, painters, shoemakers, coopers, tailors, blacksmiths, and foundry hands. By 1904, less than 10 per cent of that number appeared even though the New Orleans population had increased by more than 50 per cent."[27] Beneath the great events of the Civil War and Reconstruction, the **genocidal restructuring of the oppressed Afrikan nation continued year after year.**

This was clearly the work of the capitalists. But where did the new stratum of Euro-Amerikan workers stand on this issue? The defeat of the Slaveocracy, the political upheavals of the great conflict, and the enormous expansion of European immigration had stirred

---

* Carriers—those who hauled goods around the city for a fee.

and heartened white labor. In both North and South local unions revived and new unions began. New attempts emerged to form effective national federations of all white workers. Between 1863–73 some 130 white labor newspapers began publication.[28] The Eight-Hour Day movement "ran with express speed" from coast to coast in the wake of the war. During the long and bitter Depression of 1873–78, militant struggles broke out, ending in the famous General Strike of 1877. In this last strike the white workers won over to their side the troops sent by the government or defeated them in bloody street fighting in city after city. White labor in its rising cast a long shadow over the endless banquet table of the bourgeoisie.

Truly, white labor had become a giant in size. Even in a Deep South State such as Louisiana, by the 1860 census white laborers made up one-third of the total settler population.[29] In St. Louis (then the third-largest manufacturing center in the Empire) the 1864 census showed that slightly over one-third of that city's 76,000 white men were workers (rivermen, factory laborers, stevedores, etc.). In the Boston of the 1870s fully one-half of the total white population were workers and their families, mostly Irish.[30] In some Northern factory towns the proportion was even higher.

The ideological head on this giant body, however, still bore the cramped, little features of the old artisan/farmer mentality of previous generations. When this giant was aroused by the capitalists' cuts and kicks, its angry flailings knocked over troops and sent shockwaves of fear and uncertainty spreading through settler society. But its petit-bourgeois confusions let the capitalists easily outmaneuver it, each time herding it back to resentful acquiescence with skillful applications of "the carrot and the stick."

What was the essence of the ideology of white labor? Petit-bourgeois annexationism. Lenin pointed out in the great debates on the National Question that the heart of national oppression is annexation of the territory of the oppressed nation(s) by the oppressor nation. There is nothing abstract or mystical about this. To this new layer of European labor was denied the gross privileges of the settler bourgeoisie, who annexed whole nations. Even the particular privileges that so comforted the earlier Euro-Amerikan farmers and artisans—most particularly that of "annexing" individual plots of land every time their Empire advanced—were denied these European wage-slaves. But, typically, their petit-bourgeois vision saw for themselves a special, *better* kind of wage-slavery. The ideology of white labor held that as loyal citizens of the Empire even wage-slaves had a right to special privileges (such as "white man's wages"), beginning with the right to monopolize the labor market.

We must cut sharply through the liberal camouflage concealing this question. It is insufficient—*and therefore misleading*—to say that European workers wished to "discriminate against" or "exclude" or were "prejudiced against" colored workers. It was the labor of Afrikan and Indian workers that created the economy of the original Amerika; likewise, the economy of the Southwest was distilled from the toil of the Indian/Mexicano workers, and that of Northern California and the Pacific Northwest was built by Mexicano and Chinese labor. Immigrant European workers proposed to enter an economy *they hadn't built, and "annex," so as to speak, the jobs that the nationally oppressed had created.*

Naturally, the revisionists always want to talk about it as a matter of white workers not *sharing* equally enough—as though when a robber enters your home and takes everything you've earned, the problem is that this thief should "share" your property better! Since the ideology of white labor was annexationist and predatory, it was of necessity also rabidly pro-Empire and, despite angry outbursts, fundamentally servile towards the bourgeoisie. It was not a proletarian outlook, but the degraded outlook of a would-be labor aristocracy.

We can grasp this very concretely actually investigating the political rising of European labor in that period in relation to the nationally oppressed. Even today few comrades know how completely the establishment of the Empire in the Pacific Northwest depended upon Chinese labor.* In fact, the Chinese predate the Amerikan settler presence on the West Coast by many years.[31] When the famous Lewis & Clark expedition sent out by President Jefferson reached the Pacific in 1804, they arrived some sixteen years after the British established a major shipyard on Vancouver Bay—a shipyard manned by Chinese shipwrights and sailors.

---

* As well as the later waves of Japanese, Filipino, and Korean workers.

CHINESE FISHING VILLAGE, MONTEREY, CALIFORNIA, 1907.

For that matter, the Spanish further South in California had even earlier imported skilled Chinese workers. We know that Chinese had been present at the founding of Los Angeles in 1781. This is easy to understand when we see that California was closer to Asia than New York in practical terms; in travel time San Francisco was but 60 days' sail from Canton—but six months by wagon train from Kansas City.

The settler capitalists used Chinese labor to found virtually every aspect of their new Amerikan economy in this region. The Mexicano people, who were an outright majority in the area, couldn't be used because the settlers were engaged in reducing their numbers so as to consolidate U.S. colonial conquest. During the 1830s, '40s, and '50s the all-too-familiar settler campaign of mass terror, assassination, and land-grabbing was used against the Mexicanos. Rodolfo Acuña summarizes: *"During this time, the Chinese were used as an alternative to the Chicanos as California's labor force. Chicanos were pushed to the southern half of the State and were literally forced out of California in order to escape the lynching, abuses, and colonized status to which they had been condemned."*[32] Thus, the Chinese were not only victims of Amerika, but their very presence was a part of a genocidal campaign to dismember and colonize the Mexican Nation. In the same way, decades later Mexicano labor—now driven from the land and reduced to colonial status—would be used to replace Chinese labor by the settlers.

The full extent of Chinese labor's role is revealing. The California textile mills were originally 70–80% Chinese, as were the garment factories. As late as 1880, Chinese made up 52% of all shoe makers and 44% of all brick makers in the State, as well as one-half of all factory workers in the city of San Francisco.[33] The fish canneries were so heavily manned by Chinese—over 80%—that when a mechanical fish cleaner was introduced it was popularly called *"the Iron Chink."* The fish itself (salmon, squid, shrimp, etc.) was often caught and brought in by Chinese fishermen, who pioneered the fishing industry in the area. Chinese junks were then a common sight in California harbors, and literally thousands of Chinese seamen lived in the numerous all-Chinese fishing villages that dotted the coast from San Diego up to Oregon. As late as 1888 there were over 20 Chinese fishing villages just in San Francisco and San Pablo Bays, while 50% of the California fishing industry was still Chinese. Farms and vineyards were also founded on Chinese labor: in the 1870s when California became the largest wheat growing State in the U.S. over 85% of the farm labor was Chinese.

Chinese workers played a large part as well in bringing out the vast mineral wealth that so accelerated the growth of the U.S. in the West. In 1870 Chinese made up 25% of all miners in California, 21% in Washington, 58% in Idaho, and 61% in Oregon. In California the special monthly tax paid by each Chinese miner virtually supported local government for many years—accounting for 25–50% of all settler government revenues for 1851–70. Throughout the area Chinese also made up a service population, like Afrikans and Mexicanos in other regions of the Empire, for the settlers. Chinese cooks, laundrymen, and domestic servants were such a common part of Western settler life in the mines, cattle ranches, and cities that no Hollywood "Western" movie is complete without its stereotype Chinese cook.

But their greatest single feat in building the economy of the West was also their undoing. Between 1865 and 1869 some 15,000 Chinese laborers carved the far Western stretch of the Transcontinental rail line out of the hostile Sierra and Rocky Mountain ranges. Through severe weather they cut railbeds out of rock mountainsides, blasted tunnels, and laid the tracks of the

Central Pacific Railroad some 1,800 miles East to Ogden, Utah. It was and is a historic engineering achievement, every mile paid for in blood of the Chinese who died from exposure and avalanches. The reputation earned by Chinese workers led them to be hired to build rail lines not only in the West, but in the Midwest and South as well. This Transcontinental rail link enabled the minerals and farm produce of the West to be swiftly shipped back East, while giving Eastern industry ready access to Pacific markets, not only of the West Coast but all of Asia via the port of San Francisco.

The time-distance across the continent was now cut to two weeks, and cheap railroad tickets brought a flood of European workers to the West. There was, of course, an established settler tradition of terrorism towards Chinese. The *Shasta Republican* complained in its Dec. 12, 1856, issue that: *"Hundreds of Chinamen have been slaughtered in cold blood in the last 5 years … the murder of Chinamen was of almost daily occurrence."* Now the new legions of immigrant European workers demanded a qualitative increase in the terroristic assaults, and the 1870s and 1880s were decades of mass bloodshed.

The issue was very clear-cut—jobs. By 1870, some 42% of the whites in California were European immigrants. With their dreams of finding gold boulders lying in the streams having faded before reality, these new crowds of Europeans demanded the jobs that Chinese labor had created.[34] More than demanded, they were determined to "annex," to seize by force of conquest, all that Chinese workers had in the West. In imitation of the bourgeoisie they went about plundering with bullets and fire. In mining camps and towns from Colorado to Washington, Chinese communities came under attack. Many Chinese were shot down, beaten, their homes and stores set afire and gutted. In Los Angeles Chinese were burned alive by the European vigilantes, who also shot and tortured many others.

In perverse fashion, the traditional weapons of trade unionism were turned against the Chinese workers in this struggle. Many manufacturers who employed Chinese were warned that henceforth all desirable jobs must be filled by European immigrants. Boycotts were threatened, and in some industries (such as wineries and cigar factories) the new white unions invented the now-famous "union label"—printed tags which guaranteed that the specific product was produced solely by European unions. In 1884, when one San Francisco cigar manufacturer began replacing Chinese workers (who then made up 80–85% of the industry there) with European immigrants, the Chinese cigarmakers went on strike. Swiftly, the San Francisco white labor movement united to help the capitalists break the strike. Scabbing was praised, and the Knights of Labor and other European workers' organizations led a successful boycott of all cigar companies that employed Chinese workers. Boycotts were widely used in industry after industry to seize Chinese jobs.[35]

In the political arena a multitude of "Anti-Coolie" laws were passed on all levels of settler government. Special taxes and "license fees" on Chinese workers and tradesmen were used both to discourage them and to support settler government at their expense. Chinese who carried laundry deliveries on their backs in San Francisco had to pay the city a sixty-dollar "license fee" each year.[36] Many municipalities passed laws ordering all Chinese to leave, enforced by the trade union mobs.

The decisive point of the Empire-wide campaign to plunder what the Chinese had built up in the West was the 1882 Chinese Exclusion Act. Both Democratic and Republican parties supported this bill, which barred all Chinese immigration into the U.S. and made Chinese ineligible for citizenship. The encouragement offered by the capitalist state to the anti-Chinese offensive shows the forces at work. In their frenzy of petty plundering, European labor was being permitted to do the dirty work of the bourgeoisie. The Empire needed to promote and support this flood of European reinforcements to help take hold of the newly conquered territories. As California Gov. Henry Haight (whose name lives on in a certain San Francisco neighborhood) said in 1868: "No man is worthy of the name of patriot or statesman who countenances a policy which is opposed to the interests of the free white laboring and industrial classes ... What we desire for the permanent benefit of California is a population of white men ... We ought not to desire an effete population of Asiatics..." The national bourgeoisie used the "Anti-Coolie" movement and the resulting legislation to force individual capitalists to follow Empire policy and discharge Chinese in favor of Europeans. Now that the Chinese had built the economy of the

Pacific Northwest, it was time for them to be stripped and driven out.

The passage of the 1882 Act was taken as a "green-light," a "go-ahead" signal of approval to immigrant European labor from Congress, the White House, and the majority of Euro-Amerikans. It was taken as a license to kill, a declaration of open looting season on Chinese. Terrance Powderly, head of the Knights of Labor (which boasted that it had recruited Afrikan workers to help European labor) praised the victory of the Exclusion Act by saying that now the task for trade unionists was to finish the job—*by eliminating all Chinese left in the U.S. within the year!*[37]

The settler propaganda kept emphasizing how pure, honest Europeans had no choice but to *"defend"* themselves against the dark plots of the Chinese. Wanting to seize ("annex") Chinese jobs and small businesses, European immigrants kept shouting that they were only "defending" themselves against the vicious Chinese who were trying to steal the white man's jobs! And in case any European worker had second thoughts about the coming lynch mob, a constant ideological bombardment surrounded him by trade union and "socialist" leaders, bourgeois journalists, university professors and religious figures, politicians of all parties, and so on. Having decided to "annex" the fruits of the Chinese development of the Northwest, the usual settler propaganda about "defending" themselves was put forth.

Nor was Euro-Amerikan racial-sexual hate propaganda neglected, just as bizarre and perverted as it is about Afrikans. In 1876, for example, the *New York Times* published an alleged true interview with the Chinese operator of a local opium den. The story has the reporter asking the "Chinaman" about the "handsome but squalidly dressed young white girl" he sees in the opium den. The "Chinaman" allegedly answers: "Oh, hard time in New York. Young girl hungry. Plenty come here. Chinaman always have something to eat, and he like young white girl, He! He!"* A woman's magazine warned their

---

* Similar "news" stories are very popular today, reminding the white masses about all the runaway white teenagers who become "captives" of Afrikan "pimps and dope dealers." When we see such themes being pushed in the bourgeois media, we should know what's behind it.

readers to never leave little white girls alone with Chinese servants. The settler public was solemnly alerted that the Chinese plot was to steal white workers' jobs and thus force the starving wives to become their concubines. The most telling sign of the decision to destroy the Chinese community was the settler realization that these Chinese looked just like Afrikans in "women's garments"!

The ten years after the passage of the Exclusion Act saw the successful annexation of the Chinese economy on the West Coast. Tacoma and Seattle forced out their entire Chinese populations at gunpoint. In 1885 the infamous Rock Springs, Wyoming massacre took place, where over 20 Chinese miners were killed by a storm of rifle-fire as European miners enforced their take-over of all mining. Similar events happened all over the West. In 1886 some 35 California towns reported that they had totally eliminated their Chinese populations.

On the coast Italian immigrants burned Chinese ships and villages to take over most of the fishing industry by 1890. By that same year most of the Chinese workers in the vineyards had been replaced by Europeans. By 1894 the bulk of Chinese labor on the wheat and vegetable farms had been forced out. Step by step, as fast as they could be replaced, the Chinese who once built the foundation of the region's economy were being driven out.

Who took part in this infamous campaign? Virtually the whole of the Euro-Amerikan labor movement in the U.S., including "socialists" and "Marxists." Both of the two great nationwide union federations of the 19th century, the National Labor Union and the later Knights of Labor, played an active role.[38] The Socialist Labor Party was involved. The leading independent white labor newspaper, the *Workingman's Advocate* of Chicago, was edited by A.C. Cameron. He was a leader of the National Labor Union, a respected printing trades unionist, and the delegate from the NLU to the 1869 Switzerland conference of the Communist First International. His paper regularly printed speeches and theoretical articles by Karl Marx and other European Communists. Yet he loudly called in his newspaper for attacks on the immigrant *"Chinamen, Japanese, Malays,*

RIGHT: ANTI-CHINESE RIOT IN DENVER, COLORADO, ON OCT. 31, 1880.

and Monkeys" from Asia. Even most "Marxists" who deplored the crude violence of the labor mobs, such as Adolph Doubai (one of the leading German Communist immigrants), agreed that the Chinese had to be removed from the U.S.[39] It is easy to predict that if even European "Marxists" were so strongly pulled along by the lynch mobs, the bourgeois trade union leaders had to be running like dogs at the head of the hunt. Andrew Furuseth, the founder of the Seafarers International Union, AFL, Pat McCarthy, leader of the San Francisco Building Trades Council, Sam Gompers, leader of the cigarmakers union and later founder of the American Federation of Labor (AFL), were just a few of the many who openly led and incited the settler terror.[40]

When we say that the petit-bourgeois consciousness of European immigrant labor showed that it was a degraded stratum seeking extra-proletarian privileges, we aren't talking about a few nickels and dimes; the issue was genocide, carrying out the dirty work of the capitalists in order to reap some of the bloody fruits of national oppression. It is significant that the organizational focus of the early anti-Chinese campaign was the so-called Workingmen's Party of California, which was organized by an Irish immigrant confidence-man named Dennis Kearney. Kearney was the usual corrupt, phrase-making demagogue that the white masses love so well *("I am the voice of the people. I am the dictator ... I owe the people nothing, but they owe me a great deal.")**

This sleazy party, built on the platform of wiping out Chinese labor and federal reforms to aid white workers and farmers, attracted thousands of European workers—including most of the European "socialists" in California. Before falling apart from corruption, thugism, and factionism, Kearney's party captured seats in the State Assembly, the mayoralty in Sacramento, and controlled the Constitutional Convention which reformed the California Constitution. Even today settler historians, while deploring Kearney's racism, speak respectfully of the party's role in liberal reforms! Even revisionist CPUSA historians apparently feel no shame in praising this gang of degenerates for "arousing public support for a

---

* Unfortunately, we have Kearneys of our own.

number of important labor demands ... forcing old established parties to listen more attentively to the demands of the common people."[41] What this shows is that if the "respectable" Euro-Amerikan trade unionists and "Marxists" were scrabbling on their knees before the bourgeoisie along with known criminals such as Kearney, then they must have had much in common (is it so different today?).

The monopoly on desirable jobs that European labor had won in the West was continually "defended" by new white supremacist assaults. The campaign against Chinese was continued long into the 20th century, particularly so that its momentum could be used against Japanese, Filipino, and other Asian immigrant labor. The AFL played a major role in this. Gompers himself, a Jewish immigrant who became the most powerful bourgeois labor leader in the U.S., co-authored in 1902 a mass-distributed racist tract entitled: *Some Reasons For Chinese Exclusion: Meat vs. Rice, American Manhood vs. Asiatic Coolieism—Which Shall Survive?* In this crudely racist propaganda, the respected AFL President comforted white workers by pointing out that their cowardly violence toward Asians was justified by the victims' immoral and dangerous character: "The Yellow Man found it natural to lie, cheat and murder." Further, he suggested, in attacking Asian workers, whites were just nobly protecting their own white children, "thousands" of whom were supposed to be opium-addicted "prisoners" kept in the unseen back rooms of neighborhood Chinese laundries: "What other crimes were committed in those dark, fetid places, when those little innocent victims of the Chinamen's wiles were under the influence of the drug are too horrible to imagine..."[42] What's really hard "to imagine" is how anyone could believe this fantastical porno-propaganda; in truth, settlers will eagerly swallow *any* falsehoods that seem to justify their continuing crimes against the oppressed.

The Empire-wide campaign against the Chinese national minority played a major role in the history of Euro-Amerikan labor; it was a central rallying issue for many, a point around which immigrant European workers and other settlers could unite. It was a campaign in which *all* the major Euro-Amerikan labor federations, trade unions, and "socialist" organizations joined together. The annexation of the Chinese economy of the West during the later half of the 19th century was but another expression of the same intrusion that Afrikans met in the South and North. **All over the Empire immigrant European labor was being sent against the oppressed, to take what little we had.**

At times even their bourgeois masters wished that their dogs were on a shorter leash. Many capitalists saw, even as we were being cut down, that it would be useful to preserve us as a colonial labor force to be exploited whenever needed; but the immigrant white worker had no use for us whatsoever. Therefore, in the altered geometry of forces within the Empire, the new Euro-Amerikan working masses became willing pawns of the most vicious elements in the settler bourgeoisie, seeing only advantages in every possibility of our genocidal disappearance. And in this scramble upwards those wretched immigrants shed, like an old suit of clothes, the proletarian identity and honor of their Old European past. Now they were true Amerikans, real settlers who had done their share of the killing, annexing, and looting.

THE ARGUMENT OF NATIONALITY.

Excited Mob—"*We don't want any cheap-labor foreigners intruding upon us native-born citizens.*"

While marching through a region, the black troops would sometimes pause at a plantation, ascertain from the slaves the name of the "meanest" overseer in the neighborhood, and then, if he had not fled, "tie him backward on a horse and force him to accompany them." Although a few masters and overseers were whipped or strung up by a rope in the presence of their slaves, this appears to have been a rare occurrence. More commonly, black soldiers preferred to apportion the contents of the plantation and the Big House among those whose labor had made them possible, singling out the more "notorious" slaveholders and systematically ransacking and demolishing their dwellings. "They gutted his mansion of some of the finest furniture in the world," wrote Chaplain Henry M. Turner, in describing a regimental action in North Carolina. Having been informed of the brutal record of this slaveholder, the soldiers had resolved to pay him a visit. While the owner was forced to look on, they went to work on his "splendid mansion" and "utterly destroyed every thing on the place." Wielding their axes indiscriminately, they shattered his piano and most of the furniture and ripped his expensive carpets to pieces. What they did not destroy they distributed among his slaves.

—Leon F. Litwack, *Been in the Storm So Long*

4. The Test of Black Reconstruction

If Euro-Amerikan labor's attitude towards Chinese labor was straightforward and brutal, towards the Afrikan colony it was more complex, more tactical. Indeed, the same Euro-Amerikan labor leaders who sponsored the murderous assaults on Chinese workers kept telling Afrikan workers how "the unity of labor" was the first thing in their hearts!

Terrance Powderly, the Grand Master Workman of the Knights of Labor (who had personally called for wiping out all Chinese in North America within one year), suddenly became the apostle of brotherhood when it came to persuading Afrikans to support his organization: "The color of a candidate shall not debar him from admission; rather let the coloring of his mind and heart be the test."[43] This apparent contradiction arose from the unique position of the Afrikan colony. Where the Chinese workers had been a national minority whose numbers at any one time probably never exceeded 100,000 (roughly two-thirds of the Chinese returned to Asia), Afrikans were an entire colonized Nation; on their National Territory in the South they numbered some 4 million. This was an opponent Euro-Amerikan labor had to engage more carefully.

The relationship between Euro-Amerikan labor and Afrikan labor cannot be understood just from the world of the mine and mill. Their relationship was not separate from, but a part of, the general relation of oppressor nation to colonized oppressed nation. And at that time the struggle over the Afrikan colony was the storm center of all politics in the U.S. Empire. The end of the Civil War and the end of chattel Afrikan slavery were not the resolution of bitter struggle in the colonial South, but merely the opening of a whole new stage.

We have to see that there were two wars going on, and that both were mixed in the framework of the Civil War. The first conflict was the fratricidal, intra-settler war between Northern industrial capitalists and Southern planter capitalists. We use the phrase "Civil War" because it is the commonly known name for the war. It is more accurate to point out that the war was between two settler nations for ownership of the Afrikan colony—and ultimately for ownership of the continental Empire. The second was the protracted struggle for liberation by the colonized Afrikan Nation in the South. Neither struggle ended with the military collapse of the Confederacy in 1865. For ten years, a long heartbeat in history, both wars took focus around the Reconstruction governments.

The U.S. Empire faced the problem that its own split into two warring settler nations had provided the long-awaited strategic moment for the anti-colonial rising of the oppressed Afrikan Nation. Just as in the 1776 War of Independence, both capitalist factions in the Civil War hoped that Afrikans would remain docilely on the sidelines while Confederate Amerika and Union Amerika fought it out. But the rising of millions of Afrikans, striking off their chains, became the decisive factor in the Civil War. As Du Bois so scathingly points out:

> "Freedom for the slave was the logical result of a crazy attempt to wage war in the midst of four million black slaves, and trying the while sublimely to ignore the interests of those slaves in the outcome of the fighting.

> "Yet, these slaves had enormous power in their hands. Simply by stopping work, they could threaten the Confederacy with starvation. By walking into the Federal camps, they showed to doubting Northerners the easy possibilities of using them as workers and as servants, as farmers, and as spies, and finally, as fighting soldiers. And not only using them thus, but by the same gesture depriving their enemies of their use in just these fields. It was the fugitive slave who made the slaveholders face the alternative of surrendering to the North, or to the Negroes."

Judge John C. Underwood of Richmond, Virginia, testified later before Congress that: "I had a conversation with one of the leading men in that city, and he said to me that the enlistment of Negro troops by the United States was the turning point of the rebellion; that it was the heaviest blow they ever received. He remarked that

when the Negroes deserted their masters, and showed a general dis-
position to do so and join the forces of the United States, intelligent
men everywhere saw that the matter was ended."[44]

The U.S. Empire took advantage of this rising against the Slave
Power to conquer the Confederacy—but now its occupying Union
armies had to not only watch over the still sullen and dangerous
Confederates, but had to prevent the Afrikan masses from breaking
out. Four million strong, the Afrikan masses were on the move politically. Unless halted, this rapid march could quickly lead to mass
armed insurrection against the Union and the formation of a New
Afrikan government in the South. Events had suddenly moved to
that point.

The most perceptive settlers understood this very well. The
Boston capitalist Elizur Wright said in 1865: "... *the blacks must be
enfranchised or they will be ready and willing to fight for a government of
their own.*" Note, "*a government of their own.*" For having broken the
back of the Confederacy, having armed and trained themselves contrary to settler expectations, the Afrikan masses were in no mood to
passively submit to reenslavement. And they desired and demanded
Land, the national foundations that they themselves had created out
of the toil of three hundred years. Du Bois tells us: "*There was con-
tinual fear of insurrection in the Black Belt. This* vague fear increased
toward Christmas, 1866. The Negroes were disappointed because of
the delayed division of lands. There was a natural desire to get possession of firearms, and all through the summer and fall, they were
acquiring shotguns; muskets, and pistols, in great quantities."

All over their Nation, Afrikans had seized the land that they
had sweated on. Literally millions of Afrikans were on strike in the
wake of the Confederacy's defeat. The Southern economy—now
owned by Northern Capital—was struck dead in its tracks, unable
to operate at all against the massive, stony resistance of the Afrikan
masses. This was the greatest single labor strike in the entire history
of U.S. Empire. It was not done by any AFL-CIO-type official union
for higher wages, but was the monumental act of an oppressed people striking out for Land and Liberation. Afrikans refused to leave
the lands that were now theirs, refused to work for their former
slavemasters.

U.S. General Rufus Saxon, former head of the Freedmen's Bureau in South Carolina, reported to a Congressional committee in 1866 that Afrikan field workers in that State were arming themselves and refusing to *"submit quietly"* to the return of settler rule. Even the pro-U.S. Afrikan petit-bourgeoisie there, according to Saxon, was afraid they were losing control of the masses: *"I will tell you what the leader of the colored Union League ... said to me: they said that they feared they could not much longer control the freedmen if I left Charlestown ... they feared the freedmen would attempt to take their cause in their own hands."*[45]

The U.S. Empire's strategy for reenslaving their Afrikan colony involved two parts: (1) The military repression of the most organized and militant Afrikan communities. (2) Pacifying the Afrikan Nation by neocolonialism, using elements of the Afrikan petit bourgeoisie to lead their people into embracing U.S. citizenship as the answer to all problems. Instead of nationhood and liberation, the neocolonial agents told the masses that their democratic demands could be met by following the Northern settler capitalists (i.e. the Republican Party) and looking to the Federal government as the ultimate protector of Afrikan interests.

So all across the Afrikan Nation the occupying Union Army—supposedly the "saviors" and "emancipators" of Afrikans—invaded the most organized, most politically conscious Afrikan communities. In particular, all those communities where the Afrikan masses had seized land in a revolutionary way came under Union Army attack. In those areas the liberation of the land was a collective act, with the workers from many plantations holding meetings and electing leaders to guide the struggle. Armed resistance was the order of the day, and planter attempts to retake the land were rebuffed at rifle point. The U.S. Empire had to both crush and undermine this dangerous development that had come from the grassroots of their colony.

In August 1865 around Hampton, Virginia, for example, Union cavalry were sent to dislodge 5,000 Afrikans from liberated land. Twenty-one Afrikan leaders were captured, who had been "armed with revolvers, cutlasses, carbines, shotguns." In the Sea Islands off the South Carolina coast some 40,000 Afrikans were forced off the former plantations at bayonet point by Union soldiers. While the Afrikans had coolly told returning planters to go—and pulled out weapons to emphasize their orders—they were not able to overcome the U.S. Army. In 1865 and 1866 the Union occupation disarmed and broke up such dangerous outbreaks. *The special danger to the U.S. Empire was that the grassroots political drive to have armed power over the land, to build economically self-sufficient regions under Afrikan control, would inevitably raise the question of Afrikan sovereignty.*

Afrikan soldiers who had learned too much for the U.S. Empire's peace of mind were a special target (of both Union and Confederate alike). Even before the War's end a worried President Lincoln had written to one of his generals: *"I can hardly believe that the South and North can live in peace unless we get rid of the Negroes. Certainly they cannot, if we don't get rid of the Negroes whom we have armed and disciplined and who have fought with us, I believe, to the amount of 150,000 men. I believe it would be better to export them all..."*

Afrikan U.S. army units were hurriedly disarmed and disbanded, or sent out of the South (out West to serve as colonial troops against the Indians, for example). The U.S. Freedmen's Bureau said in 1866 that the new, secret white terrorist organizations in Mississippi placed a special priority on murdering returning Afrikan veterans of the Union Army. In New Orleans some members of the U.S. 74th Colored Infantry were arrested as "vagrants" the day after they were mustered out of the army. Everywhere in the occupied Afrikan Nation an emphasis was placed on defusing or wiping out the political guerrillas and militia of the Afrikan masses.

The U.S. Empire's second blow was more subtle. The Northern settler bourgeoisie sought to convince Afrikans that they could, and should want to, become citizens of the U.S. Empire. To this end the 14th Amendment to the Constitution involuntarily made all Afrikans here paper U.S. citizens. This neocolonial strategy offered Afrikan colonial subjects the false democracy of paper citizenship in the Empire that oppressed them and held their Nation under armed occupation.

While the U.S. Empire had regained its most valuable colony, it had major problems. The Union armies militarily held the

territory of the Afrikan Nation. But the settlers who had formerly
garrisoned the colony and overseen its economy could no longer be
trusted; even after their attempted rival Empire had been ended, the
Southern settlers remained embittered and dangerous enemies of
the U.S. bourgeoisie. The Afrikan masses, whose labor and land provided the wealth that the Empire extracted from their colony, were
rebellious and unwilling to peacefully submit to the old ways. The
Empire needed a loyalist force to hold and pacify the colony.

The U.S. Empire's solution was to turn their Afrikan colony into
a neocolony. This phase was called Black Reconstruction. Afrikans
were promised democracy, human rights, self-government, and
popular ownership of the land—but only as loyal "citizens" of the
U.S. Empire. Under the neocolonial leadership of some petit-bourgeois elements, Afrikans became the loyalist social base. Not only
were they enfranchised en masse, but Afrikans were participants and
leaders in government: Afrikan jurors, judges, State officials, militia
captains, Governors, Congressmen, and even several Afrikan U.S.
Senators were conspicuous.

This regional political role for Afrikans produced results that
would be startling in the Empire today, and by the settler standards
of a century ago were totally astonishing. The white supremacist propagandist James Pike reports angrily of State government in South
Carolina, the State with the largest Afrikan presence in government:

> "The members of the Assembly issued forth from the State
> House. About three-quarters of the crowd belonged to the
> African race. They were such a looking body of men as might
> pour out of a market-house or a courthouse at random in any
> Southern State. Every Negro type and physiognomy was here
> to be seen, from the genteel serving-man, to the rough-hewn
> customer from the rice or cotton field. Their dress was as var-
> ied as their countenances. There was the second-hand, black
> frockcoat of infirm gentility, glossy and threadbare. There was
> the stovepipe hat of many ironings and departed styles. There
> was also to be seen a total disregard of the proprieties of cos-
> tume in the coarse and dirty garments of the field.

"The Speaker is black, the Clerk is black, the doorkeepers are black, the little pages are black, the Chairman of the Ways and Means is black, and the chaplain is coal black. At some of the desks sit colored men whose types it would be hard to find outside the Congo. It was not all sham, nor all burlesque. They have a genuine interest and a genuine earnestness in the business of the assembly which we are bound to recognize and respect ... They have an earnest purpose, born of conviction that their conditions are not fully assured, which lends a sort of dignity to their proceedings."

This dramatic reversal outraged the Confederate masses—who saw their former "property" now risen over them. The liberal Reconstruction governments swept away the social garbage of centuries, releasing modern reforms throughout Southern life: public school systems, integrated juries, State highway and railroad systems, protective labor reforms, divorce and property rights for women, and so on.

What was most apparent about Black Reconstruction was its impossible contradictions. Now we can say that while it was a bold course for the Empire to embark upon, it so went against the structure of settler society that it could only have been temporary. Afrikans were organized politically into the loyalist Union Leagues (which were often armed), organized militarily into State militia companies, and all for the purpose of holding down some Euro-Amerikan settlers both for themselves and for the U.S. Empire. Yet, at the same time the Empire wanted Afrikans disarmed and disorganized. This neocolonial bourgeois government of Black Reconstruction was doomed from its first day, since it promised that Afrikans would share the land and the power with settlers.

The Afrikan petit-bourgeois leadership in government made every effort to stabilize relations with the former planter ruling class, and, in fact, to cement relations with all classes of settlers. They openly offered themselves as allies of the planters in return for settler acceptance of the new neocolony. But in vain.

The Reconstruction politicians hoped for a bourgeois democratic reconciliation, wherein the Northern industrialists, they and

even the former slave-masters could all harmoniously unite to pros-
per off the labor of the Afrikan proletariat. Beverly Nash, one of the
Afrikan leaders in the South Carolina legislature, told his people:
"We recognize the Southern white man as the true friend of the black
man ... It is not our desire to be a discordant element in the community, or to unite the poor against the rich ... The white man has
the land, the black man has the labor, and labor is worth nothing
without capital." Nash promised the banned ex-Confederates that
he would fight to not only get their voting rights restored, but to
get "our first men" (the former Confederate leaders) back in their
customary places in Congress and the judges' bench. This desire to
be accepted by the planter elite was far too common. Henry Turner,
the "most prominent" Afrikan politician in Georgia, opposed seizing tax-delinquent planter estates and campaigned to free Jefferson
Davis from prison!

But Reconstruction fell, its foundations eroded away by the
ever-growing mass terror against the Afrikan population by settler
reaction. It was militarily overthrown by the secret planter paramilitary groups of the Ku Klux Klan, White Caps, White Cross, White
Legion and so on. In town after town, county and parish one after
another, then in State after State, Reconstruction was broken in
bloody killings.

During the 1868 elections in Louisiana, for example, some
2,000 Afrikans were thought to have been killed or wounded, with
many more forced to flee. In Shreveport a gang of Italian fishermen
and market venders called "The Innocents" roamed the streets for
ten days before the elections, literally killing every Afrikan they
could find. Some 297 Afrikans were murdered in New Orleans. In
Bossier Parish "One hundred and twenty corpses were found in the
woods or were taken out of the Red River after a 'Negro' hunt..."
Although it took ten years for Reconstruction to be finally defeated
(and another twenty years before its advances were all erased), the
guerrilla war between planter and Afrikan forces was disastrously
one-sided. The war could only have had one end, since Afrikans
were disarmed militarily and politically.

By 1874 only four States—Mississippi, Louisiana, South Carolina, and Florida—still remained in the hands of Reconstruction.

The end was in sight. Secret conferences of the planter leadership mapped out the final drive to tear out the heart of Black Reconstruction, and to begin the long, hundred-year night of absolute, terroristic rule. The White League was organized as the armed united front of the KKK and all the other planter organizations. Within months it had 40,000 members. The white violence intensified.

Even at this late date the Afrikan petit-bourgeois leaders of Reconstruction remained true to their loyalty to the Empire. In 1876 there was a militant strike wave among the Afrikan plantation laborers in South Carolina. Scabs were beaten and taken prisoner, and even the local police were overpowered by the armed strikers. But the Afrikan U.S. Congressman Robert Smalls led the State militia in and pacified the angry workers, ending the strike. In Mississippi when the armed planter takeover drowned the 1876 elections in a sea of blood, Afrikan U.S. Congressman John Lynch (who had just lost his seat through vote fraud at gunpoint) reminded everyone to remain loyal to the Empire:

> "You certainly cannot expect ... to resort to mob law and brute force, or to use what may be milder language, inaugurate a revolution. My opinion is that revolution is not the remedy to be applied in such cases. Our system of government is supposed to be one of law and order ... there is patriotism enough in this country and sufficient love of justice and fair play in the hearts of the American people..."

In 1876–77, the final accommodation between Northern Capital and the Southern planters was reached in the "Hayes-Tilden deal." The South promised to accept the dominance of the Northern bourgeoisie over the entire Empire, and to permit the Republican candidate Rutherford B. Hayes to succeed Grant in the U.S. Presidency. In return, the Northern bourgeoisie agreed to let the planters have regional hegemony over the South, and to withdraw the last of the occupying Union troops so that the Klan could take care of Afrikans as they wished. While the guarded remnants of Reconstruction held out here and there for some years (Afrikan Congressmen were elected from the South until 1895), the critical year of 1877 marked their conclusive defeat.

During these fateful years, when the *central* political issue in the Empire was the war in the Afrikan colony, the white labor movement lined up on the side of the KKK terror—and against the Afrikan masses. Even the neocolonial society of Black Reconstruction was hated by white labor, since it involved giving Afrikans at least an outward form of democratic rights and government power. Even neocolonialism was too good for Afrikans in the opinion of white labor.

Some may consider it unusual that white workers opposed Black Reconstruction; particularly since Black Reconstruction not only bent over backwards to treat the entire white community, from planters to poor whites, with great respect, but introduced social reforms which gave a real boost upwards to poor whites. Poor whites were able to send their children to the new public schools, and for the first time in much of the South they were able to vote and hold minor public offices (during the "Slave Power" reign stiff property qualifications barred many whites from having political rights). These gifts failed to win the gratitude of poor whites.

Karl Marx and Friedrich Engels saw that the "mean whites" (as they called them) of the South were hopeless politically. They felt that nothing could be done with them but to render them powerless until they died out of old age. This was not a unique observation.

"Shooting Down Negroes on the Morning of May 2, 1866"
during Memphis Riots. From *Harper's Weekly*.

Wendell Phillips, the great Radical abolitionist, bluntly pleaded in 1870: *"Now is the time ... to guarantee the South against the possible domination or the anger of the white race. We adhere to our opinion that nothing, or not much, except hostility, can be expected of two-thirds of the adult white men. They will go to their graves unchanged. No one of them should ever again be trusted with political rights. And all the elemental power of civilization should be combined and brought into play to counterwork the anger and plots of such foes."[46]*

No sooner had the planter Confederacy been struck down, than poor whites began responding to the appeals of the KKK and the other planter guerrilla organizations. This was a mass phenomena. Their motivation was obvious: they desired to keep Afrikans as *colonial subjects below even wage labor.* Du Bois relates:

> "When, then, he faced the possibility of being himself compelled to compete with a Negro wage laborer, while both were hirelings of a white planter, his whole soul revolted. He turned, therefore, from war service to guerrilla warfare, particularly against Negroes. He joined secret organizations, like the Ku Klux Klan, which fed his vanity by making him co-worker with the white planter, and gave him a chance to maintain his race superiority by killing and intimidating 'niggers'; and even in secret forays of his own, he could drive away the planter's black help, leaving the land open to white labor. Or he could murder too successful freedmen."

North or South, East or West, Euro-Amerikan workingmen were intent on driving out or pushing further down all subject labor—whether Afrikan, Mexicano or Chinese. In fact, despite the divisions of the Civil War there were few qualitative differences between Northern and Southern white labor. In part this is because there was considerable merging through migration within the Empire.

So when Euro-Amerikan labor, greatly revived by the massive reinforcements immigrating from Old Europe, reorganized itself during the Civil War, it was not any strengthening of democratic forces; rather, it added new formations of oppressors, new blows

"JULIA HAYDEN, THE COLORED SCHOOL
TEACHER, ONE OF THE LATEST VIC-
TIMS OF THE WHITE MAN'S LEAGUE,
WAS ONLY SEVENTEEN YEARS OF AGE.
SHE WAS THE DAUGHTER OF RESPECT-
ABLE PARENTS IN MAURY COUNTY,
TENNESSEE, AND HAD BEEN CAREFULLY
EDUCATED AT THE CENTRAL COLLEGE,
NASHVILLE, A FAVORITE PLACE FOR
THE INSTRUCTION OF YOUTH OF BOTH
SEXES OF HER RACE."
(*HARPER'S WEEKLY*, OCTOBER 8, 1874)

being directed against the oppressed. Just as the petit-bourgeois
workingmen's movements of the 1840s and 1850s, these were
"white unions" for settlers only. So that when the representatives
from eight craft trades met in Louisville in 1864 to form the short-
lived "International Industrial Assembly of North America," there
was no mention of the emancipation of Afrikan labor.

Similarly, when the National Labor Union was formed in 1866,
most of its members and leaders clearly intended to simply push
aside Afrikan labor. The NLU was the first major labor federation
of white workers, the forerunner of today's AFL-CIO. Delegates
from 59 trade unions and craft organizations took part in its first
Baltimore meeting, with observers from much of the rest of the settler craft unions joining into the heady talking and planning. The
most "advanced" settler unionists strongly argued for "unity" with
Afrikan workers. It was repeatedly pointed out how the capitalists
had used Afrikan workers to get around strikes and demands for
higher wages by white workmen. Rather than let Afrikans compete
in the job market against settlers, it was urged to restrain them by
taking them into the NLU.

As Du Bois pointed out: "Here was a first halting note. Negroes
were welcome to the labor movement, not because they were laborers but because they might be competitors in the market, and the
logical conclusion was either to organize them or guard against their
actual competition by other methods. It was to this latter alternative

that white American labor almost unanimously turned." In other words, settler trade unionists preferred to limit job competition between whites and Afrikans *by driving the latter out of the labor market.* All motions to admit Afrikans to the NLU were defeated, as the settler trade unionists continued following the capitalists' long-range plan to use them to replace Afrikan labor. It should be remembered that in all these deeds, Euro-Amerikan labor, no matter how much it huffed and puffed itself up, was just servilely following the genocidal strategies of the industrial bourgeoisie—for which service the capitalists had imported them in the first place, rewarding their pawns with the customary mixture of table scraps and kicks.

But note, the radical/conservative difference of opinion within the ranks of settler unionism was just like that between Gov. Berkeley and Bacon; a difference between following cooptive strategies of genocide or seeking an immediate "final solution" through overwhelming force. These two opposites in the eternal settler debate are obviously inseparable and interwoven. By the National Labor Union's 1869 Convention the advocates of tactically embracing Afrikan workers had gained the upper hand, for there was serious trouble. Afrikan labor had gotten "out of control."

Throughout the Empire—but especially in their Nation—Afrikan workers were organizing their own unions, following their own leaders, launching their own strikes. In Richmond, Va. there were strikes by Afrikan stevedores and railroad workers and tobacco factory workers. On the heels of the 1867 strike wave throughout the South, Afrikan unions formed in city after city. In Savannah, Ga. the 1867 strike of Afrikan longshoremen forced the city government to lift a $10 poll tax. In Charleston, S.C., they formed the powerful Colored Longshoremen's Protective Union Association, the strongest and most respected labor organization in that State. After winning a strike for better wages, the CLPUA started helping other unions of Afrikan proletarians get organized. By 1869, State conventions of Afrikan unions were being held, following the call for the December 1869 first convention of the National Colored Labor Union. This federation was intensely political, and embraced Afrikan workers in all spheres of production, North and South. Longshoremen, carpenters, tenant farmers, printers, waiters, barbers, construction laborers, etc. were all united within it. Eventually it would have locals in 23 States.

Clearly, Euro-Amerikan labor was feeling the heat. Their colonial competitors were "out of control," building their *own* organizations to further their *own* interests. This had to be fought! The immediate decision was to warmly invite these Afrikan unions to join the white NLU, so that the settler unionists could mislead and undermine them. So at the 1869 NLU Convention, for the first time, nine Afrikan union delegates were seated. As we might expect, the speeches and pledges of eternal brotherhood flowed like some intoxicating drink. In a scene reminiscent of the festive ceremonies that marked the signing of the early "peace" treaties between settlers and Indians, the convention became imbued with the spirit of unity. So much that an amazed *New York Times* reporter wrote:

> "When a native Mississippian and an ex-confederate officer, in addressing a convention, refers to a colored delegate who has preceded him as 'the gentleman from Georgia', when a native Alabamian, who has for the first time crossed the Mason and Dixon line, and who was from boyhood taught to regard the Negro simply as chattel, sits in deliberate consultation with another delegate whose ebony face glistens with African sheen, and signs the report of his colored co-delegate, when an ardent and Democratic partisan (from New York at that*) declares with a 'rich Irish brogue' that he asks for himself no privilege as a mechanic or a citizen that he is not willing to concede to every other man, white or black—when, I say, these things can be seen or heard at a national convention, called for any purpose, then one may indeed be warranted in asserting that time works curious changes."[47]

But the celebration of unity was short-lived. The white trade unionists were, of course, only attempting to deceive Afrikan workers.

---

* The reporter remarks on this because the Democratic Party was the pro-slavery party, and New York was infamous as the seat of some of the most vicious and violent anti-Afrikan mass sentiment.

Their invitation to "join" the NLU simply meant that Afrikans would promise to honor all white strikes and organizing drives; in return, they would have the privilege of being consoled as white labor savagely and relentlessly annexed their jobs. The second aspect of this "unity" was that Afrikans would be expected to follow European labor in opposing democratic demands in the South and helping to restore the chains around their legs. The "integration" of the NLU meant not only submission to European hegemony, but was virtually suicidal. Small wonder that Afrikans quickly parted ways with the NLU.[48]

While the NLU had granted Afrikan organizations the privilege of affiliating with it as a federation, Afrikans themselves were barred out of the individual white trade unions. **Every advance, therefore, of European trade unionism meant the "clearing" of Afrikan workers out of another mill, factory, railroad, warehouse or dock.** The capitalist attack on Afrikan labor, begun in the early 1830s, continued and gathered momentum. In the most celebrated single case, Lewis Douglass (the son of Frederick Douglass) was repeatedly denied admission to the Typographers' Union. A printer at the Government Printing Office, Douglass was not only denied by the local, but his appeals were turned down by two successive conventions of the Typographers' Union—and even by the entire NLU convention.[49]

It is important to realize how strongly and overwhelmingly Euro-Amerikan workers in the Civil War period supported the concept of a settler Empire—particularly as applied to guaranteeing white workers the right to annex the jobs that Afrikan, Chinese, Mexicano, and other oppressed labor had created. Of the 130 labor newspapers started between 1863–73, in the great upsurge of white labor, exactly one (1) supported even bourgeois democratic equality for Afrikans.[50] These insurgent journals represented the "best," the most advanced trade unionists in the settler Empire. Yet only one out of one-hundred-and-thirty supported democratic rights for Afrikans.

That lone journal, the *Boston Daily Evening Voice* of the Boston printing trades, opposed President Johnson, supported Afrikan admission to the unions, backed the demand for free land for Afrikans, and so on. Such principled views lost them so many subscribers that, in a last vain effort to stay afloat, the editors promised their readers that the newspaper would stop writing about Reconstruction and the problems of Afrikans (saying that anyway that issue "is practically solved").[51] Much more typical was the *St. Louis Daily Press,* again an alternative newspaper started by local printers during a strike. The *Press* was quite "progressive"; that is, it advocated the Eight-Hour Day, the Irish Revolution, equal rights for white women, the unity of European workers around the world—even printing long Marxist documents sent by the First International in Europe. It also opposed democratic rights for Afrikans, and called on white labor to drive "the niggers" out of all desirable jobs.[52]

No one is above the reality of history. Even the masses themselves are tested in the crucible, forged, tempered or broken in the class struggle. And not in side skirmishes or paper debates either, but in great battles upon which the future waits. The attempted rising of the Afrikan colonial masses—protracted, bitter, involving millions of desperate combatants—was such a pivotal event.

As the war raged on, carrying with it the hopes of whatever democratic forces existed within the Empire, thousands upon thousands of Afrikans gave their lives. In the growing defeats eventually the entire Afrikan Nation paid the blood price of reenslavement. How should we be impressed, then, when we learn that in that hour Northern white labor was trying to tell everyone that the *real, main issue was—a shorter work day!* **If it were not so cowardly and treacherous, it would pass as comic relief.**

5. The Contradictions of White Labor

The issue of a shorter work day spread enthusiastically among the white workers between 1866 and 1873. During these years the Eight-Hour Day struggle held first place in the activities of white labor. With considerable foresight, the leaders of the National Labor Union had seen the need for such a single issue to unite and discipline their immature followers. At the founding Convention of the NLU in Baltimore, on August 20, 1866, the call was sent forth for all white workingmen in every region, trade, and industry to combine on this one front: *"... the first and great necessity of the present to free the labor of this country from capitalistic slavery is the passing of a law by which eight hours shall be the normal working day in all states of the American union."*[53]

Throughout the '60s and early '70s the Eight-Hour Day Movement grew, with immigrant German socialists playing a leading role in organizing "Eight Hour Leagues" in all the major cities of the Empire.[54] Literally millions took part in the strikes, parades and rallies. By 1868 six States, led by California, a number of cities, and the Federal government had passed Eight-Hour Day laws (the last only applying to Federal employees). In 1872, when the New York City building trades won a three-month strike for the Eight-Hour Day, a festive parade of 150,000 white workmen took over the main streets of the city.[55]

But this campaign folded like wet cardboard during the Depression of 1873–78, when it turned out that the capitalists had no intention of honoring any promises, agreements or laws. The white trade unionists found their hours of toil increasing while their pay was steadily slashed. Not until the CIO and New Deal in the 1930s would white workers attain their goal of the Eight-Hour Day.

Defeat, however, is not the same thing as failure; the Eight-Hour campaign was a success for white labor. It was a new stage of unity, the first, Empire-wide, coast-to-coast political campaign. As such it marked the historic point where the swelling settler masses emerged upwards from their earlier, pre-industrial, small craft consciousness—and entered the industrial age.

That campaign was the first time white labor actually achieved a broad, national unity in action. This was evident at the time. Alexander Kennady, head of the San Francisco Trades Assembly and a leader of both the Eight-Hour campaign and the National Labor Union, said: "…By far the most important result of this eight hour agitation—to those who look forward to the day when labor, organized and effectively drilled, shall assume its legitimate sphere in the

LEADERS OF THE KNIGHTS OF LABOR.

body politic—is visible in the marked improvement in the character of the men engaged in the movement. A few years ago the working population of California were in a chaotic state—disorganized, and at the mercy of the capitalists—with very rare exceptions. Today, nearly every branch of skilled industry has its own union, fixing its own rate of wages, and regulating its domestic differences. A spirit of independence, and a feeling of mutual confidence inspire its members..."[56]

Of course, when Kennady talks about "the working population" he isn't referring to Mexicanos, Chinese, Indians, or Afrikans—he is only discussing white settlers. When he proudly points out how "every branch of skilled industry has its own union," he means unions of white workers. While he refers to these new unions taking care of "domestic differences," it is interesting that he fails to mention the trade union role in the primary labor conflict of the time—the drive by the white unions to annex the jobs of oppressed workers. This is a curiously right-wing result from such a supposedly "class conscious" labor campaign.

This contradiction sums up the Eight-Hour struggle (and the great strike wave of 1873–77). The Eight-Hour demand was not only righteous, but it was a demand that hit home to working people across the widest variety of industries, trades, and nationalities—it became the first truly international campaign of European workers, as the First International spread it to England, France, and all of Europe. The largest single Eight-Hour demonstration was not in Europe or the U.S., however, but was in Manila; Filipino workers defied the Spanish colonial authorities and struck in a massive rally of one million. Many Afrikan, Mexicano, and Chinese workers responded militantly to the call for the Eight-Hour struggle, and in some areas Afrikan workers took an early lead in stirring up action. But the campaign, instead of *uniting* working people, furthered *disunity*.

It was no coincidence that no sooner had the early victories of the Eight-Hour campaign unified and strengthened white labor in California than they began *stepping up the attack against Chinese workers*. Nor is it true that the Eight-Hour campaign was the work of noble, class conscious trade unionists, while the anti-Chinese and anti-Afrikan campaigns were the work of some totally separate bands of declassed hoodlums and bigots. Both were the acts of the *same* hands. All of the individual craft unions, the large federations such as the National Labor Union and the Knights of Labor, the local trades assemblies, the labor press, the left organizations such as the Socialist Labor Party and the Communist-led General German Working Men's Association, were involved in these white supremacist offensives.

Unlike the experience of other nations, the Eight-Hour campaign in the U.S. Empire had an anti-democratic character, consolidating the settler masses around pro-capitalist politics. In regard to the pivotal struggle of Black Reconstruction, it is clear that the overwhelming majority of the Eight-Hour Day activists were in the camp of the enemy. While "only" a minority of a few hundreds of thousands were personally active in killing and reenslaving Afrikans, they committed their crimes *with the support of the rest* of their white kith and kin. Those "advanced" workers (particularly the German socialist and radical exiles) who loudly sympathized with the plight of the ex-slaves, didn't stop for one hour in their headlong rush to unite with the white supremacist mobs. It was as if a witness to a criminal attack were to loudly bemoan the injuries done to the victim—while trying to convince the criminals that they should become partners! The Eight-Hour campaign, the "Anti-Coolie" and anti-Afrikan campaigns were not separate and unconnected events, **but linked chapters in the development of the same movement of white labor.**

This young movement, for all its anti-capitalist noises, was unable to resist being drawn deeper and deeper into bourgeois politics. As the National Labor Union was having its first convention and first issuing the call for the Eight-Hour campaign, five representatives of the new organization were meeting with President Andrew Johnson to solicit his support. And when he threw out a gesture towards white labor by ordering the workday for government printers cut to eight hours, he was hailed as the true friend of the white masses. The leading union newspaper *National Workman* of New York City praised his "practical sympathy with labor." The Philadelphia Trades Council described his administration as "...for the benefit of the working classes." When the NLU attacked Black Reconstruction, it was clearly carrying out its part of an unholy alliance with President Johnson—who was the newfound champion of the defeated planter class.[57]

If the National Labor Union had begun life with an uncertain attitude towards class struggle—and a desire for the quick "fix" of bourgeois political deals—by 1872 it was wholly given over to these illnesses. It completely abandoned mass struggle; instead, the NLU promoted a "National Labor Reform Party" to compete with the Democrats and Republicans. This abortive party was so opportunistic and malformed that it nominated Charles O'Connor, a well-known advocate of slavery, as its Presidential candidate in the 1872 elections.[58] The NLU itself perished in this fiasco. But the class outlook it represented continued and flourished.

In this period white labor, although still young, took definite shape. Euro-Amerikan labor increasingly found itself pressed to organize, to fight the employers, to demand from the bourgeois state some relief from exploitation and some democratic rights. At the same time, these white workingmen were also a part of settler society, and felt their welfare tied up with the supremacy of the Empire. Further, pressed downward by Capital, they sought to establish a stranglehold on jobs by ruthlessly degrading or eliminating colonial labor. This consciousness was very sharply manifested in the 1870s, when these white workingmen became the eager tools of various factions in the bourgeoisie in the mass drives to reenslave Afrikans and drive out Chinese—at the same time engaging in the most vigorous and militant strike waves against the bourgeoisie.

This was a middle position—between the colonial proletariat and the settler bourgeoisie—and it had its roots in the middle position of these white masses in the class structure. It is important to see why white labor could only unite on a petit-bourgeois and opportunistic basis.

While white labor had tacked together a precarious political unity based on the commonalities of wage-status and settlerism, it was as yet so divided that it did not even constitute a class. In brief, we can point to four main aspects of this: (1) White workingmen were sharply divided by nationality; (2) The upper stratum of workmen, which contained most of the native-born "Americans," had a defi-nite petit-bourgeois character; (3) Even the bottom, most exploited layer—who were largely new European immigrants—were politi-cally retarded by the fact that their wages were considerably higher than in Old Europe; (4) Immigrant labor did not constitute a single, united proletarian class itself because they were part of separate na-tional communities (German, Swedish, etc.) each headed by their own bourgeois leaders.

The "native-born" settlers, as the citizen descendants of the original English invasion force, still kept for themselves a high, gen-eral level of privileges. They still thought of themselves as the only true "Americans," while considering the non-Anglo-Saxon, new im-migrants as "foreigners" only a step better than Afrikans or Mexicans. Among these "native-born" settlers petit-bourgeois, property-own-ing, and small tradesman status was the norm, and even wage labor-ers confidently expected to move upwards once they mastered the knack of exploiting others. Engels noted in 1886:

> "There were two factors which for a long time prevented the inevi-table consequences of the capitalist system in America from being revealed in their true light. These were the access to ownership of cheap land and the flood of immigrants. They enable the great mass of indigenous Americans, for years on end, to 'retire' from wage-labor at an early age and to become farmers, dealers, or even entrepreneurs, whereas the hard lot of the wage-laborer with his status of proletarian for life, fell mostly on the immigrant."[59]

Thus the Irish, Polish, Italian, etc. immigrants had the honor of re-placing Afrikans, Mexicanos, Indians, and Asians as the primary labor force of the U.S. Empire in the North. **But the position of "native-born," Anglo-Saxon settlers changed little if at all. The "native-born" settler masses were still above the nationally-differ-entiated proletarians,** still small property-owners and small busi-nessmen, still foremen, overseers, and skilled craftsmen.

The European immigrant workers, who were promoted to be the new, more loyal proletariat of the U.S. Empire, were themselves very divided and confused. Amerika as it entered the industrial age was a literal Tower of Babel. In the hellish brutality of the mines, mills, and factories, the bourgeoisie had assembled gangs of workers from many different nations—torn away from their native lands, desperate, and usually not even speaking a common language with each other. Engels noted the importance of these national barriers:

> "...immigration ... divides the workers into groups—native- and foreign-born, and the latter into: (1) Irish, (2) German, and (3) many small groups, the members of each of which can only understand one another, namely, Czechs, Poles, Italians, Scandinavians, etc. And then we must add the Negroes ... Sometimes there is a powerful élan; however, the bourgeoisie need merely hold out passively for the heterogeneous elements of the working masses to fall apart again."[60]

And as wretched and bitter as life in Amerika was for white workers on the bottom of settler society, it was *still far, far better* than life back in Old Europe. The Irish, for example, who became the bulk of the unskilled white labor, were used up under virtually inhuman conditions. Contemporary accounts of the 19th century usually emphasize how Irish laborers on the New York canals, the coal pits of Pennsylvania, the railroads across the Plains States, etc. were kept drunk on cheap whiskey by the labor contractors and overseers, so that they could endure their miserable lives. Along the Mississippi gangs of Irish laborers drained malarial swamps and built levees for one dollar per day and whiskey. An overseer explained: "It was much better to have the Irish do it, who cost nothing to the planter if they died, than to use up good field-hands in such severe employment."[61] While it is hard for us today to imagine that this could be *better* than life in colonial Ireland, it was. In 1846 alone some one *million* Irish died from famine. Those who emigrated did so under sure sentence of death as the alternative.

Even for those on the bottom stratum of white wage labor the actual wages were significantly higher than in Old Europe. Rural farm laborers, usually the worst-paid of workers, earned a much better wage in the U.S. Empire. Marx, as we remember, pointed out in this period that: "Now, all of you know that the average wages of the

American agricultural laborer amount to more than double that of the English agricultural laborer…"

Further, as European immigrants or poor Euro-Amerikans they were still eligible for the privileges of settlerism—and if not for them, then for their children. While this was markedly true for poor whites in the South, it applied with a few modifications throughout the Empire. Du Bois points out:

> "It must be remembered that the white group of laborers, while they received a low wage, were compensated in part by a sort of public and psychological wage. They were given public deference and titles of courtesy because they were white. They were admitted freely with all classes of white people to public functions, public parks, and the best schools. The police were drawn from their ranks, and the courts, dependent upon their votes, treated them with such leniency as to encourage lawlessness. Their vote selected public officials, and while this had small effect upon the economic situation, it had great effect upon their personal treatment and the deference shown them…"[62]

The other powerful moderating force upon the bottom, immigrant layers of white wage labor is that they were part of immigrant, national-minority communities here in the "New World." And these communities had their own culture, class structure, and leadership. The German and Scandinavian immigrant communities were on the whole fairly prosperous, with a very high degree of business- and property-ownership. The vast farming lands of the upper Midwest and the Plains States were in large measure settled by these two nationalities—the 1900 census revealed that there were 700,000 German- and Scandinavian-owned farms in the Empire then, more than *three times* the number owned by "native-born" Anglo-Saxon Amerikans.[63]

The question of the bourgeois leadership of immigrant workers is very clearly shown by the Irish here. Nor was this disconnected from settlerism. The community leaders of the Irish national minority here were not revolutionary proletarians, but ward

politicians, police chiefs, mayors, the Roman Catholic Church, etc.
It is hardly a secret that during the mid-1800s the Irish workers of
the North, under the leadership of the Church and other bourgeois
elements, were surpassed by none in their vicious hatred of Afrikans.
The Archdiocese of New York City, for example, publicly opposed
Emancipation and undoubtedly helped create the anti-Afrikan riots
that took thousands of lives during the Civil War.

It is interesting that Irish patriots, themselves engaged in the
bloody armed struggle to throw off British colonialism, saw from
across the Atlantic that their countrymen here were being led into
taking the reactionary road. In 1841 some 70,000 Irish patriots
signed a revolutionary petition to Irish-Amerikans: "Irishmen and
Irishwomen, treat the colored people as your equals, as brethren.
By all your memories of Ireland, continue to love Liberty—hate
Slavery—*Cling by the Abolitionists*—and in America you will do
honor to the name of Ireland."[64] Despite mass meetings organized
to generate support for this message of international solidarity, the
full weight of the Catholic Church, and Irish ward politicians and
trade union leaders kept the Irish immigrant masses firmly loyal to
reaction.

"Presidential Bouncer" Arthur clearing the "U.S. Hotel" lobby
of agitators. A notice on the wall states "No Bomb-Throwing;
No Incendiary Talk; No Communism; No Fenianism"; *Puck* 1883.

There was, of course, then as now a powerful national tie here towards their captive homeland. Twice the Fenian Brotherhood tried military invasions of Canada (in 1866 and 1870), trying to force loose the British deathgrip on Ireland.[65] Even after many defeats, Irish patriots and funds continued to pour into "the Cause." The modern submarine, for example, was developed by the secret Irish Clan here, and only later turned over to the U.S. Navy. Irish POWs exiled to Australia were liberated in a spectacular raid across the Pacific. So widespread was the enthusiasm for this daring attempt in the Irish-Amerikan community here than an Irish-Amerikan U.S. Senator offered to get a U.S. Customs ship for the raid if no private vessel could be obtained![66] This only underlines the process at work. The genuine national feeling towards colonial Ireland was taken over by bourgeois elements, who shaped it in bourgeois nationalist directions, and who used the appeal of "the Cause" to promote their own political careers and pocketbooks. This is still true today.

What international solidarity means can be seen by the actions of the Patricio Corps, the hundreds of Irish soldiers in the U.S. Army who broke with the Empire during the Mexican-Amerikan War. Revolted at the barbaric invasion of 1848, they defected to the Mexican forces and *took up arms against the U.S. Empire*. In contrast, the struggle of the Irish-Amerikan community here for equality with other settlers was nothing more nor less than a push to *join* the oppressor nation, to *enlist* in the ranks of the Empire. The difference is the difference between revolution and reaction.

The victorious U.S. Army inflicted barbaric punishment on any of these European soldiers who had defected that they later caught. Some eighty Irish and other Europeans were among the Mexican Army prisoners after the battle of Churubusco in 1847. Of these eighty the victorious settlers branded fifteen with the letter "D," fifteen were lashed two hundred times each with whips, and then forced to dig graves for the rest who were shot down.[67]

The U.S. Empire, then, at the dawn of industrialization, had two broad strata of white wage labor: one a true Euro-Amerikan labor aristocracy, totally petit-bourgeois in life and outlook; the second, an "ethnic," nationally-differentiated stratum of immigrant Europeans and poor whites of the defeated Confederacy, who were

both heavily exploited and yet given the bare privileges of settlerism
to keep them loyal to the U.S. Empire. Once nationally oppressed
labor was under the bourgeoisie's brutal thumb, then white wage
labor could be put into its "proper" place. In the wake of the great
strike wave of 1873–77, the white unions were severely repressed
and broken up. The mass organizations of white labor, once so sure
of their strength when they were dining at the White House and
attacking Afrikan, Mexicano, and Chinese labor at the bidding of
the capitalists, now found themselves powerless when faced with
the blacklist, the lock-out, and the deadly gunfire of company police
and the National Guard.

In taking over the tasks of the colonial proletariat, the new
white laboring masses found themselves increasingly subject to
the violent repression and exploitation that capitalism inexorably
subjects the proletariat to. Thus, the industrial age developed here
with this crucial contradiction: The U.S. Empire was founded as a
European settler society of privileged conquerors, and the new white
masses could not be both savagely exploited proletarians and also
loyal, privileged settlers. As the tremendous pressures of industrial
capitalism started molding them into a new proletariat—which we
will examine in the next section—a fundamental crisis was posed
for Amerikan capitalism.

The experience of early trade unionism in the U.S. is extremely
valuable to us. It showed that:

1. Trade unionism cannot bridge the gap between oppressor
and oppressed nations.

2. Moreover, that even among Euro-Amerikans, unionism,
political movements, etc. inescapably have a *national character*.

3. The organization of nationally oppressed workers into or
allied with the trade unions of the settler masses was only an
effort to *control and divide us.*

4. That the unity of the settler masses is counter-revolutionary,
in that the various privileged strata of the white masses can
only find common ground in petty self-interest and loyalty to
settler hegemony.

5. That whatever "advanced" or democratic-minded Euro-Amerikans do exist need to be *dis-united* from their fellow settlers, rather than welded back into the whole lock-stepping, reactionary white mass by the usual reform movements.

6. That trade unionism became a perverted mockery of its original self in a settler society, where even wage labor became corrupted.

The class antagonism latent within the settler masses had, in times of crisis, been submerged in the increased oppression of the colonial peoples. Capitalistic settlerism drastically reworked the very face of the land. A continent that was at the dawn of the 19th century primarily populated by the various oppressed nations was at the end of the 19th century the semi-sterilized home of a "New Europe." And in this cruel, bloody transformation, history forced everyone to choose, and thus to complete the realization of their class identity. Class is not like a brass badge or a diploma, which can be carried from Old Europe and hung on a wall, dusty but still intact. Class consciousness lives in the revolutionary struggles of the oppressed—or dies in the poisonous little privileges so eagerly sought by the settler servants of the bourgeoisie.

On the other hand, there is the tendency of the bourgeois and the opportunists to convert a handful of very rich and privileged nations into "eternal" parasites on the body of mankind, to "rest on the laurels" of the exploitation of Negroes, Indians, etc., keeping them in subjection with the aid of the excellent weapons of extermination provided by modern militarism. On the other hand, there is the tendency of the *masses*, who are more oppressed than before and who bear the whole brunt of imperialist wars, to cast off this yoke and to overthrow the bourgeoisie. It is in the struggle between these two tendencies that the history of the labor movement will now inevitably develop.

V.I. Lenin

V

COLONIALISM, IMPERIALISM & LABOR ARISTOCRACY

1. The "Bourgeois Proletariat"

Communism has always had to fight against not only the bourgeoisie, but also the very real opposition of some strata and masses of workers who have become corrupted and reactionary. Thus, the hostility revolutionary trends face here is neither new nor a puzzle for communist theory. In England, South Afrika, etc. the communist forces have had to recognize this opposition. Marx, Engels, Lenin—all emphasized how important this question was. It is an essential part of the world fight against imperialism.

To begin with, our criticism of the historically negative role of the settler masses here is no more pointed than Friedrich Engels's statements a century ago about the English working class. Communists have never believed that the working class was some "holy," religious object that must be enshrined away from scientific investigation. Lenin on his own part several times purposefully reminded his European comrades that the original "proletariat"—of Imperial Rome—did not work, but was supported by the surpluses of slave labor. As the lowest free class of Roman citizens, their only duty was to father new soldiers for the Roman Legions (which is why they were called "proletarii" in Latin) while they lived off government subsidies.[1] The political consciousness and material class role of the masses of any given nation cannot be assumed from historic generalizations, but must be discovered by social investigation and scientific analysis.

The phenomenon of the various capitalist ruling classes buying off and politically corrupting some portions of their own wage laboring populations begins with the European colonial systems. The British workers of the 1830s and 1840s were becoming increasingly class conscious. An early, pre-Marxian type of socialism (Owenism) had caused much interest, and the massive Chartist movement rallied millions of workers to demand democratic rights. Alarmed at this—and warned by the armed, democratic insurrections in 1848 in both France and Germany—the British capitalists grudgingly decided that the immense profits of their colonial Empire allowed them to ease up slightly on the exploitation at home.

This tossing of a few crumbs to the British workers resulted in a growing ideological stagnation, conservatism, and national chauvinism. Engels was outraged and disgusted, particularly at the corrupt spectacle of the British workers slavishly echoing their bourgeoisie as to their alleged "right" to exploit the colonial world "...There is no workers' party here ... and the workers gaily share the feast of England's monopoly of the world market and the colonies."

In 1858 Engels sarcastically described the tamed British workers in the bluntest terms: "The English proletariat is actually becoming more and more bourgeois, so that this most bourgeois of all nations is apparently aiming ultimately at the possession of a bourgeois

aristocracy and a bourgeois proletariat alongside the bourgeoisie. For a nation which exploits the whole world this is to a certain extent justifiable."[2] Britain was the Imperial Rome, the Amerikan Empire of that day—a nation which "feasted" on the exploitation of colonies around the entire world. Engels, as a communist, didn't make lame excuses for the corrupted English workers, but exposed them. He held the English workers accountable to the world proletariat for their sorry political choices.

This was not a matter of English factory hands suddenly wearing gold jewelry and "designer jeans." The change was historic: it raised the English masses past the bare floor of survival. As we discussed earlier, in the early stages of capitalist development the bourgeoisie exploited the English workers to the point of early death. Workers, women and children in particular, were overworked and starved as disposable and easily replaced objects.

The change didn't mean that English workers as a whole weren't exploited—just that their exploitation was lightened in the golden flow of colonial profits. In 1840 the wages of an "ordinary laborer" in England were 8 shillings per week, while it cost some 14 shillings per week to live on a minimal but stable basis. By 1875 both the common wages and the cost of living were up to 15 shillings per week—an event that historian Arnold Toynbee points to as the first time in British capitalist history that unskilled laborers earned enough to survive. At the same time reform legislation sponsored by the big factory owners placed restrictions on the use of child labor.

The length of the working day declined. At both Jarron Shipyards and the New Castle Chemical Works, for example, workers succeeded in lowering the work week from 61 to 54 hours.[3]

In 1892 Engels explained that the prolonged conservatism of the English workers was due to this generalized bribery: *"The truth is this: during the period of England's industrial monopoly, the English working class have, to a certain extent, shared in the benefits of monopoly. These benefits were very unequally parcelled out amongst them; the privileged minority pocketed most, but even the great mass had, at least, a temporary share now and then. And that is the reason why, since the dying out of Owenism, there has been no socialism in England."*[4]

Engels divides the workers into two groups—the "privileged minority" of the labor aristocrats, and the "great mass" of common wage labor. While the labor aristocracy engages in wage labor and grows up out of the working class, it is no longer exploited. Rather, the bourgeoisie shares with this privileged layer a part of the super-profits from colonial exploitation. Typically, these labor aristocrats are trade union officials, certain white-collar employees, foremen, the well-paid members of the restrictive craft unions, etc. They often supervise or depend upon the labor of ordinary workers, while they themselves do little or no toil.

This stratum can also include groupings of workers who are employed directly by the state, who work in the colonial system, in war industries, etc. and who therefore have a special loyalty to the bourgeoisie. The aristocracy of labor have comfortable lives, and in general associate with the petit-bourgeoisie.

The "great mass" of English workers were, in contrast, certainly exploited. They lived lives of hardship. Yet, they had in their own lifetimes seen an uneven but upward trend in their wages and working conditions—a rise dependent upon the increasing profits of the overseas Empire. Under the leadership of the aristocracy of labor—who were looked up to as the most "successful," best organized, and most unionized layer of the class—these ordinary laborers increasingly identified their own progress with the progress of "their" British Empire.

Engels felt in the late 1890s that this might be only a temporary phenomenon—and one limited to England by and large. He thought that with the growth of rival industrial empires and the sharpening of European capitalist competition, the superprofits that supported this bribery might dwindle. Exactly the reverse happened, however. With the coming of imperialism and the tremendous rise of the most modern colonial empires, the trend of social bribery of the working classes spread from England to France, Germany, Belgium, etc. Between the fall of the Paris Commune of 1871 and the eve of World War I in 1913, real per capita income in both England and Germany doubled.[5]

In 1907 Lenin wrote:

> "The class of those who own nothing but do not labor either is incapable of overthrowing the exploiters. Only the proletarian class, which maintains the whole of society, has the power to bring about a successful social revolution. And now we see that, as the result of a far-reaching colonial policy, the European proletariat has *partly* reached a situation where it is *not* its work that maintains the whole of society but that of the people of the colonies who are practically enslaved. The British bourgeoisie, for example, derives more profit from the many millions of the population of India and other colonies than from the British workers. In certain countries these circumstances create the material and economic basis for infecting the proletariat of one country or another with colonial chauvinism."[6]

Imperialism allowed the European workers—once much more exploited and revolutionary than their Amerikan cousins—to catch up in privileges and degeneracy. Lenin said that imperialism gives the bourgeoisie enough "superprofits" to *devote a part (and not a small one at that!) to bribe their own workers, to create something like an alliance ... between the workers of a given nation and their capitalists..."*

The pro-imperialist labor aristocracy—which in 1914 Lenin estimated at roughly 20% of the German working class—were the leaders of the German trade unions, the "socialist" party, etc. Using their state-sanctioned positions they led millions of workers in the more proletarian strata. This labor aristocracy succeeded in sabotaging the revolutionary movements in Western Europe, and disrupting unity between the anti-colonial revolutions and the workers of the oppressed nations.

We can sum up key lessons in this theoretical development of analyzing social bribery in the imperialist oppressor nations:

1. Lenin's insistence on a total break with those "socialists" who were unwilling to support the anti-colonial revolutions in deeds was proven correct. The shallow argument that "racist" European workers would be brought to revolutionary enlightenment by union activity and reformist economic movements (the same arguments preached here in Amerika) was proven to be totally untrue.

While in every mass there are those who have backward or chauvinistic prejudices in the yet-to-be-cleaned corners of their minds, Lenin insisted that this was not the primary problem. Under imperialism "racist" politics were an outward manifestation of a class "alliance" with the imperialists.

2. This labor aristocracy of bribed workers is not neutral, but is fighting for its capitalist masters. Therefore, they must be combatted, just like the army or police (who are the military base of the imperialists, while the labor aristocracy is its social base). Lenin told his comrades: "No preparation of the proletariat for the overthrow of the bourgeoisie is possible, even in the preliminary sense, unless an immediate, systematic, extensive and open struggle is waged against this stratum…"

3. When the new communist movement was formed, it was greatly outnumbered and out-organized everywhere in Europe outside of Russia. Lenin's answer was concise: Since the bribed, pro-imperialist masses were primarily the upper, privileged layers of workers, the communists in order to combat them had to "go down *lower* and *deeper*, to the real masses." And again he noted: "…the sufferings, miseries, and revolutionary sentiments of the ruined and impoverished masses"; he pointed to "…particularly those who are least organized and educated, who are most oppressed and least amenable to organization." (We might say that he shared the

same perception that Malcolm X had of where to find a base for revolution.)

On the global scale Lenin's strategy of "go down *lower* and *deeper*, to the real masses" meant that the communist movement became truly internationalist, organizing the masses of Asia, Latin Amerika, and Afrika—the "real masses" of imperialism. Near the end of his life, noting the unexpected setbacks in revolutionizing Western Europe, Lenin remarked that in any case the future of the world would be decided by the fact that the oppressed nations constitute the overwhelming majority of the world's population.

4. The analysis of the labor aristocracy under imperialism helps deepen the understanding of our own varied struggles, and the evolution of the U.S. Empire in general.

As the U.S. Empire jumped into the imperialist "scramble" for world domination at the turn of the 20th century, its Euro-Amerikan workers were the most privileged in the entire capitalist world. In 1900 labor in Amerika was sharply divided into three very separate and *nationally-distinct* strata (literally, of different nations—Euro-Amerikan, European, and oppressed nations).

On top was the labor aristocracy of Euro-Amerikan workers, who dominated the better-paid craft trades and their restrictive AFL unions. This "privileged stratum" of "native-born" citizens comprised roughly 25% of the industrial workforce, and edged into the ranks of their petit-bourgeois neighbors (foremen, small tradesmen, and so on).

Below them was a new proletarian stratum just imported from Eastern and Southern Europe, who comprised 50–75% of the Northern industrial workforce. They were poorly paid and heavily exploited, the main factory production force of the North. Largely unorganized, they were systematically barred from the craft unions and the better-paying factory jobs. This stratum was composed of non-citizens, was only a generation old here, and had no previous existence. The very bottom, upholding everything else, were the colonial proletariats of Afrikan, Mexicano, Indian, and Asian workers.

Even as modern industrialization and the Northern factory boom were in full swing, it was still true that the "superprofits" wrung from the oppressed nations (plus those wrung from imported labor from Asia) were the foundations of the Empire. Everything "American" was built up on top of their continuing oppression.

In the Afrikan South cotton was still "king." The Afrikan laborers (whether hired, renter or sharecropper) who produced the all-important cotton still supported the entire settler economy. Between 1870–1910 cotton production had gone up by three times, while domestic cotton usage had gone up by 600%—and "king cotton" still was the leading U.S. export product (25% of all exports). The number of Afrikan men in agriculture had increased, and in 1914 some 50% of all Afrikan workers labored in the fields. Afrikan women not only worked in the fields, as did their children, but they involuntarily continued cleaning, cooking, washing clothes, and child-raising for the upper half of Euro-Amerikan families. Over 40% of the entire Afrikan workforce was still bound into domestic labor—maintaining for the Southern settlers their conquest lifestyle.

The growing Euro-Amerikan masses in the South had benefited from the fact that Afrikans had been gradually forced out of industry and the skilled trades. While roughly 80% of all skilled workers in the South had been Afrikan in 1868, by 1900 those proportions had been reversed. In the more localized construction trades Afrikans still hung on (comprising 15% of carpenters and 36% of masons), but in the desirable mechanical trades, associated now with rising industry, they were excluded. Only 2% of machinists in the South, for example, were Afrikan. On the Southern railroads, where Afrikans once predominated—and as late as 1920 still accounted for 20–25% of all firemen, brakemen, and switchmen—the 1911 Atlanta Agreement between Southern railroads and the AFL Railroad Brotherhoods called for the gradual replacement of all Afrikans by settlers.[7]

Even the jobs in the new textile mills were reserved for "poor whites" forced off the land. So that settler labor in the South—however exploited—was grateful to the bourgeoisie for every little privilege they got. The settler masses of the South, in the tradition of the slave patrols, the Confederate Army, and the KKK, were still in the main the loyal garrison over occupied New Afrika.

Even though the Empire tried to use industry to build up a settler occupation population, Afrikan labor was necessary as the super-exploited base of Southern industry. In lumber they made up the bottom half of the workforce. In the coal mines of Alabama they were 54% of the miners at the turn of the century. In the Southern iron and steel mills we find that in 1907 Afrikans still made up 40% of the workers.[8]

In the Mexicano Southwest the same basic foundation of oppressed nation labor was present (together with Asian labor). Native Amerikan workers were present throughout the region—on cattle and sheep ranches, in the fields, and in the mines. Navaho miners, for example, played an active role in building the Western Federation of Miners local at the great Telluride, Colorado mines. Asian labor played an equally important role. Although much of the Chinese national minority had been driven by repression out of the U.S. or to retreat into the "ghetto" economy of laundries, food service, etc., new waves of Asian workers were being recruited from Japan, the Philippines, and Korea. By the many thousands they toiled on the railroads, the urban "service" economy, in canneries, and above all, in the fields.

Much less industrialized and economically developed than the North (or even the South), the Southwestern economy rested on agriculture and mining. The migrant farm laborers of the "factories in the fields" were not marginal, but the economic mainstay of the Southwest. In the key agricultural area of Southern California the majority of farm labor was Chicano-Mexicano.

Because the Southwest was much more recently conquered than other regions of the continental Empire, the labor situation was far less developed in a modern industrial sense. Armed Chicano-Mexicano resistance organizations against settler rule continued well into the 1920s. The Euro-American settlers were in general wary of concentrating masses of Mexicanos, and long into the 20th century the main interest of many "Anglo" settlers was the continuing, terroristic seizure of the remaining lands and water rights of the Chicano-Mexicano and Indian nations. Thus, the settler economy in the Southwest even in the imperialist era was still concentrated in the conquest and looting stage. Here the conquered Chicano-Mexicanos were necessary to the settlers as ranch labor and domestic labor (just as in the rural South with Afrikans).

But at the turn of the century the development of railroad systems, of large-scale commercial agriculture, and of extensive mining were also creating the imperialist need for increased masses of cheap laborers. Thousands and then tens of thousands of Mexicano workers were brought Northward to fill this need. By 1909 on both the Santa Fe and Southern Pacific railroads some 98% of the crews working west of Albuquerque were Chicano-Mexicano. While varying mixtures of Mexicano, Indian, and immigrant European nationalities were used in the mines, Mexicano labor played the largest role. In mines closest to the artificial "border," Mexicano workers were often a large majority—such as in the major copper center of Clifton, Arizona. Once driven out of much of the West by settler terrorism, Mexicanos were now being brought back to their own national land as "immigrant" or "contract" labor. Mexicanos became 60% of the miners, 80% of the agricultural workers, and 90% of the railroad laborers in the West.[9] Thus, in the West the importance of colonial labor was rapidly growing.

In terms of income and lifestyle it is easy to see the gulf between the labor of the oppressor nation of settlers, imported European national minorities, and the colonial labor of the oppressed nations and minorities. The Afrikan tenant family usually lived in debt slavery, laboring as a family for little more than some food, a few clothes and use of a shack. Those Chicano-Mexicano families trapped in the Texas peonage system earned just as little.

One Texas rancher testified in 1914: *"I was paying Pancho and his whole family 60 cents a day ... There were no hours; he worked from sun to sun."* As late as the 1920s Afrikan farm laborers in the South earned 75 cents per day when employed. For both Afrikans and Mexicanos at the turn of the century, even in industry and mining it was common to earn one-half of "white man's pay."

One step up from this was the Northern industrial proletariat from Eastern and Southern Europe—newly created, heavily exploited, but whose ultimate relationship to the imperialists was still uncertain. The "Hunky" and "Dago" commonly earned $6–10 per week in the early 1900s, for six and seven day work weeks.

One giant level up from there was the "privileged stratum" of Euro-Amerikan labor aristocrats (skilled workers, foremen,

office staff). They usually earned $15–20 per week, with the majority being homeowners and voting citizens of the Empire.

This top stratum dominated the trade unions and the socialist organizations, consistently supporting the U.S. Empire. Bribed and helped to be the imperialist leadership of all white workers as a whole, they sabotaged any militant outbreaks in the industrial ranks. Always they prevented any internationalist unity between white workers and the colonial proletariats. It is with this background (and being able to trace the continuing role of social bribery) that we can begin to examine settler mass politics in the imperialist era.

2. Settler Opposition to Imperialism

There have always been significant contradictions among the settlers, and even in the earliest stages of imperialism we have seen conflicts between the monopoly capitalists and their settler base. While the U.S. was an Empire just as soon as it started to breathe, the "Spanish-American War" of 1898 marked this early settler Empire's transition into Imperialism. The pivotal nature of this imperialist war was well-understood by the settler citizenry of that earlier day, and it caused not only a great public debate but an angry split in the settler ranks. The well-organized mass movement of settlers opposed to imperialism then foreshadowed the Anti–Vietnam War movement of our times. These are important contradictions.

In the brief 1898 war, the U.S. easily removed Puerto Rico, the Philippines, and Cuba from the feeble hands of the aging Spanish Empire. This armed robbery was so effortless because the Spanish bourgeoisie had already lost most of their former power over these colonies, due to both their own weakness and to the rise of national liberation movements. On Sept. 23, 1868, at Lares, Puerto Rican patriots proclaimed the first Republic of Puerto Rico amidst an armed uprising against the Spanish occupiers. Although crushed, the "cry of Lares" marks the start of an unbroken history of patriotic warfare by the Puerto Rican people.

Increasingly, the Puerto Rican forces controlled not only the mountains, but also the rural areas right up to the towns of the isolated Spanish garrisons. Finally, in 1897, the desperate Spanish Empire agreed in negotiations with Puerto Rican representatives to a Charter of Autonomy. This recognized the power of the Puerto Rican nation to set up its own currency, fix tariffs on imports, negotiate trade agreements with other nations, and veto if they wished any Spanish diplomatic treaties applying to Puerto Rico. The end of Spanish rule was evident.[10] Similar concessions were won by Cuban and Filipino rebels.

EL GRITO DE LARES, 23 DE SEPTIEMBRE 1868

The U.S. bourgeoisie had to move quickly if it was to annex these colonies. In addition to the possibility that Britain or some other great power would make a grab for them, there was the certainty that the oppressed nations of the Spanish Empire were raising the beacon of National Independence and anti-colonialism—as had Haiti a century before. So that on April 25, 1898, the U.S. declared war on Spain while moving to invade Puerto Rico, Cuba, and the Philippines. It was just in the nick of time as far as U.S. Imperialism was concerned.

In the Philippines the liberation struggle had already reached the formation of a new Filipino government. Spurred on by the Katipunan, the secret armed organization of workers and peasants, the revolutionaries had created a large peoples' army. By the time the first U.S. troops landed on June 30, 1898, the Filipino revolutionaries had already swept the Spanish Colonial Army and administration out of virtually the whole of the Philippines, besieging the last isolated holdouts in the old walled city of Manila. Under the pretext of being "allies" of the Filipinos, U.S. troops landed and joined the siege of the Spanish remnants. It is a fact that in the siege the Filipino patriots held 15½ miles of the lines facing the Spanish positions, while the U.S. troops held only a token 600 yards of front line.[11] More and more U.S. troops arrived, even after the hopeless Spanish surrendered on Dec. 10, 1898. Finally, on Feb. 4, 1899, the reinforced U.S. "allies" moved to wipe out the Filipino forces, even ordering that no truces or ceasefires be accepted.

The Filipino people defended their nation with the most heroic and stubborn resistance. It took over three years of the most bitter combat before the guerrilla patriots were overcome. And defeated then only because: (1) The bourgeois nationalist Filipino leaders had treacherously purged the armed movement of the most advanced proletarian elements, while they themselves vacillated in trying to reach an accommodation with the U.S. invaders. (2) Over half of the total U.S. Army (1.2 million troops) were eventually poured into the Philippines, with weapons and organization far advanced over the former Spanish foes. (3) The Filipino people were unprepared for the brutal effectiveness of the genocidal strategy used by the U.S. invaders.

The last became an international scandal when the full details became known, shaking even some settlers. Unable to cope with the guerrilla tactics of the Filipino revolutionaries, the U.S. Army decided to starve them into disintegration by destroying their social base—the Filipino population. The same genocidal "Population Regroupment" strategy (as the CIA calls it today) that settlers first used against the Indian nations was revived in the Philippines—and would be used again in Vietnam in our times. The general outlines of U.S. strategy called for destroying all organized social and economic life in guerrilla areas. Villages would be burned down, crops and livestock destroyed, diseases spread, the People killed or forced to evacuate as refugees. Large areas were declared as "free fire zones" in which all Filipinos were to be killed on sight.[12]

Of course, even Euro-Amerikan settlers needed some indoctrination in order to daily carry out such crimes. Indiscriminate killing, looting, and torture were publicly encouraged by the U.S. Army command. Amerikan reporters were invited to witness the daily torture sessions, in which Filipinos would be subjected to the

ABOVE: MEMBERS OF KATIPUNAN, A SECRET ARMED ORGANIZATION OF FILIPINO WORKERS AND PEASANTS.; RIGHT: FILIPINO GUERRILLAS KILLED IN COMBAT AGAINST U.S. INVADERS.

"watercure" (having salt water pumped into their stomachs under pressure). The *Boston Herald* said:

> "Our troops in the Philippines ... look upon all Filipinos as of one race and condition, and being dark men, they are therefore 'niggers', and entitled to all the contempt and harsh treatment administered by white overlords to the most inferior races."[13]

U.S. Imperialism took the Philippines by literally turning whole regions into smoldering graveyards. U.S. Brig. Gen. James Bell, upon returning to the U.S. in 1901, said that his men had killed *one out of every six Filipinos* on the main island of Luzon (that would be some one million deaths just there). It is certain that at least 200,000 Filipinos died in the genocidal conquest. In Samar province, where the patriotic resistance to the U.S. invaders was extremely persistent, U.S. Gen. Jacob Smith ordered his troops to shoot *every* Filipino man, woman or child they could find "over ten" (years of age).[14]

The settler anti-imperialist movement that arose in opposition to these conquests focused on the Philippines. It was not a fringe protest by a few radicals. Many of its leaders were men of wealth and standing, many of them old veterans of the abolitionist cause. The author Mark Twain, Gov. Pingree of Michigan, former U.S. Secretary of Agriculture J. Sterling Morton, and steel magnate Andrew Carnegie were but a few of the "notable" settlers involved.

From its center in New England, the movement spread coast-to-coast, and then organized itself into the American Anti-Imperialist League. The League had over 40,000 members in some forty chapters, with hundreds of thousands of settler supporters.[15] It was also closely tied to the reform wing of the Democratic Party, and to the Presidential election campaign of William Jennings Bryan. Just as Senator George McGovern would run against President Nixon on an anti-war platform in 1972, Bryan was running against the entrenched Republicans with a platform calling for an end to Asian conquests.

The politics of the League were well-developed, with an explicit class orientation. The League opposed imperialism in the first place because they correctly saw that it represented the increased power of monopoly capital. When they raised their slogan—"Republic or Empire"—they meant by it that Amerika should be a republic of free European settlers rather than a world empire, whose mixed populations would be subjects of the monopoly capitalists. They feared that the economic power gained from exploiting these new colonies, plus the permanent armed force needed to hold them, would be used as home to smother the "democracy" of the settler masses.[16]

The atrocities committed by U.S. troops in the Philippines were denounced on moral and humanitarian grounds. But the League was very careful to point out that their support for Philippine independence did not mean that they believed in any equality of colonial peoples with Europeans. Congressman Carl Schurz, the German immigrant liberal who played such a prominent role in supporting Reconstruction during the 1860s and 1870s, was a leading spokesman for the League.

In his speech "The Policy of Imperialism," Schurz began by defining Filipinos as *"the strongest and foremost tribe"* of the region. He then said: "We need not praise the Filipinos as in every way the equals of the 'embattled farmers' of Lexington and Concord ... but there is an abundance of testimony, some of it unwilling, that the Filipinos are fully the equals, and even the superiors, of the Cubans and Mexicans." The patronizing arrogance of even these settlers showed that it was possible for them to be against the new imperialism—and also be white supremacists and supporters of capitalism. That this was an impossible contradiction didn't occur to them.

The class content of the League becomes very clear as Schurz continued: "Now, it may well be that the annexation of the Philippines would pay a speculative syndicate of wealthy capitalists, without at the same time paying the American people at large. As to the people of our race, tropical countries like the Philippines may be fields of profit for rich men who can hire others to work for them, but not for those who have to work for themselves."[17] In other words, the League was articulating the interests of the liberal petit-bourgeoisie.

Settler labor was appealed to on an explicitly white supremacist basis. Congressman George S. Boutwell, the President of the League, reminded the white workers that they had just finished robbing and driving out Chinese workers—a campaign that he had supported. Now, he told white workers, a new menace had arisen of "half-civilized races" from the Philippines. If their land were to be annexed to the U.S. Empire, then in the near future these Asians would be brought to Amerika by the capitalists. He said:

> "Does anyone believe, that with safety, we can receive into this Union the millions of Asia, who have no bonds of relationship with us ... The question before this country shall be this: Should the laboring and producing classes of America be subjected to a direct and never-ending competition with the underpaid and half-clad laborers of Asia ... ?"[18]

The politics of the League did not support national liberation; they were not anti-capitalist or even anti-racist. The heart of their movement was the appeal of a false past, of the picture of Amerika as an insular European society, of an economy based on settlers' production in small farms and workshops. They feared the new imperialist world of giant industrial trusts and banks, of international production where the labor of oppressed workers in far-flung colonies would give monopoly capital a financial whip over the common settler craftsman and farmer. They believed, incorrectly, that the settler economy could be sustained without continuing Amerika's history of conquest and annexation.*

We can see the very sharply defined case the League made for counterposing the interests of settlers vs. their bourgeoisie. In his convocation address at the University of Chicago in 1899, Carl Schurz takes up the issue of explaining why the old conquests of the U.S. Empire were so "good," while the new conquests were "bad":

---

* Lenin commented: "In the United States, the imperialist war waged against Spain in 1898 stirred up the opposition of the 'anti-imperialists', the last of the Mohicans of bourgeois democracy, who declared this war to be 'criminal' ... But while all this criticism shrank from recognizing the inseverable bond between imperialism and the trusts, and, therefore, between imperialism and the foundations of capitalism, while it shrank from joining forces engendered by large scale capitalism and its development—it remained a 'pious wish.'" (*Imperialism, the Highest Stage of Capitalism.* Peking, 1970. p. 134)

> *"Has not the career of the Republic almost from its very beginning*
> *been one of territorial expansion? Has it not acquired California,*
> *Florida, Texas, the vast countries that came to us through the*
> *Mexican War, and Alaska, and has it not digested them well? If*
> *the Republic could digest the old, why not the new?"*

Schurz then gives five reasons why the old annexations worked out
so well for the settlers: (1) They were all on this continent; (2) They
were not in the tropics, but in temperate climates "where democratic institutions thrive, and where our people could migrate in
mass"; (3) They were virtually "without any population"; (4) Since
only Euro-Amerikans would populate them, they could become
territories and then States and become fully integrated into White
Amerika; (5) No permanent increase in the military was needed to
defend them from "probable foreign attack."

His political thought was that whereas the old annexations of
settlerism provided land and resources for the invading Europeans
to occupy and become the dominant population (with the aid
of genocide, of course), these new annexations in Asia and the
Caribbean brought only new millions of colonial subjects into the
U.S. Empire—but in distant colonies that the Euro-Amerikan masses would never populate.

Schurz continues: *"The scheme of Americanizing our 'new posses-*
sions' in that sense is therefore absolutely hopeless. The immutable forces
of nature are against it. Whatever we may do for their improvement,
the people of the Spanish Antilles will remain ... Spanish Creoles and
Negroes, and the people of the Philippines, Filipinos, Malays, Tagals, and
so on ... a hopelessly heterogeneous element—in some respects more
hopeless even than the colored people now living among us."[19]

These settlers were opposing imperialism from the ideologi-
cal standpoint of petit-bourgeois settlerism. It is significant that the
League refused to take a stand on the Boer War going on in South
Afrika, or on the dispatch of U.S. Marines to join other Western
Powers in crushing the "Boxer Rebellion" in China. And, obviously,
the League had no objection to colonialism "at home," in the an-
nexed and settled territories of Mexico, the Indian nations, and New
Afrika.

By 1901 the American Anti-Imperialist League was a spent force. Bryan and the Democrats had lost the 1900 elections by a large margin. More decisively, the Filipino, Puerto Rican, and Cuban patriots had been defeated, and the issue of the U.S. expanding from a continental North Amerikan Empire into a world empire had been decided.

There were other waves of petit-bourgeois settler reaction against the domination of monopoly capital. The most significant was the Populist Party, which broke the "color line" in the South uniting "poor whites" and Afrikans in voting for new government programs of reform. With heavy strength in the rural counties, the Populist Party got almost one-third of the vote in eight Northern States west of the Mississippi in 1892; in the South its strength was less but still important.[20] Led by the demagogue Tom Watson of Georgia, the Populists proposed that Afrikan sharecroppers should unite with small white farmers in forcing Big Business to give them both a better economic deal. It was the "bread and butter" coalition of two exploited forces from different nations.

But frustrated at their inability to reach their goals through this electoral coalition, the Populist leadership sharply shifted course after 1902. Watson and his cronies had discovered that the tactical position of the "poor whites" in the bourgeois elections might be improved if they drove out Afrikan voters (a conclusion the imperialists were glad to encourage). C. Vann Woodward comments: "With the Negro vote eliminated Watson and the Populists stood in much the same relation toward the two factions of the Democratic Party as the Negro had occupied towards the Populists and the Democrats: they held the balance of power."[21]

Watson himself, still the captivating spokesman of the "cracker" and "redneck," therefore moved rapidly to the right. He encouraged new waves of terrorism against Afrikans: "Lynch law is a good sign: it shows that a sense of justice lives among the people." In 1904 Watson started campaigning for disenfranchisement of the one million Afrikan voters in Georgia. With flamboyant rhetoric, Watson supported the 1905 Russian Revolution at the same time he swore that the key to a movement of "poor whites" in Amerika was disenfranchising Afrikans: *The white people dare not revolt so long as they can be intimidated by the fear of the Negro vote."*[22]

Not surprisingly, these stands only increased Watson's popularity as a leader of the "poor whites." In 1920, shortly before his death, he was finally elected to the U.S. Senate. At his death Eugene Debs, leading figure of the Euro-Amerikan Socialist Party, hailed Watson as a true hero of the white workers:

> *"He was a great man, a heroic soul who fought the power of evil his whole life long in the interests of the common people, and they loved him and honored him."*

By that time, naturally, Watson had become a wealthy plantation owner and publisher. The Populists had faded away as a party, to become just another "pressure group" lobby within the Democratic Party.

Just as in the anti-imperialism of the League, the settler-Afrikan coalition of the Populists had nothing to do with any real unity of settlers with the oppressed. Rather, these poor but still-privileged settlers were tactically maneuvering to improve their position relative to the monopoly capitalists—and recruiting Afrikans to give their settler party a boost. Historian Michael Rogin points out: "Populism, however, was a movement of the farm-owning proprietors, not property-less workers. It attempted to reassert local community control against the economic and political centralization of corporate capital..."[23]

These two movements did not cross the lines of battle between the Empire and the oppressed nations; their limitation—and their special importance—is that they represented the eruption of class contradictions within the camp of the enemy. The Vietnam War controversy of the '60s, the strange Watergate scandal that forced President Nixon out of power, are both evidence that the effects of these contradictions are considerable. And will be in the future. **If we become confused about their basic nature, we damage our strategic self-reliance. If, like the Vietnamese comrades, we can make these contradictions serve us, we will have seized an essential element of revolution.**

3. The U.S. & South Afrikan Settlerism

The same contradictions between imperialism and its settler garrison troops appeared elsewhere, most strongly in Afrika. At the same time as the American Anti-Imperialist League was denouncing the annexation of the former Spanish colonies, the Boer settlers in South Afrika were being invaded by the forces of the British Empire. The 1899–1902 Anglo-Boer War became a political issue among settlers in Amerika.

There is a historic relationship between Euro-Amerikan settlers and the colonization of South Afrika. Amerikan mercenaries, engineers, and technologies played a major role in the European exploitation of South Afrika—and, obviously, still do. The diamond and gold mines which were the economic center of British South Afrikan colonization were virtually run by the experienced Euro-Amerikans from California and Colorado.

Gardner Williams, the U.S. consular agent in Kimberley, was the manager of the DeBeers Diamond mines. John Hays Hammond was the chief engineer for the British South Africa Corporation. By 1896 one-half of all the mines were run by Euro-Amerikan mine experts. Much of the equipment, as well, came from the U.S. Empire. One U.S. company alone—Fraser & Chalmers—supplied 40% of the machinery at the Rand gold fields.[24] When the second and decisive war broke out between the Boer South African Republic and the British Empire, Euro-Amerikans became heavily involved.

The difference in Amerika over the Anglo-Boer War definitely reflected the existing strains between the monopoly capitalists and their own settler base. The U.S. bourgeoisie and its political agents were strongly pro-British. Allied to the British mining interests, they supported British imperialism as the power that would open up Southern Afrika for imperialist exploitation in general. And, like the British, they saw the backward South Afrikan Republic of the original Boer settlers from Holland as an obstacle to profits. The Boer society stressed settler family agriculture, and opposed any proletarianization of the Afrikan peoples—while it was only with mass, enforced integration of Afrikan labor into the corporate economy that the Western imperialists could fully exploit South Afrika. The British imperialists had to take state power out of the hands of those narrow, theocratic Boers and bring all of South Afrika into their colonial empire.

Euro-Amerikans were heavily involved in the 1895 Jameson Raid, the "private" British military expedition of imperialist Cecil Rhodes. In the aftermath of the Raid's well-publicized failure at overthrowing the Boer government, the facts of Euro-Amerikan involvement came out. The weapons used had been smuggled into South Afrika by Euro-Amerikan mining executives, seven of whom were arrested by the Boers.

The defense of the seven became big news back in the U.S. Mark Twain visited them in jail, afterwards supporting them as men who were innocently trying to bring about "reform." Eventually, due to diplomatic pressure, the seven were freed. Gardner Williams simply paid his fine and resumed his post as U.S. consular agent. John Hays Hammond was ousted from the colony, however, and returned to a hero's welcome in the U.S. He later became National Chairman of the Republican Party.[25]

When the war broke out in 1899 the U.S. government openly sided with the British. The Republican McKinley Administration approved the sale of much-needed provisions and munitions to the British forces. Permission was even given for the British to recruit mercenaries here.[26] Just as, covertly, the white "Rhodesians" obtained military reinforcements here in the 1970s.

But many Euro-Amerikan settlers identified with the Boers—who were, after all, just fellow European settlers ruling occupied lands like themselves—and saw the Boers as losing their "rights" to greedy monopoly capital. The parallel to the U.S. was very close in many minds. And if the Republican Administration in Washington was publicly championing the British side, still there were others who identified with the Boer "Davids" against the British "Goliath." There was so much popular sympathy for the Boer settlers among the U.S. settlers that the 1900 Democratic Party platform saluted: "...the heroic Burghers in their unequal struggle to maintain their liberty and independence."[27]

Much of the most impassioned support in the U.S. for the Boers came, to no surprise, from the Irish community. They saw the Boers not only as fellow European settlers, but as fellow rebels fighting for nationhood against British colonialism. An "Irish Brigade" was actually assembled and sent to the Transvaal to join the Boer army.[28]

As the eventual defeat of the Boers loomed closer public settler sympathy for them only increased. The States of Texas, New Mexico, and Colorado formally offered their welcome and free land (stolen from the Indians and Mexicanos) to any Boers who wished to immigrate (just as the Governor of South Carolina in 1979 officially invited the losing "Rhodesian" settlers fleeing Zimbabwe to come settle in that State).[29] So the present U.S. imperialist involvement in South Afrika has a long history—as does the Euro-Amerikan settler solidarity with their "Afrikaner" counterparts. Once these two trends were counterposed, now they are joined.

South Afrika played out, in a form much condensed, the same pattern of relations between settler workers and Afrikan labor as in the U.S. Afrikan laborers not only conducted strikes, but starting with the July 1913 mine strike Afrikans tried honoring the strikes of the white workers. Indeed, in the mines a strike by white workers alone would hardly have stopped production. But in every case the white workers themselves refused in return to support Afrikan strikes, customarily serving as scabs and "special constables" (volunteer police) to put down Afrikan struggles. The Dec. 1919 Cape Town strike by Afrikan longshoremen and the Feb. 1920 Afrikan miners' strike were both broken by the authorities with the help of white labor.[30] One Afrikaner radical comments:

> "But the white workers believed that they had nothing in common with the blacks ... the white miners earned ten times as much as the blacks, that many of them employed black servants in their homes, that a victory of the black miners would have increased the desire of the mine-owners to reduce the status of the white miners, since any increase in black wages would have to be met either by a reduction in white wages or by a reduction of profits. Such was the reality of the situation which the white workers, consciously or not, understood very well."[31]

Imperialism knows no gratitude, not even towards its servants. From 1907 on the mining companies kept pushing at the white miners, kept trying to gradually replace white miners with low-paid Afrikans, to reduce white wages, and to reduce the total numbers of expensive white miners. In response, from 1907–1922 there was a series of militant white strikes. Finally, in 1922 the Chamber of Mines announced that the companies had repudiated the existing labor agreements and had decided to lay off 2,000 white miners.[32]

This touched off the great Rand Revolt of 1922, in which an eight-week strike escalated into a general strike of all white workers, and then into a week of armed revolt with fighting between the "Red Guards" of white miners and the imperialist troops. The main slogan of this amazing explosion was "For A White South Africa!" The white "communists" marched through the streets with banners reading *"Workers of the World Fight and Unite for a White South Africa!"*[33] The main demand was obvious.

The white miners (who were Boer, British, Scottish, and Welsh) gained the support not only of the other white workers, but of the whole Boer people as well. As the strike grew, the armed "Red Guards" of the miners started attacking Afrikan workers. Between the production halts and the attacks thousands of Afrikans had to evacuate the Rand. In recognition of the reactionary character of the revolt, all the leading Afrikan political organizations, churches, and unions denounced it.[34]

The violent upheaval of settler discontent corrected the erring course of imperialism in South Afrika. In 1924 the rigidly pro-company Smuts government was voted out by the settler electorate. The new "Afrikaner" government granted the white workers all they wanted, except for driving out the Afrikan population wholesale. The "Color Bar" act was passed, which legally enforced the settler monopoly on highly-paid wage labor. Toil was now to be reserved for the Afrikan proletariat. "Afrikaner" wage labor had stabilized its position as a subsidized, non-exploited aristocracy of labor.

The main function of the "Afrikaner" masses was no longer to produce and support society, but only to serve as the social base for the occupation garrison that imperialism needed to hold down the colonial peoples. Indeed, today it is evident that South Afrikan mining, industry, and agriculture are all the products of colonial Afrikan labor alone. "Afrikaner" workers, far from supporting society, are themselves supported by the super-exploitation of the oppressed nation of Afrikans. There is no longer, in any meaningful terms, any working class struggle within settler society there.

VI

The U.S. Industrial Proletariat

1. "The Communistic and Revolutionary Races"

The industrial system in the U.S. came into full stride at the turn of the century. In 1870 the U.S. steel industry was far behind that of England in both technology and size. From its small, still relatively backward mills came less than one-sixth of the pig iron produced in England. But by 1900 U.S. steel mills were the most highly mechanized, efficient, and profitable in the world. Not only did they produce twice the tonnage that England did, but in that year even England—the pioneering center of the iron and steel industry—began to import cheaper Yankee steel.[1] That year the U.S. Empire became the world's leading industrial producer, starting to shoulder aside the factories of Old Europe.[2]

Such a tidal wave of production needed markets on a scale never seen before. The expansion of the U.S. Empire into a worldwide Power tried to provide those. Yet the new industrial Empire also needed something just as essential—an industrial proletariat. The key to the even greater army of wage-slaves was another flood of emigration from Old Europe. This time from Southern and Eastern

Europe: Poles, Italians, Slovaks, Serbs, Hungarians, Finns, Jews, Russians, etc. From the 1880s to the beginning of the First World War some 15 millions of these new emigrants arrived looking for work. And they came in numbers which dwarfed the tempo of the old Irish, German and Scandinavian immigration of the mid-1800s (and that was 3½ times as large as the Anglo-Saxon, German, and Scandinavian immigration of the 1898–1914 period).[3]

They had a central role in the mass wage labor of the new industrial Empire. The capitalists put together the raw materials and capital base extracted from the earlier colonial conquests, the labor of the Euro-Amerikan craftsman, and the new millions of industrial production workers from Southern and Eastern Europe.

In 1910 the U.S. Immigration Commission said: "A large portion of the Southern and Eastern immigrants of the past twenty-five years have entered the manufacturing and mining industries of the eastern and middle western States, mostly in the capacity of unskilled laborers. There is no basic industry in which they are not largely represented and in many cases they compose more than 50 per cent of the total numbers of persons employed in such industries. Coincident with the advent of these millions of unskilled laborers there has been an unprecedented expansion of the industries in which they have been employed."[4]

In the bottom layers of the Northern factory the role of the new, non-citizen immigrants from Eastern and Southern Europe was dominant. A labor historian writes: "More than 30,000 were steelworkers by 1900. The newcomers soon filled the unskilled jobs in the Northern mills, forcing the natives and the earlier immigrants upward or out of the industry. In the Carnegie plants* of Allegheny County in March 1907, 11,694 of 14,539 common laborers were Eastern Europeans."[5]

This was not just the arithmetic, quantitative addition of more workers. The mechanization of industrial production qualitatively transformed labor relations, reshaping the masses themselves.

---

* The Carnegie Steel Company was the leading firm in the industry. In 1901, under the guidance of J.P. Morgan, it became the main building block in the first of the giant trusts (which was named the U.S. Steel Corporation).

Instead of skilled craftsmen using individual machines as tools to personally make a tin sheet or an iron rod, the new mass-production factory had gangs of unskilled workers tending semi-automatic machines and production lines, with the worker controlling neither the shape of the product nor the ever-increasing pace of production. This was the system, so well-known to us, whose intense pressures remolded peasants and laborers into an industrial class.

This new industrial proletariat—the bottom, most exploited foundation of white wage labor—was nationally distinct. That is, it was composed primarily of the immigrant national minorities from Southern and Eastern Europe. Robert Hunter's famous exposé, *Poverty*, which in 1904 caused a public sensation in settler society, pointed this national distinction out in very stark terms:

> *"In the poorest quarters of many great American cities and industrial communities one is struck by a most peculiar fact—the poor are almost entirely foreign born. Great colonies, foreign in language, customs, habits, and institutions, are separated from each other and from distinctly American groups on national and racial lines ... These colonies often make up the main portion of our so-called 'slums'. In Baltimore 77 percent of the total population of the slums was, in the year 1894, of foreign birth or parentage. In Chicago the foreign element was 90 percent; in New York, 95 percent; and in Philadelphia, 91 percent..."*[6]

The 9th Special Report of the Federal Bureau of Labor revealed that immigrant Italian workers in Chicago had average earnings of less than $6 per week; 57% were unemployed part of the year, averaging 7 months out of work.[7] For the new mass-production system found it more profitable to run at top speed for long hours when orders were high, and then shut down the factory completely until orders built up again. In 1910, a year of high production for the steel industry, 22% of the labor force was unemployed for three months or longer, and over 60% were laid off for at least one month.[8]

Even in an industry such as steel (where the work week at that time was seven days on and on), the new immigrant workers could not earn enough to support a family. In 1910 the Pittsburgh

Associated Charities proved that if an immigrant steel laborer worked for 365 straight days he still could "not provide a family of five with the barest necessities."

And these were men who earned $10–12 per week. In the textile mills of Lawrence, Massachusetts, the 15,000 immigrant youth from age 14 who worked there earned only 12 cents per hour. A physician, Dr. Elizabeth Shapleigh, wrote: "A considerable number of boys and girls die within the first two or three years after starting work ... 36 out of every 100 of all men and women who work in the mills die before reaching the age of 25."[9]

The proletarian immigrants did not see Amerika as a "Land of Freedom" as the propaganda says, but as a hell of Satanic cruelty. One historian reminds us:

"The newcomers harbored no illusions about America. 'There in Pittsburgh, people say, the dear sun never shines brightly, the air is saturated with stench and gas,' parents in Galicia wrote their children. A workman in the South Works* warned a prospective immigrant: 'If he wants to come, he is not to complain about me for in America there are neither Sundays nor holidays; he must go to work.' Letters emphasized that 'here in America one must work for three horses.' 'There are different kinds of work, heavy and light,' explained another, 'but a man from our country cannot get the light.' An Hungarian churchman inspecting Pittsburgh steel mills exclaimed bitterly: 'Wherever the heat is most insupportable, the flames most scorching, the smoke and soot most choking, there we are certain to find compatriots bent and wasted with toil.' Returned men, it was said, were worn out by their years in America."[10] In South Works nearly one-quarter of the new immigrant steelworkers were injured or killed on the job each year.[11]

In the steel mill communities—company towns—these laborers in the pre–World War I years were usually single, with even married men having been forced to leave their families in the "old country" until they could either return or become more successful. They lived crowded into squalid boarding houses, owned by "boarding-bosses" who were fellow countrymen and often as well the foremen

---

* U.S. Steel South Works in Chicago, Illinois.

who hired them (different nationalities often worked in separate gangs, so that they had a common language).

Sleeping three or four to a room, they spent much of their free time in the saloons that were their solace. As in all oppressed communities under capitalism, cheap drink was encouraged as a pacifier. Immigrant mill communities would fester with saloons—Gary, Indiana had more than one saloon for every one hundred inhabitants. Of course, the local police and courts preyed on these "foreigners" with both abuse and shakedowns. They had few democratic rights in the major urban centers, and in the steel or mining or rubber or textile company towns they had none.

In the U.S. Empire nationality differences have always been disguised as "racial" differences (so that the Euro-Amerikan settlers can maintain the fiction that theirs is the only real nation). The Eastern and Southern European national minorities were widely defined as non-white, as members of genetically different (and backward) races from the "white" race of Anglo-Saxons. This pseudo-scientific, racist categorizing only continued an ideological characteristic of European capitalist civilization. The Euro-Amerikans have always justified their conquest and exploitation of other nationalities by depicting them as racially different. This old tactic was here applied even to other Europeans.

So Francis A. Walker, President of MIT (and the "Dr. Strangelove" figure who as U.S. Commissioner of Indian Affairs developed the Indian reservation system), popularized the Social Darwinistic theory that the new immigrants were "beaten men from beaten races; representing the worst failures in the struggle for existence..." Thus, as double failures in the "survival of the fittest," these new European immigrants were only capable of being industrial slaves.

The wildest assertions of "racial" identity were common. Some Euro-Amerikans claimed that these "swarthy" Europeans were really "Arabs" or "Syrians." U.S. Senator Simmons of North Carolina claimed that the Southern Italians were *"the degenerate progeny of the Asiatic hordes which, long centuries ago, overran the shores of the Mediterranean..."* [12]

The St. Paul, Minnesota District Attorney argued in Federal court that Finns shouldn't receive citizenship papers since "a Finn ...

is a Mongolian and not a 'white person.'" Scientists were prominent in the new campaign. Professor E.A. Hooton of Harvard University claimed that there were actually nine different "races" in Europe, each with different mental abilities and habits. As late as 1946, in the widely-used textbook, *New Horizons In Criminology,* Prof. Hooton's pseudoscience was quoted by police to "prove" how Southern Italians tended to "crimes of violence," how Slavs "show a preference for sex offenses," and so on.[13]

A widely-read *Saturday Evening Post* series of 1920 on the new immigrants warned that unless they were restricted and kept seg-regated the result would be "a hybrid race of people as worthless and futile as the good-for-nothing mongrels of Central America and Southeastern Europe."[14] On the street level, newspapers and com-mon talk sharply distinguished between "white Americans" and the "Dago" and "Hunky"—who were not considered "white" at all.

The bourgeoisie had a dual attitude of fearing these new prole-tarians during moments of unrest and eagerly encouraging their in-flux when the economy was booming. It was often stated that these "races" were prone to extreme and violent political behavior that the calm, business-like Anglo-Saxon had long since outgrown. One writer in a business journal said: "I am no race worshipper, but ... if the master race of this continent is subordinated to or overrun with the communistic and revolutionary races it will be in grave danger of social disaster."[15]

One answer—and one that became extremely impor-tant—was to "Americanize" the new laboring masses, to tame them by absorbing them into settler Amerika, to remake them into citi-zens of Empire. The Big Bourgeoisie, which very much needed this labor, was interested in this solution. In November 1918, a private dinner meeting of some fifty of the largest employers of immigrant labor discussed Americanization (this was the phrase used at the time). Previous social work and employer indoctrination campaigns directed at the immigrants had not had much success.

It was agreed by those capitalists that the spread of "Bolshevism" among the industrial immigrants was a real danger, and that big business should undercut this trend and *"Break up the nationalistic, racial groups by combining their members for America."*[16] It was thus well understood by the bourgeoisie that these European workers' consciousness of themselves as oppressed national minorities made them open to revolutionary ideas—and, on the other hand, their possible corruption into Amerikan citizens would make them more loyal to U.S. Imperialism.

The meeting formed the Inter-Racial Council, with corporate representatives and a tactical window-dressing of conservative, bourgeois "leaders" from the immigrant communities. T. Coleman DuPont became the chairman. Francis Keller, the well-known social worker and reformer became the paid coordinator of the Council's programs. It sounded just like so many of the establishment pacify-the-ghetto committees of the 1960s—only the "races" being "uplifted" were all European.

The Council's main efforts were directed at propaganda. The American Association of Foreign Language Newspapers (in actuality a private company that placed Amerikan big business advertising in the many foreign language community newspapers) was purchased. With total control over the all-important major advertising, the Council began to dictate the political line of many of those newspapers. Anti-communist and anti-union articles were pushed.

The Council also, in concert with government agencies and private capitalist charities, promoted Americanization "education" programs (i.e. political indoctrination): "adult education" night schools for immigrants, State laws requiring them to attend Americanization classes, laws prohibiting the use of any language except English in schools, etc., etc. The Americanization movement had a lasting effect on the Empire. The Inter-Racial Council was dropped by the capitalists in 1921, since by then Americanization had its own momentum.[17]

At the same time, national chauvinism and the specific class interests of the Euro-Amerikan petit-bourgeoisie and labor aristocracy led to campaigns against the new immigrants. State licensing acts in New York, Connecticut, Michigan, Wyoming, Arizona, and New Mexico barred non-citizen immigrants from competing with the settler professionals in medicine, pharmacy, architecture, engineering, and so on.[18] Under the banner of anti-Catholicism, various right-wing organizations attempted to mobilize the settler masses against the new immigrants. One such group, the Guardians of Liberty, was headed by retired U.S. Army Chief of Staff Gen. Nelson Miles (who had commanded the military repressions at both Wounded Knee and later in the invasion of Puerto Rico). The Loyal Legion, the Ku Klux Klan, and other secret paramilitary groups were also heavily involved in attacks on immigrants, particularly when they became active in socialist organizations or went out on strikes.[19]

Most significantly, the settler trade unions themselves started picturing these new proletarians as the enemy. The unions of the American Federation of Labor (AFL) were heavily imbued with the labor aristocracy viewpoint of the "native-born" settlers. This was true even though an earlier wave of German and Irish immigrants had played such a large role in founding those unions. Now they fought to bar the "Dago" and "Hunky" from the better-paid work, from union membership, and even from entering the U.S. In New York, the Bricklayers Union got Italians fired from public works projects. AFL President Samuel Gompers united with right-wing U.S. Senator Henry Cabot Lodge in campaigning to extend the anti-Asian immigration bars to the "nonwhite" Eastern and Southern Europeans as well.[20]

This process was very visible in the steel mills. It became socially unacceptable for "white" settlers to work with the Slavs and the Italians on the labor gangs. Increasingly they left the hard work to the European national minorities and either moved up to foreman, skilled positions—or out of the mills. The companies pushed the separation. Euro-Amerikans applying for ordinary labor jobs were told: "only Hunkies work on those jobs, they're too damn dirty and too damn hot for a 'white' man ... No white American works in steel-plant labor gang unless he' nuts or booze-fighter." A steel labor history tells us:

> "The English-speaking workman was in general content to ignore the immigrants. Outside the mill he rarely encountered them or entered their crowded streets. But indifference often edged into animosity ... Disdain could be read also in the stereotyped Dago and Hunky in the short stories that appeared in labor papers, and in the frankly hostile remarks of native workers.

"Eager to dissociate himself from the Hunky, the skilled man identi-fied with the middling group of small shopkeepers and artisans, and with them came to regard the merchants and managers as his models. Whatever his interests may have been, the English-speaking steelworker had a psychological commitment in favor of his employer."[21]

So the imperialist era had begun with Euro-Amerikan wage labor still a privileged, upper stratum dominated by a petit-bourgeois view-point. And although the new industrial proletariat was overwhelm-ingly European in origin, it was primarily made up of the oppressed national minorities from Eastern and Southern Europe—"foreign-ers" widely considered "nonwhite" by the settlers. The U.S. Empire's policy of relegating the work of "supporting society," of carrying out the tasks of the proletariat, to oppressed workers of other na-tionalities, was thus continued in a more complex way into the 20th century. At the same time the capitalists were raising the possibil-ity of buying off political discontent by offering these proletarians Americanization into settler society.

2. Industrial Unionism

As U.S. imperialism stumbles faster and faster into its permanent decline, once again we hear the theory expressed that some poverty and the resulting mass economic struggles will create revolutionary consciousness in Euro-Amerikan workers. The fact is that such social pressures are not new to White Amerika. For three decades—from 1890 to 1920—the new white industrial proletariat increasingly organized itself into larger and larger struggles with the capitalists.

The immigrant European proletarians wanted industrial unionism and the most advanced among them wanted socialism. A mass movement was built for both. These were the most heavily exploited, most proletarian, and most militant European workers Amerika has ever produced. Yet, in the end, they were unable to go beyond desiring the mere reform of imperialism.

The mass industrial struggles of that period were important in that they represented the *highest* level of class consciousness any major stratum of European workers in the U.S. has yet reached. And even in this exceptional period—a period of the most aggressive and openly anti-capitalist labor organizing—European workers were unable to produce an adequate revolutionary leadership, unable to defeat the settler labor aristocracy, unable to oppose U.S. imperialism, and unable to unite with the anti-colonial movements of the oppressed nations. We can sum up the shortcomings by saying that they flirted with socialism—but in the end preferred settlerism.

The Industrial Workers of the World (IWW) was the most important single organization of this period. From its founding in 1905 (the year of the first Russian Revolution) until 1920, the IWW was the center of industrial unionism in the U.S. It was the form in which the Northern and Western white industrial proletariat first emerged into mass political consciousness. Unlike the restrictive craft unions of the AFL, the IWW organized on a class basis. That is, it organized and tried to unite all sections of the white working class (copper miners, auto workers, cowboys, hotel workers, farm laborers, and even the unemployed). It was based on the European immigrant proletarians and the bottom stratum—usually migrant—of "native-born" Euro-Amerikan workers.

The IWW saw itself as not only winning better wages, but eventually overthrowing capitalism. It was a syndicalist union (the "One Big Union") meant to combine workers of all trades and nationalities literally around the world. This was a period in the development of the world proletariat where these revolutionary syndicalist ideas had wide appeal. The immature belief that workers needed

no revolutionary party or leadership, but merely had to gather into industrial unions and bring down capitalism by larger and larger strikes, was a passing phase. In 1900 these revolutionary syndicalist unions were popular in Spain, France, Italy—as well as briefly in the U.S. Empire.

While the IWW was backward in many respects, in others it displayed great strengths. It was genuinely proletarian. As an effective mass labor organization, it showed a fighting spirit long since vanished from white workers. We are referring to an open anti-Amerikanism. The IWW urged workers to reject any loyalty to the U.S. Unlike the majority of Euro-Amerikan "Socialists," the IWW linked "American" nationalism with the bourgeois culture of lynch mob patriotism. Just as the IWW was the last white union movement to be socialist, it also represented the last stratum of white workers to be in any way internationalist.

Great boldness relative to the usual settler trade unionism characterized the IWW. First, it promoted unity on the broadest scale then attempted, in the U.S. including not only the "Dago" and "Hunky" but also explicitly declaring that industrial unionism meant the inclusion of Mexicanos, Asians, Afrikans, Indians, and all nationalities. Second, it undertook the most militant campaigns of union organization and struggle, expressing the desperate needs of the most exploited white workers. Third, the IWW was able to advance industrial unionism here by learning from the more advanced and experienced immigrants from Old Europe.

Because of this, the IWW was able to launch strikes and unionization drives on a scale never seen before in the U.S. In the years after 1905 the "Wobblies" led an escalating explosion of union struggles: Hotel workers in Arizona, lumberjacks in Washington, textile workers in Massachusetts, seamen in ports from Chile to Canada, auto workers in Detroit, and so on. And there were many notable victories, many successful strikes. It must be emphasized that to workers used to seeing only defeats, the IWW's ability to help them win strikes was no small matter.

For example, in 1909 the IWW helped the immigrant workers at the McKees Rocks, Pa. plant of the Pressed Steel Car Co. (a subsidiary of the U.S. Steel trust) win their strike. This was of national importance, since it was the first time that workers had won a strike against the mammoth Steel Trust. That strike, which taught so much to union militants here, was led by an underground "Unknown Committee" representing both the IWW and the various European nationalities. The "Unknown Committee" had the knowledge of veterans of the 1905 Russian Revolution, the Italian labor resistance, the German Metal Workers Union, and the Swiss and Hungarian railway strikes. It is clear that through the IWW the more experienced and politically educated European workers taught their backward Amerikan cousins how to look out after their class interests.[22]

In 1914 the IWW's Agricultural Workers Organization (AWO) pulled off an organizing feat unequalled for fifty years. They established the "world's longest picket line," running 800 miles from Kansas up to Rapid City, South Dakota. In distant railroad yards IWW strongarm squads maintained a blockade, in which non-union workers were kept out. Confronted with a critical labor shortage at harvest time, the growers had to give in. This was the biggest agricultural labor drive in the U.S. until the 1960s. The AWO itself grew to almost 70,000 members, becoming the largest single union within the IWW. In fact, at the 1916 IWW Convention the AWO actually had a majority of the votes (252 out of 335 votes).[23]

But by 1920 the IWW had declined sharply. Not from failure in an organizational sense, but from both it and the strata that it represented having reached the limits of their political consciousness. The IWW was able to build industrial unions of the most exploited white workers and to win many strikes, but past that it was unable to advance. Its local unions usually fell apart quickly, and many of its victories were soon reversed. The landmark 1909 steel industry victories at McKees Rocks and Hammond, Indiana were reversed within a year. The 1912 Lawrence, Mass. textile strike—the single most famous strike in U.S. trade union history—was also a great victory, and the IWW also crushed there by the next year. This was the general pattern.

The external difficulties faced by the IWW were far greater than just the straightforward opposition of the factory owners. The Euro-Amerikan aristocracy of labor and its AFL unions viciously fought this upsurge from below. During the great 1912 Lawrence, Mass.

textile strike, the AFL's United Textile Workers Union scabbed throughout the strike. The AFL officially backed the mill owners. In McKees Rocks, Pa. the skilled workers of the AFL Amalgamated Association of Iron and Steel Workers used guns to break a second IWW strike.

And the factories and mines were not isolated, but were part of settler Amerika, where the masses of petit-bourgeois farmers, small merchants, and professionals joined the foremen, skilled craftsmen, and supervisors in backing up the bosses. The European immigrants represented perhaps only one-seventh of the white population, and were greatly outnumbered.

The IWW's weaknesses, however, primarily reflected its inner contradictions. The syndicalist outlook, while sincerely taken by many, was also a convenient cover to avoid dealing with the question of settlerism. Using the ultra-revolutionary sounding syndicalist philosophy the IWW could avoid any actual revolutionary work. In fact, despite its anti-capitalist enthusiasm the IWW never even made any plans to oppose the U.S. government—and never did. Similarly, its Marxist vision of all nations and peoples being merged into "One Big Union" covering the globe only covered up the fact that it had no intention of fighting colonialism and national oppression.

If the IWW had fought colonialism and national oppression, it would have lost most of its white support. What it did instead—laying out a path that the CIO would follow in the 1930s—was to convince some white workers that their immediate self-interest called for a limited, tactical cooperation with the colonial proletariats. Underneath all the fancy talk that "In the IWW the colored worker, man or woman, is on an equal footing with every other worker," was the reality that the IWW was a white organization for whites.

While this new immigrant industrial proletariat was thrown together from many different European nations, speaking different languages and having different cultures and class backgrounds, they were united by two things: their exploited state as "foreign" proletarians and their desire to achieve a better life in Amerika. The resolution of these pressures was in their Americanization, in them becoming finally integrated into settler citizens of the Empire. In changing Amerika they themselves were decisively changed. Some one-third of the immigrant workers went back to Europe, with many of the most militant being deported or forced to flee.

Looking back this underlying trend can be seen in the life of the IWW. While the IWW fancied itself as a dangerous revolutionary organization, in reality it was nothing more nor less than the best industrial union that class conscious white workers could build to "improve their condition." It was a public, fully legal union open to all. It was, therefore, just as dependent upon bourgeois legality and government toleration as the AFL. The IWW could be very strong against local employers or even the municipal government; against the imperialist state it dared only to submit in unhappy confusion. The national IWW leadership understood this unpleasant fact in an unscientific, pragmatic way.

As the Great Powers were drawn into World War I the central issue in the European oppressor nation socialist movements was the opposition to imperialist war. Not primarily because of the mass bloodshed, but because in a war for expanding empires it was the absolute duty of all oppressor nation revolutionaries to oppose the aggression of their own empire, to work for the defeat of their own bourgeoisie, and for the liberation of the oppressed nations. This is the issue that created the international communist movement of the 20th century.

On this most important struggle the IWW was revealed as being immature and lacking as a revolutionary organization. *It was simply unwilling to directly oppose U.S. imperialism.* The IWW verbally criticized the war many times. At the 1914 convention they said: "We, as members of the industrial army, will refuse to fight for any purpose except for the realization of industrial freedom."[24] But when U.S. imperialism entered the war to grab more markets and colonies, the IWW became frantic to prove to the bourgeoisie that they wouldn't oppose them in any way.

The surface problem was that since the IWW was a totally legal and public union, it was totally unable to withstand any major government repression. Therefore, the leadership said, regardless of every class conscious worker's opposition to the war the IWW dare not fight it. Walter Nef, head of the IWW Agricultural Workers Organization, said: *"We are against the war, but not organized and can do nothing."*[25] Imagine, a revolutionary organization that built for twelve years, with a membership of over 100,000, but was "not organized" to oppose its own bourgeoisie.

The many requests from IWW members for guidance as to how to fight the imperialist war went unanswered. Even "Big Bill" Haywood, the angry and militant IWW leader, had to back off: "I am at a loss as to definite steps to be taken against the War."[26] Finally, the IWW decided to duck the issue as much as possible. The word went out to white workers to stick to local economic issues of higher wages, etc. and not oppose the government. "Organize now ... for the postwar struggle should be the watchword."[27] This surface political retreat only revealed the growing settler sickness at the heart of the IWW, and sabotaged the most advanced and revolutionary-minded white proletarians within their ranks.

They never organized to oppose U.S. imperialism because that's not what even the immigrant proletarian masses wanted—they wanted militant struggle to reach some "social justice" for themselves. During the July 1915 AFL strike at the Connecticut munitions plants, the charge was made that the whole strike was a plot by German agents—with the strike secretly subsidized by the Kaiser's treasury. In a lead editorial in its national journal, *Solidarity,* the IWW hurried to put itself on record as not opposing the war effort. While admitting that they had no proof that the strike was a German conspiracy, the IWW urged the strikers to "settle quickly." The editorial angrily suggested that the strike leaders might move to Germany. Then they came to the main point, which was undermining the anti-imperialist sentiment among the workers, and urging them to think only of getting more money for themselves:

> *"The owners of these factories are making millions out of the murderfest in Europe—their slaves should likewise improve the opportunity to get a little something for themselves.*
>
> *"The point may be made here, that we should all be interested in stopping the production of war munitions. Yes, of course, but that's only a dream ... so the only thing the workers in these factories can do is to try to improve their condition..."*[28]

The line was very clear. Far from fighting U.S. imperialism, the IWW was spreading defeatism among the workers and urging them to concentrate only on getting a bigger bribe out of the imperialist superprofits. The IWW is often praised by the settler "left" as very "American," very "grassroots." We can say that their cynical, individualistic slant that workers can *only get a little something for themselves* out of the slaughter of millions does represent the essence of Amerikan settler degeneracy. In Russia the Bolsheviks were telling the Russian workers to "Turn the Imperialist War into a Revolutionary War" and overthrow the Imperialists—which they did.

The IWW's pathetic efforts to avoid antagonizing the bourgeoisie did them little good. The U.S. Empire tired of these pests, viewing the militant organization of immigrant labor as dangerous. Finally cranking its police machinery up, the imperialist state proceeded to smash the defenseless IWW clear into virtual nonexistence. It wasn't even very difficult, since throughout the West vigilante mobs of settlers declared an open reign of terror against the IWW. In Arizona some 1,300 miners suspected of IWW involvement were driven from the State at gunpoint.

In July 1918, 101 IWW leaders past and present were convicted in Chicago Federal Court of sabotaging the Imperialist War effort in a rigged trial that dwarfed the "Chicago Conspiracy Trial" of the Vietnam War–era. The political verdict was certain even though the prosecution was *unable to prove that the IWW had obstructed the war in any way!* Only one defendant out of 101 had violated the draft registration laws. While the IWW unions had led strikes that disrupted war production in Western copper and timber, the government was forced to admit that of the 521 disruptive strikes that had taken place since the U.S. Empire entered the war, only 3 were by the IWW (while 519 were by the pro-government AFL unions).[29]

Federal raids on the IWW took place from coast-to-coast. Immigration agents held mass round-ups which resulted in long jail stays while undergoing deportation hearings. In 1917 the Federal agents arrested 34 IWW organizers in Kansas, who eventually got prison terms of up to nine years. In Omaha, Nebraska, the 64 IWW delegates at the Agricultural Workers Organization Convention were arrested and held 18 months without trial. In 21 States "criminal syndicalism" laws were passed, directed at the IWW, under which thousands were arrested. In California alone between 1919–24 some 500 IWW members were indicted, 128 of whom ended up serving prison terms of up to 14 years.[30] The IWW never recovered from these blows, and from 1917 on quickly declined.

Such an unwillingness to fight U.S. imperialism could hardly come from those with anti-imperialist politics. The reason we have to underline this is that for obvious ends the settler "Left" has been emphasizing how the IWW was a mass example of anti-racist labor unity. This poisoned bait has been naively picked up by a number of Third World revolutionary organizations, and used as one more small justification to move towards revisionist-integrationist ideology.

There is no doubt that much of the IWW genuinely despised the open, white supremacist persecution of the colonial peoples. Unlike the smug, privileged AFL aristocracy of labor, the IWW represented the voice of those white workers who had suffered deeply and thus could sympathize with the persecuted. But their inability to confront the settleristic ambitions within themselves reduced these sparks of real class consciousness to vague sentiments and limited economic deals.

The IWW never attempted to educate the most exploited white workers to unite with the national liberation struggles. Instead, it argued that "racial" unity on the job to raise wages was all that mattered. This is the approach used by the AFL-CIO today; obviously, it's a way of building a union in which white supremacist workers tolerate colonial workers. This was the narrow, economic self-interest pitch underneath all the syndicalist talk. The IWW warned white workers: *"Leaving the Negro outside of your union makes him a potential, if not an actual, scab, dangerous to the organized workers..."*[31] These words reveal that the IWW's goal was to control colonial labor for the benefit of white workers—and that Afrikans were viewed as *"dangerous"* if not controlled.

So that even in 1919, after two years of severe "race riots" in the North (armed attacks by white workers on Afrikan exile communities), the IWW kept insisting that there was: "...no race problem. There is only a class problem. The economic interests of all workers, be they white, black, brown or yellow, are identical, and all are included in the IWW. It has one program for the entire working class—the abolition of the wage system."[32] The IWW's firm position of not fighting the lynch mobs, of not opposing the colonial system, allowed them to unite with the racist element in the factories—and helped prepare the immigrant proletariat for becoming loyal citizens of the Empire. It must never be forgotten that the IWW contained genuinely proletarian forces, some of whom could have been led forward towards revolution.

We can see this supposed unity actually at work in the IWW's relationship to the Japanese workers on the West Coast. In the Western region of the Empire the settler masses were deeply infected with anti-Asian hatred. Much of this at that time was directed at the new trickle of Japanese immigrant laborers, who were working mainly in agriculture, timber, and railroads.

These Japanese laborers were subjected to the most vicious persecution and exploitation, with the bourgeois politicians and press stirring up mob terror against them constantly. Both the Socialist Party of Eugene Debs and the AFL unions helped lead the anti-Asian campaign among the settler masses. In April 1903, one thousand Japanese and Mexicano sugar beet workers struck near Oxnard, California. They formed the Sugar Beet & Farm Laborers Union, and wrote the AFL asking for a union charter of affiliation.

AFL President Samuel Gompers, in his usual treacherous style, tried in his reply to split the ranks of the oppressed: "Your union must guarantee that it will under no circumstances accept membership of any Chinese or Japanese."

The union's Mexicano secretary (the President was Japanese) answered Gompers for his people: "In the past we have counseled, fought and lived on very short rations with our Japanese brothers, and toiled with them in the fields, and they have been uniformly kind and considerate. We would be false to them, and to ourselves and to the cause of unionism if we now accepted privileges for ourselves which are not accorded to them. We are going to stand by men who stood by us in the long, hard fight which ended in victory over the enemy."[33]

Japanese workers were not only unable to find unity with the settler unions, but had to deal with them as part of the oppressor forces. There was a high level of organization among us, expressed usually in small, local, Japanese national minority associations of our own. The news, therefore, that the new IWW was accepting Asian workers as members was quite welcome to us.

In 1907 two white IWW organizers went to the office of the *North American Times,* a Japanese-language newspaper in Seattle. They asked the newspaper to publish an announcement of a forth-coming meeting. As the newspaper happily informed its readers: "…every worker, no matter whether he is Japanese or Chinese, is in-vited … This new organization does not exclude you as others do, but they heartily welcome you to join. Don't lose this chance."[34]

The IWW publicly criticized those "socialists" who were part of the anti-Asian campaign. In a special pamphlet they appealed to white workers to see that Asians were good union men, who would be helpful in winning higher wages: "They are as anxious as you, to get as much as possible. This is proven by the fact that they have come to this country."[35]

But while scattered Japanese workers joined the IWW, in the main we did not. The reason, quite simply, is that while the IWW wanted our cooperation, they did not want the hated Japanese work-ers inside the IWW. In order to keep amicable relations with the mass of white supremacist settlers in the West, the IWW limited their relationship to us. Some Asians would be acceptable, but any conspicuous mass recruitment of Japanese was too controversial. A sympathetic writer about the IWW at the time noted:

> "At the Third Convention, George Speed, a delegate from California, quite accurately expressed the sentiment of the organization in regard to the Japanese Question. 'The whole fight against the Japanese,' he said, 'is the fight of the middle class of California, in which they employ the labor faker to back it up.' He added, how-ever, that he considered it 'practically useless … under present con-ditions for the IWW to take any steps' to organize the Japanese.."[36]

This position was seen in action at the 1914 Hop Pickers Strike near Maryville, California; which was the well-publicized struggle that launched the IWW's farm worker organizing drive in that State. That year the Durst Ranch hired 2,800 migrant workers at below-market wages, and forced them to toil in isolated near-slavery. IWW organizers soon started a strike in which the Japanese, Mexicano, Greek, Syrian, Puerto Rican, and other nationalities were strongly united. The strike led to a national defense campaign when the sheriff, after shooting two striking workers, arrested the two main IWW organizers as the alleged murderers.

Although the strike was victorious—and led to bigger organizing drives—the Japanese workers had disappeared. We were persuaded to withdraw (while still honoring the picket lines) in order to help the IWW, since "...the feeling of the working class against the Japanese was so general throughout the State that the association of the Japanese with the strikers would in all probability be detrimental to the latter." The IWW tried to justify everything by saying that move was on the initiative of the Japanese workers—and then praising it as an act of "solidarity." Notice that while the Japanese laborers lived, and worked, and went out on strike with the others, that the IWW statement separates *"the Japanese"* from *"the strikers."*[37]

The IWW considered it *"solidarity"* for oppressed Asian workers to be excluded from their own struggle, so that the IWW could get together with the open racists. It should be clear that while the IWW hoped to establish the "unity of all workers" as a principle, they were willing to sacrifice the interests of colonial and oppressed workers in order to gain their real goal—the unity of all white workers.

While it was advantageous for the IWW to keep Asians at arm's length, in occupied New Afrika there was literally no way to build industrial unions without winning the cooperation of Afrikan workers. In the South the Afrikan proletariat was the bedrock of everything. The IWW experience there highlights the strategic limitations of its political line.

In 1910 an independent union, the Brotherhood of Timber Workers, was formed in Louisiana and Mississippi. This was to become the main part of the IWW's Deep South organizing. These Southern settler workers were on the very bottom of the settler world. They were forced to labor for $7–9 per week—and that mostly not in cash, but in "scrip" usable only at the company stores. Their very exploited lives were comparable to that of the "Hunky" and "Dago" of the Northern industrial towns. In other words, they lived a whole level below the norm of settler society.

For that reason the settler timberworkers were driven to build themselves a union. And because half of the workforce in the industry was Afrikan, they had to recruit Afrikans as well. Half of the 35,000 BTW members were Afrikan—organized into "seg" lodges and not admitted to the settler union meetings, of course. It was not a case of radicalism or idealism: the settler worker was literally forced by practical necessity to gain the cooperation of Afrikan workers. In a major pamphlet in which he calls on settler timberworkers to join up with the IWW, the BTW's secretary, Jay Smith, reminds them that the controversial policy of integrating the union existed solely to keep Afrikans under control:

> "As far as the 'negro question' goes, it means simply this: Either the whites organize with the negroes, or the bosses will organize the negroes against the whites..."[38]

In 1912 the BTW joined the IWW, after integrating its union meetings at the demand of "Big Bill" Haywood. The IWW now had a major labor drive going in the Deep South. But a few months later the BTW was totally crushed in the Merryville, La. strike of 1912. In a four-day reign of terror the local sheriff and company thugs beat, kidnapped, and "deported" the strike activists. The BTW was dissolved by terror as hundreds of members had to flee the State and many more were white-listed and could no longer find work in that industry.

The IWW's refusal to recognize colonial oppression or the exact nature of the imperialist dictatorship over the occupied South, meant that it completely misled the strike. Industrial struggle in the Deep South could not develop separate from the tense, continuous relationship between the settler garrison and the occupied Afrikan nation. The IWW in the South swiftly fell apart. They were unable to cope with the violent, terroristic situation.

The IWW had a use for oppressed colonial workers, and it certainly didn't conduct campaigns of mob terror against us. It publicly reminded white workers of the supposed rights of the colonial peoples; but as a white workers union it had no political program, no practical answers for the problems of the colonial proletariat. And insofar as it tried to convince everyone that there was a solution for the problems of colonial workers *separate* from liberation for their oppressed nations, it did a positive disservice.*

The IWW lived, rose and fell, at the same time as the great Mexican Revolution of 1910 just across the artificial "border." For this syndicalist organization to have reached out and made common cause with the anti-colonial revolutions would have been quite easy. On November 27, 1911, the Zapatistas proclaimed the Plan of Ayala, setting forth the agrarian revolution. It was from the U.S.-occupied territory of El Paso that Francisco Villa and seven others began the guerrilla struggle in Chihuahua on March 6, 1913. Hundreds of thousands of peasants joined Zapata's Liberator Army of the South and Villa's Division of the North. Even the Villistas, less politically developed than their Southern compatriots, were social revolutionaries. Villa, a rebel who had taught himself to read while in prison, was openly anti-clerical at a time when Roman Catholicism was the official religion of Mexico. He called the Church "the greatest superstition the world has ever known." The Villista government in Chihuahua founded fifty new schools and divided the land up among the peasants.

This popular uprising spread the spirit of rebellion across the artificial "border" into the U.S.-occupied zone. One California historian writes: *"The dislocation caused by the Mexican Revolution of 1912–1917 led to an increasingly militant political attitude in Los Angeles. This led to a Chicano movement to boycott the draft. Vicente Carillo led a drive to protest the draft and to use mass meetings to focus attention upon Mexican-American economic problems."* Again, it is easy to see that the IWW didn't have far to look if they wanted alliances against the U.S. Empire.

---

* It is interesting to note that even on the Philadelphia waterfront, where the Afrikan-led IWW Marine Transport Workers Union No. 8 was the most stable local in the entire IWW, the Afrikan workers eventually felt forced to leave the IWW due to *"slander, baseless charges and race-baiting."*

Proposals were even made that the IWW and Mexicano workers join in armed uprisings in the Southwest. Ricardo Flores Magon, the revolutionary syndicalist who was the first major leader of Mexicano workers, had ties to the IWW during his long years of exile in the U.S. His organization, the Partido Liberal Mexicano (PLM), led thousands of Mexicano miners in strikes on both sides of the artificial "border." Magon was imprisoned four times by the U.S. Empire, finally being murdered by guards to prevent his scheduled release from Ft. Leavenworth. His proposal for the IWW to join forces with the Mexicano proletariat in armed struggle fell on deaf ears. Although some "Wobblies" (such as Joe Hill) went to Mexico on an individual basis for periods of time, the IWW as a whole rejected such cooperation.

Magon once angrily wrote his brother from prison: "The *norteamericanos* are incapable of feeling enthusiasm or indignation. This is truly a country of pigs ... If the *norteamericanos* do not agitate against their own domestic miseries, can we hope they will concern themselves with ours?"[39]

In outlining these things we are, of course, not just discussing the IWW. Primarily we are looking at the forming consciousness and leadership of a new class: the white industrial proletariat. The same general weaknesses of this class can be seen outside the IWW even more sharply: lack of revolutionary leadership, inability to withstand the sabotage of the labor aristocrats of the "native-born" Euro-Amerikan workers, opposition to the anti-colonial struggles. The great industrial battles in steel at the end of this period show not only these weaknesses, but emphasize the significance of what this meant.

This was evident in the 1919 steel strike, for example, in which for the first time fifteen AFL unions called an industry-wide strike. On Sept. 22, 1919, some 365,000 steelworkers walked out. But while the mass of nonunionized, immigrant European laborers held firm, the unionized Euro-Amerikan skilled workers were a weak element. Capitalist repression had an effect—most notably in Gary, Indiana, where a division of U.S. Army troops broke the strike—but the defeat was due to the incredibly bad leadership and the betrayal by the better-paid settler workers. The disaster of the strike shows why even the inadequate politics of the IWW looked so good to the proletarians of that day.

Many of the skilled Euro-Amerikan workers never joined the strike at all in places like Pittsburgh. And many who had struck started trickling back to work, afraid of losing their good jobs. In early November their union, the Amalgamated Association of Iron and Steel Workers, broke from the strike and started ordering its members back to work. By late November the mills had 75–80% of their workforce back. On January 2, 1920, the strike was officially declared over. Some of the most determined militants had to leave the industry or return to Europe.[40]

While the treachery of the labor aristocracy was very evident in this defeat, the most important event took place *after the strike*. During the strike some 30,000 Afrikan workers from the South had been imported by the steel companies. There was a strong tendency among the white steelworkers to blame the defeat of the strike on Afrikan "scabs" or "strikebreakers." And all the more so because the 10% of the Northern steel workforce that was Afrikan refused to join the strike. The bourgeoisie was guiding the white workers in this. Company officials passed the word that: "Niggers did it." In Pittsburgh one mill boss announced: "The Nigger saved the day for us."[41]

In fact, although this was widely accepted, it was clearly untrue. To begin with, 30,000 Afrikan workers fresh from the South could hardly have replaced 365,000 strikers. There also was by all accounts a tremendous turnover and desire to quit by those Afrikan workers, and within a few months supposedly few if any of them remained.

The reason is that most of them were not "strikebreakers," but workers who had been systematically deceived and brought to the mills by force. That's why they left as soon as they could. The testimony during the strike of 19-year-old Eugene Steward of Baltimore illustrates this. He was recruited along with 200 others (including whites) to work in Philadelphia for $4 per day. But once inside the railroad car they found the doors locked and guarded by armed company police. They were taken without food or water to Pittsburgh, unloaded under guard behind barbed wire, and told that they were to work at the mills. Seeing that a strike was going on, many of them wanted to quit. The guards told them that any Afrikans attempting to leave would be shot down. Steward did succeed in escaping, but was found and forcibly returned by the guards. It was only after a second attempt that he managed to get free. It is obvious that the Afrikan "strikebreakers" were deliberate propaganda set up by the capitalists—and swallowed wholesale by the white workers.

In regard to the Afrikan steelworkers already at work in the North (and who declined to join the strike), it should be remembered that this was a white strike. Many of the striking AFL unions did not admit Afrikans; those that did so (solely to get Afrikans to honor their strikes) usually kept Afrikans in "seg" locals. The Euro-Amerikan leadership of the strike had promised Afrikans nothing, and plainly meant to keep their promise. That is, this strike had a definite oppressor nation character to it and was wholly white supremacist.

Nor did the white steel strike develop separate from the continuous struggle between oppressor and oppressed nations. During the two previous years there had arisen a national movement of settler workers to bar Afrikans from Northern industry by terroristic attacks. Between 1917–19 there had been twenty major campaigns by settler mobs against Afrikan exile communities in the North. The July 1917 East St. Louis "race riot" was organized by that steel

city's AFL Central Trades Council, which had called for "violence" to remove the "growing menace" of the Afrikan exile community. In two days of attacks some 39 Afrikans were killed and hundreds injured. The hand of the capitalists was evident when the *Chicago Tribune* editorially praised the white attackers, and told its readers that Afrikans were *"happiest when the white race asserts its superiority."*[42] Again, we see the organized Euro-Amerikan workers as the social troops of one faction or another of the imperialists.

As the steel campaign was gathering steam throughout 1919 the terroristic attacks on Afrikans increased as well. In Chicago this was to climax in the infamous July 1919 "race riot," just two months before the strike began. Spear's *Black Chicago* recounts:

> *"Between 1917 and 1919, white 'athletic clubs' assaulted Negroes on the streets and 'neighborhood improvement societies' bombed Negro homes. During the Summer of 1919, the guerilla warfare in turn gave way to open armed conflict—the South Side of Chicago became a battleground for racial war ... the bombing of Negro homes and assaults on Negroes in the streets and parks became almost everyday occurrences."*[43]

On July 27, 1919, an Afrikan teenager was stoned to death on the 29th St. beach, and after Afrikans attacked his murderers generalized fighting broke out. It lasted six days, until the Illinois National Guard was called in. 23 Afrikans were killed and 342 wounded, with over 1,000 homeless after arson attacks (white losses were 15 killed and 178 wounded). Afrikans were temporarily trapped in the "Black Belt," unable to go to work or obtain food. Assisted by the police, Irish, Italian, and other white workers would make night raids into the "Black Belt"; homes were often attacked. When Afrikans gathered, police would begin firing into the crowds.

The authorities did not move to "restore order," incidentally, until after Afrikan World War I vets broke into the 8th Illinois Infantry Armory, and armed themselves with rifles to take care of the white mobs.[44]

This was the vigorous "warm-up" for the steel strike. It was not surprising that the Afrikan exile communities were less than enthusiastic about supporting the strike of the same people who had spent the past two years attacking them. Given the history of the AFL it was possible that an outright triumph of the AFL unions might have meant renewed efforts to drive Afrikan labor out of the mills altogether. It was typical settleristic thinking to make Afrikans responsible for the failure of a white strike, which was never theirs in the first place.

Both the strike leadership and the bourgeoisie cleverly promoted this hatred, encouraging the European immigrant and "native-born" settler alike to turn all their anger and bitterness onto the Afrikan nation. Perhaps the most interesting role was played by William Z. Foster, the chief leader of the strike. He was one of the leading "socialist" trade unionists of the period, and in 1920 would become a leader in the new Communist Party USA. From then on until his death he would be a leading figure of settler "communism." Even today young recruits in the CPUSA and Mao Zedong Thought organizations are often told to "study" Foster's writings in order to learn about labor organizing.

William Z. Foster had, as the saying goes, "pulled defeat out of the jaws of victory." Foster based the strike on the AFL unions, despite their proven record of treachery and hostility towards the proletarian masses. That alone guaranteed defeat. He encouraged white supremacist feeling and thus united the honest elements with the most reactionary. Despite the great popular support for a nationwide strike and the angry sentiments of the most exploited steelworkers, Foster and the other AFL leaders so sabotaged the strike that it went down to defeat. The one "smart" thing he did was to cover up his opportunistic policies by following the capitalists in using Afrikans as the scapegoats.

In his 1920 history of the strike, Foster (the supposed "communist") repeated the lie that Afrikan workers had *"lined up with the bosses."* In fact, Foster even said that in resolving the differences between Euro-Amerikan and Afrikan labor *"The negro has the more difficult part"* since the Afrikan worker was becoming *"a professional strike-breaker."* And militant white workers knew what they were supposed to do to a "professional strike-breaker."

Foster's lynch mob oratory was only restrained by the formality expected of a Euro-Amerikan "communist" leader. His white supremacist message was identical to but more politely clothed than the crude rants of the Ku Klux Klan. He warned that the capitalists were grooming Afrikans *"as a race of strike-breakers, with whom to hold the white workers in check; on much the same principle as the Czars used the Cossacks to keep in subjugation the balance of the Russian people."* It's easy to see how Foster became such a popular leader among the settler workers.

No longer was it just a question of *some* Afrikans not following the orders of white labor. Now Foster was openly saying that the *entire Afrikan "race"* was the enemy. Could the imperialists have asked for more, than to have the leading "communist" trade union leader help them whip up the oppressor nation masses to repress the Afrikan nation?

The Cossacks were the hated and feared special military of the Russian Czar, used in bloody repressions against the people. Only the most twisted, Klan-like mentality would have so explicitly compared the oppressed Afrikan nation to those infamous oppressors. And was this message not an incitement to mob terror and genocide? For the poor immigrants from Eastern Europe (much of which was under the lash of Czarist tyranny) to kill a Cossack was an act of justice, of retribution. The threat was easy to read.

In case Afrikans didn't get Foster's threat (which was also being delivered in the streets, as we know), Foster made it even more plain. He said that if Afrikans failed to obey the decisions of settler labor: "It would make our industrial disputes take on more and more the character of race wars, a consummation that would be highly injurious to the white workers and eventually ruinous to the blacks."[45]

The threat of a genocidal "race war" against Afrikans unless they followed the orders of settler labor makes it very clear just what kind of "unity" Foster and his associates had in mind. We should say that once Foster started dealing with the problem of how to build the Euro-Amerikan "Left," he discovered that it was much more effective to pose as an anti-racist and use "soft-sell" in promoting a semi-colonial mentality in oppressed nationalities. Foster the "communist" declared himself an expert on Civil Rights, poverty in Puerto Rico, Afrikan history, and so on.

The tragic failure of the new white industrial proletariat to take up its revolutionary tasks, its inability to rise above the level of reform, is not just a negative. The failure was an aspect of a growing phenomenon—the Americanization of the "foreign" proletariat from Eastern and Southern Europe. By the later part of World War I it was possible to see that these immigrants were starting the climb upwards towards becoming settlers. Revolutionary fervor, as distinct from economic activity, declines sharply among them from this point on.

This was not a smooth process. The sharp repression of 1917–1924, in which not only government forces but also the unleashed settler mob terror struck out across the U.S. Empire, was a clean-up campaign directed at the European national minorities. Thousands were forced out or returned home, many were imprisoned, killed or terrorized. Historians talk of this campaign as a "Red Scare," but it was also the next-to-final step in purifying these "foreigners" so that Amerika could adopt them.

The Chairman of the Iowa Council of Defense said: "We are going to love every foreigner who really becomes an American, and all the others we are going to ship back home." A leader of the Native Sons of the Golden West said that immigrants "must live for the United States and grow an American soul inside of him or get out of the country."[46]

The offer was on the table. The "Hunky" and "Dago" could become "white" (though barely) through Americanization if they pledged their loyalty to the U.S. Empire. In the steel mills World War I meant wholesale Americanization campaigns. "Hungarian Hollow," the immigrant slum quarter in Granite City, Ill. was renamed "Lincoln Place" at the prompting of the steel companies (with festive ceremonies and speeches). By 1918 the Gary, Ind. U.S. Steel Works had over 1,000 men enrolled in evening citizenship classes. Liberty Bond drives and Army enlistment offices in the plants were common. Immigrants were encouraged by their employers to join the U.S. Army and prove their loyalty to imperialism.[47]

Americanization was not just a mental process. To become a settler was meaningless unless it was based on the promise of privileges and the willingness to become parasitic. As "native born"

Euro-Amerikans continued to leave the factories, the immigrant Europeans could now advance. And the importation of hundreds of thousands (soon to be millions) of Mexicano, Afrikan, Puerto Rican, and other colonial workers into Northern industry gave the Americanized Europeans someone to step up on in his climb into settlerism.

In the steel mills, Mexicanos and Afrikans made up perhaps 25% of the workers in Indiana and Illinois by 1925. They were the bottom of the labor there, making up for the immigrant European who had moved up or left for better things. A steel labor history notes:

> *"Meanwhile, the Eastern Europeans were occupying the lesser positions once held by the 'English-speaking' workmen. As they rose, the numbers of Slavs in the mills shrank. At one time 58 percent of the Jones and Laughlin labor force, the immigrants comprised only 31 per cent in 1930. There were 30 per cent fewer Eastern Europeans in Illinois Steel Company mills in 1928 than in 1912. Now largely the immediate bosses of the Negroes and Mexicans, the immigrants disdained their inferiors much as the natives had once disliked them.*
>
> *"The bad feeling generated by the Red Scare abated only gradually. In Gary, the Ku Klux Klan flourished. But the respectable solidity of the immigrant communities in time put to rest unreasoning fear. The children were passing through the schools and into business and higher jobs in the mills. Each year the number of homeowners increased, the business prospered, and the churches and societies became more substantial. The immigrants were assuming a middling social and economic position in the steel towns."*[48]

The U.S. Empire could afford gradually expanding the privileged strata because it had emerged as the big winner in the First Imperialist World War. Scott Nearing pointed out how in 1870 the U.S. was the fourth ranked capitalist economy; by 1922 the U.S. had climbed to No. 1 position: "...more than equal to the wealth of Britain, Germany,

France, Italy, Russia, Belgium and Japan combined."[49] Successful imperialist war was the key to Americanization.

Throughout the Empire this movement of the immigrant proletarians into the settler ranks was evident. A history of Mexican labor importation notes: "In the beet fields of Colorado, as elsewhere in the West, other immigrant groups, such as the Italians, Slavs, Russians, or Irish, found that they could move up from worker or tenant to owner and employer through the use of Mexican migrants."[50]

This point marks a historic change. Never again would white labor be anti-Amerikan and anti-capitalist. Although it would organize itself millions strong into giant unions and wage militant economic campaigns, white labor from that time on would be branded by its servile patriotism to the U.S. Empire. As confused as the IWW might have been about revolution, its contempt for U.S. national chauvinism was genuine and healthy. It was only natural for an organization so strongly based on immigrant labor—many of whose best organizers were not U.S. citizens and who often spoke little or no English—to feel no sympathy for the U.S. Empire. It was a tragedy that this strength was overturned, that this socialist possibility faded into a reinforcement for settlerism. And yet the contradiction between the reality of exploitation in the factories and the privileges of settlerism still remained. The immigrant masses could not be both settler and proletarian. This was the historic challenge of the CIO and New Deal.

VII

BREAKTHROUGH OF THE C.I.O.

It is a revealing comparison that during the 1930s the European imperialists could only resolve the social crisis in Italy, Germany, Spain, Poland, Finland, Rumania, and so on, by introducing fascism, while in the U.S. the imperialists resolved the social crisis with the New Deal. In Germany the workers were hit with the Gestapo, while in Amerika they got the CIO industrial unions.

In that decade the white industrial proletariat unified itself, pushed aside the dead hand of the old AFL labor aristocracy, and in a crushing series of Sit-Down strikes won tremendous increases in wages and working conditions. For the first time the new white industrial proletariat forced the corporations to surrender their despotic control over industrial life.

The Eastern and Southern European immigrant national minorities won the "better life" that Americanization promised them. They became full citizens of the U.S. Empire and with the rest of the white industrial proletariat, won rights and privileges both inside and outside the factories. In return, as U.S. imperialism launched its drive for world hegemony, it could depend upon the armies of solidly united settlers serving imperialism at home and on the battlefield. To insure social stability, the new government-sponsored unions of the CIO absorbed the industrial struggle and helped discipline class relations.

1. Unification of the White Workers

The working class upsurge of the 1930s was not accumulated dis-
contents. This is the common, but shallow, view of mass outbreaks.
What is true is that material conditions, including the relation to
production, shape and reshape all classes and strata. These classes
and strata then express characteristic political consciousness, characteristic roles in the class struggle.

The unification of the white industrial workforce was the result
of immense pressures. Its long-range material basis was the mechanization and imperialist reorganization of production. In the late 19th
century it was still true that in many industries the skilled craftsmen
literally ran production. They—not the company—would decide
how the work was done. Combining the functions of artisan, foreman, and personnel office, these skilled craftsmen would directly
hire and boss their entire work crew of laborers, paying them out of
a set fee paid by the capitalist per ton or piece produced (the balance
being their wage-profit).

The master roller in the sheet metal rolling mill, the puddler
in the iron mill, the buttie in the coal mine, the carriage builder in
the early auto plant all exemplified this stage of production. The
same craft system applied to gun factories, carpet mills, stone quar-
ries etc.[1] It was these highly privileged settler craftsmen who were
the base of the old AFL unions. Their income reflected their lofty
positions above the laboring masses. In 1884, for example, master
rollers in East St. Louis earned $42 per week (a then very consider-
able wage), over four times more than laborers they bossed.[2]

This petit-bourgeois income and role gradually crumbled as
capitalists reorganized and seized ever tighter control over production. A survey by the U.S. Bureau of Labor found that the number of
skilled steel workers earning 60¢ an hour fell by 20% between 1900–
1910.[3] Mechanization cut the ranks of craftsmen, and, even where
they remained, their once-powerful role in production had shrunk.
The AFL Amalgamated Association of Iron and Steel Workers, whose
24,000 members in 1891 accounted for two thirds of all craftsmen in
the industry, had dwindled to only 6,500 members by 1914.[4]

Mechanization also wiped out whole sections of the very bottom factory laborers, replacing shovels with mechanical scoops, wheelbarrows with electric trolleys and cranes. Both top and bottom layers of the factory workforce were increasingly pulled into the growing middle stratum of semi-skilled, production line assemblers and machine operators. In the modern auto plants of the 1920s some 70% were semi-skilled production workers, while only 10% were skilled craftsmen and 15% laborers.[5] The political unification of the white workers thus had its material roots in the enforced unification of labor in the modern factory.

The 1929 Depression was also a great equalizer and a sharp blow to many settlers, knocking them off their conservative bias. During the 1930s roughly 25% of the U.S. Empire was unemployed. Office clerks, craftsmen, and college students rubbed shoulders with laborers and farmers in the relief lines. Many divisions broke down, as midwestern and Southern rural whites migrated to the industrial cities in search of jobs or relief. In 1929 it was estimated that in Detroit alone there were some 75,000 young men (the "Suitcase Brigade") who had come from the countryside to find jobs in the auto plants.[6]

The Depression not only helped unite the settler workers, but the social catastrophe pushed large sections of other settler classes towards more sympathy with social reform. Small farmers were being forced wholesale into bankruptcy and were conducting militant struggles of their own. Professionals, intellectuals, and even many small businessmen, felt victimized by corporate domination of the economy. Militancy and radicalism became temporarily respectable. When white labor started punching out it would not only be stronger than before, but much of settler society would be sympathetic to it.

2. Labor Offensive from Below

Citizenship in the Empire had very real but still limited meaning so long as many white workers remained "industrial slaves" of the corporations. The increasing centralization of monopoly capitalism repeated aspects of feudalism on a higher level. Both inside and outside the factory gates the settler workers were subject to heightened regimentation. During the 1920s it was not unusual for the persistent speed-up by management to double production per worker, even without taking mechanization into account.

At Ford, perhaps the most extreme of the industrial despots, every tenth employee was also a company spy. Workers overheard making resentful remarks would be beaten up right on the production line by the ever-present guards.[7] In the U.S. Steel plants at Homestead, Pa. the constant spying gave rise to a common saying: "If you want to talk in Homestead, you must talk to yourself."[8]

The Depression and the massive unemployment only threw more power into corporate hands. Not only were wages cut almost everywhere, but many companies laid off experienced workers and replaced them with newcomers at a fraction of the old wages. Ford Motor Company, which advertised that it was the highest paying company in the U.S., allegedly paid production workers a minimum of $7 per day (with inflation less than it paid in 1914). On the contrary, some thousands of Euro-American Ford employees in the '30s found their pay down as low as $1.40 per day; that was roughly what Afrikan women domestics had earned in Chicago.[9] It takes no genius to see that settler workers would not passively accept being reduced to a colonial wage. Companies in Detroit, Pittsburgh, etc. advertised widely in the South for workers, wishing even larger pools of jobless to intimidate and discipline their employees.

The AFL unions were not only loyal to imperialism, but in their weakened state heavily dependent on enjoying the continued favors of individual corporations by opposing any real struggle. It was for that reason that the old Amalgamated Association had betrayed the 1919 steel strike. In that same year AFL President Gompers actually told the U.S. Senate that Prohibition was a danger, because alcohol was needed to get the workers' minds off rebellion. In the new auto industry the AFL was receiving hundreds of thousands of dollars in bribes from the auto manufacturers (usually via expensive advertisements in labor newspapers or "donations" to anti-communist campaigns).[10]

But when the dam broke, the pent-up anger of millions of Euro-Amerikan industrial workers was a mighty force. New organizing drives and new strikes had never completely stopped, even during the repressive 1920s. Defeat was common. But in 1934 two city-wide general strikes in San Francisco and Minneapolis, and a near-general strike in Toledo stunned capitalist Amerika.

The victory of longshoremen in San Francisco and teamsters in Minneapolis were important, but the Toledo auto workers strike—in which thousands of unemployed supporters of the auto workers drove the Ohio National Guard off the streets in direct battle—was the clearest sign of things to come. The victory in the Auto-Lite parts plant was immediately followed by union victories at all the other major factories in town. Toledo became in 1934 the first "union city" in industrial Amerika. The tidal wave of labor unrest affected all parts of the U.S. and all industries.

The new Sit-Down strikes became a rage. It was customary strategy for employers to break strikes by keeping the plants going

with scabs, while hired thugs and police repressed the strike organization. But in the Sit-Downs the workers simply seized and occupied
the plants, not only stopping production but threatening the bosses
with physical destruction of their factories if they tried any repression. After so much abuse and powerlessness, militant young workers discovered great pleasure in temporarily taking over. In some
strikes unlucky bands of foremen and company officials trapped in
plant offices would become union prisoners for a few hours or days.

While 1935 and 1936 saw Sit-Down strikes in the rubber plants
in Akron, Ohio, in auto plants in Detroit, Cleveland, and Atlanta, it
was the Dec. 1936 Flint, Michigan Sit-Down strike against GM that
became the pivotal labor battle of the 1930s. Flint was the central
fortress of GM production, their special company town where GM
carefully kept both Afrikans and foreign-born immigrants to a minimum. Wages in the many Flint GM plants were relatively high for
the times.

Still many enthusiastic Flint auto workers organized themselves around the new CIO United Auto Workers union, and seized
both Fisher Body No. 1 and Chevy No. 4 plants. Thousands of CIO
militants from all over Michigan demonstrated in the streets as
the Sit-Downers, armed with crowbars and bats, barricaded themselves into the plants. Since the first plant was the only source of

FLINT SIT-DOWN STRIKE, 1937.

Buick, Olds, and Pontiac bodies, and the second plant was the only source of Chevrolet engines, the CIO Sit-Down strangled all GM car production.[11]

After 90 days of intense struggle around the seized plants, General Motors gave in. They recognized the UAW as the union representation in seventeen plants. This was the key victory of the entire Euro-Amerikan labor upsurge of the 1930s. It was obvious that if General Motors, the strongest corporation in the world, was unable to defeat the new industrial unions, then a new day had come. Practical advances by workers in auto, steel, rubber, electronics, maritime, meat-packing, trucking and so on, proved that this was so.

The new union upsurge, which had begun in 1933, continued into the World War II period and the immediate post-war years. The number of strikes in the U.S. jumped from 840 in 1932 to 1,700 in 1933, 2,200 in 1936, and 4,740 in 1937. By 1944 over 50% of auto workers took part in one or more strikes during the year. As many settler workers were taking part in strikes in 1944 as in 1937, at the height of the Sit-Downs.[12]

The defiant mood in the strongest union centers was very tangible. On March 14, 1944, some 5,000 Ford workers at River Rouge staged an "unauthorized" wildcat strike in which they blockaded the roads around the plant and broke into offices, "liberating" files on union militants.[13] It was common in "negotiations" for crowds of auto workers to surround the company officials or beat up company guards.

The substantial increases in wages and improvements in hours and working conditions were, for many, secondary to this new-found power in industrial life. In the great 1937 Jones & Laughlin steel strike in Aliquippa, Pa.—a company town ruled over by a near-fascistic company dictatorship—one striker commented on his union dues after the victory: *"It's worth $12 a year to be able to walk down the main street of Aliquippa, talk to anyone you want about anything you like, and feel that you are a citizen."*[14]

White Amerika reorganized then into the form we now know. The great '30s labor revolt was far more than just a series of factory disputes over wages. It was a historic social movement for democratic rights for the settler proletariat. Typically, these workers ended industrial serfdom. They won the right to maintain class organizations, to expect steady improvements in life, to express their work grievances, to accumulate some small property, and to have a small voice in the local politics of their Empire.

In the industrial North the CIO movement reformed local school boards, sought to monitor draft exemptions for the privileged classes, ended company spy systems, replaced anti-union police officials, and in myriad ways worked to reorganize the U.S. Empire so that the Euro-Amerikan proletariat would have the life they expected as settlers. That is, a freer and more prosperous life than any proletariat in history has ever had.

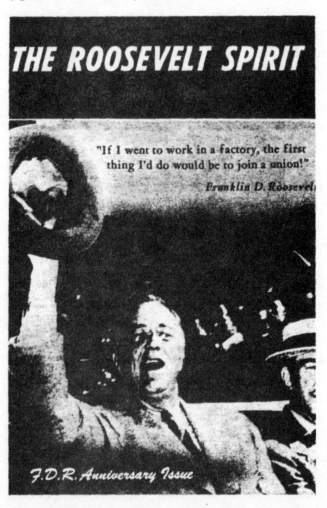

THE ROOSEVELT SPIRIT

"If I went to work in a factory, the first thing I'd do would be to join a union!"

Franklin D. Roosevelt

F.D.R. Anniversary Issue

3. New Deal & Class Struggle

The major class contradictions which had been developing since in-dustrialization were finally resolved. The European immigrant pro-letariat wanted to fully become settlers, but at the same time was determined to unleash class struggle against the employers. Settler workers as a whole, with the Depression as a final push, were de-termined to overturn the past. This growing militancy made a major force of the settler workers. While they were increasingly united—"native-born" Euro-Amerikan and immigrant alike—the capitalists were increasingly disunited. Most were trying to block the way to needed reform of the U.S. Empire.

The New Deal administration of President Franklin Roosevelt reunited all settlers old and new. It gave the European "ethnic" na-tional minorities real integration as Amerikans by sharply raising their privileges. New Deal officials and legislation promoted eco-nomic struggle and class organization by the industrial proletari-at—but only in the settler way, in government-regulated unions loyal to U.S. Imperialism. President Roosevelt himself became the political leader of the settler proletariat, and used the directed power of their aroused millions to force through his reforms of the Empire.

Most fundamentally, it was only with this shake-up, these mod-ernizing reforms, and the homogenized unity of the settler masses that U.S. Imperialism could gamble everything on solving its prob-lems through world domination. This was the desperate preparation for World War. The global economic crisis after 1929 was to be re-solved in another imperialist war, and the U.S. Empire intended to be the victor.

This social reunification could be seen in President Roosevelt's unprecedented third-term victory in the 1940 elections. Pollster Samuel Lubell analyzed the landslide election results for the *Satur-day Evening Post:*

> "Roosevelt won by the vote of Labor, unorganized as well as organized, plus that of the foreign born and their first and second generation descendants. And the Negro.

"It was a class-conscious vote for the first time in American
history, and the implications are portentous. The New Deal
appears to have accomplished what the Socialists, the IWW
and the Communists never could approach..."[15]

Lubell's investigation showed how, in a typical situation, the New
Deal Democrats won 4 to 1 in Boston's "Charlestown" neighborhood; that was a working class and small petit-bourgeois "ethnic"
Irish community. Of the 30,000 in the ward, almost every family
had directly and personally benefited from their New Deal. Perhaps
most importantly, the Democrats had very publicly "become the
champion of the Irish climb up the American ladder." While Irish
had been kept off the Boston U.S. Federal bench, Roosevelt promptly appointed two Irish lawyers as Federal judges. Other Irish from
that neighborhood got patronage as postmasters, U.S. marshals, collector of customs, and over 400 other Federal positions.

**Irish workers in the neighborhood got raises from the new
Federal minimum wage and hours law. Unemployment benefits
went to those who were still jobless. 300–500 Irish youth earned
small wages in the National Youth Administration, while thousands of adult jobless were given temporary Works Progress
Administration (WPA) jobs. Forty per cent of the older Irish
were on U.S. old-age assistance. 600 families got ADC. Many received food stamps. Federal funds built new housing and paid
for park and beach improvements. The same process was taking
place with Polish, Italian, Jewish, and other European national
minority communities throughout the North.**

It was not just crude bribery. The Depression was a shattering
crisis to settlers, upsetting far beyond the turmoil of the 1960s and
1970s. It is hard for us to fully grasp how upside-down the settler
world temporarily became. In the first week of his Administration,
for example, President Roosevelt hosted a delegation of coal mine
operators in the White House. They had come to beg the President
to nationalize the coal industry and buy them all out. They argued
that "free enterprise" had no hope of ever reviving the coal industry
or the Appalachian communities dependent upon it.[16]

Millions of settlers believed that only an end to traditional capitalism could make things run again. The new answer was to raise up the U.S. government as the coordinator and regulator of all major industries. To restabilize the banking system, Roosevelt now insured consumer deposits and also sharply restricted many former, speculative bank policies. In interstate trucking, in labor relations, in communications, in every area of economic life new Federal agencies and bureaus tried to rationalize the daily workings of capitalism by limiting competition and stabilizing prices. The New Deal consciously tried to imitate the sweeping, corporate state economic dictatorship of the Mussolini regime in Italy.

The most advanced sections of the bourgeoisie—such as Thomas Watson of IBM and David Sarnoff of RCA—backed the controversial New Deal reforms. But for most the reaction was heated. The McCormick family's *Chicago Tribune* editorially called for Roosevelt's assassination. Those capitalists who most stubbornly resisted the changes were publicly denounced by the New Dealers, who had set themselves up as the leaders of the anti-capitalist mass sentiment.

The contradictions within the bourgeoisie became so great that a fascist coup d'état was attempted against the New Deal. A group of major capitalists, headed by Irenee DuPont (of DuPont Chemicals) and the J.P. Morgan banking interests, set the conspiracy in motion in 1934. The DuPont family put up $3 million to finance a fascist stormtrooper movement, with the Remington Firearms Co. to arm as many as 1 million fascists. Gen. Douglas MacArthur was recruited to ensure the passive support of the U.S. Army. The plan was to seize state power, with a captive President Roosevelt forced to officially turn over the reins of government to a hand-picked fascist "strong-man."

As their would-be Amerikan Fuhrer the capitalists selected Gen. Smedley Butler, twice winner of the Congressional Medal of Honor and retired Commandant of the U.S. Marine Corps. But after being approached by J.P. Morgan representatives, Gen. Butler went to Congress and exposed the cabal. An ensuing Congressional investigation confirmed Gen. Butler's story. With the conspiracy shot down and keeping in mind the high position of the inept conspirators, the Roosevelt Administration let the matter just fade out of the headlines.

During the 1936 election campaign one observer recorded the New Deal's open class appeal at a Democratic Party rally in Pittsburgh's Forbes Field. The packed crowd was whipped up by lesser politicians as they expectantly awaited the Presidential motorcade. State Senator Warren Roberts recited the names of famous millionaires, pausing as the crowds thundered boos after each name. He orated: *"The President has decreed that your children shall enjoy equal opportunity with the sons of the rich."* Then Pennsylvania Governor Earle took the microphone to punch at the Republican capitalists even more:

> *"There are the Mellons, who have grown fabulously wealthy from the toil of the men of iron and steel, the men whose brain and brawn have made this great city; Grundy, whose sweatshop operators have been the shame and disgrace of Pennsylvania for a generation; Pew, who strives to build a political and economic empire with himself as dictator; the DuPonts, whose dollars were earned with the blood of American soldiers; Morgan, financier of war."*

Thousands of boos followed each name. Then, with the crowds worked up against their hated exploiters, the Presidential motorcade drove into the stadium to frenzied cheering. The observer wrote of Roosevelt's entry: *"He entered in an open car. It might have been the chariot of a Roman Emperor."*[17]

So it was not just the social concessions that the government made; the deep allegiance of the Euro-Amerikan workers to this new Leader and his New Deal movement was born in the feeling that he truly spoke for their class interests. This was no accident. Nations and classes in the long run get the leadership they deserve.

In order to end the company-town feudalism of their communities, the CIO unionists took their newfound strength into the bourgeois political arena. The massed voting base of the new unions was the bedrock of the New Deal in the industrial States. The union activists themselves merged into and became part of the imperialist New Deal. Bob Travis, the Communist Party militant who was the organizer of the Flint Sit-Down, proudly told the 1937 UAW Convention:

"We have also not remained blind to utilizing the city's political situation to the union's advantage, whenever possible.
In this way, for five months after the strike, we were able to
consolidate a 5–4 pro-labor majority bloc in the city commission, get a pro-labor city manager appointed, and bring
about the dismissal of a vicious police chief, notorious as a
strike-breaker."

By 1958, Robert Carter, the UAW Regional Director for Flint-
Lansing, could resign to become Flint City Manager. Things had
come full circle. Once outsiders challenging the local establishment,
then angry reformers, the union was now part of the local bourgeois
political structure.

This was the universal pattern in the industrial areas. In
Anderson, Indiana, the auto workers at GM Guide Lamp took
over the plant in a 1937 Sit-Down. By 1942, strike leader Riley
Etchison was a member of the local draft board. Another Sit-
Downer was the new sheriff. John Mullen, the Steelworkers
union leader at U.S. Steel's Clairton, Pa. works, went on to become the Mayor, as did Steelworkers local leader Elmer Maloy in
DuQuesne, Pa. Everywhere the young CIO activists integrated
into the local Democratic Party as a force for patriotic reform.

Nor was this limited to Euro-Amerikans. Coleman Young
(Mayor of Detroit), John Conyers (U.S. Congressman), and many
other Afrikan politicians got their start as young CIO staff members. In Hawaii, the Japanese workers in the CIO International
Longshoremen's and Warehousemen's Union became the active
base of the Democratic Party's takeover of Hawaiian bourgeois politics after the war. The CIO unions became an essential gear in the
liberal reform machine of the Democratic Party.[18]

A significant factor in the success of the 1930s union organizing drives was the U.S. government's refusal to use armed repression
against it. *No US. armed repression against Euro-Amerikan workers
took place from January 1933 (when Roosevelt took office) until the
June 1941 North American Aviation strike in California.* The U.S. government understood that the masses of Euro-Amerikan industrial
workers were still loyal settlers, committed to U.S. Imperialism. To

overreact to their economic struggles would only further radicalize them. Besides, why should President Roosevelt have ordered out the FBI or U.S. Army to break up the admiring supporters of his own Democratic Party?

Attempts by the reactionary wing of the bourgeoisie to return to the non-union past by wholesale repression were opposed by the New Deal. In the 1934 West Coast longshore strike (which in San Francisco became a general strike after the police killed two strikers), President Roosevelt refused to militarily intervene, despite the fact that the governors of Oregon and Washington requested that he do so.

In speaking for the shipping companies and business interests on the Coast, Oregon Gov. Meier telegraphed Roosevelt that troops were needed because: "We are now in a state of armed hostilities. The situation is complicated by communistic interference. It is now beyond the reach of State authorities ... insurrection which if not checked will develop into civil war." Roosevelt publicly scorned this demand. It is telling that at the most violent period of the strike a picture of President Roosevelt hung in the longshoremen's union office in San Francisco.

President Roosevelt privately said in 1934 that there was a conspiracy by "the old conservative crowd" to provoke general strikes as a pretext for wholesale repression. The President's confidential secretary wrote at the time that both he and U.S. Labor Secretary Francis Perkins believed that: "...the shipowners deliberately planned to force a general strike throughout the country and in this way they hoped they could crush the labor movement. I have no proof but I think the shipowners were selected to replace the steel people who originally started out to do this job."[19]

The reactionary wing of the bourgeoisie were no doubt enraged at the New Deal's refusal to try and return the outmoded past at bayonet point. Almost three years later, in the pivotal labor battle of the 1930s, the New Deal forced General Motors to reach a deal with their striking Flint, Michigan employees. GM had attempted to end the Flint Sit-Down with force, using both a battalion of hired thugs and the local Flint police. Lengthy street battles with the police over union food deliveries to the Sit-Downers resulted in many strikers shot and beaten (14 were shot in one day), but also in union control over the streets. In the famous "Battle of Bull's Run" the auto workers, fighting in clouds of tear gas, forced the cops to run for their lives. The local repressive forces available to GM were unequal to the task.

From the second week of the strike, GM had officially asked the government to send in the troops. But both the State and Federal governments were in the hands of the New Deal. After five weeks of stalling, Michigan Gov. Frank Murphy finally sent in 1,200 National Guardsmen to calm the street battles but not to move against either the union or the seized plants. Murphy used the leverage of the troops to pressure both sides to reach a compromise settlement. The Governor reassured the CIO: *"The military will never be used against you."* The National Guard was ordered to use force, if necessary to protect the Sit-Down from the local sheriff and any right-wing vigilantes.

The Administration had both the President's Secretary and the Secretary of Commerce call GM officials, urging settlement with the union. Roosevelt even had the head of R.J. Reynolds Tobacco Co. call his friend, the Chairman of GM to push for labor peace. The end of GM's crush-the-union strategy came on Feb. 11, 1937, after President Roosevelt had made it clear he would not approve repression, and told GM to settle with the union. GM realized that the fight was over.[20]

The important effect of the pro-CIO national strategy can be seen if we compare the '30s to earlier periods. Whenever popular struggles against business grew too strong to be put down by local police, then the government would send in the National Guard or U.S. Army. Armed repression was the drastic but brutally decisive weapon used by the bourgeoisie.

And the iron fist of the U.S. government not only inspired terror but also promoted patriotism to split the settler ranks. The U.S. Army broke the great 1877 and 1894 national railway strikes. The coast-to-coast repressive wave, led by the U.S. Dept. of Justice, against the IWW during 1917–1924 effectively destroyed that "Un-American" movement—even without Army troops. Yet no such attempt was made during the even more turbulent 1930s. President

Roosevelt himself turned to CIO leaders, in the words of the *New York Times,* "for advice on labor problems rather than to any old-line AFL leader."[21]

There was a heavy split in the capitalist class, with many major corporations viewing the CIO as the Red Menace in their backyards, and desperately using lockouts, company unions, and police violence to stop them. Not all, however. Years before the CIO came into being, Gerald Swope of General Electric had told AFL President William Green that the company would rather deal with one industrial union rather than fifteen different craft unions. And when the Communist Party–led United Electrical Workers-CIO organized at GE, they found that the company was glad to make a deal.[22]

While some corporations, such as Republic Steel, tolerated unionization only after bloody years of conflict, others wised up very quickly. U.S. Steel tried to control its employees by promoting company unions. But in plant after plant the company unions were taken over by CIO activists.[23] It was no secret that the New Deal was pushing industrial unionization. In Aliquippa, Pa., Jones & Laughlin Steel Co. had simply made union militants "disappear"—one Steelworkers organizer was later found after having been secretly committed to a State mental hospital. New Deal Gov. Pinchot changed all that, even assigning State Police bodyguards to protect CIO organizers.

In Homestead, where no public labor meeting had been held since 1919, 2,000 steelworkers and miners gathered in 1936 in a memorial to the pioneering 1892 Homestead Strike against U.S. Steel. The memorial rally was protected by State Police, and Lt. Gov. Kennedy was one of the speakers. *He told the workers that the State Police would help them if they went on strike against U.S. Steel.*[24]

With all that, it is understandable that U.S. Steel decided to reach a settlement with the CIO. Two weeks after the Flint Sit-Down defeated GM, U.S. Steel suddenly proposed a contract to the CIO. On March 2, 1937, the Steelworkers Union became the officially accepted bargaining agent at U.S. Steel plants. The Corporation not only bowed to the inevitable, but by installing the CIO it staved off even more militant possibilities. The CIO bureaucracy was unpopular in the mills. Only 7% of the U.S. Steel employees had signed union membership cards. In fact, Lee Pressman, the Communist Party lawyer for the Steelworkers Union, said afterwards that they just didn't have the support of the majority:

> "There is no question that we could not have filed a petition through the National Labor Relations Board or any other kind of machinery asking for an election. We could not have won an election..."[25]

At the U.S. Steel stockholders meeting the following year, Chairman Myron Taylor explained to his investors why the New Deal's pro-CIO approach worked:

> "The union has scrupulously followed the terms of its agreement and, in so far as I know, has made no unfair effort to bring other employees into its ranks, while the corporation subsidiaries, during a very difficult period, have been entirely free of labor disturbance of any kind."[26]

By holding back the iron fist of repression, by encouraging the CIO, the New Deal reform government cut down "labor disturbance" among the Euro-Amerikan proletariat.

It should be kept in mind that the New Deal was ready to use the most direct repression when it was felt necessary. All during the 1930s, for example, they directed an ever-increasing offensive against the Nationalist Party of Puerto Rico. Unlike the settler workers, the liberation struggle of Puerto Rico was not seeking the reform of the U.S. Empire but its ouster from their nation. The speed with which the nationalist fervor was spreading through the Puerto Rican masses alarmed U.S. Imperialism.

So the most liberal, most reform-minded U.S. government in history repressed the Nationalists in the most naked and brutal way. By 1936 the tide of pro-Independence sentiment was running high, and Don Albizu Campos, President of the Nationalist Party, was without doubt the most respected political figure among both the intellectuals and the masses. School children were starting to tear the U.S. flag down from the school flagpoles and substitute the

Puerto Rican flag. In the city of Ponce the school principal defied a police order to take the Puerto Rican banner down. The New Deal response was to directly move to violently break up the Nationalist center.

In July 1936, eight Nationalist leaders were successfully tried for conspiracy by the U.S. government. Since their first trial had ended in a dead-locked jury, the government decided to totally rig the next judge and jury (most of the jurors were Euro-Amerikans, for example). That done, the Nationalist leaders were sentenced to four to ten years in Federal prison. Meanwhile, general repression came down. U.S. Governor Winship followed a policy of denying all rights of free speech or assembly to the pro-Independence forces. Machine guns were placed in the streets of San Juan.

On Palm Sunday, 1937—one month after President Roosevelt refused to use force against the Flint Sit-Down Strike—the Ponce Massacre took place. A Nationalist parade, with a proper city permit, was met with U.S. police gunfire. The parade of 92 youth from the Cadets and Daughters of the Republic (Nationalist youth groups) was watched by 150 U.S. police with rifles and machine guns. As soon as the unarmed teenagers started marching the police began firing and kept firing. Nineteen Puerto Rican citizens were killed and over 100 wounded. Afterwards, President Roosevelt rejected

all protests and said that Governor Winship had his approval. The
goal of paralyzing the pro-Independence forces through terrorism
was obvious.[27]

Similar pressures, although different in form, were used by
the New Deal against Mexicano workers in the West and Midwest.
There, mass round-ups in the Mexicano communities and the forced
deportation of 500,000 Mexicanos (many of whom had U.S. residency or citizenship) were used to save relief funds for settlers and,
most importantly, to break up the rising Mexicano labor and national agitation. In a celebrated case in 1936, miner Jesus Pallares was
arrested and deported for the "crime" of leading the 8,000-member
La Liga Obrera De Habla Espanola in New Mexico.[28]

The U.S. government used violent terror against the Puerto
Rican people and mass repression against the Mexicano people during the 1930s. But it did nothing like that to stop Euro-Amerikan
workers because it didn't have to. The settler working class wasn't
going anywhere.

**In the larger sense, they had little class politics of their own
any more. President Roosevelt easily became their guide and
Patron Saint, just as Andrew Jackson had for the settler workmen
of almost exactly one century earlier. The class consciousness
of the European immigrant proletarians had gone bad, infected**

PONCE
MASSACRE (1937),
IN WHICH 19 PUERTO
RICANS WERE KILLED
AND OVER 100
WOUNDED (OPPOSITE
PAGE), AND FAMILY
MEMBERS OF THOSE
KILLED DURING
MASSACRE GATHER IN
FRONT OF NATIONALIST
PARTY HEADQUARTERS.
MACHINE GUN BULLET
HOLES CAN BE SEEN IN
THE WALL.

**with the settler sickness. Instead of the defiantly syndicalist IWW
they now had the capitalist CIO.**

This reflected the desires of the vast majority of Euro-Amerikan
workers. They wanted settler unionism, with a privileged relationship to the government and "their" New Deal. Settler workers accepted each new labor law passed by the imperialist government to
stabilize labor relations. But unions regulated, supervised, and reorganized by the imperialists are hardly the free working class organizations called by that name in the earlier periods of world capitalism.

One reason that this CIO settler unionism was so valuable to
the imperialists was that in a time of labor upheaval it cut down on
uncontrolled militancy and even helped calm the production lines.
Even the "Left" union militants were forced into this role. Bob Travis,
the Communist Party leader of the 1937 Flint Sit-Down, reported
only months after besting General Motors:

> "Despite this terrifically rapid growth in membership we have
> been able to conduct an intensive educational campaign
> against unauthorized strikes and for observation of our con-
> tract and in the total elimination of wild-cat actions during the
> past 3 months."[29]

Fortune, the prestigious business magazine, said in 1941:

> "... *properly directed, the UAW can hold men together in an emer-*
> *gency; it can be made a great force for morale. It has regularized*
> *many phases of production; its shop stewards, who take up griev-*
> *ances on the factory floor, can smooth things as no company union*
> *could ever succeed in smoothing them."*[30]

The Euro-Amerikan proletariat during the '30s had broken out of industrial confinement, reaching for freedoms and a material style of
life no modern proletariat had ever achieved. The immense battles
that followed obscured the nature of the victory. The victory they
gained was the firm positioning of the Euro-Amerikan working class
in the settler ranks, reestablishing the rights of all Europeans here to
share the privileges of the oppressor nation. This was the essence of

the equality that they won. This bold move was in the settler tradition, sharing the Amerikan pie with more European reinforcements so that the Empire could be strengthened. This formula had partially broken down during the transition from the Amerika of the Frontier to the Industrial Amerika. It was the brilliant accomplishment of the New Deal to mend this break.

> I watched the first shipment of "repatriated" Mexicans leave Los Angeles in February, 1931. The loading process began at six o'clock in the morning. *Repatriados* arrived by the truckload—men, women, and children—with dogs, cats, and goats, half-open suitcases, rolls of bedding, and lunchbaskets. It cost the county of Los Angeles $77,249.29 to repatriate one trainload, but the savings in relief amounted to $347,468.41 for this one shipment. In 1932 alone over eleven thousand Mexicans were repatriated from Los Angeles...
>
> The strikes in California in the thirties, moreover, were duplicated wherever Mexicans were employed in agriculture. Mexican fieldworkers struck in Arizona; in Idaho and Washington; in Colorado; in Michigan; and in the Lower Rio Grand Valley in Texas. When Mexican sheep-shearers went on strike in west Texas in 1934, one of the sheepmen made a speech in which he said: "We are a pretty poor bunch of white men if we are going to sit here and let a bunch of Mexicans tell us what to do." ...
>
> With scarcely an exception, every strike in which Mexicans participated in the borderlands in the thirties was broken by the use of violence and was followed by deportations. In most of these strikes, Mexican workers stood alone; that is, they were not supported by organized labor, for their organizations, for the most part, were affiliated neither with the CIO nor the AFL.
>
> Carey McWilliams, *North from Mexico*

4. The CIO's Integration & Imperialist Labor Policy

The CIO played an important role for U.S. imperialism in disorganizing and placing under supervision the nationally oppressed. For the first time masses of Third World workers were allowed and even conscripted into the settler trade unions. This was the result of a historic arrangement between the U.S. Empire and nationally oppressed workers in the industrial North.

On one side, this limited "unity" ensured that Third World workers didn't oppose the new, settler industrial unions, and were safely absorbed as "minorities" under tight settler control. On the other side, hungry Third World proletarians gained significant income advances and hopes of job security and advancement. It was an arrangement struck out of need on both sides, but one in which the Euro-Amerikan labor aristocracy made only tactical concessions while strengthening their hegemony over the Empire's labor market.

So while the old AFL craft unions had controlled Third World labor by driving us out of the labor market, by excluding us from the craft unions or by confining us to small, "seg" locals, the new CIO could only control us by absorbing us into their settler unions. The imperialists had decided that they needed colonial labor in certain industries. Euro-Amerikan labor could not, therefore, drive the nationally oppressed away in the old manner. The colonial proletarians could only be controlled by disorganizing them—separating their economic struggles from the national struggles of their peoples, separating them from other Third World proletarians around the world, absorbing them as "brothers" of settler unionism, and placing them under the leadership of the Euro-Amerikan labor aristocracy. The new integration was the old segregation on a higher level, the unity of opposites in everyday life.

We can see how this all worked by reviewing the CIO's relationship to Afrikan workers. Large Afrikan refugee communities had formed in the major Northern industrial centers. Well over one million refugees had fled Northwards in just the time between

1910–1924, and new thousands came every month. They were an irritating presence to the settler North; each refugee community was a foreign body in a white metropolis. Like a grain of sand in an oyster. And just as the oyster eases its irritation by encasing the foreign element in a hard, smooth coating of pearl, settler Amerika encapsulated Afrikan workers in the hard, white layer of the CIO.

Despite the "race riots" and the hostility of Euro-Amerikans the Afrikan refugees streamed to the North in the early years of the century. After all, even the troubles of the North seemed like lesser evils to those fleeing the terroristic conditions of the occupied National Territory. Many had little choice, escaping the revived Ku Klux Klan. Increasingly forced off the land, barred from the new factories in the South, Afrikans were held down by the terroristic control of their daily lives.

Each night found the Illinois Central railroad wending its way Northward through Louisiana, Mississippi, and Tennessee, following the Mississippi River up to the "Promised Land" of Gary or Chicago. Instead of sharecropping or seasonal farm labor for "Mr. John," Afrikan men during World War I might get hired for the "elite" Chicago jobs as laborers at Argo Corn Starch or International Harvester. Each week the *Chicago Defender*, in the '20s the most widely-read "race" newspaper even in the South, urged its readers to

forsake hellish Mississippi and come Northward to "freedom." One man remembers the long, Mississippi nights tossing and turning in bed, dreaming about the fabled North: "You could not rest in your bed at night for Chicago."

The refugee communities were really small New Afrikan cities, where the taut rope of settler domination had been partially loosened. Spear's *Black Chicago* says: "In the rural South, Negroes were dependent upon white landowners in an almost feudal sense. Personal supervision and personal responsibility permeated almost every aspect of life … In the factories and yards (of the North) on the other hand, the relationship with the 'boss' was formal and impersonal, and supervision limited to working hours."[31]

While there was less individual restriction, Afrikan refugees were under tight control as a national group. The free bourgeois labor market of Euro-Amerikans didn't really exist for Afrikans. Their employment was not individual, not private. They got work only when a company consciously decided to use Afrikan labor as a group. So that Afrikan labor in the industrial North still existed under colonial conditions, driven into specific workplaces and specific jobs.

Afrikans were understood by the companies as dynamite—extremely useful and potentially very dangerous. Their use in Northern

industry was the start, though little understood at the time, of gradually bringing the new European immigrants up from proletarians to real settlers. Imperialism was gradually releasing the "Hunky" and "Dago" from laboring at the very bottom of the factories. Now even more Euro-Amerikans were being pushed upward into the ranks of skilled workers and supervisors. And if the Afrikan workers were paid more than their usual colonial wages in the South, they still earned less than "white man's wages." Even the newest European immigrant on the all-white production lines could look at the Afrikan laborers and know his newfound privileges as a settler.

The capitalists also knew that too many Afrikans might turn a useful and super-profitable tool into a dangerous force. Afrikan labor was used only in a controlled way, with heavy restrictions placed upon it. One Indiana steel mill superintendent in the 1920s said: *"When we got (up to 10% Black) employees, I said, 'No more colored without discussion.' I got the colored pastors to send colored men whom they could guarantee would not organize and were not bolsheviks."* This was at a time when the Garvey Movement, the all-Afrikan labor unions, and the growth of Pan-Afrikanist and revolutionary forces were taking place within the Afrikan nation.

The Northern factories placed strict quotas on the number of Afrikan workers. Not because they weren't profitable enough. Not because the employers were "prejudiced"—as the liberals would have it—but because the imperialists believed that Afrikan labor could most safely be used when it was surrounded by a greater mass of settler labor. In 1937 an official of the U.S. Steel Gary Works admitted that for the previous 14 years corporate policy had set the percentage of Afrikan workers at the mill to 15%.[32]

The Ford Motor Co. had perhaps the most extensive system of using Afrikan labor under plantation-like control, with Henry Ford acting as the planter. A special department of Ford management was concerned with dominating not only the on-the-job life of Afrikan workers, but the refugee community as well. Ford hired only through the Afrikan churches, with each church being given money if its members stayed obedient to Ford. The company also subsidized Afrikan bourgeois organizations. His Afrikan employees and their families constituted about one-fourth of the entire Detroit

Afrikan community. Both the NAACP and the Urban League were singing Ford's praises, and warning Afrikan auto workers not to have anything to do with unions. One report on the Ford system in the 1930s said:

> *"There is hardly a Negro church, fraternal body, or other organiza-tion in which Ford workers are not represented. Scarcely a Negro professional or business man is completely independent of income derived from Ford employees. When those seeking Ford jobs are added to this group, it is readily seen that the Ford entourage was able to exercise a dominating influence in the community."*[33]

The Afrikan refugee communities, extensions of an oppressed na-tion, became themselves miniature colonies, with an Afrikan bour-geois element acting as the local agents of the foreign imperialists. Ford's system was unusual only in that one capitalist very conspicu-ously took as his role that which is usually done more quietly by a committee of capitalists through business, foundations, and their imperialist government.

This colonial existence in the midst of industrial Amerika gave rise to contradiction, to the segregation of the oppressed creating its opposite in the increasingly important role of Afrikan labor in industrial production. Having been forced to concen-trate in certain cities and certain industries and even certain plants, Afrikan labor at the end of the 1920s was discovered to have a strategic role in Northern industry far out of proportion to its still small numbers. In Cleveland Afrikans comprised 50% of the metal working industry; in Chicago they were 40–50% of the meat packing plants; in Detroit the Afrikan auto workers made up 12% of the workforce at Ford, 10% at Briggs, 30% at Midland Steel Frame.[34]

Overall, Afrikan workers employed in the industrial econ-omy were concentrated in just five industries: automotive, steel, meat-packing, coal, railroads. The first four were where settler la-bor and settler capitalists were about to fight out their differences in the 1930s and early 1940s. And Afrikan labor was right in the middle.

In a number of industrial centers, then, the CIO unions could not be secure without controlling Afrikan labor. And on their side, Afrikan workers urgently needed improvement in their economic condition. A 1929 study of the automobile industry comments:

> "As one Ford employment official has stated, 'Many of the Negroes are employed in the foundry and do work that nobody else would do.' The writer noticed in one Chevrolet plant that Negroes were engaged on the dirtiest, roughest and most disagreeable work, for example, in the painting of axles. At the Chrysler plant they are used exclusively on paint jobs, and at the Chandler-Cleveland plant certain dangerous emery wheel grinding jobs were given only to Negroes."[35]

In virtually all auto plants Afrikans were not allowed to work on the production lines, and were segregated in foundry work, painting, as janitors, drivers, and other "service" jobs. They earned 35–38 cents per hour, which was one-half of the pay of the Euro-Amerikan production line workers. This was true at Packard, at GM, and many other companies.[36]

The CIO's policy, then, became to promote integration under settler leadership where Afrikan labor was numerous and strong (such as the foundries, the meat-packing plants, etc.), and to maintain segregation and Jim Crow in situations where Afrikan labor was numerically lesser and weak. Integration and segregation were but two aspects of the same settler hegemony.

Three other imperatives shaped CIO policy: (1) To maintain settler privilege in the form of reserving the skilled crafts, more desirable production jobs, and the operation of the unions themselves to Euro-Amerikans. (2) Any tactical concessions to Afrikan labor had to conform to the CIO's need to maintain the unity of Euro-Amerikans. (3) *The CIO's policy on Afrikan labor had to be consistent with the overall colonial labor policy of the U.S. Empire.* We should underline the fact that rather than challenge U.S. imperialism's rules on the status and role of colonial labor, the CIO as settler unions loyally followed those rules.

To use the automobile industry as a case, there was considerable integration within the liberal United Auto Workers (UAW-CIO). That is, there was considerable recruiting of Afrikan labor to help Euro-Amerikan workers advance their particular class interests. The first Detroit Sit-Down was at Midland Steel Frame in 1936. The UAW not only recruited Afrikan workers to play an active role in the strike, but organized their families into the CIO support campaign. Midland Frame, which made car frames for Chrysler and Ford, was 30% Afrikan. There the UAW had no reasonable chance of victory without commanding Afrikan forces as well as its own.

But at the many plants that were overwhelmingly settler, the CIO obviously treated Afrikan labor differently. In those majority of the situations the new union supported segregation. In Flint, Michigan the General Motors plants were Jim Crow. Afrikans were employed only in the foundry or as janitors, at sub-standard wages (many, of course, did other work although still officially segregated and underpaid as "janitors"). Not only skilled jobs, but even semi-skilled production line assembly work was reserved for settlers.

While the UAW fought GM on wages, hours, civil liberties for settler workers, and so forth, it followed the general relationship to colonial labor that GM had laid down. So that the contradiction between settler labor and settler capitalists was limited, so to say, to their oppressor nation, and didn't change their common front towards the oppressed nations and their proletariats.

At the time of the Flint Sit-Down victory in February 1937 the NAACP issued a statement raising the question of more jobs: "Everywhere in Michigan colored people are asking whether the new CIO union is going to permit Negroes to work up into some of the good jobs or whether it is just going to protect them in the small jobs they already have in General Motors."[37]

That was an enlightening question. Many UAW radicals had already answered "yes." Wyndham Mortimer, the Communist Party USA trade union leader who was 1st Vice-President of the new UAW-CIO, left behind a series of autobiographical sketches of his union career when he died. Beacon Press, the publishing house of the liberal Unitarian-Universalist Church, has printed this autobiography under the stirring title *Organize!* In his own words Mortimer left us an inside view of his secret negotiations with Afrikan auto workers in Flint.

Mortimer had made an initial organizing trip to Flint in June 1936 to start setting up the new union. Anxious to get support from Afrikan workers for the coming big strike, Mortimer arranged for a secret meeting:

> "A short time later, I found a note under my hotel room door. It was hard to read because so many grimy hands had handled it. It said, 'Tonight at midnight,' followed by a number on Industrial Avenue. It was signed, 'Henry.' Promptly at midnight, I was at the number he had given. It was a small church and was totally dark. I rapped on the door and waited. Soon the door was opened and I went inside. The place was lighted by a small candle, carefully shaded to prevent light showing. Inside there were eighteen men, all of them Negroes and all of them from the Buick foundry. I told them why I was in Flint, what I hoped to do in the way of improving conditions and raising their living standards. A question period followed. The questions were interesting in that they dealt with the union's attitude toward discrimination and with what the union's policy was toward bettering the very bad conditions of the Negro people. One of them said, 'You see, we have all the problems and worries of the white folks, and then we have one more: we are Negroes.'

> "I pointed out that the old AFL leadership was gone. The CIO had a new program with a new leadership that realized that none of us was free unless we were all free. Part of our program was to fight Jim Crow. Our program would have a much better chance of success if the Negro worker joined with us and added his voice and presence on the union floor. Another man arose and asked, 'Will we have a local union of our own?' I replied, 'We are not a Jim Crow union, nor do we have any second-class citizens in our membership!'

> "The meeting ended with eighteen application cards signed and eighteen dollars in initiation fees collected. I cautioned

them not to stick their necks out, but quietly to get their
fellow workers to sign application cards and arrange other
meetings..."[38]

Mortimer's recollections are referred to over and over in Euro-
Amerikan "Left" articles on the CIO as supposed fact. In actual fact
there was little Afrikan support for the Flint Sit-Down. Only *five*
Afrikans took part in the Flint Sit-Down Strike. Nor was that an exception. In the 1937 Sit-Down at Chrysler's Dodge Main in Detroit
only *three* Afrikan auto workers stayed with the strike. During the
critical, organizing years of the UAW, Afrikan auto workers were primarily sitting *out* the fight between settler labor and settler corporations.[39] It was not their nation, not their union, and not their fight.
And the results of the UAW-CIO victory proved their point of view.

The Flint Sit-Down was viewed by Euro-Amerikan workers
there as their victory, and they absolutely intended to eat the dinner themselves. So at Flint's Chevrolet No. 4 factory the first UAW
& GM contract after the Sit-Down contained a clause on "nonin-
terchangibility" reaffirming settler privilege. The new union now
told the Afrikan workers that the contract made it *illegal* for them
to move up beyond being janitors or foundry workers. That was the
fruit of the great Flint Sit-Down—a Jim Crow labor contract.[40] The
same story was true at Buick, exposing how empty were the earlier
promises to Afrikan workers.

This was not limited to one plant or one city. A history of the
UAW notes: *"As the UAW official later conceded ... in most cases
the earliest contracts froze the existing pattern of segregation and even
discrimination."*[41] At the Atlanta GM plant, whose 1936 Sit-Down
strike is still pointed to by the settler "Left" as an example of militant "Southern labor history," only total white supremacy was good
enough for the CIO workers. The victorious settler auto workers not
only used their newfound union power to restrict Afrikan workers
to being janitors, but did away altogether with even the pretense of
having them as union members. For the next *ten years* the Atlanta
UAW was all-white.[42]

So in answer to the question raised in 1937 by the NAACP,
the true answer was "no"—the new CIO auto workers union was

not going to get Afrikans more jobs, better jobs, an equal share of jobs, or any jobs. This was not a "sell-out" by some bureaucrat, but the nature of the CIO. Was there a big struggle by union militants on this issue? No. Did at least the Euro-Amerikan "Left"—there being many members in Flint, for example, of the Communist Party USA, the Socialist Party, and the various Trotskyists—back up their Afrikan "union brothers" in a principled way? No.

It is interesting that in his 1937 UAW Convention report on the Flint Victory, Communist Party USA militant Bob Travis covered up the white supremacist nature of the Flint CIO. In his report (which covers even such topics as union baseball leagues) there was not one word about the Afrikan GM workers and the heavy situation they faced. And if that was the practice of the most advanced settler radicals, we can well estimate the political level of the ordinary Euro-Amerikan worker.

Neither integration nor segregation was basic—oppressor nation domination was basic. If the UAW-CIO practiced segregation on a broad scale, it was equally prepared to use integration. When it turned after cracking GM and Chrysler to confront Ford, the most strongly anti-union of the Big Three auto companies, the UAW had to make a convincing appeal to the 12,000 Afrikan workers there. So special literature was issued, Afrikan church and Civil Rights leaders negotiated with, and—most importantly—Afrikan organizers were hired by the CIO to directly win over their brothers at Ford.

The colonial labor policy for the U.S. Empire was, as we previously discussed, fundamentally reformed in the 1830s. The growing danger of slave revolts and the swelling Afrikan majority in many key cities led to special restrictions on the use of Afrikan labor. Once the mainstay of manufacture and mining, Afrikans were increasingly moved out of the urban economy. When the new factories spread in the 1860s, Afrikans were kept out in most cases. The general colonial labor policy of the U.S. Empire has been to strike a balance between the need to exploit colonial labor and the safeguard of keeping the keys to modern industry and technology out of colonial hands.

On an immediate level Afrikan labor—as colonial subjects—were moved into or out of specific industries as the U.S. Empire's needs evolved. The contradiction between the decision to

stabilize the Empire by giving more privilege to settler workers (ultimately by deproletarianizing them) and the need to limit the role of
Afrikan labor was just emerging in the early 20th century.

So the CIO did not move to oppose open, rigid segregation in
the Northern factories until the U.S. government told them to during World War II. Until that time the CIO supported existing segregation, while accepting those Afrikans as union members who were
already in the plants. This was only to strengthen settler unionism's
power on the shop floor. During its initial 1935–1941 organizing period the CIO maintained the existing oppressor nation/oppressed
nations job distribution: settler workers monopolized the skilled
crafts and the mass of semi-skilled production line jobs, while colonial workers had the fewer unskilled labor and broom-pushing
positions.

For its first *seven years* the CIO not only refused to help Afrikan
workers fight Jim Crow, but even refused to intervene when they
were being driven out of the factories. Even as the U.S. edged into
World War II many corporations were intensifying the already tight
restrictions on Afrikan labor. Now that employment was picking up
with the war boom, it was felt not only that Euro-Amerikans should
have the new jobs but that Afrikans were not yet to be trusted at the
heart of the imperialist war industry.

Robert C. Weaver of the Roosevelt Administration admitted:
*"When the defense program got under way, the Negro was only on the
sidelines of American industry, he seemed to be losing ground daily."*
Chrysler had decreed that only Euro-Amerikans could work at the
new Chrysler Tank Arsenal in Detroit. Ford Motor Co. was starting
many new, all-settler departments—while rejecting 99 out of 100
Afrikan men referred to Ford by the U.S. Employment Service. And
up in Flint, the 240 Afrikan janitors at Chevrolet No. 4 plant learned
that GM was going to lay them off indefinitely. During 1940 and
early 1941, while settler workers were being rehired for war production in great numbers, Afrikan labor found itself under attack.[43]

Those Afrikan workers employed in industry could not defend
their immediate class interests through the CIO, but had to step
out of the framework of settler unionism just to defend their existing jobs. In the Summer of 1941 there were three Afrikan strikes at

Dodge Main and Dodge Truck in Detroit. The Afrikan workers at Flint Chevrolet No. 4 staged protest rallies and eventually won their jobs. *As late as April 1943 some 3,000 Afrikan workers at Ford went out on strike for three days to protest Ford's hiring policies.* The point is that the CIO opposed Afrikan interests because it followed imperialist colonial labor policy—and when Afrikan workers needed to defend their class interests they had to do so on their own, organizing themselves on the basis of nationality.

It was not until mid-1942 that the CIO and the corporations, maneuvering together under imperialist coordination, started tapping Afrikan labor for the production lines. As much as settlers disliked letting masses of Afrikans into industry, there was little choice. The winning of the entire world was at stake, in a "rule or ruin" war. As the U.S. Empire strained to put forth great armies, navies, and air fleets to war on other continents, the supply of Euro-Amerikan labor had reached the bottom of the barrel. To U.S. Imperialism, if the one-and-half million Afrikan workers in war industry helped the Empire conquer Asia and Europe it would well be worth the price.

The U.S. War Production Board said: "We cannot afford the luxury of thinking in terms of white men's work." So the numbers of Afrikan workers on the production lines tripled to 8.3% of all manufacturing production workers. Now the CIO unions, however unhappily, joined the corporations in promoting Afrikans into new jobs—even as hundreds of thousands of settler workers were protesting in "hate strikes." The reality was that settler workers had government-led, imperialist unions, while colonial workers had no unions of their own at all.[44]

During World War II the CIO completed integrating itself by picking up many hundreds of thousands of colonial workers. Many of these new members, we should point out, were involuntary members. Historically, the overwhelming majority of Afrikans who have belonged to the CIO industrial unions in the past 40 years never joined voluntarily. Starting with the first Ford contract in 1941, the CIO rapidly shifted to "union shop" contracts. In these contracts all new employees were required to join the union as a condition of employment. The modern imperialist factory in most industries quickly became highly unionized—whether any of us liked it or not.

The U.S. government, depending on the CIO as a key element in labor discipline, encouraged the "union shop." The U.S. War Labor Board urged corporations to thus force their employees to join the CIO: "Too often members of unions do not maintain their membership because they resent discipline of a responsible leadership."[45] While this applied to all industrial workers, it applied most heavily to colonial labor.

The government and the labor aristocracy were impatient to get colonial workers safely tied up. If they were to be let into industry in large numbers they had to be split up and neutralized by the settler unions—voluntarily or involuntarily. In the Flint Buick plant, where 588 of the 600 Afrikan workers had been segregated in the foundry despite earlier CIO promises, the union and GM expected to win them over by finally letting them work on the production lines. To their surprise, as late as mid-1942 the majority of the Afrikan workers still refused to join the CIO.[46] The Afrikan Civil Rights organizations, the labor aristocracy, and the liberal New Deal all had to "educate" resisting workers like those to get in line with the settler unions.

The integration of the CIO, therefore, had nothing to do with increasing job opportunities for Afrikans or building "working class unity." It was a new instrument of oppressor nation control over the oppressed nation proletarians.

VIII

IMPERIALIST WAR AND THE NEW AMERIKAN ORDER

1. GI Joe Defends His Supermarket

> "The Saturday Evening Post ran a series by GIs on 'What I Am Fighting For.' One characteristic article began: 'I am fighting for that Big House with the bright green roof and the big front lawn.'"[1]

World War II was the answer to every settler's prayer—renewed conquest and renewed prosperity. The New Deal's domestic reforms alone could not get capitalism going again. And even though the CIO had won large wage increases in basic industry, the peace-time economy was incapable of providing enough jobs and profits. As late as early 1940, the unemployment rate for Euro-Amerikan workers was still almost 18%.[2] Expansion of the Empire was the necessary basis of new prosperity.

Although wars are made of mass tragedy and sacrifice, this most successful of all Amerikan wars was a happy time for most settlers. That's why they look back on it with so much nostalgia and fondness (even with a pathological TV comedy about "fun" in a Nazi POW camp). We could say that this was their last big frontier. Historian James Stokesbury notes in his summation of the war:

"One of the great ironies of the American war effort was the
way it was born disproportionately by a relatively few people.
In spite of the huge numbers of men in service, second only
to Russia among the Allies, only a limited number of them
saw combat ... For the vast majority of Americans it was
a good war, if there can be such a thing. People were more
mobile and prosperous than ever before. The demands of
the war brought the United States out of a deep depression,
created new cities, new industries, new fortunes, a new way
of life."[3]

Isolated in its Western Hemispheric Empire far from the main the-
atres of fighting, U.S. imperialism suffered relatively little. As the
Great Powers were inevitably pulled into a global war of desperation,
each driven to solve its economic crisis by new conquests, Amerika
hung back. It hoped, just as in World War I, to wait out much of the
war and slip in near the end to take the lion's share of the kill.

The millions of civilians who died from bombing raids, disease,
and famine in war-torn Europe, Asia, North Afrika, and the Middle
East have never been fully counted. The full death toll is often put at
an unimaginable 60 million lives. Amerika was spared all this, and
emerged triumphant at the war's end with citizenry, colonies, and industry completely intact. Even U.S. military forces suffered relatively
lightly compared to the rest of the world. Military deaths for the
major combatants are revealing: Germany: 7 million; Russia: 6 million; Japan: 2 million; China: 2 million; Great Britain: 250,000;
USA: 400,000. *More Russian soldiers died in the Battle of Stalingrad
alone than total U.S. military casualties for the whole war.*[4]

The war boom kicked Depression out. Factories were roaring
around the clock. The 16 million soldiers and sailors in the armed
forces had left places everywhere for the unemployed to fill. The
general prosperity that characterized Amerikan society all the way
up to the 1970s began right there, in the war economy of WWII. The
war years were such a prosperous upturn from the Depression that
the necessary propaganda about "sacrificing for the war effort" had a
farcical air to it. Lucky Strike, the biggest selling cigarette, caught the
settler mood perfectly when it changed its package color from green

to white—and then announced nonsensically in big ads: "Lucky Strike green is going off to war!"

Average family income went up by 50% compared to the Depression years. In New York City, average family income rose from $2,760 to $4,044 between 1938–1942. Nor was this just a paper gain. A historian of the wartime culture writes: *"Production for civilian use, while diminishing, remained so high that Americans knew no serious deprivations ... At the peak of the war effort in 1944, the total of all goods and services available to civilians was actually larger than it had been in 1940."*[5]

The number of supermarkets more than tripled between 1939 and 1944. Publishers reported book sales up 40% by 1943. The parimutuel gambling take at the race tracks skyrocketed 250% from 1940 to 1944. Just between 1941 and 1942 jewelry sales were up 20–100% by areas. By 1944 the cash and bank accounts held by the U.S. population reached a record $140 billion. That same year Macys department store in New York City had a sale on Pearl Harbor Day—which produced their most profitable business day ever![6] Once again, the exceptional life of settler Amerika was renewed by war and conquest. This is the mechanism within each Amerikan cycle of internal conflict and reform. The New Deal was Hiroshima and Nagasaki as well. Consumeristic Amerika was erected on top of the 60 million deaths of World War II.

2. The Political Character of the War

> "In the U.S., World War II was the principal cause of the total breakdown of the working-class movement and its revolutionary consciousness … Resistance to the war would have seemed like simple common sense. If Stalin gave the order to support the U.S. war effort he was a fool. In any case, the old vanguard's support should have been for the people's struggle inside the U.S."
>
> George Jackson

In its March 29, 1939, issue the *Pittsburgh Courier,* one of the major Afrikan newspapers, ran an editorial on the coming world war that summed up what most colonial peoples in the world thought about it:

"The 'democracies' and the 'dictatorships' are preparing to do BATTLE in the near future.

"The referee is IMPERIALISM, who stands ready to award the decision to the victor.

"The stake is the right to EXPLOIT the darker peoples of the world.

"The audience consists of the vast MAJORITY of those who happen to be NON-WHITES.

"They have NO FAVORITE, because it makes NO DIFFERENCE to them which party WINS the fight.

"They are ONLY interested in the bout taking place AS SOON AS POSSIBLE.

"The audience knows that the destruction of white civilization means the EMANCIPATION of colored people, and that explains why they eagerly await the opening gong.

"The democracies which now CONTROL the dark world have never extended DEMOCRACY to the dark world.

"THEIR meaning of democracy is for WHITE PEOPLE only, and just a FEW of them.

"The dictatorships FRANKLY DECLARE that if they win THEY will do as the democracies HAVE DONE in the past.

"The democracies as frankly declare that IF they win they will CONTINUE to do as they HAVE BEEN doing."[7]

This remarkable editorial was accurate (however unscientific its way of putting it) as to the real world situation. The "War to Save Democracy" was an obvious lie to those who had none, whose nations were enslaved by U.S. imperialism. While there was no real support for either German or Japanese imperialism, there was considerable satisfaction among the oppressed at seeing the arrogant Europeans being frightened out of their wits by their supposed "racial" inferiors. One South Afrikan Boer historian recalls:

"It seemed possible that the Japanese might capture Madagascar and that South Africa itself might be attacked. The Cape Colored people were not at all alarmed at the prospect. Indeed, they viewed the Japanese victories with almost open jubilation. Their sympathies and hopes were with the little yellow skinned men who had proved too smart for the British and Americans."[8]

Nor was this feeling just in Afrika. In colonial India the sight of the British "master" suddenly begging his subjects to help save him from the Japanese armies, revealed to many that their oppressor was a "paper tiger." The British generals soon learned that their Indian colonial troops were more and more unwilling to fight for the British Empire. The Communist Party USA was so alarmed at Afrikan disinterest in fighting Asians that it issued a special pamphlet for them recounting the crimes of the Japanese Empire against Ethiopia, urging Afrikans to honor *the alliance of the Negro people with the progressive sections of the white population.*

The sociologist St. Clair Drake relates how even among U.S. Empire forces in the Pacific, Afrikan GIs would loudly root for the

Japanese "zero" fighters overhead in the aerial dogfights against U.S. settler aviators. Robert F. Williams says that as a youth he heard many Afrikan veterans returning from the Pacific express sympathy for the Japanese soldiers, and even say that the Japanese tried not to fire at Afrikans. And studying the U.S. propaganda posters of dark-skinned Japanese trying to rape blond Euro-Amerikan women, Williams saw a connection to settler propaganda against Afrikans.[9] None of this was any approval for Japanese imperialism, but an expression of disassociation from the Euro-Amerikan oppressor. To the oppressed masses of the U.S., British, Dutch, French, German, and other Western Empires, this war was not their war.

It is important to deal with the nature of the U.S. involvement in the war. Outside of the shallow and obviously untrue "War for Democracy" propaganda, the two main arguments for the war were: (1) It was a war for European freedom, to defeat the Nazis and save the Soviet Union. (2) It was a just war of self-defense after the U.S. military was attacked by the Japanese Empire at Pearl Harbor (the main U.S. naval base in its Hawaiian colony). Both lines were often used together, particularly by the settler radicals.

Perhaps the U.S. Empire could have led a "crusade in Europe" to defeat Nazism, but it didn't. In strict fact, German fascism was defeated by the Russian people. U.S. global strategy clearly called for stalling as long as possible in fighting Hitler, in hopes that Germany and Soviet Russia would ruin and exhaust each other. As late as April 1943, Soviet forces were fighting 185 Nazi divisions while the U.S. and British Empires were together fighting 6. The heart and muscle of the German Army, almost 250 divisions, got destroyed on the Eastern front against the Russian people. That's why the Russian military lost 6 million troops fighting Germany, while the U.S. lost 160,000.

The Soviet Union's burden in the alliance against German imperialism was so visibly disproportionate that some Western imperialists were concerned. South Afrikan Gen. Jan Christian Smuts warned in 1943: *"To the ordinary man it must appear that it is Russia who is winning the war. If this impression continues, what will be our post-war position compared to that of Russia?*

Finally, in the last six months of the war, the Allies landed 2 million soldiers in France in order to get in on the German surrender and control as much of Europe as possible. Those U.S. and British divisions faced a vastly inferior German opposition (only 40% as large as the Allied force), because the bulk of Hitler's forces were tied up with the main war front against Russia.

During the war the Allies kept paratroop divisions in England, ready to be air-dropped into Berlin if Russia finished off the Nazis before Allied armies could even get into Germany.[10] U.S. imperialism's main concern was not to "liberate" anyone, but to dominate as much of Europe as it could once the Russian people had, at such terrible cost, defeated Hitler.

Amerikan war plans included being careful not to interfere with the Nazis' genocidal sterilization of Europe. Indeed, Washington and London appreciated how convenient it was to let Hitler do their dirty work for them—getting rid of millions of undesirable Jews, Communists, socialists, trade unionists, and dissenters. This cleaned up Europe from the imperialist point of view. And Hitler took the weight.

The Allies were notorious in blocking Jewish evacuation from the path of the oncoming Nazi conquest. Roosevelt refused to lift restrictions on Jewish immigration. As the war approached, on April 23, 1939, the U.S. State Dept. announced that quotas were so "filled" that Jewish immigration was to be halted except for special cases. Desperate German Jews were told that they had a minimum six year wait, until 1945. The New Deal's vicious attitude was displayed in their mocking statement that Jewish "applicants of Polish origin, even those who spent most of their life in Germany, will have to wait at least 50 years" to obtain entry visas to the U.S.! The same day the Roosevelt Administration announced that no tourist visas to Amerika would be issued to German Jews—only those Germans with "Aryan" passports could greet the Statue of Liberty.

During the war the U.S. rejected pleas from the Jewish underground that they use bombers to knock out the rail lines to the death camps (and even knock out the ovens themselves). Yet, on Sept. 13, 1944, the U.S. 15th Air Force bombed the I.G. Farben industrial complex right next to Auschwitz death camp (a few bombs fell in Auschwitz itself, killing 15 SS men and 40 other fascists). Although this proved the U.S. military's ability to strike at the Nazi death camps, U.S. imperialism still refused to interfere with the genocide. And this was when the Nazis were feverishly slaughtering as many as possible—at Auschwitz as many as 24,000 per day!

U.S. imperialism posed as being anti-fascist, but it was U.S. imperialism which had helped put Nazism in power. Henry Ford was an important early backer of Hitler, and by 1924 had started pouring money into the tiny Nazi party. Ford's portrait hung on the wall in Hitler's Party office. Every birthday until World War II Ford had sent Hitler his personal greetings (and a gift of money). Even during the War the Ford Motor Company delivered vital parts to the German Army through neutral Switzerland. On October 20, 1942, the U.S. Embassy in London complained to Washington that Ford was using his plants in Switzerland to repair 2,000 German Army trucks.

Ford was just one example out of many. GM President William Knudson told a press conference on October 6, 1933, that Nazism was "the miracle of the 20th century." GM in Germany contributed ½ of 1% out of all its employees' wages as a weekly mass donation to the Nazi Party.

While the Allied Powers wanted to defeat Germany, it had nothing to do with being anti-fascist. Both President Roosevelt and British Prime Minister Winston Churchill favored Mussolini and his Fascist regime in Italy. Even after the European war broke out in 1939, Roosevelt privately urged Mussolini to be neutral and try to mediate a British-German detente. Churchill, for his part, wanted to preserve the Mussolini Fascist regime since *"the alternative to his rule might well have been a communist Italy."* Churchill saw Fascist Italy as a possible ally. He later wrote regretfully about Mussolini:

> *"He might well have maintained Italy in a balancing position, courted and rewarded by both sides and deriving an unusual wealth and prosperity from the struggles of other countries. Even when the issue of the war became certain, Mussolini would have been welcomed by the Allies…"*

In Italy, Greece, and other nations the "liberating" U.S.-British forces put the local fascists back into power while savagely repressing the anti-fascist guerrillas who had fought them. In Greece the British had a problem since the German Army had pulled out in September 1944, harassed by guerrillas who had installed a new, democratic Greek government. The Allies invaded already-liberated Greece in order to crush the independent government; Greece was "liberated" from democracy and returned to being a fascist neocolony of Britain and the U.S. **The mercenary collaborators and the fascist "Security Battalions" organized by the German occupation were preserved by the British Army, which used them to conduct a campaign of terrorism against the Greek people. By 1945 the British were holding some 50,000 anti-fascist activists in prisons. The Allies killed more Greek workers and peasants than the Germans had.**[11]

The main focus of Amerika's military interest had nothing to do with democratic or humanitarian concerns, but with expanding the Empire at the expense of its German and Japanese rivals. Not only was a stronger position over Europe aimed at, but in the Pacific a showdown was sought with Japanese imperialism. In the 1930s both U.S. and Japanese imperialism sought to become the dominant power over Asia. Japan's 1937 invasion of China (Korea was already a Japanese colony) had upset the Pacific status quo; giant China had long been an imperialist semi-colony, shared uneasily by all the imperialist powers. Japan broke up the club by invading to take all of China for itself. The Roosevelt Administration, the main backer of Chiang Kai-Shek's corrupt and semi-colonial Kuomintang regime, was committed to a decisive war with Japan from that point on.

Both the U.S. Empire and the Japanese Empire demanded in secret negotiations the partial disarmament of the other and a free hand in exploiting China. The Roosevelt Administration and the British had secretly agreed in mid-1941 for a joint military offensive against Japan, the centerpiece of which was to be a new U.S. strategic bomber force to dominate the Pacific. We know that President Roosevelt's position was that all-out war in the Pacific was desirable for U.S. interests; his only problem was: "...the question was how we should maneuver them into the position of firing the first shot..."[12] Political necessities demanded that Roosevelt be able to picture the war as innocent "self defense."

The New Deal started embargoing strategic war materials—notably scrap iron and petroleum—going to Japan. There was a coordinated Western campaign to deny Japanese imperialism the vital oil, rubber, and iron its war machine needed. With 21 divisions bogged down trying to catch up with the Red Army in China, Japanese imperialism had to either capture these necessary resources in new wars or face collapse. The move was obvious.

To make sure that this shove would work, Roosevelt asked U.S. Admiral Stark to prepare an intelligence assessment of the probable Japanese response. In his memo of July 22, 1941 (over four months before Pearl Harbor), Admiral Stark reassured Roosevelt that Japan would be forced into a "fairly early attack" to seize British Malayan rubber and Dutch Indonesian oil, and that an attack on the U.S. Philippine colony was "certain."[13]

The New Deal wanted and expected not only an all-out war for the Pacific, but a "surprise" Japanese attack as well. Their only disappointment on Dec. 7, 1941, was that instead of concentrating on the Philippines, the Japanese military struck first at Hawaii. There was no question of "self-defense" there. The Pacific war was the mutual child of imperialist competition and imperialist appetites.

To President Roosevelt the prize was worth the risks. China was his first goal, just as it was for Japanese imperialism. A friend of the President recalls: *"At the White House, the making of FDR's China policy was almost as great a secret as the atom bomb."* Roosevelt saw that the sun had set on the old European colonial rule in Asia, and that the dynamic expansion of the small Japanese Empire proved how weak and rotten European power was. In his mind, he saw that if China were nominally free but under U.S. hegemony (via the Kuomintang regime), it could be the center for an Amerikan takeover of all Asia.*

British Prime Minister Winston Churchill, after meeting with Roosevelt and his staff, wrote a British general in some alarm: *"I*

---

* FDR was always appreciative of China's potential value because of his family's direct connection. Roosevelt often mentioned his family's long "friendship" with China—on his mother's side, the Delano family fortune was made through a leading role in the opium trade in 19th century China.

*must enlighten you about the American view. China bulks as large in the
minds of many of them as Great Britain."*[14]

Some confusion about the nature of the Second Imperialist
World War has arisen among comrades here because the war was
also a patriotic war of national defense in some nations. Both China
and the USSR, invaded and partially occupied by Axis Powers, made
alliance with competing imperialists of the Allied Powers. There is
nothing surprising or incorrect about that. Taking advantage of this
the revisionists claimed that democratic-minded people in all nations should therefore support the Allied Powers. But why should
the anti-colonial movement in an oppressed nation that was invaded
and occupied by the U.S. (or France or Great Britain) support its
own oppressor? One might just as well argue that the Chinese people should have supported the Japanese occupation during WWII
because Mexico was oppressed by U.S. imperialism (in fact, the
Japanese Empire advanced such lines of propaganda). Contrary to
the revisionists, World War II was not a war of "democracy vs. fascism," but a complex struggle between imperialist powers, and between capitalism and socialism.

The New Deal was prepared to do whatever necessary to modernize and stabilize U.S. imperialism's home base, because it was

playing for the biggest stakes
in the world. In the *Pittsburgh
Courier's* words: *"The stake is the
right to EXPLOIT the darker peoples of the world."*

3. The War on the "Home Front"

As Euro-Amerikan settlers gathered themselves to conquer Asia, Europe, Afrika, and hold onto Latin Amerika, they started their war effort by attacking the oppressed closest at hand—those already within the U.S. Empire. In Puerto Rico, the colonial occupation tightened its already deadly hold on the masses, so that their very lives could be squeezed out to help pay for the U.S. war effort. It is to the eternal honor of the Nationalist Party, already terribly wounded by repression, that it resisted this imperialist mobilization as best it could.

The Nationalist Party denounced the military conscription of Puerto Rican youth, who were to be cannon fodder for the same U.S. Army that was oppressing their own nation. On the eve of Selective Service registration in 1940, the Nationalist Party declared: *"If Puerto Ricans are the first line of defense of democracy in America, we claim the right to fight in the front line and for that reason we demand that democracy be a reality in Puerto Rico, recognizing our national sovereignty."*[15] The newspapers on the Island were afraid to print Nationalist statements for fear of U.S. prosecution—a fear that the U.S. government said was well founded.[16]

Some members of the Nationalist Party began openly refusing to register for the draft. Juan Estrada Garcia told the jury when he was tried that his concern was for "the masses who live dying of malaria, hookworm and tuberculosis for lack of food."[17] This was a just concern. Puerto Ricans had the highest death rate in the Western Hemisphere, thanks to the "Yanki" occupation that robbed them of everything needed for life. Every year 3,000 died from tuberculosis alone out of a population of 2 million. Over half were totally destitute, on relief.[18] 80% of the population had hookworm, and the life expectancy was only 46 years. Small wonder, when even those lucky ones who had jobs didn't earn enough to ensure survival—in 1941, the jibaros (the sugar cane workers) labored for an average of only 14 cents per hour.[19]

The war effort only intensified the misery. The relative prosperity that delighted Euro-Amerikans with the war was reversed in

Puerto Rico. Starvation grew much worse. The New Deal WPA jobs program closed down in 1942. Unemployment more than doubled. With food shipments deliberately restricted, prices soared 53% in less than one year. A Presbyterian woman missionary wrote Eleanor Roosevelt, the U.S. President's wife, in despair from Mayagüez: *"The children in this region are slowly starving."*[20]

U.S. Governor Winship made it clear that the New Deal's policy was not only to help subsidize the war effort out of the misery of the Puerto Rican people, but to use starvation to beat them into political submission. In his 1939 report, Winship proudly announced that the colonial administration was already extracting millions of dollars from starving Puerto Rico for the coming war.

Ten million dollars worth of valuable land had been given by the puppet colonial legislature free to the U.S. Navy for a naval base. Puerto Ricans had paid for dredging out San Juan Harbor so that it was deep enough for U.S. battleships. New U.S. Navy repair docks in San Juan were also paid for involuntarily by the Puerto Rican people. Further, local taxes had also paid for the construction of new U.S. military airstrips on Culebra, Isla Grande, Mona Island, and elsewhere.

In desperately poor Puerto Rico the local taxes collected by the imperialist occupation forces were used for their own military needs rather than clinics or food. This policy was actually quite common for WWII: for example, both the Nazi and Japanese armies also forced the local inhabitants in conquered areas to support military construction for them.[21] The U.S. imperialists were in good company.

While it may have seemed like bad propaganda to so obviously increase misery among the Puerto Rican people, the New Deal believed otherwise. It was economic terrorism. U.S. military officials said that the Nationalist resistance to the draft had been broken. They admitted that the reason hungry Puerto Ricans were submitting to the draft was that even army rations were *"pay and food exceeding prevailing Island wages."* It appeared to the military, however, that only one-third of the eligible men could be used due to the widespread physical debilitation from disease and malnutrition.[22] Still, Amerika's "War to Save Democracy" was off to a good start.

The war further accelerated the trend towards settler reunification. The stormy conflicts between settlers in the '30s had a healing effect, like draining a swollen wound. The war completed the process. Fascist and "communist," liberal and conservative alike all joined hands to follow their bourgeoisie into battle. In one small California town the press discovered that the first man in line to register for the draft was James Remochiaretta, a veteran of Mussolini's fascist Black Shirts, who proudly told everyone that he was now "100% American."[23]

The impact of Amerika's entry into the war snapped the Italian and German communities right into line. The Italian-Amerikan petit-bourgeoisie had been both loyally pro-U.S. imperialism and pro-fascist Italy. Up to Pearl Harbor 80% of the Italian community newspapers had been pro-fascist, with almost every Italian store in New York having a prominent picture of the Italian dictator Mussolini. Only the radical political exiles, most of them trade unionists who fled Italy just ahead of the Black Shirts, were openly anti-fascist.

But once the U.S. Empire declared war on the Axis, every Italian community newspaper became "anti-fascist" overnight. Every Italian was now "100% American." In recognition, Italian citizens in the U.S. were removed from the "enemy alien" category by President Roosevelt on Columbus Day, 1942.[24]

This growing, settleristic unity promoted by the war sharply increased attacks on the nationally oppressed. This was one of the major social trends of the war period. While the tightened oppression of the Puerto Rican masses was a policy of the imperialists, these attacks came from all classes and sectors of settler society—from top to bottom.

On the West Coast the settler petit-bourgeoisie, primarily farming interests and small merchants, used settler chauvinism and the identification of Japanese as members of a rival imperialist Power, to plunder and completely remove the Japanese population. Just as the Chinese had been robbed and driven out of mining, agriculture, and industry in the 19th century West, so now Japanese would be driven out. As everyone knows, some 110,000 of us were forcibly "relocated" into concentration camps by the U.S. government in 1942.

Settler rule had restricted and hemmed in Japanese labor into

the national minority economy of specialized agriculture, wholesale and retail food distribution, and domestic labor (in 1940 these
three categories accounted for 84% of all Japanese employment).[25]
But even this little was too much for the settler petit-bourgeoisie on
the West Coast.

The Euro-Amerikans not only wanted the Japanese removed
as competitors, but they wanted to take over and "annex" the
agricultural business so painstakingly built up by the Japanese
farmers. The typical Japanese farm of the period was very small,
averaging only 42 acres each (less than one-fifth the average size
of Euro-Amerikan farms in California). But these intensively
developed lands, which comprised only 3.9% of California's
farmland, produced fully 42% of the State's fresh fruits and veg-
etables.[26] The settler farm lobby wanted our business, which was
too valuable to be left to "Japs."

Austin E. Anson, representative of the Shipper-Grower Association of Salinas, told the public: "We're charged with wanting to get
rid of the Japs for selfish reasons. We might as well be honest. We do."
Through their political influence, these interests got U.S. Sen. Hiram
Johnson to pull together the West Coast congressional delegation as
a bloc and push through the concentration camp program.[27]

By military order, enforced by the U.S. Army, the whole
Japanese population was forced to leave or sell at give-away prices
all we had—houses, land, businesses, cars, refrigerators, tools, furniture, etc. The Federal Reserve Bank loosely estimated the direct
property loss alone at $400 million 1942 dollars.[28] The real loss was
in the many billions—and in lives. But it was no loss to settlers, who
ended up with much of it. West Coast settlers had a festive time, cel-
ebrating the start of their war by greedily dividing up that $400 mil-
lion in "Jap" property. *It was a gigantic garage sale held at gunpoint.*
This was just an early installment in settler prosperity from world war.

For Hawaii, a U.S. colony right in the middle of Asia, no such
simple solution was possible. Early government discussions on removing and incarcerating the Japanese population quickly floun-
dered. Over one-third of the working population there was Japanese,
and without their labor the Islands' economy might break down.
The U.S. Army said that: "...the labor shortage make it a matter of

military necessity to keep the people of Japanese blood on the islands." Army and Navy officers proposed that the Japanese be kept at work there for the U.S. Empire, but treated *"as citizens of an occupied foreign country."*[29]

The patriotic Amerikan war spirit congealed itself into the usual racist forms. Chinese were encouraged to wear self-protective placards or buttons reading "I'm No Jap" to avoid being lynched. The Kuomintang-dominated Chinese communities were lauded by the settlers as now "good" Asians. *Life* ran an article on "How To Tell Your Friends From The Japs": "...the Chinese expression is likely to be more placid, kindly, open; the Japanese more positive, dogmatic, arrogant ... Japanese walk stiffly erect ... Chinese more relaxed, *sometimes shuffle..."*[30]

Of course, these imaginary differences only expressed the settler code wherein hostile or just victimized Asians were "bad," whereas those they thought more submissive (who "shuffle") were temporarily "good." Every effort was made to whip up settler chauvinism and hatred (an easy task). The famous war indoctrination film "My Japan," produced by the Defense Department, opens to an actor portraying a Japanese soldier bayoneting a baby—with the commentary that all Japanese "like" to kill babies. German fascist

San Francisco, 1942: Family boards bus to internment camp.

propaganda about the "racial crimes" of the Jews was no more bizarre than Amerikan propaganda for its own war effort.

The Euro-Amerikan working class, now reinforced by unions
and the New Deal, brought the war "home" themselves in their massive wave of "hate strikes." These were strikes whose only demand
was the blocking of Afrikan employment or promotion. They were a
major feature of militant industrial life in the war period; a reaction
to increased wartime employment of Afrikans by U.S. imperialism.

In the auto industry (which was the heart of war production)
the "hate strikes" started in October 1941. There were twelve major
such strikes in auto plants just in the first six months of 1943. Dodge,
Hudson, Packard, Curtis-Wright, Timken Axle, and many other
plants witnessed these settler working class offensives. The UAW-
CIO and the Detroit NAACP held a "brotherhood" rally in Detroit's
Cadillac Square to counteract the openly segregationist movement.
That rally drew 10,000 people. But shortly thereafter 25,000 Packard
workers went out on "hate strike" for five days. An even bigger strike
staged by UAW Local 190 brought out 39,000 settler auto workers
to stop the threatened promotion of four Afrikans.[31]

**These "hate strikes" took place coast-to-coast, in a wave that
hit all industries. In Baltimore, Bethlehem Steel's Sparrows Point
plant went out in July 1943. In that same area a major Western
Electric plant was so solidly closed down by its December 1943
"hate strike" that the U.S. Army finally had to take it over. The
same thing happened when Philadelphia municipal transit workers closed down the city for six days in August 1944 to block the
hiring of eight Afrikan motormen. 5,000 U.S. Army troops were
needed to get transit going again. The U.S. government calculated that just in the three Spring months of 1943 alone, some
2.5 million man hours of industrial production were lost in "hate
strikes."[32]**

Mob violence against the oppressed was another war phenomenon, particularly by Euro-Amerikan servicemen. They now
constituted an important temporary stratum in settler life, drawn
together by the millions and organized into large units and bases.
*Attacks by settler sailors, marines and soldiers on Chicano-Mexicanos,
Afrikans, and Asians on the West Coast grew larger and larger in 1943.*

CHICANO-MEXICANOS LINED UP OUTSIDE LOS ANGELES JAIL
EN ROUTE TO COURT AFTER "ZOOT SUIT RIOTS."

The climax came in the "Zoot Suit Riots" in East Los Angeles on the nights of June 2–7th. They were so named because Euro-Amerikans were infuriated that the "hip" clothing styles of Chicano-Mexicano youth expressed disrespect for "American" culture. Groups of settler servicemen would beat up and cut the clothing off Chicano-Mexicano men.

The June 7th climax involved thousands of settler GIs, who with the protection of the Los Angeles police and their military commanders invaded the barrio, destroying restaurants and taking movie theater-goers captive. Street cars were seized, and one Afrikan who was pulled off had both eyes cut out. Finally, the social chaos—and the intensely angry wave of anti-U.S. feeling in Mexico—grew so large that the U.S. military ordered their troops to stop.[33]

Similar incidents took place throughout the U.S. Sailors from the Naval Armory near Detroit's Belle Isle park joined thousands of other settlers in attacking Afrikans, resulting in the city-wide fighting of the 1943 "Detroit Race Riot." 25 Afrikans and 9 settlers were killed, and many hundreds seriously wounded. The growing Afrikan resistance and community self-defense there was also seen in the August 1, 1943, great "Harlem Race Riot." Oppressed communities

in the major urban areas had now grown so large that ordinary settler mob attacks were less and less successful. The New Deal didn't
need the Northern industrial cities burning with insurrection, and
so moved to "cool" things.

Bourgeois historians in writing about the various multi-class
settler offensives on the "home front," invariably relate them to the
"tension" and "uncertainty" of the war. But these government-sponsored attacks and repressions were not random explosions of "tension." They had a clear direction.

It is easy to see this by contrasting the above events to the
treatment of the thousands of German POWs brought to the U.S.
after their defeat in North Afrika. These enemy soldiers met no mob
violence or other attacks from "tense" Euro-Amerikans. In fact, the
German Army prisoners were widely treated with hospitality and
respect by Euro-Amerikans, and fed and housed like settlers. Many
were let out on "work release" to join the civilian U.S. economy, with
some even going off on their own to live on small, Midwestern family farms.

While overseas they were enemies, here in Amerika they became honorary settlers, since they were fellow citizens of European
imperialist Powers (in contrast to the colonial subjects). Literally,
captured Nazi officers were freer than Albizu Campos or the Hon.
Elijah Muhammad. One Afrikan in the U.S. Army wrote about how
his unit was sent in 1942 to open Smoky Hill Army Air Field in
Salinas, Kansas. They discovered to no surprise that they were barred
from the town's best movie theater, the hotels, restaurants and grills,
and so on. Their only real surprise came when they saw a restaurant
serving ten German prisoners with *"the distinctive high-peaked caps
of Rommel's Afrika Korps. No guard was with them."* The owner of
the restaurant rushed over to remind them that no Afrikans were
allowed inside. Nazi soldiers ranked far above Afrikan GIs as far as
settlers were concerned.[34]

The "race riots" *were* the war, just on the "home front." This
was not the only development in the relationship between the U.S.
Empire and the nationally oppressed. Underneath the violent surface, not separated from the violence but drawing power from it,
there grew a trend of neocolonialism within the U.S. Empire.

INDIAN LAND FOR SALE

GET A HOME

OF

YOUR OWN

❈

EASY PAYMENTS

PERFECT TITLE

❈

POSSESSION

WITHIN

THIRTY DAYS

FINE LANDS IN THE WEST

IRRIGATED
IRRIGABLE
GRAZING
AGRICULTURAL
DRY FARMING

IN 1910 THE DEPARTMENT OF THE INTERIOR SOLD UNDER SEALED BIDS ALLOTTED INDIAN LAND AS FOLLOWS:

Location.	Acres.	Average Price per Acre.	Location.	Acres.	Average Price per Acre.
Colorado	5,211.21	$7.27	Oklahoma	34,664.00	$19.14
Idaho	17,013.00	24.85	Oregon	1,020.00	15.43
Kansas	1,684.50	33.45	South Dakota	120,445.00	16.53
Montana	11,034.00	9.86	Washington	4,879.00	41.37
Nebraska	5,641.00	36.65	Wisconsin	1,069.00	17.00
North Dakota	22,610.70	9.93	Wyoming	865.00	20.64

FOR THE YEAR 1911 IT IS ESTIMATED THAT **350,000** ACRES WILL BE OFFERED FOR SALE

For information as to the character of the land write for booklet, "INDIAN LANDS FOR SALE," to the Superintendent U. S. Indian School at any one of the following places:

CALIFORNIA:
  Hoopa.
COLORADO:
  Ignacio.
IDAHO:
  Lapwai.
KANSAS:
  Horton.
  Nadeau.

MINNESOTA:
  Onigum.
MONTANA:
  Crow Agency.
NEBRASKA:
  Macy.
  Santee.
  Winnebago.

NORTH DAKOTA:
  Fort Totten.
  Fort Yates.
OKLAHOMA:
  Anadarko.
  Cantonment.
  Colony.
  Darlington.
  Muskogee, ⸺ acs.
  Pawnee.

OKLAHOMA—Con.
  Sac and Fox Agency.
  Shawnee.
  Wyandotte.
OREGON:
  Klamath Agency.
  Pendleton.
  Roseburg.
  Siletz.

SOUTH DAKOTA:
  Cheyenne Agency.
  Crow Creek.
  Greenwood.
  Lower Brule.
  Pine Ridge.
  Rosebud.
  Sisseton.

WASHINGTON:
  Fort Simcoe.
  Fort Spokane.
  Tekoa.
  Tulalip.
WISCONSIN:
  Oneida.

WALTER L. FISHER,
Secretary of the Interior.

ROBERT G. VALENTINE,
Commissioner of Indian Affairs.

IX

Neocolonial Pacification in the U.S.

1. Forcing "Democracy" on Native Amerikans

We don't have to look across the world to confront neocolonialism, since some of the most sophisticated examples are right here. The New Deal reforms on the Native Amerikan reservations during the 1930s are a classic case of neocolonial strategy. The U.S. Empire has always had a special problem with the Indian nations, in that their varied ways of life were often communistic. As the U.S. Commissioner of Indian Affairs said in 1838: "Common property and civilization cannot co-exist."[1] The U.S. government enacted a genocidal campaign to erase Indian culture—including prison schools for Indian children, suppression of Indian institutions, economy, and religion. And still the Indian nations and peoples survived, resisted, endured. An AIM comrade has pointed out:

> "The Founding Fathers of the United States equated capitalism with civilization. They had to, given their mentality; to them civilization meant *their* society, which was a capitalist society. Therefore, from the earliest times the wars against

Indians were not *only* to take over the land but also to squash the threatening example of Indian communism. Jefferson was not the only man of his time to advocate imposing a capitalistic and possessive society on Indians as a way to civilize them. The 'bad example' was a real threat; the reason the Eastern Indian Nations from Florida to New York State and from the Atlantic to Ohio and Louisiana are today so racially mixed is because indentured servants, landless poor whites, escaped black slaves, *chose* our societies over the white society that oppressed them.

"Beginning in the 1890s we have been 'red-baited' and branded as 'commies' in Congress (see the Congressional Record) and in the executive boards of churches. That was a very strong weapon in the 1920s and 1930s, and in the Oklahoma area any Indian 'traditional' who was an organizer was called a communist or even a 'Wobbly.'

"So we have *always* defined our struggle not only as a struggle for land but also a struggle to retain our cultural values. Those values are communistic values. Our societies were and are communistic societies. The U.S. government has always understood that very well. It has not branded us all these years as communists because we try to form labor unions or because we hung out with the IWW or the Communist Party, but because the U.S. government correctly identified our political system. It did not make that a public issue because that would have been dangerous, and because it has been far more efficient to say that we are savages and primitive."[2]

Not only did the Indian nations resist, but this resistance included the determined refusal of many Indians to give up their collective land. This rejection of capitalism was a hindrance for the oil corporations, the mineral interests, and the ranchers. Characteristically, the New Deal decided, in the words of the U.S. Commissioner of Indian Affairs, that: *"... the Indian if given the right opportunities could do what the government had failed to do: He could arrange a place for himself and his customs in this modern America."*[3]

The New Deal pacification program for the reservations was to give Indians capitalistic "democracy" and "self-government." Under the direction of the U.S. government, bourgeois democratic (i.e. undemocratic) "tribal governments" were set up, with settleristic "tribal constitutions," paid elected officials, and new layers of Indian civil servants. In other words, Indians would be given their own capitalistic reservation governments to do from within what the settler conquests had been unable to completely succeed at from the outside.

This neocolonial strategy was led by a young, liberal anthropologist, John Collier, who had been appointed U.S. Commissioner of Indian Affairs in 1933 to reform the reservation system. Unlike the openly hostile and repressive pronouncements of his predecessors, Collier spoke sweetly of how much he respected Indian culture and how much Indians should be "freed" to change themselves. Honeyed words, indeed, covering up for a new assault:

> "In the past, the government tried to encourage economic independence and initiative by the allotment system, giving each Indian a portion of land and the right to dispose of it. As a result, of the 138,000 acres which Indians possessed in 1887 they have lost all but 47,000 acres, and the lost area includes the land that was most valuable. Further, the government sought to give the Indian the schooling of whites, teaching him to despise his old customs and habits as barbaric...

> "We have proposed in opposition to such a policy to recognize and respect the Indian as he is. We think he must be so accepted before he can be assisted to become something else..."[4]

There is the smooth talk of the welfare administrator and the colonial official in those words. Notice that the old law gave Indians only one "right"—the right to sell their land to the settlers. Having worked that strategy to its limits, the U.S. Empire now needed to switch strategies in order to keep exploiting the rest of the reservation lands. Now Washington would pose as the protector of Indian culture in order to change Indians into *something else.* Officially, Indian culture would become another respected "ethnic" remnant, like St. Patrick's Day parades, that would add "color" to settler society. But instead of Indian sovereignty, culture, economy and national development, "tribal government" was local government according to the rules of capitalist culture. It was a partial reorganization of reservation life to capitalism.

The 1934 Wheeler-Howard Act repealed the 1887 Allotment Act, authorized elections to pass new "tribal constitutions" to set up the new neocolonial reservation governments, established a $10 million loan fund to support the new governments, and officially gave Indians preference for employment with the U.S. Indian Service.

The campaign to twist Indian arms to accept this new arrangement was very heavy. U.S. Commissioner Collier himself admitted that while the government had the power to force the reservations to accept these bourgeois governments, for the strategy to work at least some number of Indians had to be persuaded to voluntarily take it in. Large numbers of Indians were hired to work in the Indian Service—their numbers reaching 40% of the total employees by 1935. 19,000 Indians were hired to work in various Federal programs, while an additional 14,000 worked in the Civilian Conservation Corps relief camps. *Close to 20% of all adult Indians were temporarily employed by the Federal government.*

The distrust and resistance were considerable. The *New York Times* commented: "This difficulty has been recognized by the cre-

CHICAGOLAND INDIANS GET GOOD JOBS.

JOBS RECENTLY OBTAINED OFFER OPPORTUNITY - SECURITY

ation by the Indian Office of an organizational unit of field agents and special men who will cooperate with tribal councils, business committees and special tribal commissions in framing the constitutions now permitted." Still, some 54 reservations, with 85,000 Indians, voted against the new "tribal governments."

History has proved that the main economic function of the neocolonial reservation governments has been to lease away (usually at bargain prices) the mineral, grazing, and water rights to the settlers. Great amounts of natural resources are involved. A very conservative Euro-Amerikan estimate said:

> "Indian lands are estimated to contain up to 13 per cent of the nation's coal reserves, 3 per cent of its oil and gas, and significant amounts of other minerals including uranium and phosphate."

Instead of the old practice of individual sale of small plots of land—which could be blocked by an Indian's refusal to sell—the new, capitalistic "tribal governments" signed wholesale mineral rights leases with major corporations. The Navaho "tribal government," led by the U.S. Bureau of Indian Affairs, signed leases as late as the 1960s that gave away Navaho coal for a mere 2% of its market value. So the impact of the 1930s "self-government" reforms was to

SHOW KNOW HOW

CHICAGOLAND INDIANS OPEN DOOR TO
HAPPINESS - SUCCESS

step up the economic exploitation of Indian nations.

At Pine Ridge the Sioux families were encouraged to end their subsistence farming and move off their land and into government-built housing projects—and then lease their "useless" land to the settler businessmen. Those Euro-Amerikan ranchers pay an average of $3 per acre each year to possess Indian land (far cheaper than buying it). While the Sioux who insist on staying on their land are deliberately denied water, electricity, seed, and livestock, so as to pressure them into leaving their land (the Euro-Amerikan ranchers who use Indian land receive constant government aid and subsidies). Control of the land and its resources still remains a steady preoccupation to the settler Empire.

Even most of the food production of the Indian Nations is taken by settlers. In 1968 the Bureau of Indian Affairs said that the reservations produced then $170 million annually in agriculture, hunting, and fishing. Of this total the BIA estimated that Indians only consumed $20 million worth, while receiving another $16 million in rent. 75% of the total reservation food production was owned by settlers.[5]

U.S. imperialism literally created bourgeois Indian governments on the reservations to give it what it wanted and to disrupt from within the national culture. These are governments led by the Dick Wilsons and Peter MacDonalds, of elements whose capitalistic ideology and income was tied to collaboration with the larger capitalist world. It is also telling that those professional Indians whose well-being is dependent upon foundation grants and government programs (such as Vine Deloria, Jr., author of the best-selling book, *Custer Died For Your Sins*) praise the Collier reorganization of the '30s as the best thing that even happened to them.

When Native Amerikans overcome the neocolonial rule and assert their sovereignty against U.S. imperialism (as AIM has) then the fixed ballot box is reinforced by assassination, frame-ups, and even massive military repression. The U.S. military moved in 1972 to prop up the neocolonial Dick Wilson regime at Pine Ridge, just as in Zaire the neocolonial Mobutu regime had to be rescued in both 1977 and 1978 by airborne French Foreign Legionnaires and Belgian paratroopers.

2. The Rise of the Afrikan Nation

The New Afrikan national struggle moved decisively into the modern period during the 1920s and 1930s. It was a key indication of this development that thousands of Afrikan communists took up the liberation struggle in those years—years in which many Afrikan workers and intellectuals dedicated themselves to the goal of an independent and socialist Afrikan Nation. The masses themselves intensified their political activities and grew increasingly nationalistic. *In this period nationalism started visibly shouldering aside all other political tendencies in the struggle for the allegiance of the oppressed Afrikan masses.* Armed self-defense activity spread among the masses. This was a critical time in the rise of the Afrikan Nation. And a critical time, therefore, for U.S. imperialism.

There is an incorrect tendency to confine the discussion of Afrikan nationalism in the 1920s and 1930s to the well-known Garvey movement, as though it was the sole manifestation of nationalist consciousness. The Garvey movement (whose specific impact we shall cover at a later point) was but the point of the emerging politics of the Afrikan Nation. In labor, in national culture, in struggles for the land, in raising the goal of socialism, in all areas of political life a great explosion of previously pent-up national consciousness took place among Afrikans in the 1920s and 1930s. It was a time of major political offensives, and of embryonic nation-building.

This outbreak of militant Afrikan anti-colonialism did not go unnoticed by the U.S. Empire. Even outside the National Territory itself, U.S. imperialism was increasingly concerned about this activity. One 1930s report on *"Radicalism Among New York Negroes"* noted:

> "The place of the Negro as a decisive minority in the political life in America received increasing attention during the early post-war years. The Department of Justice issued a twenty-seven page report on 'Radicalism and Sedition Among Negroes as Reflected in Their Publications' and the New York State Lusk Committee for the Investigation of Seditious Activities published a complete chapter in its report entitled, 'Radicalism Among Negroes.' The general anti-labor, anti-radical offensive of government and employers ... was also levelled at the trade union and radical activities of the Negro people. For a time censorship of Negro periodicals became so complete that even the mildly liberal magazine 'Crisis,' [of the NAACP –ed.] edited by W.E. Burghardt DuBois, was held up in the mails during May 1919. In August 1918, the editors of 'The Messenger' [the Afrikan trade union magazine of A. Philip Randolph –ed.] were jailed for three days and second-class mailing privileges were denied the magazine."[6]

The revisionists in general and the Euro-Amerikan "Left" in particular have falsely portrayed the Afrikan people within the U.S. Empire as having no independent revolutionary struggle at that time, but only a "civil rights" struggle. Falsely they picture Afrikan labor and Afrikan socialism as only existing as "minority" parts of the Euro-Amerikan labor and social-democratic movements. While the history of Afrikan politics lies far beyond the scope of this paper, it is necessary to briefly show why U.S. imperialism was threatened by Afrikan anti-colonialism in the 1920s and 1930s. What is central is to grasp the revolutionary nationalist character of Afrikan political trends.

In 1921 the African Blood Brotherhood (ABB), the first modern Afrikan communist organization in the U.S. Empire, was formed in New York City. Defining itself as a *"revolutionary secret order,"* the ABB raised the goal of liberating and bringing socialism to the Afrikan Nation in the Black Belt South. The Brotherhood soon claimed 2,500 members in fifty-six "posts" throughout the Empire. Most of these members were proletarians (as were most of the Garvey movement activists)—miners in Virginia, railroad workers in Chicago, garment workers in New York, etc. These Afrikan communists focused heavily on education work and on "immediate protection purposes," organizing armed self-defense units against the KKK revival that was sweeping the Empire. Soon the police and press spotlighted the Brotherhood as the supposed secret organizers of Afrikan armed activity during the Tulsa, Oklahoma "riots."[7]

The birth of modern Afrikan communism within the U.S. Empire was the most clear-cut and irrefutable evidence that the Afrikan Nation was starting to rise. It was significant that this new organization of Afrikan communists without hesitation proclaimed the goal of socialism through national liberation and independence. The existence of a socialist-minded vanguard naturally implied that at the base of that peak the masses of Afrikans were pushing upwards, awakening politically, creating new possibilities.

Much of the present written accounts of Afrikan politics in this period centers around events in the refugee communities of the North—the "Harlem Renaissance," tenants' organizations fighting evictions in the Chicago ghetto, Afrikan participation in union drives in Cleveland and Detroit, and so on. All these struggles and events were indeed important parts of the developing political awareness. But they were not the whole of what was

happening. The intensity and full scope of the Afrikan struggle can only be accurately seen when we also see the southern region of the U.S. Empire, and particularly the National Territory itself. There, under the terroristic armed rule of the settler occupation, the Afrikan Revolution started to develop despite the most bitterly difficult conditions.

While Euro-Amerikan trade unionism has always tried to restrict Afrikan labor's political role, no propaganda could change the basic fact that in the South, Afrikan labor was the primary factor in labor struggles. Notice that we say that Afrikan labor was the "primary factor"—not "minority" partners, not passive "students" awaiting the lead of Euro-Amerikan trade unionism, and certainly not just "supporters" of white trade unionism. In the South, Afrikan labor was the leading force for class struggle. But that class struggle was part of the New Afrikan liberation struggle.

Starting in the early 1920s Afrikan labor in the South struck out in a remarkable series of union organizing struggles. This was part of the same explosion of Afrikan consciousness that also produced the Garvey movement, the great breakthroughs in Afrikan culture, and the Afrikan communist movement. These things were not completely separate, but linked expressions of the same historic political upheaval of the whole oppressed Afrikan Nation.

When we think about the early organizing struggles of the United Mine Workers Union in the Southern Appalachian coal fields, we are led to picture in our minds "poor white" hillbilly miners walking picket lines with rifles in hands. This is just more settleristic propaganda. The fact is that modern unionism in the Southern Appalachian coal fields came from a "Black thing"—manned, launched, and led by Afrikan workers in their 1920s political explosion. In both the initial 1908 strike and the great 1920–1921 strikes in the Alabama coal fields the majority of strikers were Afrikan. In fact, in the main 1920–1921 strikes fully 76% of the striking miners were Afrikan. Those were Afrikan strikes. Much of the severe anti-unionism and violent repression of strikes in the 1920s South was linked by the imperialists to the need to stop the rising of Afrikans.[8]

Even outside of Alabama the coal miners' union often depended upon Afrikan struggle. One Afrikan miner who worked in the mines of Mercer County, West Virginia for forty-three years recalls: *"The white man was scared to join the union at first around here. The Black man took the organizing jobs and set it up. We went into the bushes and met in secret; and we had all the key offices. A few of the white miners would slip around and come to our meetings. After they found out that the company wasn't going to run them away, why they began to appear more often. And quite naturally, when they became the majority, they elected who they wanted for their presidents, vice presidents, and treasurers. They left a few jobs as secretaries for the Negroes. But at the beginning, most all of the main offices in the locals were held by Negroes."*[9]

The offensive was not merely about job issues, but was a political outbreak spread among Afrikan workers in general. In 1919 thousands of Afrikan workers in the South formed the National Brotherhood Workers, a common Afrikan workers union centered among the dock, shipyard, and railroad workers in Norfolk and Newport News, Virginia. In 1923 Afrikan postal workers in Washington, DC formed their own union, the National Alliance of Postal Employees. This offensive of Afrikan labor advanced throughout the 1920s and 1930s.[10]

In the mines, in the Birmingham steel mills, on the docks, the power in the South of Afrikan labor was being unchained. So much information about these struggles, so much of this story, has been obscured and put aside. The role of Afrikan labor in shaking the Empire in those years was much larger than most believe. This is no accident, for the main sources for U.S. labor history have been the various works of the Euro-Amerikan "Left." These works all have in common an oppressor nation chauvinism. In this regard such supposedly conflicting "left" writings as the CPUSA's *Labor's Untold Story* (by Boyer and Marais), the Weather Underground Organization's *Prairie Fire*, the syndicalist labor history book *Strike!* (by J. Brecher) or the *Red Papers* of the Revolutionary Union (now RCP) all commit the same distortions.

The revisionists take apart, in their mis-history, what was one great tidal wave of anti-colonial rising by oppressed Afrikans. The pieces of history are then scattered so as to leave no visible sign of the giant stature of that Afrikan development. Some pieces are "bleached" (stripped of their national character) and "annexed" by the Euro-Amerikan radicals as part of their own history. The history of Afrikan industrial workers in the North suffered this fate. Some pieces, such as the militant sharecropper struggle and the leading role of Afrikan coal miners in the Appalachian South, have been buried.

Matters as a whole are distorted to shrink the Afrikan story. To take one example: the struggle around the Scottsboro Boys (the Afrikan teenagers framed for allegedly raping two settler girls) is always brought up, while the widespread excitement and unity in the 1930s over the defense cases of armed Afrikans who fought their settler oppressors is never mentioned. This is just part of the general distortion of de-emphasizing the intense rising in the Afrikan South itself. And its nationalist character. Indeed, many of the most widely used Black Studies texts—such as the Bracey, Meier & Rudwick *Black Nationalism in America* or the Huggins, Kilson & Fox *Key Issues in the Afro-American Experience*—assure us that by 1930 Afrikans in the U.S. had lost interest in nationalism. Nationalism, they tell us, was just a passing phase back then.

On the contrary, we must underline the fact that the struggles of Afrikan labor were and are part of the political history of the entire Afrikan nation, and can only be correctly understood in that context. Those Afrikan labor struggles were far more important than

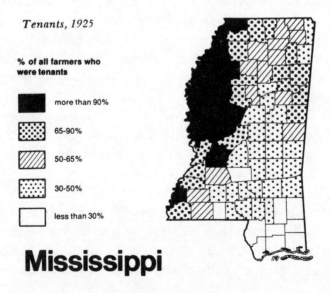

Tenants, 1925

% of all farmers who were tenants

- more than 90%
- 65-90%
- 50-65%
- 30-50%
- less than 30%

Mississippi

we have been told. In the major 1936–1937 U.S. seamen's strike, for example, Afrikan sailors played the decisive role in reaching victory. That was the strike that finally won union rights on all East Coast U.S. shipping. Led by Ferdinand Smith, the Jamaican socialist who was vice-president of the National Maritime Union (NMU-CIO), the 20,000 Afrikan seamen who were the majority of the workers in the shipping industry of the Southern and Gulf Coast ports, shut down those ports completely until the employers gave in.[11] Afrikan labor was gathering a mighty force in the South, on its own National Territory.

The colonial contradictions became most intensified when these peoples' struggles caught fire in the cotton fields, among the great oppressed mass of Afrikan tenants and sharecroppers. There the rawest nerve of the Euro-Amerikan settler occupation was touched, since the struggle was fundamentally over the land. Revisionism has tried in its mis-history to picture these sharecropper struggles as minor conflicts in a backward sector of agriculture, allegedly marginal to the main arena of struggle in auto, steel, and the rest of Northern heavy industry. The sharecropper and tenant struggles were central, however, because they involved the main laboring force of the Afrikan Nation and because they were fought over the land. That's why these struggles were fought out at gunpoint.

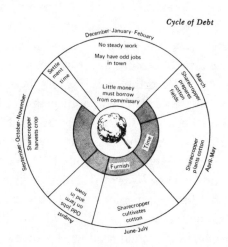

Sharecropping Causes Dependence

The Afrikan sharecroppers and tenant farmers struggles did not—and could not—take the public mass dimensions of Northern union organization. Smoldering under the heavy-handed lynch rule of the settler occupation, the Afrikan plantation struggles would suddenly break the surface in an intense confrontation. While the issues were couched in the forms of pay, rest hours, tenants' rights, etc., the underlying issue of contention was the imperialist slavery of colonial oppression. Unlike the industrial struggles in the coal mines or steel mills, the Afrikan struggle on the land immediately and directly threatened the very fabric of Euro-Amerikan society in the South. For that reason they were met by unrestrained settler violence—backed up by the imperialist state.

In July 1931 the U.S. Empire was electrified by the news that a secret organization of Afrikan sharecroppers had been uncovered in Camp Hills, Alabama. Even worse (from the settler viewpoint) was the fact that these sharecroppers had engaged in a shoot-out with the local sheriff and his planter deputies. At a time when an Afrikan man in the South would take his life in his hands just in raising his voice to a local settler, this outbreak created settler panic throughout the colony. Especially when it became known that the sharecroppers had brought in Afrikan communist organizers.

The Alabama Sharecroppers Union had begun secretly organizing in Tallapoosa County in May of 1931. Within a month they had gathered over 700 members. Under settler-colonial rule, this effort was, of course, conspiratorial; members were not only pledged to secrecy, but sworn to execute any Afrikan who betrayed the struggle to the settlers. Nevertheless it was felt necessary to risk security in order to rally sentiment behind the planned strike. Weekly mass meetings were begun, as secretly as possible, at nights in a local church. But these stirrings had alerted the police forces. At the sharecroppers' second mass meeting on July 15, 1931, the gathering was discovered and attacked by armed settlers. Tallapoosa County Sheriff Young and a force of planter deputies broke into the meeting right at the beginning, beating and cursing. Only the drawn gun held by the chairman of the meeting allowed people to escape.

The next night, after a feverish day of gathering settler reinforcements, the Sheriff and an enlarged group of 200 armed settlers

went "night-riding" to prevent a planned Afrikan meeting and to as-
sassinate the leaders.

The settlers first targeted Ralph Gray, one of the most militant
sharecroppers and one of the main organizers. Gray, who had been
out on guard that night, was shot down without parley by the settlers as soon as he was identified. Badly wounded, he told his compatriots that he had emptied his shotgun at the enemy, but had become too weak to reload and continue fighting. The settler mob left,
satisfied that Gray had been finished off. Hours later, hearing that
the wounded sharecropper had been brought home by car still alive,
the settlers regathered and attacked his house. Gray was killed and
his wife's head was fractured by a beating. But a defense guard of
Afrikans hidden in the nearby field sniped at the invading settlers;
Sheriff Young was "critically wounded" and a deputy was also shot.[12]

This unexpected organized resistance by Afrikans pushed the
settlers into a frenzy of counterinsurgency. Taft Holmes, one of the
arrested sharecroppers, said after his release: *They blew up the car
Gray was brought home in. They arrested people wherever they found
them, at home, in the store, on the road, anywhere. All the white bosses
was a sheriff that day and whenever they seen a colored man they arrested him or beat him up. I was put in jail Friday evening. The boys who
were put in Friday morning was beat up bad to make them tell—but
none of them told.* Even those mass arrests, general terrorism, and
killings failed to break the Afrikan struggle on the land.[13]

We can understand why when we look at Ralph Gray himself.
His role in the struggle grew out of his own oppression, of his own
rejection of the all-embracing colonial occupation suffocating him.
Gray had called on his brothers and sisters to refuse to do plantation labor for the then-prevailing wages in Tallapoosa County—50
cents per day for Afrikan men, 40 cents per day for Afrikan women.
He and his wife would work over the State line in Georgia, where
plantation wages were slightly higher, leaving the oldest son home
to care for their chickens and pigs.

In effect Gray had started a strike of Afrikan plantation labor,
urging everyone to withhold their labor until the settlers raised
wages. So Sheriff Young singled Gray out; he told Gray that he and
his family had to come out and chop cotton on the Sheriff's farm.

Obviously if Gray submitted then the attempted strike would be undercut. Gray refused.[14] Then Gray had a fistfight with his landlord; while the Grays owned their own shack, they had to rent farmland from the local mail carrier, Mr. Langly. Incidentally, this was very common. Not only the planters and middle classes, but even the "working class" settlers in the Afrikan colony were "bosses" over the Afrikan colonial subjects. Many landless settlers themselves rented farmland from the banks and the planters, which they then had worked by Afrikan sharecroppers or day laborers.

While Afrikan sharecroppers were in theory eligible for New Deal farm loans for seed and fertilizer, the common practice in the South was for the settler landlords to just take the money. When Ralph Gray's check arrived his landlord (who was also the postman) had him sign it under the pretext that he'd deliver it to the bank for Gray. Of course, the settler just kept the money himself. Gray finally waited for Langly at the mailbox and they got into a fistfight. Gray was a marked man because he was standing up. The colonial oppression was so suffocating that despite any dangers the Ralph Grays of the Afrikan Nation were moving towards revolution.[15] That's why the embattled sharecroppers secretly wrote away to the communists and asked their help.

Afrikans were picking up the gun. That should tell us something about their political direction. Even defense trials of individual Afrikan sharecroppers who had resorted to arms continued to draw attention throughout this period. The Odell Waller case in 1942 created newspaper headlines and demonstrations throughout the U.S. Empire. The *Richmond Times-Dispatch* said: "The most celebrated case in Virginia criminal annals ... Odell Waller's case is being watched with interest by groups of whites and Negroes in every State of the Union."[16] Waller shot and killed his settler landlord, who had seized the Waller family's entire wheat crop for himself. It's interesting that the landlord, Oscar Davis, was not a landowner, but a poor white who had Afrikan sharecroppers work part of his rented land for him.

In the Waller case the *New York Times* editorially called for commuting his execution on tactical grounds: *"The faith of colored people in their country is deeply involved in what happens to Odell*

Waller ... Our enemies would like to break down this faith. If Governor Darden grants the desired commutation he will be helping his country's reputation among all the dark-skinned and yellow-skinned peoples."[17] Waller was executed.

In these defense cases the connection to the larger anti-colonial issues was readily apparent. In the Tee Davis defense case in Edmondson, Arkansas (right across the river from Memphis, Tenn.) in 1943, the Afrikan tenant farmer was sentenced to ten years in prison for defending his family's house against settlers breaking in. Allegedly searching for stolen goods, the freshly deputized settlers were harassing Afrikan families. When Davis refused to open his door to unidentified white men, a settler "deputy" started breaking it down. When the "deputy" kicked in the bottom of the door, Tee Davis started shooting through the door to scare them off.[18]

That harassment was not just spontaneous "racism," but a campaign to drive Afrikans there off the land. That area in Crittenden County had been an Afrikan stronghold after the Civil War. Crittenden was the last county in Arkansas in the 19th century to have Afrikan sheriffs and county officials. Edmondson itself was established as an all-Afrikan town in that period with the entire population, stores, real estate, and farmland being Afrikan. Finally, the planters managed to organize a major armed attack on the town. Many of its people were driven out and the Afrikan leaders were deported from the State. Most of the Afrikan land and homes were stolen by the planters. Desiring only a limited number of Afrikans to work the occupied land as laborers, the local capitalists used terror to keep the population down and to stop any Afrikans who tried to own land.

It should be evident that behind these Afrikan sharecropper and tenant struggles loomed the larger issue and the larger rising. Despite the savage counterattacks by the settler garrison the Afrikan struggle refused to quiet down. In Alabama the 1931 mass arrests, terror, and assassinations failed to exterminate the Sharecroppers Union. The next year another shoot-out took place in Tallapoosa County. On December 19, 1932, the planter deputies killed four Afrikans in an attack on their organization. The brief battle was so intense that the settler attackers were forced to withdraw after they ran low on ammunition. (Four deputies were slightly wounded by Afrikan return fire.) Five Afrikans were sentenced to 12 to 15 years in the State penitentiary for the shoot-out.[19] As late as 1935 the Alabama Sharecroppers Union was leading almost 3,000 cotton sharecroppers on a strike that had begun in bloody Lowndes County on August 19, 1935.[20] Armed confrontations on a small scale were taking place throughout the South.

There were, of course, many Euro-Amerikan sharecroppers and tenants as well in the South. Most of them were extremely poor, a poverty whose roots lay in the original defeat of their abortive Confederate nation. For them the possible path of class conscious struggle was visible.

A unique union, the Southern Tenant Farmers Union, was formed in Tyronza, Arkansas in 1934 to follow this path. The STFU was started by two Southern Euro-Amerikan Social Democrats—H.L. Mitchell (who owned a dry cleaners) and Henry East (a gas station operator). Their union involved many thousands of sharecroppers, tried several major strikes, and was notable in the

PARKIN, ARKANSAS. THE FAMILIES OF SHARECROPPERS. LEGALLY EVICTED
THE WEEK OF JANUARY 12, 1936, THE PLANTATION HAVING CHARGED
THAT BY MEMBERSHIP IN THE SOUTHERN TENANT FARMERS UNION THEY
WERE ENGAGING IN A CONSPIRACY TO RETAIN THEIR HOMES.
THE EVICTIONS, THOUGH AT THE POINT OF A GUN, WERE QUITE LEGAL.

upper rural South of that time for being heavily "integrated." Briefly, the STFU was even a part of the national CIO (before splits between settler radicals led to its ouster), and had the same prominent role in official 1930s U.S. unionism that the farmworkers (UFW) does in today's AFL-CIO.

The STFU failed politically because it could not resolve the relationship between oppressor and oppressed nations, could find no other basis for workers' unity other than reformism under oppressor nation domination. How wide the gulf really was on the land can be seen from an incident in Oklahoma. STFU leader H.L. Mitchell had gone to Durant, Okla. on an organizing drive. Addressing a group of Choctaw Indian farm workers, Mitchell called on them to "get organized" by joining the STFU. The Choctaw leader simply ended the discussion by saying: "Indian already organized. When white man and Black man get ready to take back the land, we join them."[21]

The STFU's integrationism was just an effort to harness and use the militancy of the Afrikan masses to fight battles the poor whites could not sustain themselves. The Afrikan tenants and sharecroppers were the hard-core strength of the STFU, their steadfastness alone permitting enough organizations to hold together so that the poor whites had something to cling to. H.L. Mitchell (who always insisted on settler control of the union) himself had to admit that: "Intimidation moves were generally more successful against the whites than the Negroes. The latter have more sense of organization and the value of organization, a greater sense of solidarity."[22]

Even this social-democratic union could not successfully absorb and tame the nationalist energy of its Afrikan members. The primary organizer for the STFU in its formative years was its Afrikan vice-president, the Rev. E.B. McKinney. McKinney related to the STFU and its radical Euro-Amerikans only to the exact degree that he felt Afrikans thereby gained in self-organization and political strength. This rural preacher turned out to be both much better educated than most of the settler union activists and an Afrikan nationalist. One historian remarks: *"Though willing to work with whites, he was race-conscious, having been influenced by Marcus Garvey's Negro nationalism, and 'his people' remained primarily the Negro union members."*[23]

Badly wounded by U.S. imperialism's terroristic counter-blows, the Afrikan sharecropper struggle in the late 1930s continued to search for new directions. As late as 1939 there was considerable agitation. That year Rev. McKinney quit the STFU in protest, saying that, *"The Negro is the goat of the STFU."* All thirteen Afrikan tenant farmer union locals in Arkansas quit the STFU and joined the rival CIO union as a group. These Afrikan sharecroppers were trying to take advantage of Euro-Amerikan labor factional in-fighting, playing those factions off against each other attempting to find a situation with the most resources and leverage for themselves.

In January 1939 thousands of dispossessed, landless Afrikan sharecroppers in Southeastern Missouri took to the highways in a major demonstration. To dramatize their demand for bread and land, the sharecroppers set up a "tent city" lining the roadsides of a national highway. This protest, which lasted for months, caught Empire-wide attention and was an early forerunner to the 1960s "freedom marches" and other such actions. It was a very visible sign of the struggle of Afrikans to resist leaving their lands, to resist imperialist dispossession.[24]

Practice showed that the Afrikan sharecropper and tenant labor struggles not only had a class character but were part of a larger national struggle. They were anti-colonial struggles having the goal of removing the boot-heel of settler occupation off of Afrikan life and land. In this stirring the Afrikan masses—rural as well as urban, sharecroppers as well as steelworkers—were creating new forms of organization, trying mass struggles of varied kinds, and taking steps toward revolution. Again, it is important to recognize the meaning of the reality that Afrikans were picking up the gun. And raising the need for socialist liberation.

This gradually developing struggle was against U.S. imperialism and had a revolutionary direction. In the thirties Afrikan communism grew, taking root not only in the refugee ghettos of the North but in the South as well. Primarily this political activity took form within the Communist Party USA (which the ABB had joined). While we can recognize the CPUSA finally as a settleristic party of revisionism, it is important to see that in the Deep South at that time the CPUSA was predominantly an underground organization of

Afrikan revolutionaries. The CPUSA was accepted not only because of its labor and legal defense activities, but because in that period the CPUSA was openly espousing independence for the oppressed Afrikan Nation.

Hosea Hudson, an Afrikan steelworker who played a major role in the CPUSA in Alabama in the 1930s, points out that the party of his personal experience was in reality an Afrikan organization: **"Up in the top years, in '33, '34, '35, the Party in Birmingham and Alabama was dominated by Negroes. At one time we had estimated around Birmingham about six or seven hundred members. And in the whole State of Alabama it was considered about 1,000 members. We had only a few whites, and I mean *a few* whites."**

So that in the Afrikan Nation not just a small intellectual vanguard, not just a handful, but a significant number of Afrikans were illegally organizing for socialist revolution and national liberation. Hudson makes it plain that Afrikan communists then had very explicit ideas about their eventually leading a freed and sovereign Afrikan Nation in the South.

> **"Our struggle was around many outstanding issues in our party program in the whole South: 1) Full economic, political and social equality to the Negro people and the right of self-determination of the Negro people in the Black Belt ... When we got together, we discussed and we read the *Liberator*. The Party put out this newspaper, the *Liberator* ... It was always carrying something about the liberation of Black people, something about Africa, something about the South, Scottsboro, etc., etc.**

> **"We'd compare, we'd talk about the right of self-determination. We discussed the whole question of if we established a government, what role we comrades would play, about the relationship of the white, of the poor white, of the farmers, etc. in this area.**

> **"If you had a government in the South—they'd give you the right of self-determination in the Black Belt—you got whites there. What would you do with the whites? We say**

the whites would be recognized on the basis of their percentage, represented on all bodies and all committees. But the Negroes at all times would be in the majority..."[25]

It's revealing that at that time—when Afrikan communism had easily as much strength and numbers in the South as it did in the 1970s—they had a nationalist program. The goal of national independence very clearly made sense to the grassroots. And at that time in the early 1930s the overwhelming majority of Afrikan communists in the South were proletarians.

As we put back together some of the pieces of the New Afrikan story, we see even in incomplete outline that this struggle had indeed renewed itself and entered the modern period. The Afrikan proletariat had stood up, particularly in the South, and had spearheaded new industrial unionism campaigns (with or without the alliances with white workers). On the plantations the masses were starting to organize. Spontaneous resistance to the settler-colonial occupation was breaking out. The most politically conscious of all these were becoming communists, with Afrikan communism rapidly growing and taking on its vanguard role. Thousands of Afrikans stepped forward in those years to commit themselves to armed revolution, self-government through independence for the Afrikan Nation, and socialism. This was a program that had won respect amongst Afrikan people, particularly in the South.

The political horizons for Afrikans had opened wide in those years. It is especially important to understand that masses of Afrikans viewed themselves as part of a world struggle, that their aims and concerns encompassed but went far beyond immediate economic issues. Nothing proved this more clearly than the spontaneous mass movement to support Ethiopia in its war against Italian imperialism.

In October 1935 the Italian Empire invaded Ethiopia in a drive to expand its North Afrikan colonies (which at that time included Somalia, Eritrea, and Libya). Italian imperialists were especially glad at that new invasion since it gave them a chance to avenge their humiliating defeat at Adowa in 1896. Ethiopia was then, however feudalistic its society, the only actually independent nation left in Afrika. It had remained independent for the only possible reason, because it had repeatedly maintained its national integrity and had militarily repulsed European intrusions. The early Portuguese slavers had been driven off.

Even when the Italian Army, 40,000 soldiers armed with rifle and artillery, invaded Ethiopia in 1896, the Ethiopian nation defeated them. These Italian divisions were surrounded and wiped out at Adowa by Emperor Menelik's 250,000 Ethiopian soldiers. The humbled Italian Empire was forced after Adowa to publicly recognize the Ethiopian borders and even to pay the Ethiopian government heavy cash reparations. So in 1935, after some years of preparatory border incidents, the Mussolini regime eagerly sent its tank divisions and airplane squadrons slicing into Ethiopia.

Afrikans within the U.S. Empire reacted instantly in a great uproar of anger and solidarity. Journalist Roi Ottley pointed out that there had been *"no event in recent times that stirred the rank-and-file of Negroes more than the Italo-Ethiopian War."* It is important to grasp the full and exact significance of this political upheaval. All over the Afrikan continent and in the "New World" Afrikans were being oppressed by the European colonial powers. Why then did this one case call forth such special attention from Afrikans in the U.S. Empire? Because it involved the principle of national rights for Afrikans, the defense of Afrikan nationhood.

Even the moderate political forces rallied around this most basic issue to the nationally oppressed.[26] Even someone such as Walter White, the executive secretary of the NAACP, could angrily write: *"Italy, brazenly, has set fire under the powder keg of white arrogance and greed which seems destined to become an act of suicide for the so-called white world."* At its 1935 national convention the NAACP assailed "the imperialistic selfishness of all nations in their shameless aggression upon the sovereignty of other nations..."

The defense of Afrikan nationhood was primary in everyone's mind. Dr. L.K. Williams, President of the National Baptist Convention, told a mass rally: "We do not want to see the last black empire in Afrika lose its independence and culture..." The Fraternal Council of Negro Churches, representing the major Afrikan denominations, issued an official resolution saying: "Americans of African descent are deeply stirred in their attitudes and sympathies

for Ethiopia, a Negroid people, who represent almost the only remaining example of independent government by the black race on
the continent of Africa ..." So the concern was broadly shared by the
Afrikan Nation as a whole—not just by some strata or some political sectors.

**The support movement took many forms. Clearly the lead-
ing group in the mass mobilization was the Garvey Movement's
United Negro Improvement Association (UNIA). This was, we
should recall, the same nationalist organization that prominent
academic historians now assure us was abandoned and unimportant at that time.**

Captain A.L. King, head of the UNIA in New York, was the
chairman of the united Afrikan support committee. J.A. Rogers, the
leading intellectual of the Garvey movement in the U.S., was the
main propagandist and educator for the support movement. The
Afrikan united front committee involved not only the UNIA and
other nationalist organizations, but the CPUSA, church leaders,
Afrikan college groupings, and so on. Within several months after
the invasion the Friends of Ethiopia had 106 local branches both
North and South. There were mass church meetings, rallies, marches of thousands, and picket lines outside Italian government offices.

The national character of the movement was underlined by
the fact that virtually to the last person Afrikans boycotted the
well-funded and Euro-Amerikan-run international relief efforts.
The American Red Cross admitted that Afrikans refused to join its
Ethiopian aid campaign; Afrikans insisted on their own all-Afrikan
campaign that was highly political. The political counterattack by
U.S. imperialism struck at this point. Somehow the rumor kept
spreading that the Ethiopians thought of themselves as "Caucasian"
and that they allegedly viewed Afrikans (most especially in the U.S.
Empire) with contempt. There was a demoralizing confusion from
this rumor.

To expose this lie representatives of the Ethiopian government
came to the U.S. At a packed Harlem meeting of 3,000 people at Rev.
Adam Clayton Powell, Jr.'s Abyssinian Baptist Church, Ethiopian
envoy Tasfaye Zaphior invoked the solidarity of oppressed Afrikan
peoples: *"It is said that we despise Negroes. In the first place, you are*

not Negroes. Who told you that you were Negroes? You are the sons and daughters of Africa, your motherland, which calls you now to aid her last surviving free black people."

The "Volunteer Movement" arose spontaneously throughout the Nation. Thousands upon thousands of Afrikans volunteered to go fight in Ethiopia. The Black Legion established a military training camp in rural New York, and its leaders urged Afrikans to prepare to renounce U.S. citizenship. While the "Volunteer Movement" was blocked by U.S. imperialism, its popular nature shows how powerful were the potential forces being expressed through the Ethiopian support issue. The two Afrikans from the U.S. Empire who did fight in Ethiopia (both fighter pilots) were heroes back home, whose adventures were widely followed by the Afrikan press.

The conflict was fought out in miniature on the streets of Jersey City, Brooklyn, and Harlem between Afrikans and pro-fascist Italian immigrants. The night of August 11, 1935, over a thousand Afrikans and Italians fought with baseball bats and rocks on the streets of Jersey City. On October 4, 1935 (the day after the main invasion began) thousands of Afrikans attacked Italian shops in Harlem and Brooklyn. On the streets the masses of ordinary Afrikans viewed their fight and the fight in Ethiopia as very close.

It's indicative that in 1936 a late-night street corner rally of the African Patriotic League, called to protest Italian mass executions of Ethiopian patriots, rapidly turned into an attack on the police. Smashing Italian store windows, the crowd of 400 Afrikans marched down Lenox Ave. in Harlem looking for a particular policeman who made a point of arresting nationalists. In the mass fighting with police that followed, the New York police started shooting after the determined crowd charged them to successfully free one of their number who had been arrested.[27] Ethiopia was close to home.

The great outpouring of nationalist sentiment that accompanied the Ethiopian War was, we must emphasize, widespread throughout the U.S. Empire. One New Orleans resident wrote to the *Courier* that the Ethiopian crisis proved that *"... the time is here for the Negro to begin to look for the higher things in life—a flag of his own, a government of his own and complete liberty."* This was the developing consciousness that so threatened U.S. imperialism.

3. To Disrupt the Nation: Population Regroupment

It was only against the rise of the Afrikan Nation that we could see, in brilliant detail, how the U.S. Empire wove together the net of counterinsurgency. We know that a period that began around World War I and which continued through the 1930s, a period in which Afrikan nationalism militantly took hold of the masses, ended in the 1940s with the triumph of pro-imperialist integrationism as the dominant political philosophy in the Afrikan communities. U.S. counterinsurgency was the hidden factor in this paradoxical outcome.

In the Philippine War of 1898–1901 the U.S. Empire openly spoke of its counterinsurgency strategy. The same was true in Vietnam in the 1960s. But in the Afrikan colony of the 1930s U.S. counterinsurgency was concealed. It was none the less real, none the less genocidal for having been done without public announcements. It is when we view what happened in this light, as components of a strategy of counterinsurgency, that the political events suddenly come into full focus.

Usually counterinsurgency involves three principal components: (1) Violent suppression or extermination of the revolutionary cadre and organizations; (2) Paralyzing the mass struggle itself through genocidal population regroupment; (3) Substituting pro-imperialist bourgeois leadership and institutions for patriotic leadership and institutions within the colonial society. The terroristic suppression of Afrikan militants in the South has been discussed, and in any case should be well understood. What has been less discussed are the other two parts.

LEFT: EVICTED SHARECROPPERS ALONG HIGHWAY 60, NEW MADRID COUNTY, MISSOURI, 1939. IN THE FIELDS TENS OF THOUSANDS OF AFRIKAN FARM FAMILIES DURING THE 1930S WERE DRIVEN NOT ONLY OFF THE LAND, BUT OUT OF THE SOUTH ALTOGETHER.

POPULATION REGROUPMENT

In Mao Zedong's famous analogy, the guerrillas in People's War are "fish" while the masses are the "sea" that both sustains and conceals them. Population regroupment (in the CIA's terminology) strategy seeks to dry up that "sea" by literally uprooting the masses and disrupting the whole social fabric of the oppressed nation. In Vietnam the strategy resulted in the widespread chemical poisoning of crops and forest land, the depopulation of key areas, and the involuntary movement of one-third of the total South Vietnamese population off their lands to "protected hamlets" and "refugee centers" (i.e. the CIA's reservations for Vietnamese). These blows only show how great an effort, what magnitude of resources, is expended on imperialist counterinsurgency.

In response to growing political unrest, the U.S. Empire moved inexorably to drive Afrikans off the land, out of industry, and force them into exile. The New Deal of President Franklin Roosevelt, the major banks and corporations, and the main Euro-Amerikan political and social organizations (unions, political parties, etc.) worked together to destroy the economic base of the Afrikan Nation, to separate Afrikans from their lands, and to thus destabilize and gradually depopulate the Afrikan communities in and adjacent to the National Territory. One history of U.S. welfare programs notes:

> "...many New Deal programs ran roughshod over the most destitute. Federal agricultural policy, for example, was designed to raise farm prices by taking land out of cultivation, an action that also took many tenant farmers and sharecroppers out of the economy. The National Recovery Administration, seeking to placate organized employers and organized labor, permitted racial differentials in wages to be maintained. The Tennessee Valley Authority deferred to local prejudice by not hiring Blacks. All this was done not unknowingly, but rather out of concern for building a broad base for the new programs. It was left to FERA (Federal Emergency Relief Act) to succor the casualties of the New Deal's pragmatic policies. Since Blacks got little from (or were actually harmed by) most

programs, 30 per cent of the Black population ended up on the direct relief rolls by January 1935."[28]

Just as the 30% of the South Vietnamese people were forcibly made dependent upon direct U.S. handouts in the 1960s in order just to eat, so 30% of the Afrikan people in the U.S. were similarly reduced by 1935. But not for long. That was only the first stage. In the second, relief was turned over to the local planter governments, who proceeded to force Afrikans off the relief rolls to drive them out of the region. That history of U.S. welfare continues:

> "Under pressure from Southern congressmen, any wording that might have been interpreted as constraining the states from racial discrimination in welfare was deleted from the Social Security Act of 1935. The Southern states then proceeded to use the free hand they had been given to keep Blacks off the rolls."[29]

It is important to see that Afrikans were *not* just the victims of discrimination and blind economic circumstances ("last hired, first fired," etc.). *Africans were the targets of imperialist New Deal policy.* We must remember that the archaic, parasitic Euro-Amerikan planter capitalists were on the verge of final bankruptcy and literal dissolution in the early years of the Depression. Further, despite the 1929 Depression there was in fact relatively little agricultural unemployment among Afrikans in the rich Mississippi River cotton land of the Delta (the Kush) until the winter of 1933–34.[30] Then these two facts were suddenly reversed.

The New Deal's 1934 Agricultural Adjustment Act rescued the ruined planter capitalists, giving them cash subsidies so that they could hold on to the land and continue serving as U.S. imperialism's overseers in the Afrikan South.* But those U.S. imperialist subsidies

---

* Interestingly enough, the 1934 AAA and the entire program was administered by FDR's Secretary of Agriculture, Henry Wallace. This man was later to become the darling of the CPUSA, and the 1948 Presidential candidate of the CPUSA-led "Progressive Party."

literally gave the planters cash for each sharecropper and tenant farmer they forced off the plantation. The primary effect, then, was to forcibly destabilize and eventually depopulate the rural Afrikan communities. One 1935 evaluation of the AAA program by the lawyer for the Southern Tenant Farmers Union pointed out:

> "Before its passage most of the plantations of the south were heavily mortgaged. It was freely prophesied that the plantation system was breaking down under its own weight and that the great plantations would soon be broken up into small farms, owned by the people who cultivate them ... but by federal aid the plantation system of the South is more strongly entrenched than it had been for years.
>
> "However, this is not the most significant effect of the federal aid. By it cotton acreage was reduced about 40 per cent, and something like 40 per cent of the tenants were displaced..."[31]

This displacement was also taking place in the factories and even the coal field, where (as we noted in the previous section) Afrikan workers had played a leading role in militant unionization. As the coal mines of the South gradually became unionized during the 1930s, Afrikan miners and their families were driven out by the tens of thousands. The large coal companies and the United Mine Workers Union (UMW-CIO), while they had class differences, had oppressor nation unity. The imperialists had decided to drive rebellious Afrikan labor out of the Southern coal fields, and the pro-imperialist CIO unions eagerly cooperated. *Between 1930 and 1940 the percentage of Afrikan miners in the five Southern Appalachian States (Alabama, Virginia, Tennessee, West Virginia, and Kentucky) was deliberately cut from 23% to 16%.*[32] And it would keep on being cut year after year, regardless of economic boom or bust.

The drive by capital to strike down Afrikan labor, to force the colonial masses out of the main economy, intensified throughout the 1930s. Between 1930–36 some 50% of all Afrikan skilled workers were pushed out of their jobs.[33] Careful observers at that time made the point that this was *not* caused by the Depression alone, but

clearly reflected a strategy used by imperialism against the Afrikan
Nation as a whole. W.E.B. Du Bois said in the main address of the
1933 Fisk University commencement ceremony:

> **"We do not know that American Negroes will survive. There
> are sinister signs about us, antecedent to and unconnected
> with the Great Depression. The organized might of indus-
> try North and South is relegating the Negro to the edge of
> survival and using him as a labor reservoir on starvation
> wage…"[34]**

In the fields tens of thousands of Afrikan farm families during the
1930s were driven not only off the land, but out of the South altogether. As we have seen, this was clearly not the result of "blind economic circumstances," but was the genocidal result of imperialist
policy (as enacted by the most liberal settler administration in U.S.
history). The social disruption and de-population were no less significant for Afrikans than for other dispersed colonial peoples, such
as the Palestinians.

The militant struggle on the land and the turn of Afrikan workers toward revolution was not only blunted by violent repression;
increasingly the Afrikan masses were involuntarily dispersed, scattered into the refugee camps of the Northern ghettoes, removed
from established positions in industries and trades that were an irreplaceable part of the modern Nation. It was not just a matter of
dollars, important as income is to the oppressed; what was happening ravaged the national culture. The "sea" of Afrikan society was
stricken at its material base.

4. Neocolonialism & Leadership

The U.S. Empire has had a long and successful history of applying neocolonialism to hold down the oppressed. In Latin America and in New Afrika during the mid-1800s the U.S. Empire utilized neocolonialism prior even to the advent of world imperialism. But in the 1920s and early 1930s U.S. imperialism's neocolonial instruments lost control over the Afrikan masses. In order to re-establish pro-imperialist leadership over Afrikan politics, U.S. imperialism had to forge new neocolonial instruments. These neocolonial instruments were not only traditional but also radical and even socialistic in outward form, and had the special task of controlling the modern forces of Afrikan trade unionism and Afrikan socialism that had arisen so widely.

We should remember that the essence of neocolonialism is an outward form of national self-determination and popular democracy concealing a submissive relationship with imperialism on the part of the new bourgeois forces. As Amilcar Cabral pointed out almost twenty years ago concerning neocolonialism:

> "The objective of the imperialist countries was to prevent the en-
> largement of the socialist camp, to liberate the reactionary forces in
> our countries which were being stifled by colonialism and to enable

*these forces to ally themselves with the international bourgeoisie.
The fundamental idea was to create a bourgeoisie where one did
not exist, in order specifically to strengthen the imperialist and the
capitalist camp."*[35]

The U.S. Empire had literally done exactly that in the 1870s. The
neocolonial stage known as Black Reconstruction had qualitatively
changed and enlarged the New Afrikan petit-bourgeoisie. This class,
even in defeat by the Euro-Amerikan planter capitalists, were to a
degree held up by and patronized by U.S. imperialism—and they retained like a religion their loyalty and dependence upon the Federal
government. Washington, DC was their Mecca or Rome. Indeed,
the Federal government was for many years the prime employer of
the Afrikan petit-bourgeoisie.

Many Afrikan politicians of the 19th century were consoled
by Federal patronage jobs for the lost glories of Reconstruction.
U.S. Senator Blanche Bruce from Mississippi was the last Afrikan
in the Senate. When his term ended in 1881, Mississippi politics
were back under planter control and he was replaced. For his loyal example the Empire awarded him the position in Washington
of U.S. Register of the Treasury (for the next thirty-two years that
post would be reserved for loyal Afrikan leaders). Even Frederick
Douglass was not immune to the ideological bent of his class. He
was appointed U.S. Marshall for the District of Columbia, and later
in his life was U.S. Consul to Haiti. Small wonder that the former
radical abolitionist spent years preaching how Afrikans should always remain loyal to the Republican Party, Northern capital, and
the Federal government.

By 1892 the Federal offices in Washington employed some
1,500 Afrikans. While most of these jobs were as cleaning women
and the lowliest of clerks, a trickle of professional and official positions were reserved for hand-picked Afrikan petit-bourgeois leaders.
Washington, DC was then the "capitol" in exile of Afrikans, the center of "Negro society." Some eight bureaucratic positions with status
eventually were reserved for them: DC Municipal Judge, Register of
the Treasury, Deputy Register, Assistant District Attorney for DC,
Auditor of the Navy Department, Chief Surgeon at DC Freedman's

Hospital, Collector of Customs at Georgetown, and U.S. Assistant Attorney-General.

In 1913 a journalist light-heartedly labeled these eight "the Black Cabinet." But what began in jest was eagerly taken up by petit-bourgeois Afrikans in seriousness. **The custom began of regarding the "Black Cabinet" as the representatives to the U.S. government of the whole Afrikan population within the U.S. So a petit bourgeois Afrikan national leadership had been created which was, in fact, both employed by and solely picked by the imperialist government.**[36]

At this time the most prominent Afrikan in these circles, standing in reality even above the "Black Cabinet," was Booker T. Washington of the Tuskegee Institute. Washington was viewed by the imperialists as their chief Afrikan advisor, and served them as a leading propagandist and apologist for white supremacy and colonialism. In return, any Afrikan who sought position or funds from the imperialists had to be approved by him. During the Theodore Roosevelt and Taft Administrations even the "Black Cabinet" appointments were cleared first with him. Washington had great fame and, acting for the Empire, some influence over Afrikan education, newspapers, community institutions, and so on. But, of course, neither he nor the other imperialist-selected Afrikan leaders represented the will of the masses.

At the end of World War I an anti-colonial movement of incredible vigor burst forth—seemingly almost overnight—that rejected both the U.S. Empire and the bourgeois leadership that it had installed for Afrikans. This was the historic movement touched off and led by the Jamaican Marcus Garvey. Even its enemies conceded that the Afrikan masses were expressing their deep desires through this rebellious movement of Afrikan nationalism.

The Garvey movement at its peak in the early 1920s was the greatest outbreak of Afrikan political activity since the Civil War. It said that Afrikans could find their liberation in building a new, modern Afrikan Nation of their own back on the soil of the Afrikan continent. The proposed Nation would eventually unite and protect Afrikans everywhere—in the U.S. Empire and the West Indies as well as on the Afrikan continent itself.

This new nation would expand to liberate all Afrika from colonialism and unite it into one continental Afrikan Power. There Afrikans would shape their own destiny in great industries, universities, agricultural cooperatives, and cultural institutions of their own. As a beginning toward the day, Garveyism organized national institutions here in all spheres of life. However modest, these medical, religious, military, economic, and other organizations were designed to develop Afrikan self-reliance and national independence. If Garveyism suffered from practical shortcomings, nevertheless its imposing sweep of vision expressed the burning national aspirations of the suppressed Afrikan peoples (and not only within the U.S., but worldwide).

Garveyism's great contribution consisted of the fact that it raised high for all to see a vision of Afrikan life that was completely self-reliant, built around their own national economy and culture,

MARCUS GARVEY

that waited on no European to "accept" them or "emancipate" them, that was dependent solely on Afrikan energies and will. In this Garveyism was expressing the strongest desires of the Afrikan masses. It is no accident that Garveyism and its successor, the Nation of Islam, were the two largest outbreaks of Afrikan activity and organization-building within the continental Empire of our century. Even such a self-admitted "skeptic" as Richard Wright was profoundly moved by Garveyism in his youth:

> "The one group I met during those exploring days whose lives enthralled me was the Garveyites, an organization of black men and women who were forlornly seeking to return to Africa. Theirs was a passionate rejection of America, for they sensed with that directness of which only the simple are capable that they had no chance to live a full human life in America. Their lives were not cluttered with ideas in which they could only half believe; they could not create illusions which made them think they were living when they were not; their daily lives were too nakedly harsh to permit of camouflage. I understood their emotions, for I partly shared them.

> "The Garveyites had embraced a totally racialistic outlook which endowed them with a dignity that I had never seen before in Negroes. On the walls of their dingy flats were maps of Africa and India and Japan, pictures of Japanese generals and admirals, portraits of Marcus Garvey in gaudy regalia, the faces of colored men and women from all parts of the world. I gave no credence to the ideology of Garveyism; it was, rather, the emotional dynamics of its adherents that evoked my admiration. Those Garveyites I knew could never understand why I liked them but would never follow them, and I pitied them too much to tell them that they could never achieve their goal...

> "It was when the Garveyites spoke fervently of building their own country, of someday living within the boundaries of a culture of their own making, that I sensed the passionate hunger of their lives, that I caught a glimpse of the potential strength of the American Negro."

The Garvey Movement's ambitious economic ventures—in particular the ill-fated Black Star ship line—became centers of controversy.
There is no doubt, however, that at the time they were often considered as very difficult but necessary steps for Afrikan progress. Even
W.E.B. Du Bois of the NAACP, who was one of Garvey's favorite
targets for scorn as "a white man's nigger," initially spoke out in favor
of Garvey's program (but not his personal leadership):

> "...the main lines of the Garvey plan are perfectly feasible. What
> he is trying to say and do is this: America Negroes can, by ac-
> cumulating and ministering their own capital, organize indus-
> try, join the black centers of the South Atlantic by commercial
> enterprise and in this way ultimately redeem Africa as a fit and
> free home for black men. This is true. It is *feasible* ... The plan
> is not original with Garvey but he had popularized it, made it a
> living, vocal ideal and swept thousands with him with intense
> belief in the possible accomplishment of the ideal."[37]

To the extent that Garveyism was naive about capitalism (which it
obviously was) this was a stage of development widely shared by
its critics as well. Garveyism's weakness was that it saw in capitalism—the form of social organization of the colonizer—the instruments that Afrikans could use to free themselves. So that the essence
of nation-building was expressed in forms precisely paralleling those
of European society—businesses, churches, Black Cross, etc., etc.
Garveyism's predilection for Western titles of nobility ("Duke of
Nigeria") and full-dress European court uniforms was but a symp-
tom of this. While this made the concept of independent Afrikan
nationhood instantly understandable, it also was a contradiction
and a blind alley.

Millions of Afrikans responded to the call of Garvey's United
Negro Improvement Association (UNIA), read its newspaper *The
Negro World,* bought stock in its Afrikan business ventures, came out
to its meetings and rallies. In 1920 some 50,000 Afrikans marched
in a mass UNIA rally in Harlem. Garvey claimed 4.5 million members for the UNIA. His critics charged that an examination of the
UNIA's public financial reports revealed that the Garvey Movement

had "only" 90,000 members of whom "only" 20,000 were paid up at that time in dues. The UNIA was so overwhelming that its critics could try to belittle it by saying that it had "only" 90,000 members.[38]

The UNIA's international effect was very profound. Claude McKay reminds us that: "In the interior of West Africa new legends arose of an African who had been lost in America, but would return to save his people."[39] On the Nigerian coast Afrikans would light great bonfires, sleeping on the beaches, waiting to guide in the ships of "Moses Garvey." Kwame Nkrumah of Ghana and Ho Chi Minh of Vietnam both said that Garvey had been an important "inspiration" for them.

Clements Kadalie, whose 250,000 member Industrial & Commercial Workers Union (ICU) was the first Afrikan working class political organization in Azania, said that he had been much influenced by the UNIA. In British Kenya the separationist KiKuyu Christians brought in UNIA ministers from the U.S. to train and ordain their own first ministers—and it was from these congregations that much of the Kenya Land & Freedom Army (called "Mau-Mau" by the British) would come a generation later. The Garvey Movement, in Nkrumah's words, "raised the banner of African liberation" on three continents.[40]

In Haiti U.S. Marines violently put down the UNIA. In Costa Rica and Cuba the United Fruit Company used police power to repress it. George Padmore, a bitter opponent of Garvey, recounts that:

> "In certain places the punishment for being seen with a *Negro World* was five years at hard labor, and in French Dahomey it was life imprisonment. It was suppressed in such places as Trinidad, British Guiana, Barbados, etc., in the West Indies and all French, Portuguese, Belgian, and some of the British colonies of Africa."

In the continental U.S. the Garvey Movement was met with varying degrees of repression (Malcolm X's father, we should recall, was assassinated by the KKK because he was an organizer for the UNIA). But overall U.S. imperialism moved against this surprising upsurge with some care. After several of Garvey's former lieutenants were suborned by the U.S. government, the imperialists had Garvey arrested for alleged mail fraud.

This tactic of posing Garvey as a common criminal was conceived by none other than J. Edgar Hoover, who at that time was a rising FBI official. In an Oct. 11, 1919, memorandum Hoover noted that Garvey was: *"Agitating the negro movement. Unfortunately, however, he has not as yet violated any federal law. It occurs to me, however, from the attached clipping that there might be some proceeding against him for fraud in connection with his Black Star Line..."*[41] Eventually *Garvey was convicted, imprisoned in Atlanta Federal Prison and later deported in 1927. The door, however, had been opened.*

What was most apparent was that the old, conservative, imperialist-sponsored Afrikan leadership had been shoved aside and left behind by this outbreak. They could no longer even pretend to lead or control the Afrikan people. It is significant that even the liberal, Civil Rights integrationists had been overshadowed by the new militant nationalism.

This was a time of rich ideological struggle and transformation in the Afrikan Nation. That, however, is not the precise focus of our investigation. What we are looking at is the neocolonial relationship between the forming petit-bourgeois Civil Rights leadership and U.S. imperialism. We are analyzing how in a time of mass unrest and the beginnings of rebellion among Afrikans, U.S. imperialism helped promote a neocolonial Afrikan leadership that in outward form was integrationist, protest-oriented, radical, and even "socialist."

The political attack against the Garvey Movement within the Afrikan Nation was most aggressively spearheaded by a young Afrikan "socialist" and labor organizer, Asa Philip Randolph (who used only his first initial "A."). Since those years of the early 1920s Randolph, even then one of the leading Afrikan radical intellectuals, would grow in stature and influence. A. Philip Randolph became the organizer, and then the President, of the Brotherhood of Sleeping Car Porters. He would become for decades the most important Afrikan union leader, eventually rising to be the only Afrikan member of the AFL-CIO Executive Council. As the leader of the historic 1941 March On Washington Movement, he was credited with forcing the Federal government to desegregate industry.

To most today Randolph is at best a dim name somehow associated with dusty events in the past. In 1969 he had an 80th birthday dinner at the Waldorf-Astoria Hotel in New York, where he was personally congratulated not only by Coretta King and other Afrikan notables, but by Gov. Nelson Rockefeller and AFL-CIO President George Meany. It's hard for activists today to view him as anything but another of the faceless Uncle Toms.

This greatly underestimates his historic role. To grasp how useful he was to the U.S. Empire we have to see that the young A. Philip Randolph was a radical star in the Afrikan community. He was an angry, provocative troublemaker with an image as bold as a James Forman or a Cesar Chavez. Randolph published the first socialist Afrikan journal aimed at workers, promoting Afrikan unionism. The

A. PHILIP RANDOLPH

Messenger carried the motto "The Only Radical Negro Magazine In America," and had 45,000 readers. He was arrested and briefly held by Federal authorities for speaking out against World War I. The New York State Legislature's investigative committee called him *"the most dangerous Negro in America."* Randolph did his work *inside* the Afrikan struggle, as a radical mass leader (not as a conservative-talking conciliator sitting in a fancy office somewhere).

His long tenure as the lone recognized Afrikan leader on a "national level" in the AFL-CIO was so striking that it led the Rev. Martin Luther King, Jr. to query in an article why:

"The absence of Negro trade-union leadership. 85% of Negroes are working people. Some 2,000,000 are in trade unions, but in 50 years we have produced only one national leader—A. Philip Randolph."[42] This is a question whose answer will become apparent to us.

At the beginning of Randolph's political career, this ambitious young intellectual was taken in and helped by the UNIA. Garvey appointed him as head of the UNIA delegation to the League of Nations conference at the end of World War I (Randolph was de-nied a U.S. passport and was unable to go). When Randolph and his close associate Chandler Owen needed assistance for the *Messenger,* the UNIA provided them with offices in the Harlem building that it owned.[43] The UNIA attempted to be broadly encouraging to Afrikan ventures, even those of a socialist nature, so long as they were Afrikan-run and oriented.

Randolph's integrationism and ambition led him to break with the UNIA. *It was not, we should emphasize, only a political struggle within Afrikan ranks alone.* The U.S. oppressor nation was also in-volved in the dispute. While Randolph and his fellow integrationists, totally impressed with the might of the U.S. Empire, never believed that national liberation could succeed, they feared that the growing mass agitation would antagonize settlers. To these neocolonialists, settler "goodwill" and patronage was more important than almost anything. Further, Randolph's immediate career as a would-be labor leader was threatened by Garveyism's hold on the Afrikan masses.

Randolph and his associates were fanatically determined to destroy Garvey and the UNIA at any cost. They pursued this end using any and every means. In their magazine, the *Messenger,* Garvey was sneeringly referred to as "monumental monkey" and "supreme Negro Jamaican jackass." Randolph's near-racist rhetoric reflected his assertion that Garvey was an "alien" West Indian and not a true "American Negro." National speaking tours with the NAACP for a "Garvey Must Go" campaign failed.[44]

In a telling move, Randolph—the supposed "socialist"—and his integrationist allies turned to the U.S. Empire for help. They openly encouraged the repression of the UNIA. In early January 1923 this grouping became alarmed when the chief government witness against Garvey in his coming mail fraud trial was killed. This traitor, Rev. J.W. Easton of New Orleans, had formerly been a leader in the UNIA, but had been ousted for embezzlement. The dying Easton had allegedly identified his assailants as two workers, a longshoreman and a painter, who were UNIA security cadre.

The anti-Garvey grouping was seized with fear that they themselves would be corrected for their treasonous collaboration with the state. On January 15, 1923, constituting themselves as a "Committee of Eight," they wrote to U.S. Attorney General Daugherty begging him to strike down the Afrikan nationalists without any delay. This historic letter is informative:

"Dear Sir;

"(1) As the chief law enforcement officer of the nation we wish to call your attention to a heretofore unconsidered menace to a harmonious race relations. There are in our midst certain Negro criminals and potential murderers, both foreign and American born, who are moved and actuated by intense hatred of the white race. These undesirables continually proclaim that all white people are enemies to the Negro. They have become so fanatical that they have threatened and attempted the death of their opponents...

"(2) The movement known as the Universal Negro Improvement Association has done much to stimulate the violent temper of this dangerous movement. Its President and moving spirit is one Marcus Garvey, an unscrupulous demagogue, who has ceaselessly and assiduously sought to spread among Negroes distrust and hatred of all white people.

[...]

"(5) The UNIA is chiefly composed of the most primitive and ignorant element of West Indian and American Negroes...

[...]

"(25) For the above reasons we advocate that the Attorney General use his full influence completely to disband and extirpate this vicious movement, and that he vigorously and speedily push the government's case against Marcus Garvey for using the mails to defraud ... its future meetings should be carefully watched by officers of the law and infractions promptly and severely punished."[45]

The eight who signed this slavish appeal (Randolph dishonestly professed to know nothing about it) were:

Chandler Owen—Co-editor of the *Messenger* and Randolph's closest political associate

William Pickens—Field Secretary of the NAACP

Robert Bagnall—NAACP Director of Branches

Robert Abbott—Publisher of the *Chicago Defender*

Julia Coleman—"Hair-Vim" cosmetics company

John Nail—Real estate broker

George W. Harris—NY City Councilman, editor of the newspaper *New York News*

Harry Pace—Pace Phonograph Company

It is useful to examine this move. In practice it turned out that Randolph's grouping of moderate "socialists"—supposedly dedicated to overthrowing capitalism—were blocked with the liberal, pro-capitalist petit-bourgeois elements of the NAACP, and with the marginal Afrikan business interests who fed off the degradation of colonial oppression. *And that in practice all these elements looked upon the U.S. Empire as their ultimate protector—against their own people.*

While it was obviously true that Randolph was an agent of U.S. imperialism, it wasn't true that he was a simple tool just following orders, such as a police informer might be. To understand neocolonialism we have to see that Randolph represented a certain class viewpoint—the viewpoint of a Munoz Marin in Puerto Rico or the young Mike Masaoka in the Japanese-American national minority. This is a viewpoint of the section of the petit-bourgeoisie that sees advancement and progress not from leaving the struggle, but from coopting it and using it as a bargaining tool in winning concessions from the Empire in return for loyal submission. It is only a seeming paradox that these activist petit-bourgeois elements encouraged—and needed—both democratic struggles and violent repression. They are the leaders that U.S. imperialism promotes to ensure that even Third World protest and organization is ultimately loyal to it.

A. Philip Randolph's career makes us recall Cabral's warning that: *"imperialism is quite prepared to change both its men and its tactics in order to perpetuate itself … it will kill its own puppets when they no longer serve its purposes. If need be, it will even create a kind of socialism, which people may soon start calling 'neo-socialism.'"*[46]

Randolph became a leading advocate of all-Afrikan unionism and political organizations. He publicly argued against integrated Civil Rights organizations, such as the NAACP, on the grounds that only Afrikans should decide how their struggle was conducted. But his goal was only to weld Afrikans together as a bloc so that he and his fellow pro-imperialist leaders could demand a price from the U.S. Empire in return for Afrikan submission. Randolph's integrationistic "socialism" was used to fill a void, to ideologically portray a far off, glittering social vision to Afrikan workers that didn't relate to national liberation or breaking away from the U.S. Empire.

Randolph had been indoctrinated in Euro-Amerikan social democracy and settler unionism. That is, he shared the Euro-Amerikan reformist view on how social betterment for Afrikans should take

place. Randolph argued that Afrikans could be protected by unionism and Civil Rights if they carefully convinced settlers of their
nonviolent submissiveness and their desire to be ruled by Euro-
Amerikans. While the *Messenger* abused both communism and nationalism in print in the most vulgar and crude ways, towards AFL
President Samuel Gompers—who was a segregationist, an open
advocate of white supremacy, and a public spokesman of the doctrine of the "racial" inferiority of Afrikans—Randolph was never
less than humble and praising. In 1924, when Gompers died, the
Messenger excused him as a "diplomatically silent" friend. Randolph
feared and hated the Garvey Movement, not because of its faults,
but because of its virtues.

All this is made abundantly clear by Randolph's relationship
to Gompers's successor, AFL President William Green. Morehouse
College Professor Brailsford Brazeal admitted in his laudatory 1946
book on the Porter's Union: "Randolph, although a socialist, had
by this time convinced Green that Pullman porters were anxious
to demonstrate that the Negro would help to further the program
of American workers through conventional channels. Randolph had
condemned the Communists and their tactics in the *Messenger* ...
*All this must have reaffirmed Green's convictions that here were the man
and the organization that could serve as an instrument for rallying Negro
workers under the hegemony of the Federation.*"[47]

Bayard Rustin, Randolph's leading disciple, has said of him: "...
he realized that separatism, whether espoused by Marcus Garvey or
latter day nationalists, is grounded in fantasy and myth despite its
emotional appeal to an oppressed people ... Black people, he realized, could never advance without the good feelings and assistance
of many whites."[48]

And now we can see the answer to the question that Dr. King
raised.

There was only one A. Philip Randolph because U.S. imperialism only wanted one. Randolph was pushed forward and made a big
leader by his Euro-Amerikan mentors. When we look at his magazine, the *Messenger,* during the years when it was fighting Garveyism,
we see in issue after issue large "solidarity" advertisements paid for
by the Euro-Amerikan radicals who ran the International Ladies'

STRIKE NOTICE

To All Pullman Porters and Maids

On account of the refusal of the Pullman Company to settle the dispute on Recognition of Wages and Rules governing Working Conditions with the Brotherhood of Sleeping Car Porters, a strike has been declared and shall be enforced on all Pullman Cars effective

FRIDAY, JUNE 8th
12 O'clock Noon

For further information call Glendale **6373.** You are requested to attend the meetings to be held each evening from 4 until 6 o'clock at **2382 18th street.**

BENNIE SMITH
Field Organiser

By Order of Strike Committee

Garment Workers Union and the Amalgamated Clothing Workers Union. Social-democratic settler labor was indirectly subsidizing Randolph to attack nationalism from *within* the Afrikan Nation—to be their agent and do what they from the outside could not. His whole career was similarly aided and arranged. Imperialism needed its own militant-sounding Afrikan leaders.

A. Philip Randolph's actual record as President of the Brotherhood of Sleeping Car Porters is instructive. He and Chandler Owen were approached by a committee of porters, who were looking for an Afrikan intellectual who could help them to organize a union. The porters' previous attempts had been clumsy. Several efforts had been smashed by the company in a series of firings. Randolph took up the opportunity, and in 1925 the union was formed. The *Messenger* became the official journal of the Brotherhood.

In terms of leading labor struggles, Randolph was a peculiar "success." After years of difficult building, the new 7,000 member union had called for a coast-to-coast Pullman strike in 1928. A mood of tense anticipation was prevalent among the porters. Knowing that the settler train crews wouldn't honor their strike and would try to roll the trains anyway, large groups of Afrikan workers began arming themselves and preparing to take over the rail yards in Oakland and on the East Coast.

Randolph was upset, for he had never really intended to lead a strike. He had not prepared for one, and had told union associates that it was all a bluff. He felt certain that the Federal Mediation Board would step in and arrange a negotiated settlement—just as they did for the Euro-Amerikan railroad Brotherhoods. As a precaution Randolph had even had a White House meeting with President Coolidge and told him of his secret hopes for a government-sponsored settlement. But as the strike deadline neared, the Federal government refused to intervene. The imperialists were unwilling to publicly admit that an Afrikan union could force a "national emergency."

As a desperate hope, Randolph then went begging to AFL President William Green. In a last-minute meeting he implored Green for AFL support of the porters' strike, getting the settler railroads Brotherhoods to close down the trains. Green told him that: "The public isn't ready to accept a strike by Negroes." He told Randolph to give up and call off the strike. Randolph sadly obeyed. On the eve of the first coast-to-coast strike of Afrikan railroad workers the word went out to go back to work, to offer no resistance to the companies.

Disillusioned and confused, the Afrikan porters left the union by the thousands. Two-thirds of the union's 7,000 members quit in the next few months. Randolph's only plan was for them to wait and wait until Euro-Amerikans decided to finally approve of them. Many porters were fired by the triumphant company, knowing that Randolph had left them defenseless. Dues slowed to a trickle, and even the *Messenger* stopped appearing. A. Philip Randolph had won acceptance from the AFL leadership but the workers who had followed him paid the bill. And he had succeeded in defusing a potentially explosive struggle of Afrikan workers.

Randolph's vindication came with the New Deal, with the entry into state power of liberal Democratic Party politicians who understood him

STRIKE Postponed

To All Pullman Porters and Maids

Strike - set for
FRIDAY, JUNE 8th
12 O'clock Noon

Has been Postponed this action taken upon advice of Wm. GREEN-PRESIDENT of the American Federation of Labor.

Who promises immediate Co-Operation.

BENNIE SMITH
Field Organiser B. S. C. P.

By Order of Strike Committee
A. PHILIP RANDOLPH and M. P. WEBSTER

and why he was so useful. In 1937 the National Labor Relations Board ordered the Pullman Company to recognize the Brotherhood and give in to its main demands (during this same period, we should note, Afrikan nationalists in the North who were trying to form unions independent from Euro-Amerikan unionism were subjected to both legal and police disruption). Under the imperialist-ordered settlement porters' wages went up by 30%, while working hours were cut. Randolph was promoted as the very successful leader of an all-Afrikan union, who had gotten his members sizeable rewards in wages and working conditions.[49]

His greatest hour of fame lay still ahead—the 1941 March On Washington Movement, when for one month Randolph was the most important Afrikan in the U.S. This was the event that ensured him a place as a national leader of Afrikans for the U.S. Empire. Instead of Booker T. Washington, an avowed "socialist" labor leader was now meeting and advising at the White House.

So a new, militant nationalism and a new, protest-oriented integrationism engaged in ideological struggle for leadership of the Afrikan masses. It was not, however, a symmetrical struggle or an equal one (struggle rarely is). The insurgent nationalism had the far greater share of popular support, particularly from the laboring masses. It was also true that Afrikan revolutionaries of that time had not yet developed successful strategies for liberation. The Civil Rights integrationists, however slim their own forces, had the powerful resources of the oppressor nation backing their play. The full range of forces, from the U.S. Department of Justice and the police to the foundations, the social-democrats and the settler trade unions, all worked in their various ways to promote the hegemony of a modernized, neocolonial leadership allied to the U.S. Empire.

5. World War II and "Americanization"

World War II marks a definite point at which national movements of the oppressed within the U.S. Empire were thrown back, and the growing hegemony of neocolonial politics firmly established. At home this neocolonialism took the well-prepared form of "Americanization"—of offering and forcing the colonially oppressed to assume supposed "citizenship" in the U.S. Empire in place of national liberation. Of course, while the "Americanization" of the European immigrants during the World War I period meant that they voluntarily became settlers and Euro-Amerikans, the "Americanization" of the colonially oppressed meant involuntary confinement as supposed "minorities" camped on the edges of settler society. This was the ultimate in Civil Rights.

The global war and the U.S. Empire's expansion moved in a new stage in colonial relations. On the one hand, the liberal Roosevelt Administration had gone out of its way to try to convince Third World peoples that the New Deal was their "friend" and protector. This was done in a manner by now very familiar to us.

New Deal Secretary of the Interior Harold Ickes was an aggressive patron of Civil Rights. Ickes was, in fact, the former President

MARY McLEOD BETHUNE, WHO SERVED IN THE "BLACK CABINET,"
AND ELEANOR ROOSEVELT.

of the Chicago NAACP chapter. He and Mrs. Eleanor Roosevelt, the President's wife, arranged for Afrikan intellectuals and professionals to get Federal appointments. The practices of the "lynch-belt South" were sympathetically deplored. In the urban North welfare programs were opened up for Afrikans, and by 1934 some 52%—a majority—of the Afrikan refugee population in the North were on relief.[50] This act was smoothly performed. Pollster Samuel Lubell described how it looked to many petit-bourgeois Afrikans who supported the New Deal:

> "To the younger Negroes the WPA and relief mean not only material aid but a guaranty that no longer must they work at any salary given them, that they are entitled—they emphasize the word—to a living wage. Through the WPA, Harlem's Negroes have had opened to them white-collar opportunities which before had been shut, such as the music and art and writers' projects. Negroes, too, remember that Mrs. Roosevelt visited Harlem personally, that President Roosevelt has appointed more Negroes to administrative positions ... than any President before him. Each time Roosevelt makes such an appointment, the *Amsterdam News*, Harlem's leading newspaper, headlines it in 72-point type. Every young Negro gets a vicarious thrill thinking, 'There may be a chance up there for me.'"[51]

While the liberal Roosevelt Administration kept up a steady propaganda campaign throughout the 1930s and early 1940s, claiming to be "the best friend Negroes ever had," the period was a time of savage attacks to destabilize the Afrikan Nation. There was a conspicuous deindustrialization of Afrikan employment, as they were pushed out of the main imperialist economy.

For awhile it appeared on the surface as though Afrikans were simply victims of the Depression, suffering a heightened version of the commonly-shared joblessness. But by 1940 the voices of Du Bois and others who pointed out a genocidal pattern were proven right. In 1940 and 1941 the Depression finally broke. The war in Europe in 1939 had brought new orders for steel, munitions, ships, trucks, and other industrial products, factories were adding shifts for the first time in years, and Euro-Amerikan unemployment was going down rapidly throughout the last half of 1940 and in 1941.

Afrikans were barred from the new production, however. Their industrial employment was going down as more and more new jobs opened up. Corporation after corporation issued public statements that their new plants would be 100% Euro-Amerikan. Led by Colt Firearms, Consolidated Aircraft, Chrysler Corporation, North American Aviation, and similar industrial giants, Corporate Amerika openly was saying that patriotism required keeping Afrikans out. Imperialism itself well recognized the boundary between oppressor and oppressed nations. After the war began the Anaconda Company's wire and steel division in New York ordered a bar on hiring laborers from enemy countries—*"No Italians, Germans, or Negroes."*[52] Colonial Afrikans were untrustworthy from the viewpoint of imperialism.

The U.S. government itself reflected this genocidal program once we go past the White House's propaganda campaign. Between October 1940 and April 1941, the Afrikan percentage of those placed in factory jobs by the U.S. Employment Service dropped by over half, from a mere 5.40% down to only 2.5%.[53] The U.S. Navy instituted a new policy in its shipyards wherein all "Negro" workers would have to wear an arm badge with a big letter "N". The Navy rejected an NAACP protest that the "N" badges were just like *"the labels used by the Nazis to designate Jews."* In May 1941 Chairman Arthur Altmeyer of the Social Security Board issued an official statement that the Board would continue to support white supremacy.[54]

The liberal, pro-imperialist Afrikan leadership were being pushed to the wall. They had urged Afrikans to remain loyal to the settler Empire and had increasingly little to show for it. While they had taken swift advantage of both repression and the internal contradictions of the nationalist movement to gain a political predominance over Afrikan communities, their top position was unsteady.

Many signs indicated that the nationalist political current was strong on the streets, at the grassroots of the Nation. In 1933 the "Jobs for Negroes Movement" spread from Chicago to Harlem. Surprising as it may sound today, many of the community's jobs were held by Euro-Amerikans.* In the retail stores (which were mostly Euro-Amerikan owned) all the sales clerks, cashiers, managers, and secretaries were Euro-Amerikans. Even 75% of the bartenders in Harlem were settlers. Although all the customers were Afrikan and the stores were in the Afrikan community, even the most pathetic white-collar job was reserved for a Euro-Amerikan only. Particularly under the grim conditions of the Depression, many in the community had angrily pointed out this contradiction.[55]

A nationalist campaign sprung up around this issue in Harlem, led by a "street-corner agitator" named Sufi Abdul Hamid (Eugene Brown). The Sufi was a self-taught Pan-Afrikanist and a teacher of Eastern mystic philosophy. In retrospect it may appear unusual that such a lone political figure could play such an important role, but this only underscores the tremendous leadership vacuum that existed. Together with a core of unemployed college students the Sufi had recruited, he organized the picketing and illegal boycotts of Harlem stores. The campaign continued for five years, with merchant after merchant having to compromise and hire Afrikans.

During these years the "Jobs for Negroes Movement" was illegal, subjected to court injunctions and arrests, as well as the opposition of both the liberal Civil Rights leadership (NAACP, Urban League, Rev. Adam Clayton Powell, Jr., etc.) and the CIO and CPUSA.[56] For years only the small, grassroots nationalist groups fought for more jobs in a jobless community. While both the CPUSA and the Harlem churches started "Jobs" committees, these carefully obeyed the law and did nothing except try to divert support from the nationalist struggle.

In March 1935 the smoldering anger over the genocidal pressures squeezing Afrikan life burst out in a spontaneous uprising. The early "Harlem Riot" saw tens of thousands of Afrikans taking over the streets for 3 days, attacking police and liberating the contents of stores. The liberal, pro-imperialist leadership were helpless and ignored by the people. Indeed, afterwards the Euro-Amerikan capitalists and politicians bitterly castigated their Afrikan allies for

---

* This was before desegregation, while Afrikans still did their shopping, dining out, etc. in their own community.

having failed to control the masses. Everyone agreed that the popular response to the nationalists' "Jobs for Negroes" campaign was an important factor in the uprising.

The *New York Times,* in their obituary on Sufi Abdul Hamid, in 1938, gave hostile acknowledgement:*

> *"The death of the Sufi ended a career that had affected Harlem more deeply than that of any other cult leader … Sufi put his followers on the picket line with placards saying 'Buy Where You Can Work,' in front of stores whose proprietors he accused of refusing to hire Negro help. He reached the height of his power in the Winter of 1934–35 and his picket lines were a sore trial to Harlem merchants. The tension that resulted from this, combined with other causes of friction, resulted in the fatal Harlem race riots of March 1936."*[57]

Imperialism's response was to help their hand-picked Afrikan Civil Rights leaders take over the issue, with a big propaganda campaign picturing the liberal integrationists as the "militant leaders" who had supposedly won new jobs for jobless Afrikans. In 1938 the U.S. Supreme Court ruled the "Jobs" boycotts finally legal. At this a big-name, integrationist coalition took over the "Jobs for Negroes" struggle in Harlem. The YMCA, the Urban League, the major Protestant denominations, the CIO, the CPUSA all joined to support the new leadership of the Rev. Adam Clayton Powell, Jr. over the campaign.[58] Newspaper headlines and joyous victory celebrations greeted the wave of unprecedented agreements between Powell's coalition and business. It appeared as though pro-imperialist integrationism was the key to bringing economic improvement to Harlem.

What was absolutely true was that while concessions were gained, Afrikans were being fronted off. An example was the

---

* It's interesting that virtually all histories that mention the "Jobs" Movement credit its leadership solely to Rev. Adam Clayton Powell, Jr., who for it first five years was a vocal opponent of its illegal boycotts. The nationalist role is never mentioned. This is even true of most historical accounts written by Afrikans (the contemporary account by Claude McKay is a notable exception). As late as 1941 the nationalists were still the cutting edge of the struggle.

"historic" 1938 pact between Powell's coalition and the Uptown Chamber of Commerce, which was hailed in newspaper headlines. *"Harlem Compact Gives Negroes Third of Jobs in Stores There."* But in the fine print there were no specific number of jobs promised. In return for agreeing to end all protests and boycotts, the coalition got a promise that Afrikans would eventually be hired for only one-third of the clerical jobs only in the Harlem stores—and even there only as replacements whenever Euro-Amerikan employees quit.

In a joint statement, Rev. Powell and Col. Philipp of the Chamber of Commerce said, "The settlement reached today is historic. It is the first agreement of its kind ... and will help quiet unrest in Harlem because it is proof that white business leaders have a sympathetic interest in the economic problems of the colored race." Even more to the point the *New York Times* said that the pact was reached because of *"fear of racial uprisings."*[59] So whatever jobs were gained were really won by the Afrikan masses in violent uprising—and by the grassroots nationalism which alone spoke to their needs and interests.

The tamed and carefully-controlled "Jobs" campaign was used to picture Rev. Adam Clayton Powell, Jr. and other pro-imperialist leaders as "militants," as leaders who really fought the "white power structure" and won all kinds of things for Afrikans. In 1941 Powell won a seat on the NY City Council. His campaign was supported by Mayor Fiorello LaGuardia, the Republican Party, and the radical American Labor Party. (Powell was a prominent member of this radical settler party.) In 1944 he became a U.S. Congressman, where he achieved national fame for leading a fight to desegregate Congressional facilities. In the press he was named "Mr. Civil Rights."

There were small concessions and cosmetic victories, but there was still no change in the basic situation. Afrikans were still being driven off the land, out of the industrial economy. Their Nation was being destabilized. In 1938 the great, spontaneous movement over the Italo-Ethiopian War swept the dispersed Afrikan Nation. Nationalist politics again revived in the Afrikan mainstream. Walter White, head of the NAACP, wrote of 1941: *"Discontent and bitterness were growing like wildfire among Negroes all over the Country."*[60]

THE MARCH ON WASHINGTON MOVEMENT

In this situation, their backs against the wall, the integrationist lead-ership was forced to put pressure on their imperialist masters. The A. Philip Randolphs and the Roy Wilkinses desperately needed some real concessions that they could take back to their community. They also saw that it was in a long-range sense in imperialism's own interest to make concessions, to ease up, to give Afrikan neocolo-nial leadership a stronger hand against revolutionary sentiments. It was out of this crisis that the March On Washington Movement was born.[61]

In early 1941 A. Philip Randolph, together with Walter White of the NAACP, called for a massive Afrikan demonstration in Washington, DC. The goal was to force the New Deal to integrate the military, and to open up jobs in defense industry and federal agencies. Randolph said: *"Black people will not get justice until the ad-ministration leaders in Washington see masses of Negroes—ten, twenty, fifty thousands—on the White House lawn."* This was to be the first Afrikan mass march on the Empire's capitol. It was a confrontation between imperialism and its own Afrikan allies.

The March On Washington Movement issued a "Call to Negro America to march on Washington for jobs and equal par-ticipation in a national defense on July 1, 1941":

> *"Dear fellow Negro Americans, be not dismayed in these terrible times. You possess power, great power. Our problem is to hitch it up for action on the broadest, daring and most gigantic scale ... shake up White America."*

President Roosevelt ignored the MOW demands. By June of 1941 there were strong signs that masses of Afrikans were preparing to come. Churches were chartering fleets of buses. Worried, the President's wife and Mayor LaGuardia met with Randolph in New York City, urging him to cancel the March. Mrs. Roosevelt told Randolph that there might be repression if the March took place. Besides, she said, "Such a march is impractical. You say you will be able to get 25,000 or more Negroes to come to Washington. Where will they stay, where will they eat?" Washington of 1941 was a Southern city, rigidly Jim Crow, with virtually no public facilities for "colored."

Mrs. Roosevelt had laid down one threat; Randolph politely answered with another: "Why, they'll stay in the hotels and eat in the restaurants." Randolph was threatening a massive breaking of the Color Bar, crowds of Afrikans pushing into "white" areas all over the capital—and the resultant "race riots" as thousands of Afrikans and settler police clashed! The stakes were high, and the integrationist leaders were preparing to have an open confrontation. That alone should tell us how critical their situation was. The very next day the White House invited the MOW leaders to come for negotiations on cancelling the March.

Randolph and Walter White met with President Roosevelt, who had brought in William Knudson, Chairman of General Motors, and Sidney Hillman of the CIO. The MOW leaders rejected the offer of the usual study commission. Finally, on June 24, 1941, the White House offered to meet Randolph's demands on employment. The next day Roosevelt signed Executive Order No. 8802, which for the first time ordered: "…there shall be no discrimination in the employment of workers in defense industries or government…" For the first time a Fair Employment Practices Commission (FEPC) was set up to pretend to do something about job discrimination. Randolph called the March off in a network radio address.

The threat of touching off the Afrikan masses had produced a surprising turnabout in public imperialist policy. The breakthrough was credited to Randolph, who became Amerika's officially-endorsed protest leader. He was showered with awards. The *Amsterdam News* said: "A. Philip Randolph, courageous champion of the rights of his people, takes the helm as the nation's No. 1 Negro leader … already he is being ranked with the great Frederick Douglass."[62]

As we know from the 1960s, these official promises of themselves mean very little in the way of real change. The gathering pressure from the masses below, the still unorganized militant nationalist sentiment building among the grassroots, had crowded, pushed on U.S. imperialism. A nodal point was being reached. Notice was taken that Afrikans were not willing to be passively starved. Further,

U.S. imperialism understood the meaning of the startling fact that even their chosen Afrikan allies could not shrug off the pressure from the Afrikan people on the streets, but had to either lead them into struggle or be left behind. Imperialism's contradiction was that it had to both strike down the Afrikan Nation—and also grant sufficient concessions to the Afrikan masses in order to stave off rebellion.

We must remember that there was a strong, rising tide of Afrikan struggle. The armed sharecropper outbreaks on the National Territory, the violent uprising that took over Harlem for three days, the mass anger that finally forced even imperialism's loyal Afrikan allies to make threats against it, all were convincing signs of even larger rebellion soon to come. Locked into a "rule-or-ruin" global war, could the U.S. Empire afford to also divert troops and energy to fight major colonial wars at home? This was the heat that finally bent even the iron rule of Empire.

THE NEED FOR COLONIAL LABOR

This contradiction was resolved through the specific form of "Americanization" imperialism enforced on Afrikans. The genocidal campaign to change the population balance and repressively disrupt the Afrikan South would continue without letup—but the pill would be sugar-coated. In Northern exile Afrikans could suddenly get not only "democracy" but "integration" into middle-wage jobs in industrial production.

The New Deal's willingness to "integrate" imperialist industry was a 180-degree turnabout from previously existing policy, and was also a tardy recognition that the unprecedented demands of waging a global war required the recruitment of colonial labor on a vast scale. These jobs were no "gift" from White Amerika, but a necessity forced upon it both by threat of revolt and by the urgent needs of world conquest.

The transformation was dramatic. Robert C. Weaver, one of Roosevelt's "Black Cabinet," wrote that the various rules that kept Afrikans out of industry were changed because: *"...after Pearl*

Harbor they were too costly—too costly for a nation at war to afford."[63]
He noted further:

> "This occupational pattern was slowly changing by 1942.
> While the majority of new colored workers were entering un-
> skilled and janitorial jobs, other Negroes were slowly finding
> jobs as welders, as riveters, and on other production opera-
> tions ... Negroes replaced white workers who formerly were
> employed as cooks, waiters, garage attendants ... and who
> now entered defense work."[64]

Between 1942 and 1944 the percentage of industrial labor that was
Afrikan tripled from 2.5% to 8%. By 1944 the numbers of Afrikan
skilled craftsmen had suddenly doubled, as had the numbers
of Afrikans in Federal civil service jobs. By 1945 the numbers of
Afrikans in the AFL and CIO unions had gone up some 600%, to
1.25 million. As Afrikan families left sharecropping and day labor in
the rural South and were forced up North, their incomes rose. Even
the lowliest factory job in Detroit or Chicago paid better than the
rural plantation. **The real average incomes of Afrikan workers rose
by 73% during 1939–1947, the largest gain in Afrikan income
since the end of slavery.**[65]

This was the material basis in mass life for neocolonial "Americanization." This sudden windfall of "white man's wages" was for some a convincing argument that loyalty to the U.S. Empire made sense. It allowed A. Philip Randolph and Rev. Adam Clayton Powell, Jr. to "prove" that their leadership paid off in cash—and that imperialist World War was "good" for Afrikans. *And, of course, this process once again reinforced the neocolonial ideology in which Third World people are told that they must look to the Federal government in Washington as their ultimate "friend" and protector.* Roosevelt just replaced Lincoln on the altar. The process sugarcoated the forced exodus from the Afrikan South, and even allowed pro-imperialist propaganda to assert that the depopulation of the Afrikan Nation was a "benefit" to Afrikans.

This "integration" into the main industrial economy, however dramatic its effects, only directly reached a minority of the nationally oppressed. For the first time, however, some significant number of colonial workers could struggle for the "American" lifestyle, with houses, automobiles, appliances, consumer items, college education for the children, and so on. Again, this was a semi-European standard of living—a miniaturized version of that of Euro-Amerikans, but materially well above that of other colonial peoples in Latin Amerika, Asia, and Afrika. Imperialism cared little that

most of the nationally oppressed here did not have those middle-wage jobs or the new petit-bourgeois positions opened up by token integration. What was important to imperialism was that these inviting possibilities for some created ideological confusion, pro-imperialist tendencies, and social disunity. They also were a magnet to draw people to the Northern industrial centers and out of the National Territory.

THE DISLOCATION OF IMPERIALIST WAR

Amerika's colonies were forced to bear a heavy—and often disproportionate—share of the human cost of World War II. This was no accident. The Roosevelt Administration promoted this "Americanization" of the nationally oppressed, pushing and pulling as many Puerto Ricans, Indians, Asians, Chicano-Mexicanos, and Afrikans as possible to become involved in the U.S. war effort. Not only because we were needed as cannon fodder and war industry labor, but because mass participation in the war disrupted our communities and encouraged pro-imperialist loyalties.

Close to a million Afrikans alone served in the U.S. military during the 1940s. When we think about what it would have meant to subtract a million soldiers, sailors, and airmen from the Empire's global efforts we can see how important colonial troops were. In many Third World communities the war burdens were very disproportionate. The Chinese community in New York, being so heavily unmarried men due to immigration laws, saw 40% of its total population drafted into the military.[66] In colonial Puerto Rico the imperialist draft drained the island; many did not return. One Puerto Rican writer recalls of his small town:

> "I saw many bodies of young Puerto Ricans in coffins covered with the American flag. They were brought in by military vehicles and placed in living rooms where they were mourned and viewed. The mournings never ceased in Salsipuedes!

> Almost every day I was awakened by the moans and wails of
> widows, parents, grandparents, and orphans whose loved one
> had died 'defending their country.'"[67]

The same was true in the Chicano-Mexicano Southwest. Acuña
notes that: "The percentage of Chicanos who served in the armed
forces was disproportionate to the percentage of Chicanos in the
general population." He further notes: *"Chicanos, however, can readily remember how families proudly displayed banners with blue stars
(each blue star representing a family member in the armed forces). Many
families had as many as eight stars, with fathers, sons, and uncles all serving the U.S. war effort. Everyone recalls the absence of men between the
ages of 17 through 30 in the barrios. As the war progressed, gold stars
replaced the blue (gold representing men killed in action), giving the barrios the appearance of a sea of death."[68]*

Third World people were told, in effect, that if they helped the
U.S. Empire win its greatest war, then at long last they too would
get a share of the "democracy" as a reward. In every oppressed nation and national minority, many elements mobilized to push this
deal. We should note that those political forces most opposed to this
ideological "Americanization" were driven under or rendered inef-
fective by severe repression.

Civil Rights leaders fell all over themselves in urging their
people to go kill and die for the U.S. Empire. The rhetorical contor-
tions were amazing. A. Philip Randolph, the supposed socialist, said
that Afrikans should enlist in the admittedly unjust war in order to
reform it! He admitted that: "This is not a war for freedom ... It is
a war between the imperialism of Fascism and Nazism and the imperialism of monopoly capitalistic democracy." But, he told Afrikan
workers, by getting an integrated war effort "the people can make
it a peoples' revolution."[69] An avowed pacifist and advocate of total
Afrikan nonviolence in the U.S., Randolph nevertheless said that it
was right for Afrikans to fight in Asia and Europe.

Following the same "Two Front War" thesis, Rev. Adam
Clayton Powell, Jr. enthusiastically agreed that the Japanese attack
on "our" base at Pearl Harbor forced Afrikans to fight—so long as
the government was going to give them integration:

> "On December 7, 1941, America for the first time in its his-
> tory entered upon two wars simultaneously. One was a world
> war and the other a civil war. One was to be a bloody fight
> for the preservation and extension of democracy on a world
> basis—the other a bloodless revolution within these shores
> against a bastard democracy.

> "The sneak attack of the Japanese upon our mid-Pacific
> base was no more vicious than the open attacks that had
> been waged consistently for four hundred years against the
> Declaration of Independence, the Constitution and the Bill of
> Rights."[70]

Taking part in the imperialist war was praised as patriotic—not only
to the U.S. but to "the race." By Asians or Chicano-Mexicanos or
Afrikans serving in the U.S. military we were supposedly helping
our peoples "earn" full citizenship rights by "proving" our loyalty to
Amerika. So the war period saw strange contradictions.

Perhaps the sharpest irony of the "win your freedom" game
was that of Japanese-Americans. We were drafted right out of the
U.S. concentration camps and told that our willingness to fight for
U.S. imperialism would show whether or not our people were "dis-
loyal." The all-Japanese military unit, the 442nd Regimental Combat
Team, was used by the U.S. Army as disposable shock troops to be
thrown into every bloody situation in Europe. The 442nd had over
9,000 Purple Hearts awarded for a 3,000-soldier unit.

Ordered to break through and rescue the "Lost Battalion" of
Texas National Guard settlers cut off and surrounded by the German
Army in France, the 442nd took more casualties than the number of
settler GIs saved. One Nisei sergeant remembers how K Company
of the 442nd *"went in with 187 men and when we got to the Texans,
there were 17 of us left. I was in command, because all the officers were
gone. But I Company was down to 8 men."*[71]

The political effects of the war were not simple. It definitely
marked the end of one period and the start of another. The Depression
had been replaced by the fruits of military victory—high employment fueled by new world markets and U.S. international supremacy.

The massive dislocation of the war, coming after the harsh repression of the 1930s and the war period itself, and the jet-propelled rise of neocolonial "citizenship" had definitely sidetracked many people. Acuña writes of the Chicano-Mexicano movement:

> "...much of the momentum of the movement of the 1930s was lost. Many Chicano leaders entered the armed forces; many were killed; others, when they returned, were frankly tired of crusades ... Understandably, during the war and when they returned, many Chicano veterans were proud of their records. They believed that they were entitled to all the benefits and rights of U.S. citizenship. A sort of euphoria settled among many Chicanos, with only a few realizing that the community had to reorganize ... Many Chicanos believed the propaganda emanating from World War II about brotherhood and democracy in the United States. They thought that they had won their rights as U.S. citizens. For a time, the GI Bill of Rights lulled many Chicanos into complacency, with many taking advantage of education and housing benefits...
>
> *"Many Chicanos, because of their involvement in the armed forces, realized that they would never return to Mexico. Many also became superpatriots who did not want to be identified with the collective community. In the urban barrio, many parents, remembering their own tribulations, taught their children only English. Middle-class organizations and, for that matter, civic organizations became increasingly integrationist in the face of the Red-baiting of the 1950s."*[72]

The neocolonial pacification that came out of the WWII years was not a calm, but the stillness that came after devastation. We must remember how, once again, in the Deep South returning Afrikan GIs were singled out for assassination by the KKK. In the Chicano-Mexicano Southwest the Empire conducted a genocidal mass deportation drive of unequaled severity. Even the savage immigration raids and deportations of the New Deal were outdone by the new imperialist offensive after WWII.

Believing that the wartime labor shortage had permitted "too many" Chicano-Mexicanos to live inside the occupied territories, the Empire started a gigantic military campaign to partially depopulate and terrorize the Southwest. Under the cover of the 1952 McCarran-Walter Immigration and Nationality Act, a reign of armed terror descended upon the Chicano-Mexicano communities. This was CIA population regroupment strategy in textbook form.

Command of the campaign was held by INS Commissioner Lt. General Joseph Swing (an open racist and a veteran of Gen. Pershing's U.S. expedition into Mexico in 1916). Swing organized a series of barrio sweeps, with pedestrians stopped and homes broken into; often without hearing or any bourgeois legal formalities, the selected Mexicanos would be taken at gunpoint to trains and deported. Homes were broken up and communities terrorized. Some with valid residency papers and U.S. "citizenship" were deported. Others, suspected of being revolutionaries, were arrested for "immigration" offenses. Virtually all the militant Chicano-Mexicano labor activists were victims of this campaign.

The overall numbers are staggering. In 1953 Swing's paramilitary units deported 875,000 Mexicanos. In 1954 the number seized and deported was 1,035,282—more than were deported throughout the 1930s. Even in 1955 and 1956, after the main job was done, 256,000 and 90,000 Mexicanos respectively were deported. How massive this was can be seen from the fact that in 1941 an estimated 2.7 million Chicano-Mexicanos lived in the U.S.-occupied territories, while the 1953–56 population regroupment drive uprooted and deported 2.2 million Chicano-Mexicanos. This was the fruit of "The War for Democracy."

The Chinese community, which had been largely spared during WWII, was the target of a new repressive campaign. The U.S. Empire had discovered that the imperialist contradictions of World War had helped communism and national liberation advance. Long sought-after China had stood up and brushed off the clutching hands of U.S. imperialism. In 1945 over 50,000 U.S. Marines landed in China to take over Peking, the Kailan coal mines, and the North China railroad lines. By 1946 there were over 120,000 GIs in China, backing up the reactionary Kuomintang armies. The Red Army and the

Chinese people swept these forces away.

During the war years the Empire had professed friendship towards the Chinese community, since China itself was an Allied nation in the war against Japan. Now the situation reversed itself: Japan was the new U.S. "junior partner" in Asia, while Communist China was hated and feared by imperialism. The FBI and INS moved against the Chinese community, breaking up patriotic and class organizations.

The main patriotic mass organization of the 1930s and 1940s, the Chinese Hand Laundry Association, was destroyed. The popular China Youth Club, which had fought gambling, drugs, and sexism by introducing a modern community life, was forcibly dissolved as a "communist front." *China Daily News,* which had been the leading patriotic newspaper, lost most of its advertising and readers. In a frameup, the newspaper's manager was imprisoned under the Federal "Trading With the Enemy Act" because the newspaper had accepted an advertisement from the Bank of China. **The supposedly "silent" Chinese community had actually been a stronghold of activity for national liberation and socialism—and was silenced.**[73]

IMPERIALIST CIVIL RIGHTS

It is also true that this genocidal campaign illustrated how well neocolonial "Americanization" served imperialism. Once, in the early years of the century, oppressed Mexicano and Japanese workers shared the hardships of the fields, and naturally shared labor organizing drives. In the abortive 1915 Texas uprising to establish a Chicano-Mexicano Nation, Japanese were recognized as not only allies but as citizens of the to-be-liberated nation. But by the 1950s this had changed. Civil Rights had replaced the unity of the oppressed.

The Japanese-American national minority had been politically broken by the repression of World War II. Uprooted and recombined into scattered concentration camps, we had faced an intense physical and psychological terrorism. The resistance and defiance, even while in the hands of the enemy, was considerable. Many of the camp inmates refused to sign U.S. loyalty oaths. Demonstrations took place behind barbed wire. Some 10% were under even harsher incarceration at the Tule Lake Camp for dissidents and resisters. But this popular current of resistance had no strategic direction to advance along.

The main dissenting political views had been crushed. Some Japanese rejected U.S. "citizenship" and the oppressor nation that had imprisoned them, but sought their identity by looking backwards towards the Japanese Empire. Clandestine pro-Imperial groups and propaganda flourished. Claims of U.S. military advances were denied and the day of Japanese Imperial victory eagerly looked forward to. The unconditional Japanese surrender in 1945, plus the news of Hiroshima and Nagasaki, made a vain hope out of this perspective.

The other major dissenting view was communism. A number of young Japanese college students and union activists had joined the CPUSA during the 1930s. Japanese-American communists had been very active in CIO organizing drives in the fish canneries, in opposing the Imperial invasion of China, and in rallying people to fight anti-Asian oppression. All this had been smashed on Dec. 7, 1941, when Pearl Harbor happened. In a panic to assure their fellow Euro-Amerikans that the CPUSA was loyally "American," this revisionist party came out in *full support of the government's concentration camp program for Japanese-Americans.* Even further, the CPUSA ordered its Japanese-American members to rally the community for its own imprisonment—*and then publicly expelled all its Japanese-American members to show White Amerika that even the "Communists" were against the "Japs."* Communism was completely discredited for an entire generation inside the Japanese-American community.

Leadership of the community was left completely in the hands of the pro-imperialist Japanese-American Citizens League (JACL), which for forty years has been the main Civil Rights organization. The JACL, in the name of those who suffered in the concentration camps, publicly called for and lobbied for the passage of the 1952 McCarran-Walter Immigration & Nationality Act. This was in the best tradition of "Americanization," and, for that matter, of Civil Rights.

In 1952 A. Philip Randolph was saying that civil rights meant that Afrikans should go to Korea and help U.S. imperialism kill Asians—provided that the Empire gave them equal wages. In the same way, in 1952 the JACL was saying that so long as Japanese-Americans got some benefits from it, white supremacist depopulation of the Chicano-Mexicano communities was fine. This is the sewer philosophy of "I've Got Mine."

Having mutilated themselves to fit into Babylon, the JACL is even quite proud of what they did. U.S. Senator Pat McCarran (D-Nevada) was a white supremacist, and a known Mexican-hater. He devised his new immigration law to genocidally cut down Third World population in general (and Chicano-Mexicanos in specific). He warned White Amerika that unless they restricted Third World population "we will, in the course of a generation or so, change the ethnic and cultural composition of this nation." In his crusade for settler purity he joined forces with Congressman Francis Walter, the Chairman of the rabid House Un-American Activities Committee (HUAC).[74]

Congressman Walter was, of course, a fanatical anti-Communist. Led by Mike Masaoka, the JACL developed a close relationship to Congressman Walter. In any case, JACL leader Bill Hosokawa called Walter *"a strong friend of the JACL."* The JACL eventually gave Walter a special award. Walter and McCarran added clauses in their repressive legislation giving some concessions to Asians—primarily ending the 1924 Oriental Exclusion Act—which made it possible for non-citizen Japanese to become U.S. citizens. With this the JACL was glad to help sponsor this vicious legislation and give cover to the reactionary wing of U.S. imperialism. Hosokawa, who has been a senior editor for the *Denver Post,* writes that the final passage of this repressive law was *"a supreme triumph"* of the JACL.[75] Two million Mexicano men, women, and children, victims of "Migra" terror raids, saw very well whose "triumph" that was.

That's why the shallow rhetoric that says all Third World people automatically "unite against racism" is dangerously untrue. Pro-imperialist civil rights is a pawn in the crimes of the Empire against the oppressed nations. The example of the JACL was just the opening wedge of a strategic process in which the Empire was promoting

Asians as a "buffer" between settlers and the oppressed nations. We can see this in daily life, by the numbers of Asian professionals and small retailers entering the inner city. This process began, however, with Japanese-Americans in the years right after World War II.

A PAUSE AND A BEGINNING

It may have appeared to some in those years that the U.S. Empire had consolidated its Fortress Amerika, that it had won "a supreme triumph." But the streams of national consciousness ran deep within the colonial masses. If the Adam Clayton Powells and the Roy Wilkinses occupied the public mainstream of Afrikan politics, we can see that nationalism was only forced down out of sight. It still lived in the grassroots and continued to develop. This pause was historically necessary, since anti-colonial struggles and leaders of the 1920s and 1930s had many strengths, but did not yet have programs for liberation that could successfully lead the masses. Now we can see that this was a stage in development, in opening up new doors. And so we can also see literally everywhere we choose to look, the "seeds beneath the snow."

An Afrikan GI named Robert Williams went home from Asia to Monroe, North Carolina, having learned something about self-defense and world politics. In Los Angeles in the early '40s Chicano teenagers formed the *Pachuco* youth subculture, flaunting "Zoot suits" and openly rejecting Euro-Amerikan culture. Chicano-Mexicano historians now see the defiant *Pachuco* movement as "the first large current within the Chicano movement towards separatism." An Afrikan ex-convict and draft resister was building the "Nation of the Lost-Found." The revolutionary explosions of the 1960s had their seeds, in countless ways, in the submerged but not lost gains and developments of the 1920s, 1930s, and 1940s.

X

1950s Repression and the Decline of the Communist Party U.S.A.

1. The End of the Euro-Amerikan "Left"

The post–World War II collapse of the Communist Party USA, the main organization of the Euro-Amerikan "left," was an important indicator of disappearing working class consciousness in the oppressor nation. *It is not true that the Euro-Amerikan "left" was destroyed by the McCarthyite repression of the 1950s.* What was true was that the anti-Communist repression effortlessly shattered the decaying, hollow shell of the '30s "old left"—hollow because the white workers who once gave it at least a limited vitality had left. The class struggle within the oppressor nation had once again effectively ended. Mass settler unity in service of the U.S. Empire was heightened.

Looking back we can see the Communist Party USA in that period as a mass party for reformism that penetrated every sector of Euro-American life. At its numerical peak in 1944–1945 the CPUSA had close to 100,000 members. Approximately one-quarter of the entire CIO union membership was within those industrial unions that it directly led. Thousands of Communist Party trade union activists and officials were present throughout the union movement, from shop stewards up to the CIO Executive Council.

The Party's influence among the liberal intelligentsia in the '30s was just as large. Nathan Witt, chief executive officer of the Federal National Labor Relations Board during 1937–1940, was a CPUSA member. Tens of thousands of administrators, school teachers, scientists, social workers, writers, and officials belonged to the CPUSA. That was a period in which writers as prominent as Ernest Hemingway and artists such as Rockwell Kent and Ben Shahn contributed to CPUSA publications. Prominent modern dancers gave benefit performances in Greenwich Village for the *Daily Worker.* Maxim Lieber, one of the most exclusive Madison Avenue literary agents (with clients like John Cheever, Carson McCullers, John O'Hara, and Langston Hughes), was not only a CPUSA member, but was using his business as a cover to send clandestine communications between New York and Eastern Europe. The CPUSA, then, was a common presence in Euro-American life, from the textile mills to Hollywood.[1]

This seeming success story only concealed the growing alienation from the CPUSA by the white workers who had once started it. In the early 1920s the infant Communist Party was overwhelmingly European immigrant proletarian. In its first year half of its members spoke no English—for that matter, two-thirds of the total Party then were Finnish immigrants who had left the Social Democracy and the IWW to embrace Bolshevism. Virtually all the rest were Russian, Polish, Jewish, Latvian, and other East European immigrants. The CPUSA was once a white proletarian party not just in words but in material fact.

The rapid expansion of the Party's influence and size during the late '30s and the World War II years was an illusion. Euro-Amerikans were not fighting for Revolution but for settleristic reforms, and those years the CPUSA was just the radical wing of President Roosevelt's New Deal. As soon as Euro-Amerikan industrial workers had won the settler equality and better life they sought, they had no more use for the CPUSA.

The facts about the changing class base of the CPUSA are very clear. Between 1939 and 1942 the number of CPUSA members in the steel mills fell from over 2,000 to 852; the number of CPUSA miners fell from 1,300 to 289. Similar losses took place among the Party's ranks in construction, garment, auto, and textile. And while more and more workers drifted away from the Euro-Amerikan "left," the CPUSA was swelling up with a junk food diet of rapid recruitment from the petit-bourgeoisie. Middle class members composed only 5% of the Party in 1932, but an astonishing 41% in 1938 (a proportion soon to go even higher). By World War II 50% of the CPUSA's membership was in New York, and the typical member a New York City professional or minor trade union official.[2]

Joseph Starobin, CPUSA leader, later admitted: "In retrospect, the war had been for thousands of Communists a great turning point. Many from the cities came for the first time to grasp America's magnitude, the immense political space between the labor-democratic-progressive milieu in which the left had been sheltered and the real level of consciousness of the millions who were recruited to fight for flag and country. A good part of the Party's cadre never returned to its life and orbit. The war was a caesura, a break. Many migrated to other parts of the country, many began to build families and change their lives. Communism became a warm memory for some; for others it was a mistake."[3]

So we can be certain that there was no repression involved in ending the radical current within the masses of Euro-Amerikan workers. Long before McCarthyism was spawned, during the very years of the 1930s when the CPUSA reached its greatest organizational power, Euro-Amerikan workers started voluntarily walking out. By 1945 it was definite. Nor did they leave for other radical parties or more revolutionary activity. This is one of the reasons why the crudely revisionist policies of CPUSA leaders like Earl Browder and William Z. Foster were never effectively opposed—the working class supporters of the Party had lost interest in reformism and were leaving to occupy themselves with the fruits of settlerism.

2. McCarthyism & Repression

The false view that the CPUSA (and the rest of the Euro-Amerikan "left") were crushed by "McCarthyite repression" not only serves to conceal the mass shift away from class consciousness on the part of the settler masses, but also helped U.S. imperialism to conceal the violent colonial struggles of that period. The post-war years were the Golden Age of the U.S. Empire, when it tried to enforce its "Pax Americana" on a devastated world.

We are really discussing *three* related but different phenomena—

1. Cold War political repression aimed at limiting pro-Russian sympathies among liberal and radical "New Deal" Euro-Amerikans,

2. the McCarthyite purges of the U.S. government itself in an intra-imperialist policy struggle, and

3. the violent, terroristic counterinsurgency campaigns to crush revolutionary struggles throughout the expanded U.S. Empire.

It is a particular trait of Euro-Amerikan "left" revisionism to blur these three phenomena together, while picturing itself as the main victim of U.S. Imperialism. This is an outrageous lie.

When we actually analyze the repression of the CPUSA it is striking how mild it was—more like a warning from the Great White Father than repression. In contrast, the Euro-American "left" pictures its role as one of steadfast and heroic sacrifice against the unleashed imperialist juggernaut. Len DeCaux, a former CPUSA activist who was Publicity Director of the national CIO, recalls in self-congratulation:

"...The United States was now officially launched on a bipartisan Cold War course with the appearance of a popular mandate. Every vote against it was a protest, a promise of resistance. Without this effort, few American progressives could have held up their heads … Like those Germans who resisted the advent of Hitlerism, the Americans who opposed Cold War imperialism were overwhelmed, almost obliterated. Perhaps they were not 'smart' to throw their weak bodies, their strong minds, their breakable spirits, against the trampling onrush of reaction. But they did."[4]

This is easy to check out. DeCaux says that he and his CPUSA compatriots were *"almost obliterated"* just *"like those Germans who resisted the advent of Hitlerism."* Just to throw some light on his comparison, we should note that the casualty rate of the German Communist underground against Nazism was almost 100%. Hundreds of thousands of German Communists and Communists from other European nations died in actual battle against the Nazis and in the Nazi death camps. In Italy alone the Communists lost 60,000 comrades in the 1943–45 armed partisan struggle against Fascism. Were DeCaux and his CPUSA compatriots *"almost obliterated"* like other Communists who *fought* imperialism?

In 1947 DeCaux was forced out of his comfortable job as Publicity Director of the CIO (and editor of the union newspaper "CIO News"). For many years thereafter he worked as a paid journalist for the CPUSA in California. He was never beaten or tortured, never faced assassination from the death squads, never had to outwit the police, never had to spend long years of his life in prison, never knew hunger and misery, never saw his family destroyed, never was prevented from exercising his rights as a settler. Throughout, he went to public demonstrations and worked in bourgeois elections. DeCaux *was* arrested and had to face trial (he won on appeal while out on bail), had to give up his prestigious job and salary, and was threatened by U.S. government disapproval. Truly, we could say that the average welfare family in "Bed-Stuy" faces *more repression* than DeCaux went through.

The U.S. government repression that *"almost obliterated"* the CPUSA (in DeCaux's words) was a series of warnings, of mild cuffs, to push Euro-Amerikans back into line with imperialist policy against the USSR. There were no death squads, no shoot-outs,

Robert Thompson and Benjamin J. Davis, CPUSA leaders charged under Smith Act in 1949, surrounded by supporters.

no long prison sentences—the CPUSA wasn't even outlawed, and published its newspaper and held activities throughout this period.

The CPUSA at the time usually called this repression a "witch hunt," because it was a government campaign to promote mass political conformity by singling out "Communists" for public abuse and scorn. It was not repression of the usual type, in which the Empire tries to *wipe out,* to *eliminate* through legal and extra-legal force an entire revolutionary movement. In 1949 some 160 CPUSAers were arrested and tried under the Smith Act for advocating "the over-throw of the U.S. government through force and violence." Of these 114 were convicted, with 29 CPUSA leaders serving Federal prison sentences of 2–5 years. Two obscure CPUSA members, Julius and Ethel Rosenberg, were executed amidst worldwide publicity in an "atomic espionage" hysteria. Some 400 non-citizen radicals, most of them Third World members or allies of the CPUSA, were arrested for deportation under the McCarran-Walter Immigration Act of 1952. Many of these radicals later won in court.[5]

This warning harassment by Washington totally broke the back of a supposedly "Communist" Party that counted 70,000 members in its ranks in 1947. *In contrast, the American Indian Movement just at Pine Ridge sustained casualties between 1972–1976 that were quantitatively greater than that of the CPUSA coast-to-coast during the entire 1950s.* At Pine Ridge alone AIM has lost over ninety members killed and over 200 imprisoned. The Nationalist Party of Puerto Rico in 1950–1957 alone suffered many times the losses in dead, injured, and imprisoned than those borne by the CPUSA during the entire McCarthyite period. For that matter, both SNCC and the BPP alone also sustained far greater casualties from struggle in the 1960s than the whole CPUSA did during the 1950s. What was so great, so large, so historic about the slap that the CPUSA suffered was the loud panic it caused among the pampered Euro-Amerikan "left." "An empty drum makes the loudest noise."

This mild repression knocked the CPUSA clear off its tracks. In a panic, their leadership concocted the delusional "one minute to midnight" perspective, which held that world nuclear war and total fascism were about to happen. Peggy Dennis, wife of party leader Gene Dennis, recalls the shambles of their focus on survivalism:

"The FBI knew, the news media knew, the remnants of the Peoples' movements knew. Our Party had taken a severe beating under the assaults of McCarthyism, the Smith Act arrests and imprisonments, the continuing anti-Communist hysteria. It was reeling on the defensive. But the almost fatal blow was self-inflicted when the Party leadership took the whole organization underground, placing control of daily operative financial and political decision-making into the hands of this subterranean structure. [...]

"Thousands of militants — in the labor movement, former anti-fascists, New Dealers, Progressive Party activists, former Communist members — went into personal 'underground,' dropping out of all activity, rebuilding lives in enclaves of suburban and urban obscurity."[6]

What was most telling is that for 4 years the CPUSA structure went underground not to wage renewed and heightened struggle, but to passively hide until full bourgeois democracy returned. Their whole movement surrendered and fell apart under the first pressure from Washington. They never even faced any real repression.

When Russian Prime Minister Khrushchev made his disillusioning revelations about Stalin's rule at the 1956 20th Party Congress of the CPSU, it was just "the icing on the cake." Once a white workers vanguard and later a mass party for reform within the oppressor nation, the CPUSA had finally been reduced by U.S. imperialism to a thoroughly housebroken and frightened remnant. From 70,000 members in 1947 the CPUSA evaporated down to 7,000 in 1957. Working class radicalism had effectively ceased within the settler society, and its former main organization had politically collapsed.

The capitalist newspaper headlines of that day paid little attention to that phenomenon, however. The media of the late 1940s and early 1950s was preoccupied with the larger aspects of this same imperialist campaign to whip up Euro-Amerikan society for the global confrontation with communism. The bourgeoisie then demanded only the most rigid, reactionary, and monolithic outlook from its settler followers. All had to fall in line. This McCarthyism was aimed not so much at the bottom of settler society but at the middle—at purging the ranks of generals, educators, congressmen, diplomats, and so on. All government employees had to sign new loyalty oaths. *We must remember that the infamous U.S. Senator Joseph McCarthy never harassed revolutionaries.* His targets were all U.S. government employees and officials, from Army officers to clerks. In a telling statement, the well-known liberal journalist George Seldes wrote at the time:

> "There is fear in Washington, not only among government employees but among the few remaining liberals and democrats who hoped to salvage something in the New Deal. There is fear in Hollywood ... There is fear among writers, scientists, school teachers, among all who are not part of the reactionary movement."[7]

So that McCarthyism reflected a power struggle within the imperialist ranks between liberal and conservative forces, as well as being part of the general move of the Empire to tighten up and prepare for world domination. In no sense was this 1950s repressive campaign directed at crushing some non-existent revolutionary upsurge within settler society. At the same time—on fronts of battle *outside* of Euro-Amerikan society—U.S. imperialism was conducting the most bloody counterinsurgency campaigns against the colonial peoples. This had little to do with the CPUSA and the rest of the oppressor nation "left."

3. The Case of Puerto Rico: Clearing the Ground for Neocolonialism

It is generally known that U.S. imperialism chose neocolonialism as the main form for its expanding Empire in the immediate post-WWII years. In 1946 the U.S. Philippine colony was converted with much fanfare to the supposedly independent "Republic of the Philippines" (to this day occupied by major U.S. military bases). In 1951 the Puerto Rican colony was converted into a "Commonwealth" with limited bourgeois self-government under strict U.S. rule. What is less discussed is that neocolonialism is no less terroristic than colonialism itself. Neocolonialism, after all, still requires the military suppression and elimination of the revolutionary and national democratic forces. Without this political sterilization after WWII imperialism's local agents would not have been able to do their job. This was true in the Mexicano-Chicano Southwest, in the Philippines, and other occupied territories.

The 1950 U.S. counterinsurgency campaign in Puerto Rico is a clear example of this. It also gives us a comparison to further illuminate the CPUSA by. By 1950 U.S. imperialism had decided that its hold over Puerto Rico would not be safe until the Nationalist Party was finally wiped out. That year U.S. Secretary of War Louis Johnson spent three days in Puerto Rico planning the counterinsurgency campaign. The puppet Governor, Munoz Marin, was told to arrest or kill the Nationalist leaders. Police pressure on the revolutionaries increased. Nationalist Party leader Don Albizu Campos was openly threatened. U.S. Congressman Vito Marcantonio complained on October 19, 1949:

> "The home of Pedro Albizu Campos is surrounded day and night by police patrols, police cars, and jeeps with mounted machine guns. When Dr. Albizu Campos walks along the streets of San Juan, he is closely followed by four or five plainclothes policemen on foot, and a load of fully armed policemen in a car a few paces behind.

> *"Every shop he enters, every person to whom he talks, is subsequent-*
> *ly visited by representatives of the police department. A reign of*
> *terror descends on the luckless citizens of Puerto Rico who spend a*
> *few minutes talking to Dr. Albizu Campos."*[8]

By late October of that year the colonial police had begun a series of "incidents"—of ever more serious arrests and raids against
Nationalist Party activists on various charges. Finally in one raid police and Nationalists engaged in a firefight. Faced with certain annihilation piecemeal by mounting police attacks, the Nationalists took
to arms in the *Grito de Jayuya*. On October 30, 1950, Nationalist
forces captured the police station and liberated the town of Jayuya.
They immediately proclaimed the Second Republic of Puerto Rico,
as more uprisings broke out all over the island.[9]

The defeat of the Second Republic required not only the police,
but the full efforts of the colonial National Guard. It was an uprising
drowned in blood. The seriousness of the combat can be seen from
the Associated Press dispatch:

> *"National Guard troops smashed today at violently anti–United*
> *States Nationalist rebels and drove them out of two of their strong-*
> *holds with planes and tanks...*
>
> *"Striking at dawn, troops armed with machine guns, bazookas*
> *and tanks recaptured Jayuya, fifty miles southwest of San Juan,*
> *and the neighboring town of Utuado. Fighter planes strafed the*
> *rebels. They had seized control of the two towns last night after*
> *bombing police stations, killing some policemen and setting many*
> *fires ... Jayuya looked as if an earthquake had struck it, with sev-*
> *eral blocks destroyed and most of the other buildings in the town*
> *of 1,500 charred by fire. Another Guard spearhead was racing*
> *towards Arecibo to crush the uprising there."*[10]

Even in defeat the heroic Nationalist struggle had great effect. In
the 1951 referendum for "Commonwealth" status Governor Marin
could only muster enough votes for passage by falsely promising
the people that it was only a temporary stage leading to national

independence. The revolution had exposed the lie that colonialism was accepted by the Puerto Rican people. Throughout Latin Amerika mass solidarity with the Puerto Rican Struggle blossomed. In Cuba the cause of Puerto Rican independence had won such sympathy that even the pro-U.S. Cuban President, Carlos Prio Socarras, sent off a public message interceding for the safety of Don Albizu Campos and the other Nationalists. The Cuban House of Representatives sent a resolution to President Truman asking that the lives of Don Albizu Campos and other captured leaders be guaranteed.[11] In Mexico, in Central Amerika, throughout Latin Amerika the 1950 *Grito de Jayuya* stirred up anti-imperialist sentiment.

The defeat of the patriotic uprising was followed by an intense reign of terror over all of Puerto Rico. In addition to the many martyrs who fell on the field of battle, some 3,000 Puerto Ricans were arrested by U.S. imperialism. Many were sent to prison under the infamous "Little Smith Act" (the 1948 Law 53), which made it a crime to advocate revolution against the colonial administration. Many were charged with murder, arson, and other crimes. One woman, for example, was sentenced to life imprisonment for having cooked some food for her husband and sons before they went to join the uprising. The neocolonial "Commonwealth" scheme was only possible because of the terroristic violence used by U.S. imperialism to pacify the patriotic movement and the Puerto Rican masses.

It isn't difficult to see that the level of imperialist repression inflicted upon the Puerto Rican Nationalists was qualitatively far greater than that used on the CPUSA. It is somewhat obscene to even compare the two. It is enough to say that U.S. Imperialism had to use tanks, air attacks, machine guns, mass imprisonment, and terror to crush the Puerto Rican Nationalists, for they were genuine revolutionaries.

What did the CPUSA and the U.S. oppressor nation "left" do in solidarity to help their supposed allies in Puerto Rico? Absolutely nothing and less than nothing. The CPUSA's main response was to concern itself only with saving its own skin. The single Euro-Amerikan imprisoned with the Nationalists after Jayuya—the anti-war activist Ruth Reynolds—did more in solidarity with the anti-colonial struggle than did the entire CPUSA with its thousands of members.

For years during the 1930s the CPUSA had won support from Puerto Ricans in the barrios of the continental U.S. by posing as proponents of Puerto Rican independence. In order to win over Puerto Ricans the CPUSA pretended to be allies of the Nationalist Party. One Euro-Amerikan CPUSA organizer in New York's Spanish Harlem recalls: *"The main issues were unemployment and Puerto Rican independence. 'Viva Puerto Rico Libre' was the popular slogan. The Nationalist movement in Puerto Rico, headed by Pedro Albizu Campos, dominated the politics of 'El Barrio.'"*[12] In 1948 CPUSA leader William Z. foster made a well-publicized trip to Puerto Rico, in which he met with Don Albizu Campos. Afterwards, Foster wrote a mass pamphlet on poverty in Puerto Rico (*The Crime of El Fangito*) to show CPUSA solidarity with the Nationalists.

But when U.S. Imperialism unleashed its counterinsurgency, when the Revolution joined battle with the mighty U.S. Empire, where was the CPUSA? On its knees proclaiming its loyalty to the U.S. Empire, begging in the most cowardly fashion to be spared by its masters. On November 1, 1950—the second day of fighting—two Puerto Rican patriots, Griselio Torresola and Oscar Collazo, attacked Blair House in Washington, DC (the temporary residence of President Truman). This bold, sacrificial action against the U.S. tyranny occupied the headlines in newspapers around the world. Joining the rest of the oppressor nation media the CPUSA's *Daily Worker* also made the heroic attack on Blair House its main, front-page story.

This issue is completely revealing. Tucked away on its inside pages, as a second-rate story, the CPUSA's *Daily Worker* routinely reported the revolution in Puerto Rico and gave some very routine, lukewarm words of sympathy. But on its front page it carried an official Party statement on the Blair House attack. That statement was signed by CPUSA leaders William Z. Foster and Gus Hall. It was not only under a major headline, but the full text was printed in extra-large heavy type. And what was the meaning of this obviously very important statement? A cowardly and shameful slander of the heroic patriots Torresola and Collazo, and a cowardly assurance that the CPUSA joined ranks with the rest of their oppressor nation in supporting President Truman. The treacherous statement read:

CP ASSAILS TERRORIST ATTEMPT IN WASHINGTON

"Like all our fellow Americans we Communists were profoundly shocked by this afternoon's report of an attempt to enter Blair House with the apparent purpose of taking President Truman's life.

"As is well known, the Communist Party condemns and rejects assassination and all acts of violence and terror. This can only be the act of terrorists, deranged men, or agents..."[13]

With war raging in Puerto Rico, was it a shock for the struggle to be brought to the front door of imperialism? What kind of "Communists" reject *"all acts of violence"*? What kind of "anti-imperialists" would join the imperialists in saying that the martyr Griselio Torresola, who so willingly gave his life for the oppressed, was either *"deranged"* or an *"agent"*? This disgusting statement was transparently begging U.S. imperialism to spare the CPUSA. Far from being the main victims of the 1950s repression, as they so falsely claim, the Euro-American "left" were still housebroken accomplices to the crimes of U.S. imperialism. They were the U.S. Empire's loyal opposition.

GRISELIO TORRESOLA LIES DEAD FOLLOWING ATTACK ON BLAIR HOUSE.

"We Have Nothing to Repent"

Four Puerto Rican terrorists go home to a heroes' welcome

For a brief moment last week San Juan's international airport took on the atmosphere of a revolutionary carnival as some 5,000 Puerto Ricans gathered... Airline 132...

For nearly an hour the nationalists hammered home the need for unity among independence supporters. The sympathetic audience interrupted frequently with bursts of applause. From the...

Lebrón kneels at grave of Nationalist Hero Pedro Albizu Campos

PUERTO RICO IS AMERICA.

It's serving our country.

Puerto Rico's Air National Guard calls itself the watchdogs on the Caribbean. For five straight years, this unit had the best safety record in America.

gement skills.

nesses have come to
rto Rican leader-
tzational abilities
on, in marketing,
anking and legal
matters.

Terrorist bombs hit 8 planes at U.S. base

Guard planes blown up in Puerto Rico

From Sun-Times Wires
SAN JUAN, Puerto Rico—Bombs blew seven to 10 Air National Guard planes in quick succession early Monday at Muñiz Base next to San Juan's Isla Verde tional Airport, police said.

No one was hurt and there was speculation the attack was ate claim of responsibility independence group draft or the U.S. Rico.

The plan apart on and

e Texas, we're simply a different America. Our heritage is h, but our virtues are strictly me town. Walk through any town, any city ico. You'll see Spanish tile roofs and Spanish gns. But the people you meet will seem familiar

to you. We're American citizens. Every one of us.

We're ambitious for ourselves and our families, just like other Americans. We work hard. We work skillfully. We're proud of our way of life, and we're ready to protect it. Our voluntary enlistments in all U.S. Armed Service branches far outpace the national average.

We're productive. And we're committed to our

Which is why made Puerto

and less absen-
there's an ever-
the second
th largest con-

tainer shipping facility in the world.

In skill, in motivation, in the business environment, Puerto Rico is America. Puerto Rico and industry is a partnership that works.

Puerto Rico, U.S.A.
The ideal second home for American Business.

There have been 5 wars and 17 military coups; there emerged a diabolical dictator who carried out, in God's name, the first Latin American ethnocide of our time. In the meantime, 20 million Latin American children died before the age of one—more than have been born in Europe since 1970.

Those missing because of repression number nearly 120,000, which is as if no one could account for all the inhabitants of Upsala. Numerous women arrested while pregnant have given birth in Argentine prisons, yet nobody knows the whereabouts and identity of their children … Because they tried to change this state of things, nearly 200,000 men and women have died throughout the continent, and over 100,000 have lost their lives in three small and ill-fated countries of Central America: Nicaragua, El Salvador, and Guatemala. If this had happened in the United States, the corresponding figure would be that of 1,600,000 violent deaths in four years.

One million people have fled Chile, a country with a tradition of hospitality—that is, 10 percent of its population. Uruguay, a tiny nation of two and a half million inhabitants, which considered itself the continent's most civilized country, has lost to exile one out of every five citizens … The country that could be formed of all the exiles and forced emigrants of Latin America would have a population larger than that of Norway.

Colombian novelist Gabriel García Márquez, in his 1982 Nobel Prize lecture in Stockholm, reminding the world how in the previous eleven years Latin America had suffered from imperialist violence

XI

THIS GREAT HUMANITY
HAS CRIED "ENOUGH!"

Parasitism is still the principal characteristic of Euro-Amerikan society. Only now the crude parasitism of the early settler conquest society has grown into and merged its blood with the greater parasitism of world imperialism. The imperialist oppressor nations of North Amerika, Western Europe, and Japan have in the post–World War II years reached a mass standard of living unparalleled in human history. These nations of the imperialist metropolis are choked in an orgy of extravagance, of fetishistic "consumerism," of industrial production without limit. Even now, in the lengthening shadows of imperialism's twilight, in the confusion of the U.S. Empire's decline, the settler masses still can hardly believe that their revels are drawing to an end.

It must be emphasized that Euro-Amerikan society is not self-supporting. The imperialist mythology is that factories simply multiply themselves, that trains beget airlines and mines beget computers. In other words, that the enormous material wealth of the imperialist metropolis is supposedly self-generated, and supposedly comes to birth clean of blood.

The unprecedented rise in the wealth of the oppressor nations is directly and solely based on the increased immiseration of the oppressed nations on a global scale. The looting and killing of early colonialism continue in a more sophisticated and rationalized system of neocolonialism. But continue they do. It was Karl Marx, a century and a half ago, who first defined the accumulation of world capital as rising out of an accumulation of world proletarianization, oppression, and misery.

> "The greater the social wealth, the functioning of capital, the extent and energy of its growth, and therefore, also the absolute mass of the proletariat and the productiveness of its labor, the greater is the industrial reserve army ... the more extensive, finally, the Lazarus-layers of the working class, and the industrial reserve army, the greater is the official pauperism. *This is the absolute general law of capitalist accumulation ... It establishes an accumulation of misery, corresponding with the accumulation of capital.*"[1]

Zaire, for example, is the richest mineral-producing nation in the entire world, its great mines overshadowing even such nations as Azania and Canada. The Belgian, French, British, and Euro-Amerikan imperialists have taken literally billions of dollars in copper, diamonds, cobalt, and other minerals out of Zaire since the anti-colonial Lumumba government was destroyed in 1960–61. This frenzy of looting has so infected the neocolonial Mobutu

CHILD KILLED AT SABRA REFUGEE CAMP IN LEBANON, 1982.

regime that the Belgians laughingly call their allies a "kleptocracy." In a typical little amusement during the Winter of 1982, Zaire's President Mobutu and his entourage of 93 wives, concubines, servants, and bodyguards spent $2 million visiting Disneyworld. His make-believe government is perpetually bankrupt, unable to pay even its phone bills, permanently indebted to Western banks. And the Afrikan masses, how do they relate to this great wealth? Real wages in Zaire have declined by 80% between 1960–1978. This is the source of the wealth.[2] In Zaire, as in Ghana, Philippines, Mexico, and elsewhere in the neocolonial world, the bottom half live worse than they did twenty years ago. For that matter, worse than they did five centuries ago.

The majority of the world's population, the proletarian and peasant masses of the neocolonial Third World, exist under conditions of *increasing* hunger and landlessness, of *increasing* terror and dislocation. Millions have died that Euro-Amerikans may walk on the moon; people die of hunger and disease that Euro-Amerikans may overeat. This is the bloody secret at the roots of imperialist technological prosperity.

Just as unequal treaties, arrived at through invasion and gunboat diplomacy, were common mechanisms of global capital transfer for much of the 19th century, so today unequal trade in the imperialist

PEASANTS KILLED BY SALVADOREAN
ARMED FORCES AT EL MOZOTE, IN 1983.

world market effectively strips and plunders the neocolonial world. This is well-known, and we need only discuss it in a brief, general way.

The amazing, post–World War II economic recovery of the imperialist powers was not solely a process of creation, but also a process of extraction and transfer. Western Europe was refertilized and rebuilt in large part with new capital extracted from the Third World, extracted under a process of involuntarily tightening trade terms. In the 1960s Sékou Touré of Guinea pointed out:

> "In the course of the last ten years alone, the prices of industrial goods in international trade have increased by 24%, while the prices of raw materials have fallen by 5%. In other words, the underdeveloped countries exporting raw materials were, towards the end of the fifties, purchasing one-third less industrial goods for a determined quantity of raw materials, as compared with ten years ago."

Touré related this to the fact that the average per capita income in the U.S., which in 1945 was *ten times* greater than the average income in Asia, Afrika, and Latin Amerika, had by 1960 become even more extreme—no less than *seventeen times* as much as the average Third World income![3]

This extractive process has since 1960 only stepped up its tempo, driven to new levels by imperialism's crisis of profitability. The *New York Times* recently said: *"Commodity prices have in fact reached their lowest levels in 30 years ... For Central America's agricultural economies, the terms of trade—the relative prices of exports and imports—have deteriorated 40 per cent since 1977 ... the gap between the richest and poorest nations has widened ... Moreover, many rural societies are no longer able to feed themselves. In Africa, for example, there is less food per capita today than there was 20 years ago, with sub-Saharan Africa frequently ravaged by starvation."[4]

Behind the neocolonial facade of international airports, of tourist hotels, of Mercedes-Benz society in the capital cities, is a world of oppressed nations increasingly war-torn, looted and socially disorganized. No less than the *Wall Street Journal* clinically described this in the example of the Dominican Republic:

"Sugar had been like oil to the Dominican Republic, allowing the country to import its needs without learning to develop them locally. 'Over the past few years we've been able to create the illusion of being a developed country—we have the latest computers, automobiles and appliances,' says Felipe Vicini. 'But we aren't developed at all.'

"Stripped of its imported goods, the Dominican Republic is essentially what it was 100 years ago—a plantation society with thousands of acres of sugar cane, some bananas and cocoa, and several gold and silver mines. Today, in this plantation society, about 6% of the population owns 40% of the wealth. Most of the people are peasants, living in areas where unemployment is 50%, illiteracy is 80% and many of the adults and children are malnourished. The impoverished population spills over into urban barrios and in the city streets children beg...

"In the sugar fields, wages average $3.50 a day, at least during the six-month cutting season when work is available. Much of the cutting is done by Haitians ... some half million of them roam the Dominican countryside often working in conditions approaching slavery."[5]

In 1965, when a reform government was attempted by a faction of the Dominican military, the U.S. promptly invaded with 23,000 troops to restore the old order. *The neocolonial societies are not, of themselves, stable or viable. To maintain them imperialism subjects the world to a neverending series of search-and-destroy missions.* There is both the "white death" by starvation and disease and the literally millions of Third World casualties from endless war. Jon Stewart of the Pacific News Service has written:

"According to *War In Peace*, a new book published in London, about 35 million people have died in 130 military conflicts in more than 100 countries (all but a handful in the Third World) since the end of World War II. In the vast majority of these conflicts, the four original powers of the UN Security

Council—Britain, France, the United States and the Soviet Union—have played prominent direct or indirect roles.

"One thinks especially of Korea, which claimed 2½ million lives and involved all the great powers; of Indochina, which involved all the great powers but Britain; of France's bloody colonial wars in Africa, which claimed several million...

"The argument that these Third World wars—which, taken together, really represent a third World War—are mostly the products of nation-building among backward and blood-thirsty societies simply doesn't wash. At least it doesn't explain why the four great powers ... have engaged in as many as 71 direct military interventions outside their own borders in the postwar period, all but 4 of which have been in the Third World."[6]

Thus, there is nothing "benign" about imperialistic parasitism. The so-called world market is not a neutral trading ground, but a system of rigged transactions and economic crimes at gunpoint. There is a direct, one-to-one relationship between world hunger, mass un-employment, and proletarian *"conditions approaching slavery"* (to use the words of the *Wall Street Journal*) on the one hand, and a forti-fied Babylon filled with consumer decadence and arms factories on the other hand. For generations the increasingly proletarian masses of Afrika, Asia, and Latin Amerika have labored—and yet live in misery.

No society would freely enter into such self-destructive rela-tionships. A world of colonies and neocolonies create the only con-ditions for the imperialist "free market." In addition to its own armies, imperialism maintains in every nation that it dominates puppet mili-tary and police forces, amounting worldwide to millions of armed men, in order to extend capitalistic repression into the smallest and remotest village. The Third World War is already going on.

XII

THE GLOBAL PLANTATION

1. The Promotion of the Proletariat and Replacement by Third World Labor

The short era of "Pax Americana" after World War II was one of completing profound changes for Euro-Amerikan society. Those expansionist years of 1945–1965, when U.S. military and economic power lorded over the entire non-socialist world, saw the final promotion of the white proletariat. *This was an en masse promotion so profound that it eliminated not only consciousness, but the class itself.*

Just as in the 19th century, the Euro-Amerikan bourgeoisie both watered down class contradictions and reinforced its settler garrison over the continental Empire by absorbing immigrant European nationalities fully into the U.S. oppressor nation. This 20th century cycle had begun in the anti-communist "Americanization" campaign of the World War I period; it reached its decisive point in the accommodation between the imperialist state and the dependent, settleristic CIO unions of the 1930s. The process was sealed by the post–World War II imperialist feast, finally laying to rest the class contradictions of the period of industrial unionism. While the deproletarianization of the white masses was a historic pacification, it led to an increase in decadence and parasitism that has today reached a nodal point.

This mass promotion rewarded settlers for the U.S. Empire's "supreme triumph" as the world's No. 1 imperialist. Super-privileged life for the Euro-Amerikan masses was made possible by two factors: U.S. domination of world markets and the Empire's giant reserve armies of colonial proletarians, who took over a greater and greater burden of essential production from white workers. We must remember that World War II had physically devastated and bankrupted all the major imperialist nations save one. In the late 1940s U.S. steel mills supplied 50% of the world's steel (and now supply only 15%). U.S. aircraft plants manufactured almost 100% of the world's commercial airplanes. As late as 1949 the flow of U.S. trucks, diesel engines, elevators, pharmaceuticals, industrial tools, wheat, etc. accounted for roughly 25% of all world trade.[1] Of course, the largest single market in the entire world—the continental U.S. Empire—was "owned" by U.S. corporations. This produced the economic surpluses that started Euro-Amerikan society on its long retreat from essential production.

In these years the Euro-Amerikan workers moved upwards, increasingly handing over their places in basic production to colonial workers. Broom and Glenn summarized in the 1960s: *"Between 1940 and 1960, the total number of employed white workers increased by nearly 12 million, or 81 per cent, while the total employed labor force increased by only 37 per cent. Hundreds of thousands of white workers have moved up into higher-level jobs, leaving vacancies at intermediate levels that could be filled by Negroes ... Negroes are now well represented in semi-skilled work and in industrial unions..."*[2] Once driven, step-by-step during the 19th century, out of U.S. industry they had created, Afrikans were recruited anew into the factories. They, along with Chicano-Mexicano and Puerto Rican labor, would keep production growing while most Euro-Amerikan workers laid down their tools, one by one.

By the early 1950s Armour's main Chicago meatpacking plant was 66% Afrikan. Of the 7,500 workers there almost all the younger men and women were Afrikan. The younger Euro-Amerikans hired by Armour went into white-collar jobs at the nearby, 4,000-person Armour main office, which was all-white. Swift's meatpacking plant in Chicago was also 55% Afrikan by 1950. The desperate Swift personnel department fruitlessly begged young Euro-Amerikans to work at their plant, with one white woman complaining: "We had so many colored people during the war and now we can't get rid of them." This had more than local significance, since at that time some 75% of all packinghouse workers in the U.S. were employed in Illinois-Wisconsin.[3] In Houston, Texas, as well, Afrikans and Chicano-Mexicanos made up 60% of the packinghouse workers by 1949.[4]

By the 1960s the transformation of labor was very visible. In the great Chicago-Gary steel mill district over 50% of the workers were Third World (primarily Chicano-Mexicano and Afrikan). In the 26 Detroit area Chrysler plants at that time the clear majority of production workers were Afrikan (while the skilled trades, supervisors, and office staffs were Euro-Amerikan). In some plants, such as Dodge Main, the percentage of Afrikan workers was 80–90%. Chrysler Tank Arsenal, the main producer of U.S. Army heavy tanks, was overwhelmingly Afrikan. (When it had first opened in 1942, Chrysler had decreed that only Euro-Amerikans could work there.) The UAW officially estimated in 1970 that 25% of all auto workers were Afrikan. The League of Revolutionary Black Workers disagreed, saying instead that Afrikan workers were then closer to 45% of the primary auto production force.[5]

Chicano-Mexicano and Puerto Rican labor played growing industrial roles as well, particularly in the Southwest and on the East Coast. For example, in the 1920s and 1930s the garment industry was composed primarily of East European Jewish and Italian workers. By the 1950s young Euro-Amerikans were no longer entering the needle trades. The children of European immigrant sewing machine operators and cutters were going off to college, becoming white collar workers, or going into business. The AFL-CIO garment unions, while still Jewish and Italian in their bureaucracy, retirees, and older membership, increasingly tried to control an industry workforce that was Chicano-Mexicano, Puerto Rican, Chinese, Dominican, Afrikan, etc. on the shop floor.[6]

In the urban infrastructure we saw these changes as well. In 1940 only whites had jobs as transit bus drivers, mechanics or motormen in New York, Washington, DC, etc. By the 1960s Afrikans, Puerto

Ricans, and Chicano-Mexicanos made up a majority or a near-majority of the municipal transit workers in Chicago, Washington, New York, and other urban centers. The same for postal workers. Young Euro-Amerikans didn't want these jobs, which were difficult and might force them into physical contact with the ghetto.

This tendency could not reach the theoretical totality of having no settler workers at all, of course (any more than the capitalist tendency toward the concentration of Capital could reach its theoretical totality of only one capitalist who would employ the rest of humanity). The growing re-dependence on colonial labor has been masked not only by industry and regional variations, but by the fact that at all times a numerical majority of manufacturing corporation employees within the continental U.S. are Euro-Amerikans (although this represents only a small minority of their settler society). This seeming productive vigor was only outward. U.S. imperialism was moving the weight of Euro-Amerikan society away from toil and into a subsidized decadence.

Essential production and socially useful work occupy a gradually diminishing place in the domestic activity of U.S. corporations, in the work of its settler citizens, in the imperial culture. Decadence is taking over in an even deeper way, in which non-essential and parasitic things become the most profitable, while worthless activities are thought the most important. Always present within imperialism, this decadence now becomes dominant within the oppressor nation.

We can see this in the dramatic increase of the non-productive layers in economic life. While this phenomenon is centered in the rule of finance capital, its manifestation appears in all imperialist institutions. Advertising, marketing, package design, finance, "corporate planning," etc. mushroom with each corporation. *Management on all levels grows as numbers of production workers shrink. When one includes the large army of white-collar clerical workers needed to maintain management and carry out its work, the proportions become visibly lopsided.* At Weyerhaeuser, the large timberland and natural resources corporation, top executives and professionals alone (not including supervisors, foremen, and clerical workers) account for one out of every six employees. At the Southern Pacific Railroad, one out of every ten employees is in management.[7]

There has been a historic trend, as an expression of decadence, for the growth of management. The *New York Times* recently noted: "By December 1982, there were nearly 9 percent more managers and administrators in the American economy than in January 1980, according to the Bureau of Labor Statistics. This is in sharp contrast to the nearly 1 percent decline in overall employment and the 12 percent drop in blue-collar jobs ... In manufacturing businesses that are thriving, such as office and computing companies and pharmaceutical concerns, administrators and managers account for 11 percent of total employment."[8]

This is an aspect of an overall change, in which technology plays its part but is secondary to the corpulence, the affordable self-indulgence of an oppressor nation. Peter Drucker, the management "guru," writes on capitalism's "Midriff Bulge":

> "...instead of disappearing or even shrinking, middle management has been exploding in the last few decades. In many companies the 'middle' between the first-line supervisor and the corporate top has been growing three or four times faster than sales ... The growth hasn't been confined to big business; middle management in small and medium-sized companies may have grown even faster ... And it hasn't been confined to business; managerial growth has been even greater in government, the military and a host of non-profit institutions ... A liberal arts college I know had, in 1950, a president, a dean, and an assistant dean of students who also handled admissions and a chief clerk who kept the books. Enrollment has doubled, from 500 to 1,000; but administrative staff has increased six-fold, with three vice-presidents, four deans and 17 assistant deans and assistant vice-presidents ... five secretaries did the same work now being done by seven or eight deans, assistant deans and assistant vice-presidents—and did it very well."[9]

The historic trend has been to sharply dilute the role of productive workers even in vital industries. In food products, for example, the percentage of total employment that is non-production (managerial, supervisory, technical, and clerical) rose from 13% in 1933 to 32% in 1970. A similar development took place in the chemical industry, where non-production employees rose from 16% of all employees in 1933 to 37% in 1970.[10] In manufacturing industries as a whole the percentage of non-productive employees went up from 18% to 30% in 1950–1980.[11]

When we look at the overall distribution of employed Euro-Amerikans, we see that in 1980 white-collar workers, profession-als, and managers were 54%—a majority—and service employ-ees an additional 12%. Only 13.5% were ordinary production and transportation workers. That is only 13 out of every 100 em-ployed Euro-Amerikans. By 1982 there were thought to be more Third World domestic servants in California alone than Euro-Amerikan workers in the entire U.S. steel industry.[12]

2. New Babylon

The observation was made by the Black Liberation Movement during the 1960s that modern Amerika was just "slavery days" on a higher level—in which U.S. imperialism as slavemaster made the entire Third World its plantation and Amerika itself its "Big House." The real economy of the U.S. Empire is not continental but global in its structural dimensions.

The U.S. oppressor nation itself has increasingly specialized into a headquarters society, heavily dependent upon the superprofits of looting the entire Third World. This is more than just a matter of dollar transactions. Born out of the slave trade and the conquest of Indian lands, raised up to power through colonial labor, the U.S. oppressor nation has again developed a one-sided dependence, even for its daily necessities, on the labor and resources of the oppressed nations.

The *Wall Street Journal* said recently: "By last year the U.S. sales to Third World countries had swelled to 39% of its exports, from 29% in 1970."[13] This even understates the relationship. Afrika, for example, accounts for 10% of all U.S. export earnings by official statistics.[14] These figures conceal more than they reveal, not including, for example, the profits taken out of Afrika directly and indirectly by the European subsidiaries of U.S. multinationals, or the sale of third-party commodities—such as Saudi oil—by U.S. multinationals. Nor can such figures express the superprofits gained through unequal trade terms. The U.S. and other imperialists purchase from Afrika at bargain basement prices (often only a fraction of what they were 30 years ago) cocoa, coffee beans, iron, ore, chromium, coal, mica, nickel, cobalt, copper, manganese, and so on. The basic raw materials of industrial life are taken by U.S. imperialism so cheaply they are the next thing to free.

This economic dependency on the rest of the world was recently admitted by former U.S. Vice President Mondale: "Unless our exports grow, we cannot hope to recover from the recession ... More than 20 percent of American industrial output is exported. One out of every six manufacturing jobs is linked to exports; *four out of every*

five created between 1977 and 1980 were export-related. Almost one-third of all corporate profits derive from foreign investment and trade.* Two-fifths or our farmland produces for export..."[15]

The most significant trend to us, however, has been the export of capital in the form of production. This is the latest step in moving the work of essential production out of the oppressor nation. In the 1945–1965 period the loyal Euro-Amerikan workers received a mass promotion away from the proletariat, raising the majority of them out of the factories and fields and into the white-collar professional, office, and sales world. Even in its origins this was only possible by replacing them with colonial labor, Afrikan, Puerto Rican, and Chicano-Mexicano.

That early stage, in which the Afrikan proletariat took such a heavy role in industrial production, is now over. In the second stage the Empire is continuing to move productive work out of the oppressor nation. This is accelerating on a global basis now, with factories moving across the Pacific and southward below the Rio Grande. Even within the continental Empire new millions of colonial proletarians are being brought in from Asia, Latin Amerika, and the

---

* Many of the largest corporations—such as Ford, GM, Exxon, Citibank, Coca-Cola—obtain over 50% of their profits overseas.

Caribbean to both provide even cheaper industrial and service labor, and to permit the dispossession of Afrikans.

Alarmed at the rising anti-colonial movement of the 1960s, the Empire has been replacing Afrikan workers as rapidly as possible. Images of the past persist. We recall how Afrikan proletarians, at the point of rebellion, were systematically dispersed out of the urban South of the 1830s, and later throughout the 19th century driven out of the industry and skilled trades they had created.

We recall how the early settlers in New England kept Indian women and children as slaves, but disposed of all the Indian men as too dangerous. The *New York Times*, in reporting new studies on Afrikan unemployment, said:

> "... in addition to the men counted in the statistics who have no jobs, about 15 to 20 percent of black men aged 20 to 40 could not be found by the Census Bureau and are presumed to have neither jobs nor permanent residences ... more than half of black adult males do not have jobs."[16]

The jobless rate for New Afrikan men in the U.S. is adjusting toward the usual world level, the 40–50% seen in Mexico City or Kinshasa. Thus, the growing integration of the entire Third World into the U.S. economy is increasing national dislocation and misery.

THE EXPORT OF PRODUCTION

The unoccupied zone of Mexico, just south of the artificial border, provides a clear example. There in 1982 some 128,000 Mexicano women labored in the *maquilas,* the factories set up by U.S. corporations to assemble parts from the U.S. into finished products, which are then shipped back north across the artificial border. The average wage is less than $1 an hour, with a 48-hour workweek. RCA, Caterpillar Tractor, Ford, Chrysler, American Motors, and many other major corporations have *maquilas*. GM has ten such plants in the unoccupied zone. Foster Grant sunglasses, Samsonite luggage,

Mattel toys, and many other familiar products come in part out of the *maquilas*.[17]

The rate of profit is enormous. In 1978 the Mexicano women assemblers and machine-operators in the *maquilas* added a total of $12.7 billion in value to the products they made for U.S. corporations. At the same time, total wages paid to the then 90,000 workers were less than $336 million (roughly ⅟₃₆ of the value they created). These profits of billions of dollars each year never even pass through neocolonial Mexico, of course. The U.S. oppressor nation receives a flow of inexpensively-produced consumer and industrial goods, U.S. finance capital and the multinationals are aided in shoring up their rate of profits, while a shrinking number of Euro-Amerikan workers are still enabled to receive their necessary high wages.

While everyone understands instantly the unemployment problem caused by corporations moving their factories abroad, there is much less light shed on how some Euro-Amerikan workers benefit from it. To be sure, every trade union favors full factory employment with $20,000 per year wages (average U.S. wages for manufacturing production workers are slightly above $16,000 per year). Those days are gone forever, the monetary fruits of "boom" economy and monopoly markets. Now, for at least some Euro-Amerikan workers to retain those high-wage jobs (and the bosses to still profitably use U.S. factories with considerable capital invested in them), labor costs have to be "averaged down" by blending in super-exploited colonial labor.

American Motors, for example, says this explicitly. An AMC spokesman said: *"We established a strategy to continue to operate U.S. plants, but to expand in Mexico to average our cost downward."* Fisher Price has five toy factories in the U.S., but its Mexican plant—the smallest—produced the toy tape recorder that was their No. 1 profit-maker in 1982. Reason? Dollar an hour wages.

Or take GM's modernization to compete with imports. Recently General Motors announced a $200 million plan to frankly imitate "Toyota City" (Toyota's primary, highly-integrated complex in Japan). GM hopes that reorganization and robotizing its main Buick plants into a "Buick City" in Flint, Michigan, will let it reduce costs by $1,500 per car. Of course, today's 8,600 Buick workers in

Flint will be slashed by 3,600 (40%) by 1986. GM, which even now employs one skilled technician for every 5.6 production workers, hopes for the ratio to be one-to-one by the robotized future of year 2000. Many auto workers will lose their jobs, but a large minority will still have their high-wage positions.

Where does GM get the $200 million to modernize Buick production, to stay competitive (and, incidental to that, still employ high-wage Euro-Amerikan workers)? While GM might say "retained earnings" or "raising capital on the bond market," we note that the labor costs saved by GM in producing some auto parts for the U.S. in its 10 Mexican plants instead of Detroit, *is over $200 million per year. That is not their profits, but their superprofits, above and beyond normal profits, gotten from $1-an-hour labor.* GM can have renewed factories, and a number of Euro-Amerikan auto workers can still keep their high-wage jobs.

So while the liberals and radicals see high-wage U.S. production and low-wage colonial production as opposed to each other, it is truer that there is an interrelationship and even a dependency. The flashy production of robots and automation, of oppressor nation technicians and workers drawing advanced wages, draws sustenance from the ordinary physical labor and skills of the Mexicano proletariat. *"Nations become almost as classes."*[18]

The *maquilas* do not constitute any economic development for Mexico. They are just labor-intensive intrusions of U.S. manufacturing. It isn't just the profits that go to the U.S. oppressor nation. The U.S. receives both the superprofits and the consumer products themselves, while retaining all the white-collar managerial, professional, clerical, technical, and distributive jobs made possible by the production. Even in this form—of giving Mexican women employment at wages five times the usual rate in the rural areas—the imperialist looting has a destructive effect on the social fabric. The border *maquilas* gather women from all over the unoccupied zone, while helping to force jobless men north across the artificial border.

So this export of production is often a Trojan horse to the Third World. Even worse is the parasitic trend of looting the Third World for foodstuffs, shifting agricultural production for U.S. consumption in part to the oppressed nations. The entire imperialist bloc is joining in on this. In 1980 the *Far East Economic Review* noted that in poor Asian nations *"the new export-oriented luxury food agribusiness is undoubtedly the fastest growing agriculture sector. Fruit, vegetables, seafood and poultry are filling European, American and, above all, Japanese supermarket shelves."*[19]

In Mexico this has reached grotesque proportions. Within the unoccupied zone the area of Western Sinaloa alone supplies some 50% of all winter vegetables consumed in the U.S. Thousands of peasants have been displaced, driven off traditional lands to make way for the large plantations (and their gunmen) that are neocolonial agents for the U.S. supermarket chains. *The land is Mexicano; the labor is Mexicano. Only the profits and consumption are Euro-Amerikan.* There is nothing too subtle about this. White Amerika is parasitic on the Mexicano nation, taking food from the starving to help fill up the fabled Amerikan supermarket. A report from Mexico in the *New York Times* tells the price paid by that oppressed nation for involuntarily maintaining the "American Way of Life:"

> "Reliable statistics on nutrition levels do not exist, although the 1970 census concluded that 30 percent of the population, then over 60 million, were undernourished, another 30 percent suffered malnutrition and at least 20 per cent were obese because of poorly balanced diets…

> "'The first indicator is when we see infant mortality rising again,' said Dr. Adolfo Chavez, head of nutrition in the National Nutrition Institute. *'In some really depressed rural communities few children born since 1974 have survived. We have what we call generational holes.* But infant mortality is also growing in slum areas of the cities … More than 100,000 children die here each year because of the relationship between malnutrition and transmittable diseases' he said, 'and of the two million or so born each year at least 1.5 million will not adequately develop their mental, physical and social functions.'

> "As in many developing countries, agricultural priorities are, first, food for export, second, food for industrial processing, and only third, food for the population at large. While winter

vegetables, strawberries, tomatoes and coffee are being produced for export, for example, the government must import
corn and beans. Similarly, according to official figures, more
basic grains are consumed for animal forage than by 20 million peasants."[20]

We should note here that the peculiar chemical-mechanized U.S.
agriculture is itself highly specialized, primarily oriented around
the subsidized mass production of feed grains. *Two-thirds* of all U.S.
agricultural exports are feed grains used in raising livestock. Most
of these exports are to the industrial powers—Europe, Japan, and
the USSR—while much of the $16 billion in foodstuffs the U.S. im-
ports each year is from the Third World. In Mexico the neocolonial
economy imports grain from the U.S. to raise meat for the upper and
middle classes, while exporting significant amounts of its own food
productivity.[21]

So all over the Third World the oppressed not only supply U.S.
imperialism with raw materials, but increasingly labor in both the
factories and "the factories in the fields" to send the U.S. a growing
stream of consumer and industrial products, and even foodstuffs.
The world plantation is still very real in the age of the computer. We
say that the first makes the second possible.

HI-TECH & THE THIRD WORLD

This trend now accelerates. As early as 1970 the U.S. electrical equipment industry had one-third of its total workforce outside the U.S. borders. Ford Motor Co., which already takes over 50% of its profits overseas, has announced plans to sharply increase foreign production. Already investing $1 billion each year in foreign plants Ford's spokesman emphasized: "We plan to spend at an even higher rate…" Even Hewlett-Packard, the computer giant that is one of the largest California "hi-tech" employers, is building its newest major plants in Mexico and the UK. Hewlett-Packard has said that its future production growth will be outside the U.S.[22]

Paradoxically, the uproar over the Atari Corporation's decision to close out U.S. production itself verifies this trend. While radicals denounce this move "to shift manufacturing of its video games and home computers from the U.S. to Hong Kong and Taiwan," Atari production has *always* been in the Third World. Its game cartridges are made in Puerto Rico, its Asian plants were established years ago, and its U.S. production employees primarily Chicano-Mexicano and Asian immigrant women. It was only a question for Atari of *which* Third World workers to lay off.[23]

Decadence is revealed anew in unexpected ways. Everyone has heard that "hi-tech" is the industrial future. These are the new industries based on sophisticated products that keep rapidly changing, keeping on the "cutting edge of technology," rather than just stamping out standard products year after year. In other words, instead of steel bars and diesel engines, computer chips or biogenetics or robotics. These "hi-tech" industries today, by their very nature, employ one engineer for every 3.6 production workers in the U.S. And there is today a relative shortage of engineers in key specialities.[24]

The U.S. Empire's answer has been to drain engineers from the rest of the world, in particular the Third World (India, Taiwan, Mexico, Palestine, etc.). A recent study funded by the Mellon Foundation reported that *"… many graduate engineering programs, even at some of the most prestigious institutions draw 70 percent or more of their students from abroad. 'Several engineering deans,' the report says, 'suggest that without foreign students they would have had to close down their graduate program in the short run and their whole operation ultimately.' Since graduate students are essential labor in university laboratories, much research vital to the national interest would 'grind to a halt,' without foreign students, the report warns."*[25]

It turns out that many of the engineering school faculty as well—at some universities close to a majority—are from the Third World. *In 1982, for the first time, a majority of the U.S. doctorates awarded in engineering went to foreign students.* In testimony before a House of Representatives immigration subcommittee, John Calhoun of the Intel Corporation (advanced electronics) said: "We in the industry have been forced to hire immigrants in order to grow." He said that just considering graduates of U.S. universities, 50% of the masters degree engineers and 66% of the Ph.D. engineers hired by Intel were foreign immigrants.

The U.S. Empire's absorption of Third World scientists and engineers (the "brain drain") is so significant that last year the UN General Assembly passed a resolution urging a halt to "reverse transfer of technology" out of the Third World. The U.S. and the other NATO powers voted against it. Even when it comes to high technology, it turns out that part of the U.S. Empire's superiority comes from looting the Third World.[26]

Just as interesting is the question of why aren't there enough Euro-Amerikan engineers? Answer: Engineering doesn't pay well enough for settlers. In 1981 a survey found an average engineering income, according to the Institute of Electrical and Electronics Engineers, of $36,867. This isn't good enough for them. Engineering requires years of study, taking difficult courses in college, and then constant reeducation to keep up with new advances.[27]

The overwhelming majority of U.S. engineers leave the field, primarily for management and entrepreneurial careers. A 1970 survey of 878 MIT engineering graduates found that 726 had left engineering. **For Euro-Amerikans, in other words, engineering is primarily a good foundation to become a business executive.** While U.S. universities are producing 67,000 engineers per year, the American Electronics Association says that through 1985 there will be an annual shortfall of 20,000 engineers just in its sector.

The shortfall only exists because as many as 50,000 U.S. engineers per year leave the profession.[28] Technical education becomes only a step to swell the numbers of Euro-Amerikan businessmen, while the Third World is drained of educated men and women to do essential parts of the actual technological work for the U.S. Empire. Decadence manifests itself even in the most advanced aspects of the oppressor nation. Babylon with computers is still Babylon.

UNDOCUMENTED COLONIAL LABOR

The growing dependence on undocumented workers just transfers new Third World production inside the borders of the continental Empire. Numbering a minimum of 6 million at this time, these workers are primarily Mexicano, but include Dominicans, Chinese, Haitians, and others from all over the world. Their role in production is by now essential and irreplaceable to the U.S. oppressor nation.

Undocumented workers play both a specific and a general role. In specific they are *the* proletariat in U.S. agriculture and garment industries. In general they are a mobile, continental labor army, constituting the low-wage, proletarian base in many enterprises, upon which a superstructure of skilled, white collar, and management jobs for Euro-Amerikans is erected. Douglas S. Massey of the Princeton University Office of Population Research has noted that: *"Illegal aliens typically work in menial low-paying positions shunned by citizens, who often work in supervisory and administrative positions in the same firms."*[29]

Undocumented colonial labor pervades the imperialist economy. Undocumented workers haul in nets on shrimp boats off Texas,
repair railroad tracks near Houston, assemble furniture in California
factories, unload trucks at a Chicago food-processing plant, trim
tree branches away from suburban Illinois electric power lines,
clean rooms in Connecticut hotels, sell fast food in Manhattan, mop
floors in corporate offices, and operate canning machines in Florida
factories. The undocumented worker drives trucks, puts together
electrical goods, slaughters beef, harvests crops, and in general does
those necessary jobs at wages too low to sustain the "white" lifestyle.

In supplying the settler society with cheap food and clothing,
undocumented workers supply two of the three basic necessities
of life, literally feeding and clothing Euro-Amerikans. Even within
the continental U.S. it is well-known that effectively all agricultural
labor is Third World. The tractor dealers and mechanics, fertilizer
salesmen and county agricultural agents, the farm owners and managers, may all be Euro-Amerikan—but the agricultural laborers in
the fields are Afrikan, Puerto Rican or Dominican, and, most of all,
Chicano-Mexicano (as is much of the workforce in foods process-
ing). It is hard for a Euro-Amerikan family to have a day's meals
without eating the products of immiserated Third World labor.

This applies, only more so, to clothing. The clothes Euro-
Amerikans wear are appropriated from Third World labor. Los
Angeles has become a major garment manufacturing center, with an
estimated 100,000 workers. Even by AFL-CIO estimates, some 80%
of these workers are Chicano-Mexicano. *An absolute majority are undocumented workers.* This is a sweatshop industry, with the conditions that Euro-Amerikans left behind them over a generation ago. A
1979 investigation by the California Division of Labor showed that
of 1,083 garment manufacturers some 999 (92%) were paying less
than the minimum wage. Some 376 of these manufacturers (34%)
did not have workers' compensation insurance. Many used illegal
child labor.[30]

These Chicano-Mexicano workers join the other Third World
garment workers furnishing Amerika with clothes. In New York
over a quarter of all garment workers—some 50,000—work in
supposedly-illegal sweatshops. Not only Chinese women (the

traditional sweatshop workers in New York), but also Koreans, Haitians, Dominicans, Chicano-Mexicanos, etc.

Undocumented workers make up a growing and perhaps majority part of New York garment workers. It is certainly indicative that over 30% of all International Ladies Garment Workers Union (ILGWU-AFL-CIO) members there are undocumented. New York's Department of Labor admits that *"in most cases"* these workers earn under the minimum wage (union or not), and that their agency had found sweatshops where the Third World women averaged $1.50 an hour in pay for 50-hour weeks. (Even that is more than the garment workers in Asia and Latin Amerika earn; imports accounted for 41% of clothing sales in the U.S. in 1981.)[31]

Charles B. Keely, immigration policy analyst for the Population Council in New York City, told the *Washington Post*: *"Could the economy continue to function if all the illegal aliens were deported? 'Are they really deportable?'* he asked. *'Would Americans do those jobs?'* Some industries, such as agriculture, food services and garment manufacturing are virtually dependent on illegal immigrant labor..."[32] The "Big House" needs the plantation.

As Lenin pointed out: *"The class of those who own nothing but do not labor either is incapable of overthrowing the exploiters. Only the proletarian class, which maintains the whole of society, has the power to bring about a successful social revolution."* The meaning of this for us is obvious.

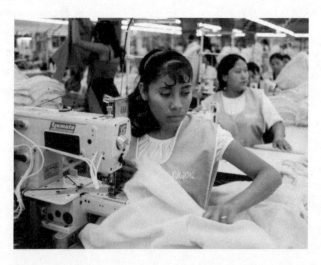

Thousands of Aliens Held In Virtual Slavery in U.S.

By JOHN M. CREWDSON
Special to The New York Times

IMMOKALEE, Fla. — Uncounted thousands of Spanish-speaking aliens who flee to this country each year to escape the crushing poverty of their homelands are being virtually enslaved, bought and sold on sophisticated underground labor exchanges. They are trucked around the country in consignments by self-described labor contractors who deliver them to farmers and growers for hundreds of dollars a head.

Exactly how many find themselves bound to employers who take advantage of their illegal status, their naïveté and their cultural alienation is not known.

But dozens of Immigration and Naturalization Service officials, migrant aid lawyers, prosecutors, social workers, farm union organizers and others who work closely with migrant laborers said in interviews that they believed the practice, while not common, was probably a growing one involving thousands of migrants from the tomato fields of Arkansas to the apple orchards of Virginia, from the cotton fields of North Texas to the orange groves of Florida.

Rising Tide of Immigration

"You're not talking about something isolated," said William Burk, an assistant Border Patrol chief in Del Rio, Tex. Humberto Moreno, a senior official of the immigration service, agreed. "There's a significant amount of that going on," he said.

* * * * * *

Existence is hard enough for the illegal aliens who toil in the fields from sunup to sundown, picking lemons in Arizona, lettuce in California or melons in south Texas for a few dollars a day, cooking over open fires, sleeping in the fields at night and watching, always, for the green-uniformed agents of La Migra, the United States Border Patrol.

But for those who unwittingly stumble into the underworld of the slave traders, life can be infinitely worse. Shackled with inflated debts they can never repay, they may find themselves locked up by night and guarded by day, beaten or threatened with harm or even death if they try to escape, their children held hostage to insure their continued servitude. Sometimes the workers held in bondage are little more than children themselves.

Of the 25,000 or so agricultural workers who come to Florida at the peak of the winter harvest season, Mr. Williams estimates, perhaps 2,000 are "trapped in camps where they can't leave."

"A lot of people try," he said, "especially when they find the working conditions not to their liking, and that brings in the nastier elements of violence."

When the harvest ends, the worker, if he is lucky, is set free, often with only a few dollars to show for weeks of labor. If he is not so lucky he is sold by the farmer to another farmer for several hundred dollars, and the process begins again.

* * * * *

Peonage Moves With Migrants

Peonage, though it exists on farms and ranches of the Southwest, is relatively uncommon there because of the proximity to the Mexican border. California, Arizona and Texas are flooded with illegal alien workers, and "there just isn't that much excess demand for labor here," said Lupe Sanchez of the Arizona Farmworkers Union.

Rather, it is in the citrus and winter vegetable belts of Florida and the potato fields of Idaho and on the tobacco farms of Virginia and North Carolina that farmworkers are at a premium, so much so that the coyotes who smuggle them north or east can easily command fees of $500 a worker.

* * * * *

Federal officials say one of the largest smuggling operations is run by two Florida men who operate a tomato farm. They are under investigation by the immigration service and the Justice Department, and a Federal grand jury is hearing evidence in the case.

Until recently, the vast majority of farmworkers in the South and Southeast were black. But the makeup of the farm labor force is changing rapidly all along the Eastern Seaboard.

Virtual Enslavement Awaits Some Illegal Aliens

Continued From Page 1

ers," said Gary Bryant, a lawyer with Migrant Legal Action in Washington. Formal complaints about involuntary ...

...ly few ...

were closely watched by one of the Cisneros, who "would often force many of the younger members of the crew to buy them 'gifts' while they ... shopping," ... his work "promised ...ect' ...

Mr. Cisn ...

planning to run away doesn't ... liams said. "That's the way ... works. It really is peonage." — the Federal laws can ... 'hough ... seldom ...

XIII

"Klass, Kulture & Kommunity"

"A UE international officer said, in November 1968, to a group of shop stewards and local union officers:

"'For the past two years, as you know, we have been having widespread discussion in our union on the general feeling of rebellion, cynicism and disgust among young workers. Let's examine, now, why these young workers coming into the shops today feel and act as they do. [...]

"'When this young guy starts getting his weekly paycheck it looks pretty good, but not for long. Soon he buys a house with a thirty-year mortgage. He puts some furniture in the house. He buys a car, a refrigerator, washer and dryer. A TV—likely a color TV. On top of all that, his young wife is pregnant again.

"'As the monthly bills start piling up, his pay envelope looks ridiculous. He sees no reason at all why America, the richest country in the world, can't give him a job that will provide him with all of the necessities and some of the luxuries of life—and what's wrong with that? He is frustrated, he is mad, he is ready to fight the Establishment that fails to give him what he needs.'"

Matles & Higgins, *Them and Us*

"'I'd like to tell you why we are troubled … First, we are tired of being politically courted and then legally extorted. Second, we are sick and tired of institutions, both public and private, not being responsive … Third, we feel powerless in our dealings with these monoliths. Fourth, we do not like being blamed for all the problems of Black America. Fifth, and perhaps the key, we anguish at all of the class prejudice that is forced upon us.'

"The speaker is Barbara Mikulski, a third-generation Polish-American from Baltimore and there is little question but that she speaks for millions of the inhabitants of what Peter Binzen calls *Whitetown USA* …

"People forget that, in the metropolitan areas, twice as many white as non-white families live in 'official' poverty, and of course many Whitetowners don't quite qualify for that governmental distinction. They are poor but not poor enough … The Whitetown husband and father works hard as a truck-driver or turret lathe operator or policeman or longshoreman or white-collar clerk—perhaps at more than one of these jobs—to buy and hold on to his fourteen-foot-wide house and new color television set.

"'The only place we feel any sense of identity, community, or control is that little home we prize,' says Mikulski. 'But there again we feel threatened by Black people.'"

Carnegie Quarterly, Fall 1970

Euro-Amerikan workers are absorbed, as are Boer-Afrikaner workers in Azania, into supra-class settler communities where the petit-bourgeoisie is leadership and the labor aristocracy is the largest and most characteristic element.

There is a distinct and exceptional Euro-Amerikan way of life that materially and ideologically fuses together the settler masses—shopkeeper, trade unionist, and school teacher alike. The general command of bourgeois ideology over these settler communities is reinforced by the mobilization of tens of millions

of Euro-Amerikans into special reactionary organizations. Those Euro-Amerikans who are immiserated or heavily exploited are not only still commanded by loyalty to "their" Empire, but are submerged and disconnected amongst the far larger, heavily privileged mass of their fellow citizens. These "white poor" are truly the lost; the abandoned remnants of the old class struggle existing without direction inside Babylon.

While there are numbers of Euro-Amerikan workers, they no longer combine into a separate proletarian class. The old white industrial proletariat of the 1930s has been dissolved by promotion and privilege, and its place taken by the colonial proletariats. The abnormal and historically brief contradiction of proletarian class conflict *within* the settler garrison has been ended. Just as in the 17th, 18th, and 19th centuries, the U.S. oppressor nation is again a nonproletarian society that is purely capitalistic in character.

The level of decadence and general privilege can be measured by examining the class structure. Revisionist analyses of the U.S. class structure are, of course, deliberately misleading. Most typically, the revisionists lump together the U.S. oppressor nation with the various Third World oppressed nations and national minorities as one society. Their scheme is to try and hide Babylon behind the masses of colonial workers. They typically say: "America has a working class majority." This implies about settler society what is not true.

A more subtle distortion is to focus on Euro-Amerikans, but to determine "class" by sorting each individual man and woman into different occupational groupings (roughly correlating to a private relationship to the means of production and distribution). This approach lets the revisionists claim that "the majority of white Americans are working class."

This approach denies the "sensuous" reality of human society. Classes are huge, self-defined, living social formations, with general aspects and aspects unique to their own history, time, and nation. Engels, in this regard, notes: "The working classes have always, according to the different states of the development of society, lived in different circumstances and had different relations to the owning and ruling classes."[1] It is our task to discover and explore the tangible class formations that have their own existence in material

life (completely independent of our investigation). The revisionist distortion on the contrary, seeks to arbitrarily concoct statistical categories, fill them up (on paper, anyway) with abstract individuals—and call this "classes." This is just bourgeois sociology with "left" rhetoric.

The U.S. oppressor nation *is a patriarchal settler society* of some complexity. In general Euro-Amerikans exist in family units, with the class identity of the family primarily dependent on the husband or father. We should say that we neither advocate this situation nor see it as eternal. It is the prevailing reality at this time, in this century, and it is our task to understand it.

The revisionist methodology comes up with conclusions like: "all secretaries are in the clerical sector of the working class." That sounds reasonable to many. *Factually, however, it isn't true.* For example, if a young Euro-Amerikan woman works as a secretary, came from a petit-bourgeois family background, is married to a professional, lives in an exclusive white residential suburb or "arty" urban community, shares in a family income of $30,000 per year—is she working class? Could she be working class but her husband and children petit-bourgeois? Obviously, such a person would, in the actual social world that exists, be solidly flourishing within the petit bourgeoisie.

This is not such a far-fetched example. Fully 25% of Euro-Amerikan women employed as clerical-sales personnel are married

to men who are managers or professionals. 17% of the wage-employed wives of male managers (includes small retail businesses) are blue-collar workers.[2] Due to the patriarchal nature of Euro-Amerikan society, most women from the middle classes are forced, when seeking employment, to accept non-professional clerical and retail sales jobs. This does not necessarily change their class identity. One study shows that roughly one-third of all secretaries under 30 years of age are graduates of colleges or junior colleges.[3] This is commonplace knowledge. We have to *describe* classes as they exist, not *define* them as concocted categories of our making.

We can gain a better idea of this patriarchal settler society's class structure by looking at Euro-Amerikan male occupations alone. While this is nowhere near as accurate as conducting social investigation, actually going out and surveying the masses in all aspects of their lives, it should help us see the general outlines of the class situation.* This outline is not a full class analysis, we must caution; for our purposes here we do not need to separately delineate the big bourgeoisie, regional and local bourgeoisie, and the varied middle

---

* Mao Zedong, for example, in his social investigation of China's countryside, found significance not just in economic roles, but in concomitant social changes: "As to the authority of the husband, it has always been comparatively weak among poor peasants, because the poor peasant women, for financial reasons compelled to engage more in manual work than women in the wealthier classes, have obtained greater rights to speak and more power to make decisions in family affairs. They also enjoy considerable sexual freedom. Among the poor peasants triangular and multilateral relationships are most universal."

classes (small business proprietors, salaried managers, land-owning farmers, professionals, etc.). All these are placed into one bourgeois-petit-bourgeois grouping (which contains what are separate classes). This is based on the 1970 Census:

BOURGEOIS & MIDDLE CLASSES   37%[*]

Managers	12.17%
Professionals	15.34%
Salesmen, Agents & Brokers	5.20%
Farmowners & Managers	3.11%
Clerical-Admin.	1.15%

CORE OF LABOR ARISTOCRACY   24%

Craftsmen	21.82%
Protective security (police, firemen, etc.)	1.90%

WORKERS (INCLUDES MUCH OF LABOR ARISTOCRACY)   39%

Factory & Transport, Machine Operators	18.31%
Laborers	6.87%
Clerical	6.45%
Retail Sales Clerks	2.31%
General Service	5.30%[4]

---

[*] The actual U.S. bourgeoisie is abnormally large. The wealthiest 1% of the U.S. Empire's population—one out of every 100 adults of all nationalities (primarily Euro-Amerikan)—own an average of $1.32 million each.[5] This is the zone where the upper petit-bourgeoisie and local bourgeoisie meet. Earlier studies indicate that the actual Big Bourgeoisie (DuPonts, Rockefellers, Morgans, etc.) is only a fraction of this number, perhaps as few as 15,000 individuals.

This breakdown of Euro-Amerikan male occupations has a very clear meaning, verifying everything about White Amerika that daily life has told us.

The bourgeois, the middle classes, and the core of the labor aristocracy are the absolute majority (over 60%). The labor aristocracy is swollen in size. Almost 2 out of every 100 male Euro-Amerikans are policemen, firemen or other protective security workers. Highly-paid construction tradesmen, machinists, mechanics, and other skilled craftsmen *outnumber* ordinary production and transportation workers. Even this greatly understates the extent of the settler labor aristocracy. Many Euro-Amerikan factory workers, technicians, clerical workers, and even general laborers (such as municipal Park Department "laborers" in the major cities) receive extra-proletarian wages, sometimes doing light labor and usually no toil at all. The settler labor aristocracy is considerably larger than its hard core, perhaps comprising as much as 50% of all male Euro-Amerikans.

PHILISTINE MODE OF LIFE

Most importantly, Euro-Amerikans share an exceptional way of life. What is so exceptional about it is that almost all get to live in a bourgeois way, *"quite Philistine in the mode of life, in the size of their earnings and in their entire outlook..."* Thus, the mass of the lower middle classes, the huge labor aristocracy, and most workers are fused together by a common national way of life and a common national ideology as oppressors. The masses share a way of life that apes the bourgeoisie, dominated by a decadent preoccupation with private consumption. Consuming things and owning things, no matter how shoddy or trivial, is the mass religion. The real world of desperate toil, the world of the proletarians who own nothing but their labor power, is looked down upon with contempt and fear by the Euro-Amerikans.

Euro-Amerikans know how privileged they have it on a world scale, how exceptional they are. Interviews by one reporter in an Iowa industrial city found: "...the prevailing attitude expressed here was capsuled in this comment from Don Schatzberg, the 46-year-old foreman of a concrete-pipe plant:

> "'If you had a chance to pick your country, where else would you go? Where else can a working man own his own house and two cars and take a vacation every year? I'd say I'm a happy man, not a bit unhappy with my lifestyle...'

> "Like Mr. Schatzberg and many other Americans elsewhere, workers here often seemed to equate success with ownership of homes, cars, campers, boats and the like.

> "'I work a lot of hours,' said James Dirkes, Teamster union shop steward at Zeidler, 'but I've got a car, a truck, a boat and a camper to show for it.'

> "And LaVone Feldpouch, a 36-year-old wife and mother who works as a clerk for Deere, where her husband is also employed, said: 'I feel my life is an upward curve,' She noted that she and her husband had accumulated three houses and

added: 'We're not going to stop there.' They also own two cars, a truck, a boat and a motorcycle and take two vacation trips a year, one with their children and one without."[6]

All statistics show that the amount of consumption in Euro-Amerikan society is staggering. Enough so that it establishes for the mass a certain culture. In the settler tradition today's Euro-Amerikan culture is one of home-owning, with 68.4% of all settler households in 1979 owning their own home (up 50% from 1940). These households share a cornucopia of private electric appliances: 89.8% of all U.S. homes in 1979 had color TVs (watched an average of over 6 hours per day), 55% had air-conditioning, 77.3% had washing machines and 61% had clothes dryers, 43% had dishwashers, 52% had blenders and food processors, and so on.[7] Much of the world's health products are hoarded in the U.S., with, for example, one out of every three pairs of prescription eyeglasses in the world sold here.

In terms of the "basics," the most characteristic for Euro-Amerikans is the automobile. In 1980 there were a total of 104.6 million cars on the road. 84.1% of all U.S. households had cars, with 36.6% having two or more.[8] Everyone says that owning automobiles is a "necessity," without which transportation to work (83% drive to work), shopping, and childcare cannot be done.

A Bureau of Labor Statistics study shows how the "average wage owner" in Boston of 1875 had to spend 94% of the family income on *"necessities: food, clothing and housing."* A "Century of Progress to 'the Good Life'" later, the study found that the "average wage earner" in 1972–73 in Boston spent only 62% on these necessities, meaning they *"could afford to spend 38 percent … on nonessentials."*[9] We should note that few Euro-Amerikans would agree with this elemental definition—since in their society such things as automobiles, sleeping pills, college education, drycleaning, telephones, etc. are viewed as "necessities."

These by no means exhaust the list of Euro-Amerikan private possessions. Stocks—one of every seven Euro-Amerikans owns at least some corporate stocks—vacation homes, land, hair dryers, motorcycles, exercise equipment, guns, boats, annual changes of clothing styles, and on and on. We have brought up these boring, almost

mind-numbing lists of possessions to drive home the point that consuming is a disease among settlers, an infection that is dominant in
that culture. *Euro-Amerikan life is no longer centered around production but around consumption. This is the near-final stage of decadence.*

All this is only made possible by the generalized high income
that characterizes Euro-Amerikan mass life. The median Euro-
Amerikan family income in 1981 was $23,517.[10] This is not equally
distributed, quite obviously, but the extent to which many Euro-
Amerikans in all classes—an absolute majority—shared this generalized high income is striking. Between 1960 and 1979 the percentage of settler families earning over $25,000 per year (in constant
1979 dollars) *doubled, making up 40% of the settler population.* When
we examine Euro-Amerikan families earning over $20,000 per year
in terms of different occupations, this income sameness is very conspicuous: [11]

HUSBAND'S OCCUPATION	% EARNING OVER $20,000 IN 1978 DOLLARS
Manager	75%
Professional	67%
Clerical/Sales	69%
Skilled Worker	49%
Unskilled Worker	35%

This generalized high income has come to characterize even industrial production workers, who in previous historical periods were
highly exploited, and lived in abject misery. An upper stratum of
unionized production workers in heavy industry earn on an approximate level with the petit-bourgeoisie. At the end of 1982 General
Motors was paying its blue-collar workers an average base wage of
$11.53 per hour, plus an additional .99 per hour average in shift
and overtime premiums, and an additional $7.13 per hour in aver-
age benefits (health insurance, SUB, holiday and vacation pay, etc.).
This is a total package of some $40,000 per year. Steelworkers' aver-
age 1981 total wage package was $19.42 an hour. This compares to
craft incomes in the most fortunate high-wage areas—in San Jose,

California the latest pact raises union electricians' total wage to $24.40 an hour.[12]

Most Euro-Amerikan workers no longer can go into such industries, however. Much more typical and more exploited would be Maureen Akin, recently written about as one of the 9,000 Motorola workers in Phoenix, Arizona. A 41-year-old divorcee, Ms. Akin earns $7.02 per hour (for a 36-hour work week) as a production worker making semi-conductors. Living on a restricted budget, she saw only one movie last year in order to pay for her son's orthodontic work and her daughter's college. When we go down even lower, we find the notoriously low-wage North Carolina textile mills (which in a low-wage industry have the poorest-paid workers of those in any State). Virtual symbols of backward, "poor white" exploitation, they paid an average production wage in 1982 of $5.24 per hour, or $10,900 per year.[13]

This low wage of North Carolina textile mill workers is much higher than world standards. This is roughly *30 times the wage* that the Del Monte Division of the R.J. Reynolds Corp. pays the women workers who toil 10–12 hours each day on their vast Philippine plantations.[14] It is *11½ times the wage* that Rawlings Co. pays the Haitian women who stitch together *all* the major league baseballs. It is *5 times the wage* that General Motors pays its Afrikan autoworkers in Azania.[15] The *most exploited* Euro-Amerikan workers live whole

levels above the standard of the world proletariat, since they may be on the bottom, but they are on the bottom of a privileged nation of oppressors. Nation is the dominant factor, modifying class relations.

No matter where we look, the mass, extra-proletarian privileges of Euro-Amerikans have structurally insulated them within their exceptional way of life. "Problems" like high mortgage rates for homes are problems of a particular way of life. The full extent of what the Euro-Amerikan masses get from their special relationship serving imperialism cannot be measured in dollars alone. Everyone in the Empire understands the saying: "If you're white, you're alright." To the settler garrison goes the first pick of whatever is available—homes, jobs, schools, food, health care, government services, and so on. Whatever security is available under imperialism is theirs as well. This is taken for granted.

A 1977 survey by the Center for Policy Research among Vietnam veterans in the Northeast showed that while Afrikan Vietnam-era vets surveyed had an unemployment rate of 28%, corresponding Euro-Amerikan veterans had an unemployment rate of only 3%. Further, the employed Euro-Amerikan veterans earned an average of $4,212 per year more than even those Afrikan veterans who were working.[16]

Even the Women's Movement became a real factor in preserving their exceptional way of life. While the Women's Movement both expressed anger at sexism and greatly improved Euro-Amerikan women's lives, it was largely co-opted as a political movement by imperialism at its birth. The imperialist-sponsored "liberation" of settler women has been a major prop to reinforce and modernize the patriarchal family structure; for that matter, to transfuse the whole settler society. Just as the Empire called out white women from the kitchen during World War II, to be "Rosie the Riveter" in war industry, so in the 1970s white women were again freed by imperialism to enter the labor force in new areas and in unprecedented numbers.

First, at a time when the Empire had decided that Afrikans were again too rebellious to be employed in any great numbers in key industrial, commercial, and professional institutions, Euro-Amerikan women were recruited to stand by their men in filling up the jobs. "Equal Opportunity" in medical schools, law schools, business, etc.

meant a large influx of Euro-Amerikan women—and few Afrikans. This is noticeable even in the blue-collar skilled trades, which have long been male sectors of employment. During 1970–1980 the percentage of women in these restricted crafts rose at a rate 3 *times* that for Third World workers. This was like a new wave of European immigration to reinforce the settler hold on their job market.

And it was a "breath of fresh air," modernizing settler society. Now, for instance even the *New York Times* has a very literary "women's consciousness" column (called *"Hers"*), where feminist leaders and writers can reach a mass audience. The fractures of the sixties are being reconciled and reunited among settlers. Novelist Gail Sheehy wrote in this column: "Behind just about every successful woman I know with a public as well as a private life there is another woman. The dirty little secret is, all but one of the female leaders interviewed here has household help..." Sheehy herself tried Filipino and Argentinian domestics unsuccessfully (too "hostile") before going back to the tried and true Afrikan woman domestic.[17]

While Women's Liberation is an essential part of the world revolutionary future, the struggles of women in various societies have their own national characteristics. In the U.S. oppressor nation the politics of Women's Liberation form but one small current within the much larger, overall Women's Movement. This larger Movement is pro-imperialist, and is concerned only with equality of privilege among male and female settlers. It is opposed to any liberation in general. The revolutionary ideas of Women's Liberation rested lightly upon the surface of the Women's Movement, and some individual women did pick them up.

Real wages in the U.S. began to stagnate in 1967, when imperialism ran aground on the Vietnamese Revolution. For the first time since World War II rapid inflation was eating at the upward spiral of Euro-Amerikan income. In this continuing crisis the new income of Euro-Amerikan women saved the settler family from "loss of buying power" (a phrase of the oppressor nation economy that carries an almost traumatic weight). The new income of employed women contributed to the 22% increase in real per capita income in the U.S. between 1970–1980. The Euro-Amerikan family continued its way of life by becoming a two-wage-earner family (at a time when Afrikan proletarian families, for example, were increasingly becoming the reverse). By 1978 some 75% of the U.S. families with incomes over $25,000 per year had two wage-earners. The *New York Times* reported.

> "Across the nation women have swarmed into the workforce by the millions, swelling the numbers of multi-income families. That trend can mask the effects of inflation, since a substantial number of families are living better than they did."[18]

We are not just describing simple social bribery, as in the bourgeoisification of European workers in Germany, France, England, etc.

In Europe the bribed workers came from a long history of class war, in societies with centuries of sharply defined and rigid class divisions. Their classes, however bribed and infected, still exist as formations in the actual social world—occupying traditional communities, continuing a definite class culture. Politically, the European working class still swell the large, nominally-"socialist," voluntary industrial unions (which do not exist in the U.S. oppressor nation), and are electorally represented by their traditional working-class parties—the German Social-Democratic Party, the French Communist Party, etc. **Of course, the long-range trends of world polarization and internationalization mean that all oppressor nation societies have become more alike and will become even more so.**

In Amerika this bribery, this bourgeoisification, took place within the context of a settler society, which has its own history, culture, and traditions—based not on class struggle, but on their material role as the privileged garrison over the continental Empire. The immigrant European proletarians were bribed by being absorbed—"integrated" if you will—into this specific society.

So in Amerika intra-oppressor class distinctions have always been muted on the mass level by the fact that the main distinction was whether you were a settler or a subject, whether you were in the slave patrols or enslaved in the fields, whether you were in the frontier garrison community or imprisoned in the reservation. This was the all-important identity, to which everything else was subordinate. Only someone with no contact with reality can fail to see this.

THE GARRISON COMMUNITY

The Euro-Amerikan community is not just a conglomeration of stores and residences. It is a physical structure for settler life, in which the common culture of the Empire garrison still lives on. These garrison communities are enforcers of the oppressor nation way of life among its citizens, demanding social conformity and ideological regimentation. They have certain specific characteristics: the most glaring of which is that colonial subjects are generally barred out. Why should the settler garrison let the "Indians" live inside the walls of the fort? There is an arrogance but at the same time an underlying feeling of being threatened or besieged by "those people"—which occasionally breaks out in collective hysteria (during which guns are flourished and the laggards rush to buy out the local gunshops). The confining, boring, and philistine way of life of these communities is one reason Euro-Amerikan youth "dropped out" of them in such numbers during the 1960s.

There are, of course, different types of settler communities, distinguished by a number of things, including by class. The community of multimillionaires in Palm Springs or Aspen is very different from the communities of Canarsie or Skokie or Charlestown. As are the "hip-eoisie" communities of Berkeley or Greenwich Village. *On the mass level, however, a certain type of supra-class Euro-Amerikan community has been characteristic for over a century.* It is a small home-owning, small-propertied community. In it the lower middle class, the labor aristocracy, and other workers share the tight but generally comfortable life of the settler garrison. This is where community life is supported by the conspicuous concentration of state services—parks, garbage collection, swimming pools, better schools, medical facilities, and so on. In contrast to the reservation or ghetto, the settler community is full of the resources of modern industrial life.

Increasingly such communities are suburbs (or "exurbs"), filled with the Euro-Amerikans who are regrouping away from the old central cities. Today the suburban population is 103 million, roughly half of the U.S. population. These suburbs are fundamentally "all-white," averaging around 90% Euro-Amerikan. Those numbers are misleading, since most Third World people in the suburbs are either tightly segregated into ghettoized small towns and residential pockets or are Asian. The social character of the typical suburb is relentlessly, monolithically "white."

We can see in such garrison communities, urban "ethnic" enclave as well as suburb, how the shared exceptional way of life materially and ideologically fuses together the masses. There, on the same block and street, the families of electricians and small retailers, truck drivers and schoolteachers, policemen and grill owners, book-keepers and telephone repairmen, white-collar supervisors and factory workers, computer programmers and legal secretaries grow up together, go to the same schools together, and intermarry. Nominal class distinctions on the common level pale beside their supra-class unification as a settler mass, most characterized by the labor aristocracy.

Here also is the home of the state labor force. Policemen and firemen are quite common, and in some communities almost everyone is related to, friends or neighbors with police. Literally thousands of "all-white" voluntary organizations criss-cross settler communities. Tens of millions of settlers are organized into special reactionary groupings of the most diverse kinds. Some, such as the KKK or the Moral Majority, are overt. Far more respectable and wide-reaching are reactionary organizations such as the AFL craft unions, "ethnic" organizations like the Sons of Italy, the "all-white" Roman Catholic parishes, the "Right-To-Life" groupings, the Mormon Church, the NRA, the

Betar and other Zionist-fascist groups, sports leagues, thousands of neighborhood "Improvement Associations," ranchers associations, military reserve units, and on and on. The list of special "all-white" organizations with reactionary politics is endless.

The National Rifle Association in the State of Pennsylvania alone has ties to over 1,000 local gun clubs with 200,000 members. One report shows how Jim Price, a part-time farmer and factory worker, is also a "power broker" as president of the State Federation of Sportsmen's Clubs. This grouping was credited for electing Republican Richard Schweiker to the U.S. Senate when the Democratic incumbent spoke out for gun controls. The report goes on: *"Mr. Price's forebears were original settlers here, so when he talks of the threat of government dictatorship through gun controls his sense of history sounds personal. 'My people were chased off twice by the Indians before they stayed for good,' he said."*[19] Everyone who has had any contact with the NRA network of gunmen knows exactly how they expect to use their weapons. This network alone mobilizes millions of armed Euro-Amerikans.

Such special reactionary organizations are far from all-commanding even within the settler community, but their strength

is considerable. What is most important is to realize that White Amerika is not a political "blank." The Euro-Amerikan "left" sometimes discusses things as if this were true, discussing "organizing white workers" as though they were frozen in place. Settlers are not waiting passively for "the Movement" to come organize them—the point is they already have many movements, causes, and organizations of their own. That's the problem.

THE POOR & EXPLOITED

The U.S. oppressor nation does have its own casualties and its broken remnants of the industrial past. These constitute an insufficient base for revolutionary change, however. Approximately 10% of the Euro-Amerikan population has been living in poverty by government statistics. This minority is not a cohesive, proletarian stratum, but a miscellaneous fringe of the unlucky and the outcast: older workers trapped by fading industries, retired poor, physically and emotionally disabled, and some families supported by a single woman. The whole culture silently reminds them that if they are poor and white the fault must be theirs. The rate of alcoholism in this layer is considerable. They are scattered and socially diffused.

Some entire industrial communities do exist as outmoded but surviving pockets of the old way of life. It's interesting to see how imperialism controls them. The Appalachian coal mining communities are the sharpest example, having their own economic, cultural, and union tradition going back to the 19th century. What a great contrast between these old, torn-up mountain miner communities and the new Euro-Amerikan white-collar suburbs. Yet, there is an "inner interrelationship," even in the exceptions to the trends.

Precisely because of this stark, deeply ingrained tradition the Appalachian mining communities have been special targets of radical organizing efforts. The Communist Party USA has had organizers in the mountains for some 60 years. It was there during the 1920s that the most famous of the CPUSA's "Red Unions"—the National Miners Union—led the coal miners into the bitter, violent Harlan

County strike. Even during the reactionary 1950s the Southern Conference Education Fund maintained a radical presence.

In the 1960s we find numerous Appalachian organizing projects, including those of the Progressive Labor Party, SDS, and Southern Student Organizing Committee. By the 1970s many radical groupings were helping promote dissident movements, such as for community reforms or the Miners for Democracy (MFD) that eventually won control of the United Mine Workers Union. In the mid-1970s the Revolutionary Communist Party had its own rank-and-file miners organizations (just as the CPUSA had over 40 years before), which for a time had some following.

Despite the 60 years of repeated radical organizing drives there has been, in fact, zero revolutionary progress among the mining communities. Despite the history of bloody union battles, class consciousness has never moved beyond an embryonic form, at best. There is no indigenous revolutionary activity—none—or traditions. Loyalty to U.S. imperialism and hatred of the colonial peoples is very intense. We can see a derailment of the connection between simple exploitation and class consciousness.

To see why we can look at Martin County, Kentucky. This has long been one of the poorest counties in the U.S. There are no highways, no sewage system, no garbage collection, no hospitals or even movie theaters, and one radio station and one fast food franchise restaurant for its 14,000 citizens. The community is ripped off, exploited to an extreme degree. Even the government, while spending close to $20 million a year in Martin County for school programs, job retraining, etc. takes out twice that much, $40 million a year, in taxes.

One corporation dominates the economy. In fact, owns it. The Norfolk & Western Railroad has mineral rights to some 129,000 acres, over half of the total land area of the county (the second largest landowner is Harvard University). The 13 million tons of coal taken out every year not only brings large profits to the mine operators (Occidental Petroleum, Fluor Corporation, Ashland Oil, and MAPCO) but gives N&W coal royalties and freight fees of over $30 million annually. This is an annual rate of return on their investment of 120%. Over the fifty year life of the coal field, N&W's

total return will be something like $1.5 billion—or 6,000% on their investment. As everyone knows, the rampant stripmining is rapidly destroying the area's simple road system, choking the streams with corrosive coal refuse, fouling the underground water supply, and generally causing more physical and ecological destruction than repeated bombings. Harry Caudill, author of *Night Comes to the Cumberlands,* says: *"They've treated the region as if it were a colony. When they finish taking what they want from it, they'll just let it go to hell."*[20]

Why don't the workers in this ripped-off "colony" organize, seeing in a revolutionary change a way to keep the wealth for the community of their children's generation? In fact, to really have a community? Why don't they resist? The answer is that the majority of them welcome such exploitation, whatever the future price. Their community may have nothing, may be sliding back into an eventual future of undeveloped desolation, but right now those who have jobs are making "good bucks." The 5,000 coal miners have been earning around $30,000 per year, while the county's per capita annual income is up to $7,000.

The employed miners who are getting those "good bucks" are unconcerned about the poverty right at their side. Disabled miners and the elderly live in poverty, children are uneducated, while what income exists in the community is eagerly thrown away on individual consumerism. This points out the fact that what is poverty-stricken about settlers is their culture.

The Euro-Amerikan coal miners are just concentrating on "getting theirs" while it lasts. In the settler tradition it's "every man for himself." They have no class goals or even community goals, just private goals involving private income and private consumerism. Meanwhile, the local N&W land manager says that they do have future plans for Appalachia: "We don't intend to walk off and leave this land to the Indians." Of that we can be certain.

The most significant fact about the real consciousness of the Euro-Amerikan masses is how anti-communal and private it is. Settlers recognize no common bond with the rest of humanity. That is why everything they build is perverted: why settler trade unions are anti-proletarian, and settler "Women's Liberation" is happy to exploit the women of other nations. It means nothing to Euro-Amerikans that the winter fruit they eat was really paid for by the lives of Mexican or Chilean or Filipino children. For them the flavor is so sweet. Euro-Amerikans don't even really care too much about each other. Lower taxes are more important than food for their own elderly. This is a diseased culture, with a mass political consciousness that is centered around parasitism.

The mere recognition that there are rich and poor, or even that corporations exploit people—any idiot can see this—cannot constitute class consciousness. The long, long history of unionism in the coal counties shows this. Class consciousness implies a participation in the class war. While such a consciousness certainly can involve fighting for better wages, it cannot be limited to or even centered on this.

The Euro-Amerikan "left" has completely mystified the question of class consciousness. They see in every labor strike, in the slightest twitch for reform, examples of proletarianism. Some "socialist scholars" (a self-awarded title, to be sure) conduct almost anthropological expeditions into the settler masses, seeing in every remembered folk song or cultural nuance some profound but hidden nuggets of working class consciousness. Others, who have spent years as working class "experts," find proletarian vision in every joke about the bosses told during coffee breaks. This is not politics, whatever else it may be.

There is nothing mystical, elusive or hidden about real working class consciousness. It is the political awareness that the exploiting class and its state must be fought, that the laboring masses of the world have unity in their need for socialism. The Red Army is class consciousness. An action for higher wages or better working conditions need not embody any real class consciousness whatsoever. Narrow self-interest is not the same as consciousness of class interests. "More for me" is not the same slogan as "liberate humanity."

Lenin wrote on this: "Only when the individual worker realizes that he is a member of the entire working class, only when he recognizes the fact that his petty day-to-day struggle against individual employers and individual government officials is a struggle against the entire bourgeoisie and the entire government, does his struggle become a class struggle."[21]

This famous and often-quoted passage set forth a clear threshold—by which the coal miners or any other significant grouping of Euro-Amerikan workers do not in a scientific sense have any real working-class consciousness. Much more than this, however, is the reality that practice is the proof, that the actual struggle reveals more than any theoretical criteria. Lenin pointed this out at the 2nd Congress of the Communist International:

> "We cannot—nor can anybody else—calculate exactly what portion of the proletariat is following and will follow the social-chauvinists and opportunists. This will only be revealed by the struggle, it will be definitely decided only by the socialist revolution."[22]

We have lived through two decades of the most tumultuous political struggle on a global scale. The Afrikan masses broke through the colonial repression in massive urban uprisings during the 1960s. The Chicano-Mexicano Land struggle revived in the Southwest. Armed self-defense became a popular concept. Wounded Knee lit a signal fire for the Indian Nations. Socialist ideas and international solidarity took root in the new insurgencies. The Puerto Rican revolution brought an armed struggle once again to the front door of the Empire. The answer to their actual consciousness, to what class awareness the Euro-Amerikan workers had, can be found in what side they supported in the wars to overthrow "their" U.S. Empire.

U.S. SETTLERISM & ZIONISM

The connection between Euro-Amerikan settlerism and Zionist settlerism—twin servants of imperialism—is shown in all the recent reactionary political developments within the U.S. Jewish communities. Repeated propaganda about the Holocaust is used as fascistic indoctrination, to whip up a belligerent sentimentality that both justifies Euro-Amerikans as victims ("no more guilt trips about racism") and powers new terroristic attacks on colonial peoples. The same ultra-Orthodox Zionist elements are killing Afrikan youth in

Brooklyn and shooting Palestinian youth on the West Bank. Now even the anti-semitic bigots of the Moral Majority recognize the Zionists as their "kith and kin."

This Zionist example has stirred many of the Russian Jewry, and brought some 175,000 of them here to become settlers in the "New World." Again we can see how the division of the world into oppressed nations pervades all relations and events. The Russian Jewish immigration is not like the Puerto Rican immigration, for example, which is the forced dislocation of a colonial people in search of employment. In contrast, the Russian Jewry come as more reinforcements for the U.S. oppressor nation; come not for survival or bread, but for the rich, privileged lifestyle of settlerism. Beneath the propaganda, this is all very evident. A recent *New York Times* report from Russia's Jewish "human rights" underground is revealing:

> "About 30 Moscow Jews and a few Westerners gathered in a private apartment recently to mark Purim with poetry and amateur theatricals. The players shifted easily from Russian to Hebrew, and some members of the hopelessly cramped audience joined in the songs. Even the children readily recognized Queen Esther and the other characters in the ancient legend of how Persian Jews triumphed over a devious plot to massacre them by the wicked Haman, done up for the evening as a Palestinian guerrilla ... The Six-Day War of 1967 is generally recognized as a turning point in the self-esteem of Russian Jews and in their identification with Israel. 'There was a sense of colossal national rehabilitation,' recalled Naum Meiman, a 72-year-old physicist and human rights activist."[23]

We see the same pattern—how the conquering and killing of Arabs, Afrikans, etc. is felt by Zionist settlers as therapeutic "rehabilitation," restoring them to European dimensions. This is the same virile restoration through mass murder that was so ecstatically praised by Adolf Hitler.

Jews do face an entrenched anti-semitism, which in Russia definitely makes them "second-class citizens," restricts advancement into upper management, and limits religious and cultural expression (such as the "human rights" get-together described). About 30% of the Russian Jewish immigrants here are university graduates. One such family are the Resnikovs, interviewed in Forest Hills, NY: *"'Russia was a beautiful country. But not for us,' said Mrs. Resnikov, a brief sorrow in her huge dark eyes. She was a technician in an electronics plant and her husband, a squarely built man of 42, was a construction engineer. 'Higher I couldn't go in Russia—a Jew for them is an enemy,' he said ... Now, after four years here, Mr. Resnikov is impatient with 'working like a worker' in his $6.50-an-hour job as a roofer but has found nothing better ... 'We live nice,' he said, 'but we didn't live bad in Kiev or Haifa. I would like to have my own American business...'"[24]*

Some two-thirds of all Russian Jewish emigrants have come to the U.S. rather than Israel. A survey for the council of Jewish Federations found that in 1981 the median family income of these new settlers was $19,632; other surveys have found that less than 1%, mostly the elderly, have to stay on welfare.[25] Coming from thousands of miles away, often speaking no English, their new citizenship in the U.S. oppressor nation gives them an instant lifestyle above the colonial world.

Night on the Town for Soviet Imn

A Playboy Bunny escorting the party of Russian immigrants at the club.

The New York Times / Jim Wilson

XIV

TACTICAL & STRATEGIC

The settler nature of the Euro-Amerikan oppressor nation is the decisive factor in their political struggles. It is the decisive factor in relations between Third World struggles and the Euro-Amerikan masses. This was true in 1776 and true in 1976. True for the Ku Klux Klan and true for the Communist Party USA—not that these two organizations have the same politics, but that their settler national character is the decisive factor in both.

It is only by grasping this that the question of broader unity can be correctly answered. This is a particular problem for Asian-Amerikans, who as relatively small national minorities within the continental Empire have a high organic need for political coalitions and alliances. It is difficult to evaluate different forms of unity just from our own experiences alone. Asian national minorities here have had a limited history of political unity with each other, much less with Euro-Amerikans or the oppressed nations.

Settler radicalism has taught us that two types of unity are important: proletarian internationalism (strategic unity of communists and workers of all nations) and immediate trade union unity (tactical unity of all workers in unions and other mass organizations). Since historically most Asian workers here have been nationally segregated, there has been little opportunity to test out this trade union unity. The often-cited example is that of the Filipino-Japanese plantation workers in the Hawaiian ILWU (the radical-led Longshoremen's Union on the West Coast), who by the 1970s were the highest-paid agricultural workers in the world.* This is cited as proof that by uniting inside the settler unions we will be able to not only get immediate economic benefits, but will be laying the foundations for eventual strategic unity with our "brother and sister" Euro-Amerikan workers. In that viewpoint, money-based tactical unity with settlers will eventually produce a heartfelt strategic unity, wherein Euro-Amerikan workers will join us as true comrades in making revolution against their Empire. What our analysis has proved is that this view is worse than simple-minded.

To better examine the question of strategic and tactical relations, we need to turn to the broader history of "Black-White workers unity," which has been used in the U.S. Empire as the classic example of the supposed superiority of radical integrationism. We need to begin with the theoretical framework constructed by *Message to the Black Movement*. *Message* performed a mentally liberating deed by taking the question of unity out of the fog of "racial" or "interracial" sentiment—posing it instead in terms of national interests and class interests:

> *"Black-White worker solidarity cannot be attained at any cost, but at a particular cost. We do not agree with white leftist revisionists that Black and White workers share the same interest because they are both workers. While this may be true on a tactical level (specific struggles around certain issues) it is not true on a strategic level. Strategically speaking (long range) the Black workers ultimate goal is the same as the masses of Blacks, which is toward national self-determination as a people … Both the establishment of a Black revolutionary Nation based on socialist relations, and overthrowing the present capitalist system and establishment of a predominantly white workers state are complementary struggles, and as such there will be tactical unity around issues that effect both Black and white workers."[1]*

---

* They are the first and last such, as the Hawaiian plantations are closing down and shifting production further into the Third World.

While this view was an important advance, it also contained certain contradictions. It assumed, despite settlerism, that the Euro-Amerikan masses and the Afrikan masses had nationally separate but parallel struggles, both moving in the same direction. Because of this "complementary" relationship, there would naturally "be tactical unity" between "Black and white workers."

First of all, tactical unity should be understood as temporary, short-run unity around a specific issue by forces that can even be fundamentally antagonistic. The Chinese Revolution and the U.S. Empire had for a few years a tactical unity against the Japanese Empire. The unity between proletarians of different nations, struggling towards socialism, is not tactical but strategic. There is nothing temporary or tactical about the deep bond, for example, between the Vietnamese Revolution and the guerillas of El Salvador. We ourselves have deep feelings of unity—more *strategic* than any national boundary—towards our comrades in Vietnam.

If "both Black and white workers" were indeed moving towards socialism in their respective nations, then the unity would be more than tactical. In reality this is not the situation. *Message* becomes confused when it tries to deal with the fact that immediate issues (higher wages in a factory, tenants' rights legislation, etc.) call for some tactical relationship between "Black and white workers." This is a relationship in the larger framework of national antagonism.

It is necessary to deepen this to see more fully what is tactical and what is strategic in the linked struggles of Euro-Amerikan and Third World workers. Particularly, in seeing that revolutionaries are not the only ones with tactics and strategies. *What is the relationship of tactical unity to genocide?*

The classic and most cited example of "Black-White workers unity" has always been the United Mine Workers. From its founding in 1890, the UMW constitution admitted all coal miners regardless of "race, creed or nationality." As early as 1900 the UMW had some 20,000 Afrikan members, while even in the earliest years an Afrikan miner, Richard L. Davis, was a union leader (Davis was elected to the UMW National Executive Board in 1896 and 1897). Davis himself said after many white miners voted to put him on the Board that the "... question of color in our miners organization will soon be a thing of the past." By 1939 the UMW had as many as 100,000 Afrikan members, and Horace Cayton and George Mitchell wrote that year in *Black Workers and the New Unions* that the UMW was "... from the point of view of the participation of Negroes, the most important in the country."

One of the earliest modern industrial unions in the U.S., the UMW was the only major union with significant Afrikan membership. The most integrated union in the AFL, the UMW under John L. Lewis led the breakaway from the old AFL to form the more militant CIO. To this very day the Mine Workers Union has Afrikan local and district officers and the original constitutional provisions still making discrimination by any member grounds for expulsion.

The historic place assigned the UMW as an example of "working class unity" and integration is unique. The *Negro Almanac* says, for instance: "It has been said that no other CIO leader better understood 'the importance of equalitarian racial policies for successful unionism than John L. Lewis of the United Mine Workers.' In this union, the common economic and occupational hardships endured by all minimized—although they did not totally eliminate—racial differences among members, even in the South ... CIO policies ultimately prompted Thurgood Marshall to declare that 'The program (of this organization) has become a bill of rights for Negro labor in America.'"

In the UMW we can examine tactical unity over a 90-year period in a major industry. The fundamental reality was that Afrikan miners and Euro-Amerikan miners had *tactical* unity, but different *strategic* interests. Afrikan miners attempted to pursue their tactical interests by uniting within settler unionism, helping to organize all coal miners and thus building a strong enough union to significantly increase wages and improve working conditions. This tactical unity was very practical and easily understood. *But the strategic contradictions are now equally clear, while seldom brought to light.* While Afrikan workers had the strategic goal of liberating their nation from the U.S. Empire, the settler workers had the strategic goal of preserving the U.S. Empire's exploitation of the oppressed nations. The mythology that they had "common class interests" proved factually untrue.

Since Afrikan miners were perhaps 20% of all coal miners and a majority in the Southern mines, it was impractical for settler miners to build a union that excluded them. As early as 1899, UMW president John Mitchell told an astonished Congressional investigation that even in Alabama "There are cases where a colored man will be the officer of a local union" with both Afrikan and Euro-Amerikan members:

> "I will say there is no difference as far as our organization is concerned. They recognize—as a matter of necessity they were forced to recognize—the identity of interest. I suppose among miners, the same as other white men in the South, there is the same class differences, but they have been forced down, so they must raise the colored man up or they go down, and they consequently have mixed together in their organization."[2]

Both Euro-Amerikan and Afrikan miners wanted tactical unity. However, since they had different strategic interests their tactical unity meant different things to each group. The Euro-Amerikan miners wanted tactical unity in order to advance their own narrow economic interests and take away Afrikan jobs.

In the early 1920s the UMW could in practice be divided into two regions: the unionized North, where most UMW locals in Illinois, Indiana, Ohio, and Pennsylvania used their settler organization to keep Afrikan miners out; the unorganized Appalachian South, where the UMW needed Afrikan miners to build the settler union.

While the UMW welcomed Afrikan workers as unpaid organizers and militants, when a mining community in the North became organized very often the Afrikan "union brothers" were told to get out. At the 1921 UMW Pittsburgh District Convention an experienced Afrikan delegate, recalling how he and hundreds of other Afrikan miners had taken up rifles to join the union's "Armed Marches" in West Virginia, complained bitterly:

> "Those colored men from the State of West Virginia put their shoul-
> ders to the shoulders of white brothers, and our newspapers tell us
> that they have sacrificed their lives for this great movement.
>
> "I think it looks very embarrassing when a man would sacrifice his
> life for this movement, and after the victory is won then his brother
> would say: 'We need you no longer.' A livelihood belongs to every
> man and when you deprive me of it … you have almost commit-
> ted murder to the whole entire race."

Richard L. Davis, whom we mentioned as the first Afrikan to be elected to the UMW Board, spent sixteen years as an unpaid labor organizer—not only in Ohio, but in Alabama and West Virginia as well. Finally he was white-listed, unable to get work from the mine operators and unable despite his leading role to get either financial aid or paid organizer's position with the UMW. Living in great want, unable to provide for his children, ill, he finally died of "lung fever" at the age of thirty-five.[3] He was used and then discarded. This is why Euro-Amerikan historians write of him as the best possible example for Third World workers to follow.

The union actually depended upon a fighting base of Afrikan miners to get established in the South. As we discussed earlier, in both the 1908 and 1920–21 Alabama strikes the majority of strikers were Afrikans (76% of the 1920–21 UMW strikers were Afrikan). An Afrikan miner who worked in Mercer County, West Virginia for 43 years recalled:

> "The white man was scared to join the union at first around here.
> The Black man took the organizing jobs and set it up. We went into
> the bushes and met in secret; and we held all the key offices. A few
> of the white miners would slip around and come to our meetings.

After they found out that the company wasn't going to run them
away, why they began to appear more often. And quite naturally,
when they became the majority, they elected who they wanted for
their Presidents, Vice Presidents and Treasurers. This left a few
jobs as Secretaries for the Negroes. But at the beginning, most all
of the main offices in the locals were held by Negroes."

The UMW's triumph in the mid-1930s meant that at last the Euro-Amerikan miners held enough power to defend their settler class interests. Much higher wages, per-ton production royalties for union pension and medical plans, seniority and safety regulations, and other benefits all resulted from this triumph. Today, while underground mining is still very hard and dangerous work, the union mines are highly mechanized and workers regularly earn $20,000 to $30,000 per year.* These are very desirable jobs by the standards of the imperialist labor market. Even the weakened position of the UMW since the 1960s has not completely wiped out the gains made.

Now that the fruits of successful union struggle have been placed in view, we can evaluate in practice the gains that Afrikan miners won by sacrificing to build the settler UMW and steadfastly uniting with their Euro-Amerikan "union brothers." The gains, objectively speaking, are non-existent. There are no gains because Afrikan coal miners have been virtually wiped out by the alliance of settler capitalists and settler miners. Driven out of the industry by the tens of thousands, Afrikan miners found their share of the jobs taken over by their Euro-Amerikan "union brothers."

In 1930 Afrikan coal miners comprised 22% of the industry in Southern Appalachia (Alabama, Kentucky, Tennessee, West Virginia, Virginia). *By 1960 their share of the coal mining jobs in Southern Appalachia had been cut to only 6%.* Even during the boom

---

* In 1980 the President's Coal Commission said that the 233,400 coal miners in the U.S. earned an average wage of $20,000 per year (with average weekly gross earnings of $434.70). Of these 50% owned their own homes and an added 24% owned mobile homes. 87% owned their own cars and 24% owned 2 cars. While imperialism is literally destroying much of Appalachia through physical and social environmental dislocation, it is paying high wages in the union mines in order to maintain mass acceptance of its policies.

years of the 1940s and early 1950s, when tens of thousands of new
Euro-Amerikan miners were getting hired, thousands of Afrikan
miners were being fired and not replaced.

In doing this the imperialists were merely carrying out their
general policy on colonial labor, restricting its role in strategic industries and reserving the best jobs for Euro-Amerikans in order to
ensure the loyalty of settler society. When most coal mining jobs
were brutal hand-loading of the coal while working in two foot high
tunnels, there were many jobs for Afrikan labor. But as unionization and mechanization raised the wages and improved the work, it
became "too good" for Afrikans, and the companies and the UMW
started pushing Afrikans out.

Denied jobs operating the new machinery, Afrikan laborers
with ten years seniority found themselves being permanently laid
off (in other words, fired) at the same time as the company would
be hiring Euro-Amerikan teenagers for high-wage jobs on the new
equipment. The other favored tactic was to transfer large numbers of
Afrikan miners into the oldest mines, working them to exhaustion
without investing even a penny in modernization, and then closing
the worked out mine and firing the Afrikan men. At the same time
the same company would be opening new mines elsewhere with an
all-white workforce. The United Mine Workers actively conspired
with all the mine companies in this campaign against Afrikan labor—it would not have been possible otherwise.

Today surface mining accounts for over 60% of all coal production, double its percentage just ten years ago. The growing sector of the industry, it is also the best paid, safest, cleanest, and most
mechanized. It should be no surprise that these jobs are reserved for
Euro-Amerikans. Alabama is traditionally the most heavily Afrikan
area in the coal industry. **Yet in 1974, the UMW's district 20 in
Alabama had only ten Afrikan members among the 1,500 surface
miners—while Afrikans are over 26% of the area's population.**

The "Black-Out" of Afrikan workers in the coal industry
has reached a point where the 1980 report on *The American Coal
Miner* by the President's Coal Commission (chaired by John D.
Rockefeller IV) has an entire chapter on the Navaho miners who
produce 3% of the U.S. coal, but not even one page on Afrikan

miners. In a few paragraphs, the study praises the UMW as an example of integration, and notes that past "discrimination" is being corrected by corporate civil rights programs. It ends these few words by noting that the coal companies would supposedly like to hire more Afrikans for these well-paying jobs, but they can't find any job-seekers: *"Coal companies contend that the major problem in finding Black miners is that many Black families have migrated to the large urban centers and that few live in the coal fields."*[4]

We can see, then, that the *tactical unity* of settler and Afrikan miners cannot be understood without examining the *strategy* of both groups. *Euro-Amerikan labor used that tactical unity to get Afrikan workers to carry out the strategy of preserving the settler Empire.* Some Afrikan miners received tactical gains from this unity in the form of higher wages and better working conditions. But in return, Afrikan miners disorganized themselves, giving themselves up to the hegemony of settler unionism. Thus disarmed and disorganized, they soon discovered that the result of the *tactical unity* was to take their jobs and drive them out. There are no tactics without a larger strategy, and in the U.S. Empire that strategy has a national and class character.

As that Afrikan miner so correctly pointed out in 1921: *"A livelihood belongs to every man and when you deprive me of it ... you have almost committed murder to the whole entire race."* Without that economic base, the Afrikan communities in West Virginia lost 25% of their total population during 1960–1970, as families were forced out of the coal areas. This, then, is the bitter fruit of "Black-white workers unity" over ninety years in the coal industry.

While such integration was shocking to many settlers, we can now understand why Richard L. Davis was elected to the UMW National Board in 1896. He was the chosen "Judas goat," selected to help lure Afrikan miners into following settler unionism. The UMW *Journal* reminded white miners at the same time that with his new position: *"He will in a special way be able to appear before our colored miners and preach the gospel of trade unions..."*

When Afrikan miners in Ohio complained that the UMW was *"A White man's organization,"* Davis answered them: *"Now, my dear people, I, as a colored man, would ask of you to dispell all such ideas as they are not only false but foolish and unwise ... you have the same inter-ests at stake as your white brother..."*[5] While Davis proved his sincer-ity by literally giving his life to build industrial unionism, it isn't very hard to see that he was elevated into a high union office by white miners because that actually represented their own narrow interests. He was the mis-leader (although idealistic and honest) they helped create for Afrikan miners.

Even today, after the decisive blows have fallen, we find mis-leaders telling Afrikan coal miners that *better unity* with settler work-ers, and *reforming* the settler unions, are the answers to their prob-lems. The damage in this case is limited solely by the fact that no one can be killed twice.

Bill Worthington, past President of the Black Lung Association (of miners disabled from breathing coal dust), is a prominent retired Afrikan miner. He often speaks at national labor rallies, community and settler "left" events. And he trots out with shameless disregard for the truth the whole tired line of settleristic lies: *"The operators try to divide Black and white. It's a master plan to keep confusion among the workers. Keep the poor people fighting one another."*

This is the classic line invented by the settler "left" to explain away national oppression. In point of fact, Afrikan and Euro-Amerikan coal miners are not actually fighting each other in the coal fields. By cooperating with the imperialists, Euro-Amerikan miners have forced most Afrikans out and now have whatever remains of the jobs. Afrikan miners have been forced out and are in a difficult position to fight. Imperialism has the coal mines, the settlers have the jobs—and are going to try to hold on to them—and the unem-ployed Afrikan workers get the inspiring propaganda about "Black-white workers' unity."

This history proves concretely that the *strategy* of settleristic assimilation and the tactics that flowed from it were incorrect for Afrikan miners, and that their true *strategic interests* lay not only in national liberation but in developing their *own* fighting organi-zations which alone could defend their true class interests. It was only from that foundation that correct tactical relations could have been made with Euro-Amerikan workers. **Correct alliances must be based on correct strategy.**

We also see how the Euro-Amerikan labor aristocracy uses tactical unity and the surface appearance of advancing the common good, but only really acts to protect settler privilege and maintain settler hegemony over labor. It is always important to go beneath the surface appearances of such tactical unity, no matter how good it looks.

In the summer of 1974 the United Mine Workers and the Euro-Amerikan "left" announced that a wonderful breakthrough had just happened: the union was leading thousands of settler miners to make common cause with the Afrikan liberation struggle in South Afrika! This was an event so improbable as to surpass anything but the propaganda of the settler "left."

In its June 5, 1974, issue, the radical weekly *Guardian* ran a large head-line: "MINERS HALT WORK TO PROTEST S. AFRICA COAL." In the article underneath they proclaimed that *"spirited action"* had *"united the worker's movement with the Black liberation struggle."* The article details how: *"nearly 8,000 miners went on a one-day walkout throughout Alabama May 22. On the same day 1,500 people, also mainly miners, staged a militant rally in common cause with the Black workers of South Afrika. Carrying picket signs which read, 'Stop Imperialism in South Africa', 'End Racism and Slavery', and 'Stop The Southern Co.', the workers blasted the plans of U.S. energy companies to import coal from racist South Africa."*

The "militant rally" was organized by the Birmingham-based Coalition to Stop South African Coal and endorsed by UMW District 20. The next week the *Guardian* ran follow-up material in its June 12, 1974, issue, including a large photograph of a Euro-Amerikan and an Afrikan kneeling together wearing miner's helmets, holding a sign urging "Do Not Buy South African Coal." Another photograph showed a Euro-Amerikan miner holding a sign saying "Oppose Racism—In Africa And At Home!" The *Guardian* further said:

> "Times are changing in the U.S. labor movement. When a major union recognizes the unity between the struggles of U.S. workers and workers abroad, it is a sharp departure from the usual union campaign of 'Be American, Buy American', which

> fails to distinguish the common interests of workers through-
> out the world. It is even more significant when the U.S. work-
> ers are from the South and the workers abroad are Afrikan..."

This was truly unbelievable. How could the UMW and its mass of Euro-Amerikan members—who had a proven record of white su-premacist attacks on Afrikan workers—literally overnight without a struggle be converted to Proletarian Internationalism? Yet the Euro-Amerikan "left" was responsible for that new alliance. Some of the organizations involved in uniting with the UMW were the Rev-olutionary Union (now the Revolutionary Communist Party), the October League (now CPUSA-ML), The Black Workers Congress, some elements from the Southern Conference Education Fund, and the Atlanta African Liberation Support Committee.

On the basis of its newfound "solidarity" with Afrikan Liberation, the UMW District 20 officers approached the Afrikan dockworkers in Mobile, Alabama (where the South Afrikan coal was to be unloaded) and asked them to join the campaign and not unload the coal. *The Afrikan dockworkers in Mobile refused.* And at that point the whole treacherous scheme by the UMW and the set-tler radicals blew apart at the seams.

It turned out that the UMW District 20 leadership was, of course, totally reactionary and white supremacist. They were, in fact, the labor arm in the area of the rabid George Wallace "American Independence Party" movement. Their settler union had also en-dorsed the then Attorney-General Bill Baxley, who was appealing to Euro-Amerikan voters by personally trying to get the death penalty for the Atmore-Holman Brothers. Inside the mines they openly pro-moted the most vicious race-baiting—knowing all this, the Afrikan dockworkers refused to have anything to do with them.[6]

The genesis of that strange charade began with the UMW's decision to fight importation of all foreign coal. The decision by the Southern Power Co. to import $50 million worth of low-sulfur South Afrikan coal was singled out. At that point the District 20 re-actionaries were quietly approached by some Euro-Amerikan radi-cals, who convinced them that by falsely adopting "anti-imperialist" slogans they could trick the Afrikan dockworkers into fighting to

save Euro-Amerikan jobs (stolen from Afrikans, of course). That's
what all that treachery was about—"tactical unity" based on settler self-interest. That's why we saw the unreal spectacle of racist
Alabama settlers marching around with signs saying "Support South
African Liberation."

Frustrated, the Klan-like unionists turned on the settler radicals and denounced them. Soon the *Guardian* and the other settler
"left" organizations had to admit that the UMW leaders were not as
they'd originally pictured them. Even after the UMW admitted that
they didn't care about any Afrikan liberation, but only wanted to
boycott all foreign coal to save settler jobs, the Euro-Amerikan radicals kept trying to support them.

Finally, the UMW miners had to tell the radicals to leave the
boycott picket lines or get tossed out. An article in the Sept. 11,
1974, *Guardian* said that even though the Alabama UMW was now
cooperating with the FBI and the Alabama State Police, the radical
Coalition to Stop South African Coal still wanted to unite with them
and still supported their settler boycott.

The entire example of attempted tactical unity shows how
strongly the oppressor nation character of both the settler unions
and the settler "Left" determines their actions. The settler "Left"
tried to reach an opportunistic deal with reactionary labor leaders,
hoping that Afrikan workers could be used to pay the price for their
alliance.

PATRIOT

VOL. 32, NO. 5   MAY, 1974   PUBLISHED BY SOUTHERN CONFERENCE EDUCATIONAL FUND (SCEF), LOUISVILLE, KY.

Coal From South Africa

Apartheid in The Mines

The following article is taken from a memorandum written by Tom Bethell of the United Mine Workers of America. It describes the new development of coal imports from South Africa, the threat this is to the job security of U.S. miners, and the added strength it will give to the repressive apartheid policies of the South African government.

Arrangements are currently being made to bring substantial quantities of low-sulfur steam coal into the United States from the Republic of South Africa. This move on the part of the coal and utilities industries requires a strong response on the part of the UMWA, because it takes jobs away from American miners and because coal is produced in South Africa under conditions very close to slave labor.   (Continued on page 7)

Alabama Miners Say "No"

BIRMINGHAM, Ala.–Almost 1,000 people took part in a rally and picket line here on May 22. They were letting the stockholders of the Southern Company know that they were opposed to coal being imported from South Africa.

The occasion was the annual stockholders' meeting of the Southern Company, a holding company which owns Georgia Power Company, Alabama Power Company, Mississippi Power Company, and Gulf Power Company.

At issue was a contract signed by the Southern Company to import 2 million tons ($50 million worth) of coal from South African coal producers over the next 3 years. The first shipment will be brought into the Port of Mobile in mid-July and burned at generating stations in Florida.

Rank and file members, particularly from District 20 of the UMWA and other unions, as well as people from various community organizations made the rally the largest and most militant gathering in Alabama in over a decade.

The coal companies employing District 20 members reported absenteeism at around 90%. The miners said they were not on strike but that they were "taking time off to take care of business."

Approximately 100 miners went to the state capitol in Montgomery to see elected government officials. Governor Wallace was out of town and the politicians told the miners that they couldn't do anything to prevent American corporations from importing coal.

At the Birmingham picket line the men were angry, and they manifested their attitude both in their conversation and in the slogans on their signs: "Pull the switch on Southern Co.", "Stop Southern Company Imperialism" and "No Slave Coal".

After two hours of picketing, the miners held a rally on a corner of the hotel lot. Acting as coordinator was Andy Himes of the Selma Project, an Alabama political action group which worked in the last United Mine Workers election to help throw out the corrupt Tony Boyle machine.

Among the speakers was Mrs. John Marchant, the wife of a retired miner from Brookwood, a coal town outside Birmingham. Mrs. Marchant talked about the lynchings, lockouts, and "yellow dog" (anti-union) contracts the companies had used against the miners in the twenties and about how her own brother had been killed in a roof fall in the thirties. She said it was profit that they had to fight then and it was profit they had to fight now.

Don Stone of the Black Workers Congress spoke about the conditions in the South African coal fields and stressed the importance of fighting in both places against the same enemy, the monopoly capitalist corporations.

Andy Himes wound things up with a statement about how the Company was not only chiseling the miners of Alabama out of jobs but that the electric ratepayers of the Southeast were being expected to pick up the tab. "They say that they're concerned about Alabama because they live here too. Well, that's a damn lie. Look at the top ten stockholders of the Southern Company. They're all New York City banks and all they care about is more profit."

(Information from Andy Himes and the Georgia Power Project).

Above: South African miners.   *Below: Food in South African mining camps served with a shovel and miners in Birmingham demonstrating against the Southern Company.*

    While the settler radicals professed a heartfelt concern with helping the liberation struggle in South Afrika, we notice that they were totally unconcerned with the long-standing genocidal attack of the UMW against the economic base of Afrikans in the occupied South. Further, they covered up for their settler fellow citizens as much as possible. What is evident is that despite the tactical division between the rabid, George Wallace-loving settlers and the radical settlers, their common national position as oppressors gave them a strategic unity in opposing the interests of the oppressed.

    After an emotional meeting in their local union hall with a representative from Zimbabwe, the Afrikan longshoremen temporarily held off the orders of their local union president and stalled for a day in unloading the South Afrikan coal. They desired to show support for the liberation struggle of their brothers and sisters in Southern Afrika. However incomplete and still undeveloped, that desire for solidarity was real. But in regards to the attempted UMW boycott, the Afrikan longshoremen were firm in their refusal to have anything to do with it.

That attempted maneuver was crude and obvious, no matter how lovingly the settler radicals wrapped it up in a camouflage of "anti-imperialist" slogans and postures. The Afrikan longshoremen saw right through it, right to its rip-off, reactionary essence. How come the Black Workers Congress couldn't unmask it? How come all the assorted Third World comrades involved in those radical "multinational" organizations couldn't unmask it? They thought they were "Communists," but in practice their political framework of settleristic revisionism left them politically simple-minded, unable to prevent themselves from being pawns in the most vulgar white supremacist maneuvers.

Exposed and defeated, this fiasco was dug up out of its grave four years later. This time by a new crew—the Chinese-Amerikan-led Workers Viewpoint Organization (now called the Communist Workers Party). In their campaign to recruit Afrikans, this grouping had organized an "African Liberation Support Committee" under its leadership to stage a large Afrikan Liberation Day 1978 rally in Washington, DC.*

They dug up and reprinted the old, staged UMW photograph of the Euro-Amerikan and Afrikan miners kneeling together, even going so far as to say that the 1974 white supremacist UMW boycott gives *"lessons for future struggles"* by its *"examples of international solidarity between all working people by supporting Afrikan miners."* That old lie of four years earlier was revived as evidence to justify another round of integrationism. This organization certainly shows that even an entire group of radical Chinese-Amerikans can be indoctrinated into settler ideology.[7] While proletarian ideology has a clear relationship to the oppressed, it is not transmitted genetically.

So we see that tactical unity is not just some neutral, momentary alliances of convenience. Tactical unity flows out of strategy as well as immediate circumstances. Nor is tactical unity with

---

* We place "African Liberation Support Committee" in quotation marks to distinguish it from the earlier, genuine ALSC.

Euro-American workers simply the non-antagonistic working to-gether of "complementary" but different movements. Even the sim-plest rank-and-file reform coalition inside a settler union is linked to the strategic conflict of oppressor and oppressed nations.

The alliances formed around the fiery League of Revolutionary Black Workers in Detroit illustrate all this. The rise of the League's Revolutionary Union Movements in 1967, first at the old Chrysler Dodge Main plant, had alarmed the United Auto Workers labor ar-istocracy. The League represented the militant, anti-capitalist, and anti-settler union sentiment of the young Afrikan workers in the Detroit auto plants. At least at Chrysler's Dodge Main and Eldon Ave. Gear and Axle plants the LRBW had won a clear majority sup-port of young Afrikan workers *against* the UAW.

The UAW leadership responded with numerous attacks of dif-ferent kinds—from verbal to violence. Emil Mazey, UAW Secretary-Treasurer and the most prominent figure in the liberal grouping of settler trade unionists against the Vietnam War, denounced the LRBW as *"black fascists."* He called upon Euro-Amerikan auto work-ers to respond to this new *"black peril"* (his words): *"We can no longer tolerate the tactics of these young militants."*[8] And when the UAW used direct police intimidation to defeat the LRBW's Ron March candi-dacy for union trustee at Dodge Main, the liberal settler union didn't look too much different from George Wallace.

But the UAW was different. One of the key ways it reacted to contain the League was to promote alternative, non-revolutionary Afrikan unionists. The International UAW had always intervened everywhere in the local unions to keep settlers in charge. This be-came particularly important with the gradual rise of Afrikan mem-bership—the UAW officially placed Afrikans then at 25% of the UAW membership. But the breakout of revolutionary leadership in the form of the LRBW had outflanked the Euro-Amerikan labor bosses.

The UAW leadership selectively stopped organizing against those non-revolutionary Afrikan unionists who had been seeking the top offices in Detroit locals. After the LRBW broke out, moder-ate Afrikans were elected as the UAW local presidents at Ford Wayne Local 900, Chrysler Forge Local 47, Plymouth Local 51, Chrysler

Mopar Local 1248, etc. etc.[9] So that in addition to cooperating with the companies to fire LRBW cadre, using police intimidation, etc., the settler union bureaucracy tried to undercut the League—that is to undercut revolutionary Afrikan leadership which rejected settler hegemony—by advancing alternative, moderate leaders for Afrikan auto workers.*

Now, the League itself had made alliances with Euro-Amerikan radicals in the auto plants. Most importantly, they had responded positively to suggestions from the United National Caucus for a cooperative working relationship against the UAW leadership. The United National Caucus was (and still is) the more-or-less official opposition coalition to the UAW leadership, with members from reform caucuses in locals throughout the UAW.

It had grown out of the "Dollar An Hour Now Caucus," a caucus of Euro-Amerikan skilled craftsmen who were pressuring for an immediate dollar an hour raise for themselves alone. The UNC was organized by Euro-Amerikan radicals, and had an Afrikan co-chairman.

He was Jordan Sims, an experienced activist and union reformer at Chrysler's Eldon Ave. Gear and Axle—an LRBW center of strength. Sims, while not a revolutionary, had defended the League in his attempts to win the local presidency. (After several stolen elections and getting fired, Sims finally became local President in 1973.) So this broad, "Black-white workers' unity" had some constructive possibilities.

But the world of the automobile plants is, however important, not the entire world. In April 1968 Martin Luther King, Jr. was assassinated in Memphis. Detroit blew up—and settler Detroit armed up. In the Detroit white suburbs gun sales soared as settlers prepared

---

* Bayard Rustin, arch-flunky for the AFL-CIO and Zionism, crowed about this in his article, "The Failure of Black Separatism": "Some of the most interesting election victories were won at the Chrysler Eldon Gear and Axle Local 961 and Dodge No. 3 in Hamtramck, where the separatist Eldon Revolutionary Union Movement (ELRUM) and Dodge Revolutionary Union Movement (DRUM) have been active. At both locals the DRUM and ELRUM candidates were handily defeated by Black trade unionists who campaigned on a platform of militant integrationism..."

to keep Afrikans out of their communities. Euro-Amerikan house-wives were signed up in special handgun classes. A publication associated with the League reprinted a newspaper photograph of suburban Euro-Amerikan women practicing with their new guns—and referring to the settler women in unfriendly words.

The problem was that one of the settler women photographed was the wife of a leading member of the United National Caucus! Incensed, the skilled Euro-Amerikan auto workers demanded that their caucus either break off ties with the "Black nationalists" or force the League to print an apology. The settler skilled tradesmen were raging mad that "their" women had been insulted by Afrikans. Naturally, the LRBW was unlikely to apologize for pointing out a true fact about Euro-Amerikan behavior. The relationship between the UNC and the LRBW was off, a casualty of the sudden lightning-bolt of truth that flashed across Amerika after King's assassination.

Privately, the leader of the Euro-Amerikan skilled tradesmen admitted that his people were wrong, that their attitude towards the LRBW was racist. But to be principled at that moment, he said, would be to *"throw away"* his years of work founding the United National Caucus and organizing settler auto workers into joining it. As a Euro-Amerikan radical he was unwilling to see his "rank-and-file" settler organization torn apart over their racism.

Besides, he continued, to be overly principled would be meaningless since *"the League is through."* With a smile, he revealed that the UNC had been secretly dealing with key Afrikan supporters of the League. As an example, he said that at a plant of the Ford River Rouge complex the UNC had convinced a League activist that if he split with the League and took some of its base of support with him, that together with the UNC's Euro-Amerikan voting bloc they would have enough votes to make him the next local union President! The UNC leader felt certain that with such practical bribes, they would be able to gradually win over enough Afrikan workers to undermine the League.[10]*

---

* The complex reasons for the League's demise and the outcome of the various counterinsurgency tactics against it is far beyond the scope of this paper. This case study does not answer these questions.

It is interesting that the supporters of this radical-led, "rank-and-file" workers caucus were busy arming themselves against Afrikans—at the same time tactical unity for union reform was being proposed. The most interesting fact that emerges, however, is that this radical-led settler caucus—organized to fight the established UAW bureaucracy—was using the exact same tactic against Afrikan revolutionaries as was the UAW bureaucracy! Both were working to divide the ranks of Afrikan auto workers, both promoting moderate Afrikan leaders who accepted settler hegemony, in order to undercut the threatened leadership of Afrikan revolutionaries. So where was the real unity?

In earlier chapters we primarily focused on the larger picture of Euro-Amerikan workers in relation to the expansion of the U.S. Empire and the development within that of settlerism. Here we have examined the politics of settler unionism in the workplace, in its tactical relations with Third World workers.

What is important about these case histories is that they should push us to think, to question, to closely examine many of the neocolonial remnants in our minds. "Working class unity" of oppressor and oppressed is both theoretically good, and is immediately practical we are told. It supposedly pays off in higher wages, stronger unions, and more organization. But did it?

Some Afrikan coal miners did indeed get higher wages, better working conditions and so on from this unity. But to pay for that most got driven out of their jobs. Many Afrikan families who once mined coal now live in exile and on welfare in the North. A part of the economic foundation of New Afrika was taken over and occupied by settler workers—acting as social troops of the U.S. Empire. It was a national setback. In all this the UMW, the union organization, was guarding only the strategic interests of U.S. Imperialism. Afrikan miners proved to be without organization, merely prisoners within an organization of their oppressors.

Was this just an isolated, untypical example? No. Afrikan workers were gradually herded into the oldest, least mechanized mines. Their exploitation helped provide the capital for modernization and economic investment elsewhere—and then they were laid off and the industry was gradually de-Afrikanized. Sounds like Detroit, doesn't it? What happened to the many thousands of Afrikan workers who were once the majority force in the now-closed Chicago meat-packing industry?

The actual history disproves the thesis that in settler Amerika "common working class interests" override the imperialist contradictions of oppressor and oppressed nations when it comes to tactical unity around economic issues. The same applies to the thesis that supposed ideological unity with the Euro-Amerikan "Left" also overrides imperialist contradictions, and hence, even with their admitted shortcomings, they are supposed allies of the oppressed against U.S. Imperialism. *Could it be the other way around?* That despite their tactical contradictions with the bourgeoisie, that Euro-Amerikan workers and revisionistic radicals have strategic unity *with* U.S. Imperialism? Most importantly, how has imperialism been so successful in using this tactical unity against the oppressed?

The thesis we have advanced about the settleristic and non-proletarian nature of the U.S. oppressor nation is a historic truth, and thereby a key to leading the concrete struggles of today. Self-reliance and building mass institutions and movements of a specific national character, under the leadership of a communist party, are absolute necessities for the oppressed. Without these there can be no national liberation. This thesis is not "anti-white" or "racialist" or "narrow nationalism." Rather, it is the advocates of oppressor nation hegemony over all struggles of the masses that are promoting the narrowest of nationalisms—that of the U.S. settler nation. *When we say that the principal characteristic of imperialism is parasitism, we are also saying that the principal characteristic of settler trade unionism is parasitism, and that the principal characteristic of settler radicalism is parasitism.*

Every nation and people has its own contribution to make to the world revolution. This is true for all of us, and obviously for Euro-Amerikans as well. But this is another discussion, one that can only really take place in the context of breaking up the U.S. Empire and ending the U.S. oppressor nation.

THE END

When the new Republic is established there will never be any more army in Mexico. Armies are the greatest support of tyranny. There can be no Dictator without an army.

We will put the army to work. In all parts of the Republic we will establish military colonies composed of the veterans of the Revolution. The state will give them grants of agricultural lands and establish big industrial enterprises to give them work.

Three days a week they will work and work hard, because honest work is more important than fighting, and only honest work makes good citizens. And the other three days they will receive military instruction and go out and teach all the people how to fight.

Then, when the Patria is invaded, we will just have to telephone from the palace at Mexico City, and in half a day all the Mexican people will rise from their fields and factories, fully armed, equipped and organized to defend their children and their homes.

My ambition is to live my life in one of those military colonies, among my compañeros whom I love, who have suffered so long and so deeply with me.

Francisco "Pancho" Villa

ENDNOTES

I. THE HEART OF WHITENESS

1. William Bradford, *Of Plymouth Plantation* (NY, 1952), p. 23.

2. Mildred Campbell, "Social Origins of Some Early Americans" in Smith, ed., *17th Century America* (NY, 1972), p. 68. Other accounts are similar. For example, see: C.E. Banks, *The Winthrop Fleet of 1630* (Cambridge, 1930); Morison's account of Sir Walter Raleigh's second Virginia Colony of 1587 describes the colonists as: "All were middle-class English or Irish" (Morison, p. 657).

3. Campbell, op. cit., p. 82.

4. Treasury Papers 47: 9–11. Quoted in Richard B. Morris, *Government and Labor in Early America* (NY, 1946), p. 48.

5. Christopher Hill, *Reformation to Industrial Revolution* (NY, 1967), pp. 48, 64.

6. Richard Hofstadter, *America at 1750* (NY, 1973), pp. 11–12. This is but one source out of many, all essentially in agreement.

7. Morris, op. cit., p. 48.

8. Campbell, op. cit., p. 83.

9. Theodore Roosevelt, *The Winning of the West, Vol. I* (NY, 1900), p. 90.

10. Wilcomb E. Washburn, "The Moral and Legal Justification for Dispossessing the Indians." In Smith, ed., p. 23.

11. Testimony of Wilbur R. Jacobs at Sioux Treaty Hearing. In R. Dunbar-Ortiz, *The Great Sioux Nation* (San Francisco, 1971), p. 60; Henry F. Dobyns, "Estimating Aboriginal American Population. An Appraisal of Techniques With a New Hemispheric Estimate." *Current Anthropology*, Vol. III, No. 4, p. 395.

12. Philip Gibson, quoted in Hofstadter, op. cit, p. 69; also see Cook & Simpson (1948).

13. Harold E. Driver, *Indians of North America* (Chicago, 1968), p. 604.

14. *New York Times*, May 18, 1899.

15. Karl Marx, *The Poverty of Philosophy* (NY, 1963), p. 111.

16. See: Hofstadter, op. cit, p. 99; Ottley & Weatherby, eds., *The Negro In New York* (NY, 1967); Edith Evans Asbury, "Freed Black Farmers Tilled Manhattan's Soil in the 1600s," *New York Times*, Dec. 7, 1977.

17. See: Verner W. Crane, *The Southern Frontier, 1670–1732* (Ann Arbor, 1956); Dunbar-Ortiz, op. cit, p. 86.

18. Gary B. Nash, *Red, White, and Black* (Englewood Cliffs, 1974), pp. 112–113.

19. Ibid.

20. Ibid.

21. Samuel Eliot Morison, *The European Discovery of America: The Northern Voyages* (NY, 1971), p. 678.

22. Clinton Rossiter, *The First American Revolution* (NY, 1956), p. 41.

23. Hofstadter, op. cit, pp. 89–90.

24. Robert E. & B. Katherine Brown, *Virginia 1705–1786: Democracy or Aristocracy?* (East Lansing, 1964), p. 22.

25. Philip S. Foner, *Labor and the American Revolution* (Westport, 1976), pp. 8–9.

26. Jackson Turner Main, *The Social Structure of Revolutionary America* (Princeton, 1965), pp. 66–67. While we use Main's findings, it is evident that although Euro-Amerikan historians have widely differing conclusions about class stratification in this period, their factual bases are very similar.

For example, James A. Henretta, in his well-known essay, "Economic Development and Social Structure in Colonial Boston," concludes that the Colonial era was one of rapidly growing settler class inequality, with the "appearance of ... 'proletarians.'"

This is an often-quoted conclusion. Yet, a careful examination of his research shows that: (1) In rural Massachusetts of the 1770s land ownership was near-universal among the settlers (over 90%); (2) Even in Boston, a major urban center, the clear majority of settler men were self-employed property-owners (60–70%); (3) Henretta himself points out that many settler men who were without taxable property were not poor, but had comfortable incomes and were respected enough to be elected to public office. So, although Henretta chose to stress the appearance of inequality among settlers, his own research confirms the general picture of shared privilege and an exceptional way of life for the Euro-Amerikan conquerors.

27. Hofstadter, op. cit, p. 161.

28. Audrey C. Land, *Bases of the Plantation Society* (NY, 1969), p. 105.

29. Morris, op. cit, p. 40.

30. Karl Marx, *18th Brumaire ...* In *Selected Works* (NY, 1960), p. 104.

31. Karl Marx, *Wages, Price and Profit.* In *Selected Works* (NY, 1960), p. 192.

32. Foner, op. cit., p. 12.

33. Morris, op. cit., p. 46; Brown & Brown, op. cit., p. 22.

34. Morris, op. cit., p. 45.

35. Karl Marx, *Selected Works* (NY, 1960), p. 226.

36. Fred Shannon, *American Farmers Movements* (Princeton, 1957), p. 9; Morris, op. cit., p. 36.

37. Hill, op. cit., p. 74.

38. Morris, op. cit., pp. 36–37.

39. Thomas J. Wertenbaker, *The Shaping of Colonial Virginia* (NY, 1958), p. 134.

40. Morris, op. cit., p. 29.

II. STRUGGLES & ALLIANCES

1. Herbert Aptheker, *The Colonial Era* (NY, 1959), p. 62.

2. Theodore W. Allen, *Class Struggle and the Origins of Slavery* (Somerville, 1976), pp. 3–4.

3. A photograph of this plaque can be seen in: Charles W.H. Warner, *Road to Revolution* (Richmond, 1961).

4. Except as otherwise noted, events in Bacon's Rebellion are taken from Wilcomb E. Washburn, *The Governor and the Rebel* (Chapel Hill, 1957).

5. Bernard Bailyn, "Politics and Social Structure in Virginia." In Smith, op. cit., pp. 103–104; also Washburn, pp. 17–19.

6. Shannon, op. cit., pp. 109–110. Bacon's own account, written on June 8, 1676, is there as well.

7. Warner, op. cit., pp. 21–22.

8. Philip S. Foner, *History of the Labor Movement of the United States, Vol. I* (NY, 1978), p. 29.

9. Louis Adamic, *A Nation of Nations* (NY, 1945), p. 288.

10. For a brief account, see: Samuel Eliot Morison, *Oxford History of the American People* (NY, 1965), pp. 119–122.

11. Jack Hardy, *The First American Revolution* (NY, 1937), pp. 37–38.

12. Ibid, p. 72.

13. Richard C. Wade, *The Urban Frontier* (Chicago, 1971), p. 2.

14. Foner, *Labor and the American Revolution* op. cit., pp. 182–183.

15. Winthrop D. Jordan, *White Over Black* (NY, 1969), p. 115.

16. Thomas Paine, *Selected Writings* (NY, 1945), p. 29. John C. Miller states in his *Origins of the American Revolution* that "the patriots proclaimed themselves the champions of white supremacy against the British Government..." (pp. 478–479).

17. Roi Ottley, *Black Odyssey* (London, 1949), p. 63.

18. Benjamin Quarles, *The Negro in the American Revolution* (Chapel Hill, 1961), p. x.

19. Ibid, pp. 118–119.

20. Ibid, p. 131.

21. Lerone Bennett, Jr., *Before the Mayflower* (Baltimore, 1968), p. 62; Ottley, op. cit., p. 65; etc.

22. Quarles, op. cit., p. 28; Ottley, op. cit., p. 63.

23. Ottley, op. cit., p. 65.

24. Bennett, Jr., op. cit., p. 58.

25. Quarles, op. cit., p. 30.

26. Bennett, Jr., op. cit., p. 59; Ottley, op. cit., pp. 73–74.

27. Bennett, Jr., op. cit., p. 59; Ottley, op. cit., pp. 73–74.

28. Foner, *Labor and the American Revolution* op. cit., p. 184.

29. Quarles, op. cit., pp. 171–172.

III. THE CONTRADICTIONS OF NATION AND CLASS

1. Hofstadter, op. cit., p. 4.

2. Ottley, op. cit., p. 57.

3. See: Ronald T. Takaki, *Iron Cages* (NY, 1979), pp. 42–45; Winthrop D. Jordan, op. cit., pp. 429–440.

4. Takaki, op. cit., p. 44.

5. Stephen B. Oates, *The Fires of Jubilee* (NY, 1975), pp. 135–136.

6. Richard C. Wade, *Slavery in the Cities* (NY, 1964), pp. 1–27.

7. J.G. Tregle, Jr. "Early New Orleans Society: A Reappraisal." *Journal of Southern History*, Feb. 1952, p. 34.

8. Wade, *Slavery in the Cities* op. cit., p. 245.

9. Ibid., p. 219.

10. Ottley, p. 83.

11. Robert S. Starobin, *Industrial Slavery in the Old South* (NY, 1975), p. 88; Herbert Aptheker, *To Be Free* (NY, 1969), p. 73.

12. Ibid.

13. Wade, *Slavery in the Cities* op. cit., p. 235.

14. Ibid., pp. 16–19.

15. Ibid., p. 264.

16. Starobin, op. cit., pp. 157–160.

17. Eugene D. Genovese, *The Political Economy of Slavery* (NY, 1965), p. 163.

18. Henry Nash Smith, *Virgin Land* (NY, 1950), p. 243.

19. Genovese, op. cit., p. 231.

IV. SETTLER TRADE UNIONISM

1. Richard B. Morris, ed., *Encyclopedia of American History*, pp. 444–448.

2. Roger W. Shugg, *Origins of Class Struggle In Louisiana* (Baton Rouge, 1972), p. 79.

3. Stuart Blumin, "Mobility and Change in Ante-Bellum Philadelphia." In Thernstrom & Sennet, *Nineteenth-Century Cities* (New Haven, 1971), pp. 198–200.

4. Ibid.

5. Leon F. Litwack, *North of Slavery* (Chicago, 1961), p. 82.

6. Edward Pessen, *Jacksonian America* (Homewood, 1969), p. 63.

7. Litwack, op. cit., pp. 90–91, 271.

8. Foner, *History of the Labor Movement of the United States, Vol. I* op. cit., pp. 142–149.

9. Mary E. Young, "Indian Removal and Land Allotment: The Civilized Tribes and Jacksonian Justice." *American Historical Review*, Oct. 1958, pp. 31–45.

10. Peter Farb, *Man's Rise to Civilization* (NY, 1968), pp. 250–254.

11. Ibid.

12. Takaki, op. cit., p. 96.

13. Richard Maxwell Brown, *Strain of Violence* (NY, 1975), pp. 200–207.

14. Takaki, op. cit., p. 102.

15. Foner, *History of the Labor Movement of the United States, Vol. I* op. cit., p. 145.

16. Pessen, op. cit., p. 261; Foner, *History of the Labor Movement of the United States, Vol. I* op. cit., pp. 144–150; Lee Benson, *The Concept of Jacksonian Democracy* (NY, 1966), pp. 171–175.

17. Foner, *History of the Labor Movement of the United States, Vol. I* op. cit., p. 150.

18. Pessen, op. cit., p. 215.

19. Foner, *History of the Labor Movement of the United States, Vol. I* op. cit., pp. 183–188.

20. George M. Fredrickson, *The Black Image in the White Mind* (NY, 1971), p. 133.

21. See: Leonard L. Richards, *Gentlemen of Property and Standing* (Oxford, 1970), pp. 14, 114, 140, 153, 156–157.

22. Fredrickson, op. cit.

23. Ibid.

24. Ibid., p. 146.

25. Litwack, op. cit., pp. 162–166.

26. Roger W. Shugg, *Origins of Class Struggle in Louisiana* (Baton Rouge, 1972), p. 118.

27. Herbert G. Gutman, "Persistent Myths About the Afro-American Family." In Michael Gordon, ed., *The American Family In Social-Historical Perspective* (NY, 1978), p. 485.

28. Philip S. Foner, "A Labor Voice for Black Equality: The Boston Daily Evening Voice, 1864–1867." *Science & Society*, 1974, pp. 304–305.

29. Shugg, op. cit., pp. 319–320.

30. David Roediger, "Racism, Reconstruction, and the Labor Press..." *Science & Society*, 1978, pp. 156–178; Sam B. Warner, Jr., *Streetcar Suburbs* (NY, 1973), p. 53.

31. Unless otherwise noted, Chinese history in the U.S. West based on: Jack Chen, *The Chinese of America* (NY, 1981).

32. Rodolfo Acuña, *Occupied America* (San Francisco, 1972), p. 118.

33. Takaki, op. cit., p. 232.

34. Chen. op. cit, p. 137.

35. Herbert Hill, "Anti-Oriental Agitation and the Rise of Working Class Racism." *Society*, Jan.–Feb. 1973, pp. 43–54.

36. Ibid.

37. Ibid.

38. Ibid.

39. Foner, *History of the Labor Movement of the United States, Vol. I* op. cit., p. 489.

40. Hill, op. cit.

41. Foner, *History of the Labor Movement of the United States, Vol. I* op. cit., pp. 490–493.

42. Hill, op. cit.

43. Foner, *History of the Labor Movement of the United States, Vol. I* op. cit., p. 511.

44. W.E.B. Du Bois, *Black Reconstruction In America. 1860–1880* (NY, 1972), pp. 120–121. Unless otherwise noted, the events of the U.S. Civil War and Reconstruction are based on Du Bois's monumental work.

45. Fredrickson, op. cit.

46. Wendell Phillips, "Warnings." *National Anti-Slavery Standard*, April 9, 1870.

47. Foner, *History of the Labor Movement of the United States, Vol. I* op. cit., p. 400.

48. Ibid., pp. 393–394.

49. Ibid., p. 401.

50. Foner, "A Labor Voice..." op. cit., p. 304.

51. Ibid., pp. 322–323.

52. Roediger, op. cit.

53. Foner, *History of the Labor Movement of the United States, Vol. I* op. cit., p. 374.

54. Felix S. Cohen, *Immigration and National Welfare* (NY, 1940), p. 14.

55. Foner, *History of the Labor Movement of the United States, Vol. I* op. cit., pp. 377–382.

56. Ibid., pp. 381–382.

57. Ibid., pp. 377, 393–394.

58. Ibid., pp. 428–429.

59. Quoted in Jürgen Kuczynski, *The Rise of the Working Class*, p. 161.

60. Quoted in A. Lozovsky, *Marx and the Trade Unions* (NY, 1935), p. 91.

61. Shugg, op. cit., p. 90.

62. Du Bois, op. cit., p. 700.

63. Adamic, op. cit., p. 182.

64. Foner, *History of the Labor Movement of the United States, Vol. I* op. cit., pp. 269–270.

65. Thomas N. Brown, *Irish-American Nationalism, 1870–1890* (Philadelphia, 1966), pp. 38–41.

66. Ibid., pp. 67–69.

67. Acuña, op. cit., pp. 25–26.

V. COLONIALISM, IMPERIALISM & LABOR ARISTOCRACY

1. Eric Hobsbawm, "Lenin and the Aristocracy of Labor." In Sweezy & Magdorf, *Lenin Today* (NY, 1970), p. 47.

2. V.I. Lenin, *Imperialism, The Highest Stage of Capitalism* (Peking, 1970), p. 129.

3. Robert L. Heilbroner, *The Worldly Philosophers* (NY, 1964), p. 144.

4. Martin Nicolaus, "The Theory of the Labor Aristocracy." In Sweezy & Magdorf, pp. 91–101.

5. Gerhard Bry, *Wages In Germany 1871–1945* (Princeton, 1960), p. 267.

6. Hobsbawm, op. cit.; V.I. Lenin, "Thesis on the Fundamental Tasks of the 2nd Congress of the C.I." *Collected Works*. Vol. 31, pp. 184–201.

7. Sterling D. Spero & Abram Harris, *The Black Worker* (NY, 1931), pp. 150–260; Harold Baron, "The Demand for Black Labor: Historical Notes on the Political Economy of Racism." *Radical America*, March–April 1971.

8. Spero & Harris, op. cit.; Paul Nyden, *Black Coal Miners in the U.S.* AIMS. No. 15 (NY, 1974), p. 18.

9. Acuña, op. cit., pp. 94–98, 132–134; "The Struggle for Chicano Liberation." *Forward*, August 1979.

10. National Committee To Free Puerto Rican POWs, *Petition to the United Nations* (n.d.), pp. 4–6.

11. Hon. John F. Shafroth, *The Army Bill and Philippine Policy* (Washington DC, December 5, 1900), p. 3.

12. Daniel Boone Schirmer, *Republic or Empire* (Boston, 1972), pp. 230–240.

13. Ibid.

14. Ibid.; Amado Guerrero, *Philippine Society and Revolution* (Oakland, 1979), pp. 16–19.

15. Ibid., pp. 174–176.

16. Carl Schurz, *The Policy of Imperialism*. American Anti-Imperialist League Liberty Tract No. 19 (Chicago, 1899), inside cover. This was an address at the League Convention.

17. Ibid., pp. 4, 21.

18. Hon. George S. Boutwell, *War and Conquest Abroad, Degradation of Labor at Home*. A.A.L. Liberty Tract No. 7 (Chicago, 1900), pp. 5–11.

19. Carl Schurz, *American Imperialism*. Convocation Address at the University of Chicago. January 4, 1899, p. 6.

20. Michael Rogin, "Comment." In John H.M. Laslett & S.M. Upsett, eds., *Failure of a Dream?* (Garden City, 1974), p. 147.

21. C. Vann Woodward. *Tom Watson. Agrarian Rebel* (NY, 1963), pp. 370–380.

22. Ibid.

23. Daniel Bell, *Marxian Socialism in the United States* (Princeton, 1967), p. 89; Rogin, op. cit.

24. Thomas J. Noer, *Briton, Boer and Yankee* (Kent, 1978), pp. 30–34.

25. Ibid., pp. 48–55.

26. Ibid., pp. 69–70.

27. Ibid., p. 85.

28. Ibid., pp. 80–81.

29. Ibid., p. 88.

30. Edward Roux, *Time Longer Than Rope* (Madison, 1964), pp. 132–134, 154–155.

31. Ibid., p. 134.

32. Ibid., p. 147.

33. Ibid., p. 148.

34. Ibid., pp. 149–151.

VI. THE U.S. INDUSTRIAL PROLETARIAT

1. David Brody, *Steelworkers in America, The Nonunion Era* (NY, 1969), p. 1.

2. Robert W. Dunn, *The Americanization of Labor* (NY, 1927), p. 9.

3. John Higham, *Strangers in the Land* (NY, 1975), p. 159.

4. U.S. Immigration Commission, *Reports*, 61st Congress, 3rd Session, Senate Document No. 747, I, pp. 37–39.

5. Brody, op. cit., p. 96.

6. Robert Hunter, *Poverty* (NY, 1912), p. 261.

7. Ibid., p. 33.

8. Brody, op. cit., p. 40.

9. Ibid., p. 98; Irving Werstein, *Pie in the Sky* (NY, 1969), pp. 67–68.

10. Ibid., p. 99.

11. Ibid., p. 101.

12. Higham, op. cit., pp. 143, 164.

13. Victor Paananen, "Rebels All: The Finns in America." *In These Times,* April 5–11, 1978; Harry Elmer Barnes & Negley K. Teeters, *New Horizons in Criminology* (NY, 1946), p. 184.

14. Higham, op. cit., p. 273.

15. Ibid., p. 138.

16. Ibid., p. 257.

17. Ibid., pp. 259–262.

18. Ibid., p. 301.

19. Ibid., p. 182.

20. Ibid., pp. 163–164, 183.

21. Brody, op. cit., pp. 120–121.

22. Len De Caux, *The Living Spirit of the Wobblies* (NY, 1978), p. 60.

23. Patrick Renshaw, *The Wobblies* (Garden City, 1967), p. 178.

24. Paul Brissenden, *The IWW: A Study of American Syndicalism* (NY, 1919), p. 329.

25. Renshaw, op. cit., p. 329.

26. Ibid., p. 217.

27. Philip S. Foner, *History of the Labor Movement in the United States. Vol. IV* (NY, 1965), pp. 554–559.

28. *Solidarity,* July 24, 1915.

29. Renshaw, op. cit., pp. 220–230.

30. De Caux, op. cit., pp. 134–135.

31. Foner, *History of the Labor Movement in the United States. Vol. IV* op. cit., p. 124.

32. Ibid., p. 127.

33. Philip S. Foner, *History of the Labor Movement in the United States. Vol. III* (NY, 1964), pp. 276–277.

34. Foner. *History of the Labor Movement in the United States. Vol. IV* op. cit., p. 70.

35. Ibid., p. 82.

36. Brissenden, op. cit., pp. 208–209.

37. *Solidarity*, July 24, 1915.

38. Foner, *History of the Labor Movement in the United States. Vol. IV* op. cit., p. 243.

39. John Reed, *Insurgent Mexico* (NY, 1974), pp. 13–15, 125–140; Howard A. Dewitt, *Images of Ethnic and Radical Violence in California Politics, 1917–1930: A Survey* (San Francisco, 1975), p. 11; Renshaw, op. cit., pp. 249, 289; Acuña, op. cit., pp. 156–157; Ben Fletcher, "Philadelphia Waterfront Unionism." *Messenger,* June 1923, pp. 740–741.

40. Brody, op. cit., pp. 231–262.

41. Ibid., p. 255; Spero & Harris, op. cit., p. 251.

42. Philips S. Foner, *Organized Labor and the Black Worker, 1619–1973* (NY, 1974), p. 137; Allan H. Spear, *Black Chicago* (Chicago, 1967), p. 202.

43. Spear, op. cit., pp. 201, 212.

44. Ibid., pp. 215–216.

45. William Z. Foster, *The Great Steel Strike and Its Lessons* (NY, 1920), pp. 205–212.

46. Higham, op. cit., p. 221.

47. Brody, op. cit., pp. 188–196.

48. Ibid., p. 266–268.

49. Dunn, op. cit.

50. Arthur Corwin & Lawrence Cardoso, *"Vamos Al Norte."* In Corwin, ed., *Immigrants—and Immigrants* (San Francisco, 1972), p. 47.

VII. BREAKTHROUGH OF THE C.I.O.

1. Harry Braverman, *Labor and Monopoly Capital* (NY, 1974), pp. 61–62.

2. Brody, op. cit., p. 44.

3. Ibid., p. 47.

4. Ibid., pp. 50–75.

5. Robert W. Dunn, *Labor and Automobiles* (NY, 1929), p. 61.

6. Ibid., pp. 62–63.

7. Wyndham Mortimer, *Organize!* (Boston, 1971), p. 41; Irving Howe & B.J. Widick, *The UAW and Walter Reuther* (NY, 1949), p. 93.

8. Brody, op. cit., p. 84.

9. Howe & Widick, op. cit., p. 94; Spear, op. cit., p. 157.

10. Dunn, *Labor and Automobiles*, pp. 182–183, 191.

11. Sidney Fine, *Sit Down: The General Motors Strike of 1936–1937* (Ann Arbor, 1969), pp. 266–270.

12. George Rawick, "Working Class Self-Activity." *Radical America, No. 2,* 1969; Ed Jennings, *Wildcat! The Strike Wave and the No-Strike Pledge in the Auto Industry.* Manuscript, p. 12.

13. Jennings, op. cit., p. 17.

14. Robert R. Brooks, *As Steel Goes* ... (New Haven, 1940), p. 129.

15. Samuel Lubell, "Post Mortem: Who Elected Roosevelt?" In William E. Lechtenburg, ed., *The New Deal* (NY, 1968), pp. 162–166.

16. Francis Perkins, *The Roosevelt I Knew* (NY, 1946), pp. 228–231.

17. Lechtenburg, op. cit., pp. 151–152; Charles Higham, *Trading With the Enemy* (NY, 1983), p. 163.

18. Robert Travis, *Flint; A True Report* (Flint, 1937), p. 4; Jack Steiber, *Governing the UAW* (NY, 1962), p. 63; Claude E. Hoffman, *Sit-Down in Anderson; UAW Local 663* ... (Detroit, 1968), p. 91; Robert R. Brooks, op. cit., pp. 83–85; August Meier & Elliot Rudwick, *Black Detroit and the Rise of the UAW* (NY, 1979), p. 66; Charles P. Larrowe, *Harry Bridges* (NY, 1972), pp. 284–286; *New York Times,* December 8, 1981.

19. Larrowe, op. cit., pp. 74–84.

20. Fine, op. cit., pp. 272–274, 293, 302, 233.

21. Murray Edelman, "New Deal Sensitivity to Labor Interests." In Milton Derber & Edwin Young, eds., *Labor and the New Deal* (Madison, 1957), p. 167.

22. Ben Stolberg, *Tailor's Progress* (NY, 1944), p. 205.

23. Brooks, op. cit, pp. 83–106.

24. Ibid., pp. 110–119.

25. Op. cit., p. 106; Saul Alinsky, *John L. Lewis* (NY, 1949), p. 149.

26. Brooks, op. cit., p. 194.

27. Thomas Mathews, *Puerto Rican Politics and the New Deal* (Gainesville, 1960), pp. 261–314.

28. Acuña, op. cit., pp. 190–195.

29. Travis, op. cit., p. 3.

30. Jennings, op. cit., p. 36.

31. Spear, op. cit., p. 157.

32. Edward Greer, "Racism and U.S. Steel, 1906–1974." *Radical America,* Sept.–Oct. 1976.

33. Meier & Rudwick, op. cit., pp. 16–20.

34. Spero & Harris, op. cit., pp. 152–166; Meier & Rudwick, op. cit., pp. 6–8.

35. Dunn, *Labor and Automobiles*, pp. 68–69.

36. Ibid.

37. Meier & Rudwick, op. cit., p. 38.

38. Mortimer, op. cit., p. 111.

39. Meier & Rudwick, op. cit., pp. 36–37; Interviews with two radical participants in the Flint Sit-Down.

40. Flint interviews.

41. Meier & Rudwick, op. cit., p. 50.

42. Ray Marshall, "The Negro in Southern Illinois." In Julius Jacobsen, ed., *The Negro and the American Labor Movement* (NY, 1968), p. 149.

43. Robert C. Weaver, *Negro Labor: A National Problem* (NY, 1946), p. 15; Meier & Rudwick, op. cit., pp. 124–125.

44. Weaver, op. cit., p. 27.

45. Jeremy Brecher, *Strike!* (Oakland, 2014), p. 211.

46. Weaver, op. cit., p. 75.

VIII. IMPERIALIST WAR & THE NEW AMERIKAN ORDER

1. John Morton Blum, *V Was for Victory, Politics and American Culture During World War II* (NY, 1976), p. 67.

2. Baron, op. cit.

3. James L. Stokesbury, *A Short History of World War II* (NY, 1980), pp. 378–380.

4. Ibid.

5. Blum, op. cit., pp. 90–91.

6. Ibid., pp. 91–99.

7. J.R. Johnson, "What Do Negroes Themselves Think About the War?" *Socialist Appeal*, October 20, 1939.

8. Roux, op. cit., p. 306.

9. Summer M. Rosen, "The CIO Era, 1935–55." In Julius Jacobsen, ed., op. cit., p. 196; Interview with St. Clair Drake, 1960.

10. David Horowitz, *Empire and Revolution* (NY, 1970), p. 70; *Biennial Report of the Chief of Staff of the U.S. Army* (Washington DC, 1945); Matthew Cooper, *The German Army 1933-1945* (NY, 1978), p. 471; Gabriel Kolko, *Politics of War* (NY, 1968), p. 22.

11. William R. Perl, *The Four-Front War* (NY, 1979), pp. 2, 218; Bernard Wasserstein, *Britain and the Jews of Europe. 1939-1945* (NY, 1979), pp. 309–320; Kolko, op. cit., pp. 44, 182–193, 429; Higham, op. cit., pp. 155–163.

12. Letter from John E. Costello, *New York Times*, January 17, 1982; Diary of U.S. Secretary of War Henry Stimson, quoted in Charles A. Beard, *President Roosevelt and the Coming of the War, 1941* (New Haven, 1948), p. 517; Barbara Tuchman, *Stilwell and the American Experience in China. 1911–45* (NY, 1970), p. 224.

13. Beard, op. cit., pp. 178–179.

14. Tuchman, op. cit., pp. 238–240.

15. *New York Times*, November 20, 1940.

16. *New York Times*, November 21, 1940.

17. *New York Times*, February 19, 1941.

18. Matthews, op. cit., pp. 17–18, 324.

19. Charles T. Goodsell, *Administration of a Revolution* (Cambridge, 1965), pp. 3–9.

20. Ibid.

21. Rodolfo O. Rivera, "Puerto Rico Pays." *Nation*, May 25, 1940.

22. *New York Times*, December 4, 1940.

23. "Ex-Soldier of Il Duce Volunteers in Draft." *New York Times*, Nov. 21, 1940.

24. Blum, op. cit., pp. 147–152.

25. Setsuko Nishi, *Facts About Japanese-Americans* (Chicago, 1946), pp. 2–3.

26. Ibid.

27. Ibid., p. 20.

28. Bill Hosokawa, *Nisei* (NY, 1969), p. 440.

29. Ibid., pp. 457–467.

30. Blum, op. cit., p. 45.

31. Meier & Rudwick, op. cit., p. 164.

32. Foner, *Organized Labor and the Black Worker* op. cit., pp. 264–265.

33. Acuña, op. cit., pp. 203–206.

34. *New York Times*, February 26, 1973.

IX. NEO-COLONIAL PACIFICATION IN THE U.S.

1. Takaki, op. cit., p. 189.

2. Jimmie Durham, *American Indian Culture: Traditionalism & Spiritualism in a Revolutionary Struggle* (NY, 1974), pp. 5–6.

3. Frank Ernest Hill, "A New Pattern of Life for the Indian." *New York Times Magazine*, July 14, 1935.

4. Ibid.

5. Ibid.; *New York Times,* January 26, 1982; Peter Mewick, "Navajos Levy Taxes On Energy Giants." *In These Times*, August 30, 1978; Jan Stites, "Native Land." *Village Voice*, May 4, 1982; E. Shusky, *The Right To Be Indian* (San Francisco, 1970), p. vi.

Note that due to a typesetting error in the original 1983 edition of *Settlers*, on which the present volume is based, sources for endnotes 6–9 were lost. The endnote references in the text have been retained, as they were in previous editions of *Settlers*.

10. Foner, *Organized Labor and the Black Worker* op. cit., pp. 158–161.

11. Peter Kwong, *Chinatown. New York* (NY, 1979), pp. 120–121.

12. "Crop Sharers in Ala. Fight Hostile Posse." *Louisiana Weekly,* July 25, 1931; Eugene Gordon, "Alabama Massacre." *New Masses*, August 1931.

13. Jane Dillon, "Fighting for Bread in Dixie Land." *Labor Defender*, Oct. 1931.

14. "A Sharecropper Tells the Story." *Labor Defender,* September 1931.

15. Dillon, op. cit.

16. *Richmond Times-Dispatch,* June 7, 1942.

17. "Odell Waller: A Test Case." *New York Times,* June 11, 1942.

18. Morris Milgram, "Aid Sought for Arkansas Negro Imprisoned for Defending Home." *The Call*, December 12, 1943.

19. "Five Farmers in Alabama Convicted." *Chicago Defender*, May 6, 1933.

20. Albert Jackson, "On the Alabama Front." *Nation*, September 18, 1935.

21. Donald Grubbs, *Cry from the Cotton* (Chapel Hill, 1971), p. 81.

22. Ibid., p. 24.

23. Ibid., p. 67.

24. Louis Cantor, *A Prologue to the Protest Movement: The Missouri Sharecropper Roadside Demonstrations of 1939* (Durham, 1969).

25. Nell Painter & Hosea Hudson, "Hosea Hudson: A Negro Communist in the Deep South." *Radical America* Vol. II, No. 4., July–August 1977.

26. William R. Scott, "Black Nationalism and the Italo-Ethiopian Conflict." *Journal of Negro History*, 1978, pp. 118–134. Unless otherwise noted, all quotations and references on this movement are from Scott's work. This important essay shows the nationalist orientation of the support movement, and rescues a deliberately suppressed history of popular political struggle.

27. Ibid.; "Mob of 400 Battles the Police in Harlem: Italian Stores Raided, Man Shot in Crowd." *New York Times*, May 19, 1936.

28. Frances Fox Piven & Richard A. Cloward, *Regulating the Poor* (NY, 1971), p. 76.

29. Ibid., p. 133.

30. William R. Amberson, "The New Deal for Share-Croppers." *Nations*, Feb. 13, 1935.

31. C.T. Carpenter, "Federal Aid in South Helps Rich Owner. Oppresses Poor." *NY World-Telegram*, May 11, 1935.

32. Nyden, op. cit., pp. 17–22.

33. Weaver, op. cit., p. 9.

34. Julius Lester, ed., *The Seventh Son: The Thought & Writing of W.E.B. DuBois. Vol. I* (NY, 1971), p. 104.

35. Amilcar Cabral, *The Struggle in Guinea* (Cambridge, n.d.—reprint of speech in Milan, Italy, May 1964), p. 442.

36. Constance McLaughun Green, *The Secret City* (Princeton, 1967), pp. 129, 157–158.

37. Lester, ed., op. cit., p. 89; Richard Wright, *American Hunger* (NY, 1983), pp. 28–29.

38. *Crusader*, Nov. 1921, p. 23.

39. Claude McKay, *Harlem: Negro Metropolis* (NY, 1940), p. 168.

40. St. Claire Darke, "Hide My Face." In Herbert Hill, ed., *Soon, One Morning* (NY, 1969), pp. 78–105; Cohen, op. cit., p. 284.

41. Drake, op. cit.; W.F. Elkins, "Marcus Garvey, the Negro World, and the British West Indies, 1919–1920," *Science & Society*, Spring 1972, pp. 74–75.

42. Martin Luther King. Jr. "Behavioral Scientists in the Civil Rights Movement." In Glenn & Bonjean, eds., *Blacks In the United States* (San Francisco, 1969), p. 8.

43. Jeff Henderson, "A. Philip Randolph and the Dilemmas of Socialism and Black Nationalism in the United States, 1917–1941." *Race & Class*, Autumn 1978, pp. 143–159.

44. Ibid.

45. Amy Jacques-Garvey, ed., *Philosophy and Opinions of Marcus Garvey* (NY, 1980), p. 295.

46. Cabral, op. cit., p. 444.

47. Foner, *Organized Labor and the Black Worker* op. cit., p. 124; Brailsford R. Brazeal, *The Brotherhood of Sleeping Car Porters* (NY, 1946), p. 132.

48. Daniel S. Davis, *Mr. Black Labor* (NY, 1972), p. xii.

49. Henderson, op. cit.; Davis op. cit, pp. 62–69.

50. Harry A. Ploski & Warren Marr II, eds., *The Negro Almanac.* 3rd Edition (NY, 1976), p. 27.

51. Lubell, op. cit., p. 165.

52. W.D.L., *The Case of Sharecropper Waller* (NY, 1942), 12 p. mimeo factsheet.

53. Foner, *Organized Labor and the Black Worker* op. cit., pp. 238–239.

54. W.D.L., op. cit.

55. McKay, op. cit., pp. 188–229.

56. Ibid.

57. *New York Times*, August 1, 1983.

58. McKay, op. cit., pp. 188–229.

59. *New York Times*, August 1938.

60. Davis, op. cit., pp. 102–112.

61. Ibid.

62. Ibid.; Constance M. Green, op. cit., pp. 254–258.

63. Weaver, op. cit., pp. 27–33.

64. Ibid.

65. Foner, *Organized Labor and the Black Worker* op. cit., p. 243; Davis, op. cit., p. 111; Greer, op. cit., p. 57.

66. Kwong, op. cit., p. 114.

67. Jose Chegui Torres, "A Contempt Pure and Dangerous." *Village Voice*, March 10, 1980.

68. Acuña, op. cit., p. 198.

69. Davis, op. cit., pp. 113–114.

70. Adam Clayton Powell, Jr., *Marching Blacks* (NY, 1945), p. 125.

71. *New York Times*, August 3, 1981.

72. Acuña, op. cit., pp. 198–199, 209.

73. Acuña, op. cit., pp. 212–214; Kwong, op. cit., pp. 144–147.

74. Ibid.

75. Hosokawa, op. cit., pp. 451–453.

X. 1950S REPRESSION & THE DECLINE OF THE COMMUNIST PARTY USA

1. There are many, many histories and personal memoirs detailing CPUSA involvement in the CIO and other Amerikan institutional structures; most agreeing on the facts of the CPUSA's significance. Just two of many referred to are: B. Karsh & Philips Garman, "The Impact of the Political Left." In Milton Derber, ed., *Labor and the New Deal* (Madison, 1957); Albert Halper, *Good-Bye. Union Square* (Chicago, 1971).

2. Ben Rose, "The Communist Party and the CIO." *Theoretical Review,* May–June 1981, p. 13.

3. Ibid.

4. Len De Caux, *Labor Radical* (Boston, 1971), p. 521.

5. John Abt, "Review of Cold War Political Justice: the Smith Act, the Communist Party and American Civil Liberties." *Science & Society*, Spring 1979, p. 92; Peggy Dennis, *The Autobiography of an American Communist* (Westport, 1977), p. 206; Charles Rubin, *The Log of Rubin the Sailor* (NY, 1973), pp. 337–340.

6. Peggy Dennis, op. cit., pp. 203–206.

7. Kwong, op. cit., p. 141.

8. "Vito Marcantonio on Puerto Rico and Puerto Rican Nationalism." In Jose E. Lopez, ed., *Puerto Rican Nationalism: A Reader.* Puerto Rican Cultural Center (Chicago, 1977), pp. 119–120.

9. Jose E. Lopez, "Introduction." In Lopez, op. cit., pp. 22–24.

10. *New York Times*, November 1, 1950.

11. Ibid.

12. George Charney, *A Long Journey* (Chicago, 1968), p. 107.

13. *Daily Worker*, November 2, 1950.

XI. THIS GREAT HUMANITY HAS CRIED "ENOUGH!"

1. Karl Marx, *Capital. Vol. 1* (Moscow, 1960), pp. 603–604.

2. *Wall Street Journal,* January 22, 1983; *Financial Times,* February 12, 1979.

3. Edwards, op. cit., pp. 135–136.

4. *New York Times*, December 6, 1982.

5. *Wall Street Journal,* January 7, 1983.

6. *Newsday,* November 29, 1982.

XII. THE GLOBAL PLANTATION

1. William Serrin, "The Collapse of Our Industrial Heartland." *New York Times Magazine,* June 6, 1982.

2. Leonard Broom & Norval D. Glenn, "The Occupations and Income of Black Americans." In Glenn & Bonjean, op. cit., pp. 24, 41.

3. *Daily Worker,* January 30, 1953.

4. John Hope II, *Equality of Opportunity* (Washington DC, 1956), p. 10.

5. Ken Cockrel, "Our Thing is DRUM." Detroit, n.d, p. 11; Foner, *Organized Labor and the Black Worker* op. cit., p. 421.

6. See: Herbert Hill, "The ILGWU Today, The Decay of a Labor Union." *New Politics,* Vol. I, No. 4.

7. Figures derived from comparing number of management and professional employees as given in *Wall Street Journal,* March 22, 1983, to total employees as given in *Standard & Poor's Register 1983.*

8. *New York Times,* April 14, 1983.

9. Peter F. Drucker, "Squeezing the Firm's Midriff Bulge." *Wall Street Journal,* March 25, 1983.

10. Bureau of the Census, *Historical Statistics of the United States. Part II* (Washington DC, 1975), p. 669.

11. Cook, op. cit.

12. *Statistical Abstract...* , p. 400; Comparison derived from: *New York Times,* March 3, 1983; Larry Remer, "Organizing Begins at Home." *Mother Jones,* May 1983.

13. *Wall Street Journal,* March 28, 1983.

14. *Wall Street Journal,* March 21, 1983.

15. Walter F. Mondale, "The U.S. Can Compete." *New York Times,* November 8, 1982.

16. *New York Times,* July 18, 1983.

17. *New York Times,* July 25, 1982; September 30, 1982.

18. Ibid.

19. Frances Moore Lappé, *Diet for a Small Planet* (NY, 1982), p. 63.

20. *New York Times,* September 9, 1979.

21. *New York Times*, March 6, 1978.

22. Peter Baird & Ed MacCaughan, "Power Struggle: Labor and Imperialism In Mexico's Electrical Industry." *NACLA Report*, Sept.–Oct. 1977, p. 13; *New York Times*, March 31, 1983; *Business Week*, March 1983, p. 87.

23. *Business Week*, March 14, 1983, p. 102.

24. *Business Week*, March 28, 1983.

25. *New York Times*, March 15, 1983.

26. *New York Times*, March 27, 1983.

27. Ibid.

28. Ibid.

29. Douglas S. Massey, "Hordes of 'Illegals'? No." *New York Times*, May 31, 1979.

30. *New York Times*, June 3, 1979.

31. *New York Times*, February 26, 1981; March 27, 1983.

32. *Washington Post*, July 26, 1982.

XIII. "KLASS, KULTURE & KOMMUNITY"

1. Friedrich Engels, *Principles of Communism* (NY, 1952), p. 7.

2. Stephen J. Rose, *Social Stratification in the United States* (Baltimore, 1979), p. 18.

3. *New York Times*, March 14, 1983.

4. Percentages based on figures given in: Bureau of the Census, *1970 Census of Population. Vol. 1: Characteristics of the Population, Part 1: U.S. Summary. Section 2*. GPO. (Washington DC, 1973), pp. 739–745.

5. Rose, op. cit., p. 28.

6. *New York Times*, September 18, 1979.

7. Bureau of the Census, *Statistical Abstract of the U.S. 1981* (Washington DC, 1981), pp. 763–766; *New York Times*, September 25, 1977.

8. *Statistical Abstract* ... , pp. 624–628.

9. *New York Times*, November 25, 1979.

10. *Newsweek*, January 17, 1983. "The Work Revolution."

11. *Statistical Abstract* ..., p. 420; Rose, op. cit., pp. 20–26.

12. *New York Times*, January 8, 1982; *In These Times*, December 15–21, 1982; *San Jose News*, June 10, 1982.

13. *New York Times*, May 30, 1982; *Wall Street Journal*, April 7, 1983.

14. Lappé, op. cit., pp. 37–38.

15. *Wall Street Journal*, April 7, 1983.

16. Lee Sloan, "Maligning Black Veterans." *New York Times*, September 14, 1980.

17. *Statistical Abstract* ... , p. 403; *New York Times*, January 17, 1980.

18. Christopher Jencks, "How We Live Now." *New York Times Book Review*, April 10, 1983; *New York Times*, December 21, 1978.

19. *New York Times*, April 9, 1983.

20. John Egerton, "Boom or Bust in the Hollows of Appalachia." *New York Times Magazine*, October 18, 1981.

21. Lenin op. cit., p. 187.

22. Ibid., p. 151.

23. *New York Times*, March 20, 1983.

24. *New York Times*, August 21, 1979.

25. *New York Times*, November 16, 1981.

XIV. TACTICAL & STRATEGIC

1. *Message to the Black Movement: A Political Statement from the Black Underground*. n.d, p. 18.

2. Herbert G. Gutman, "The Negro and the United Mine Workers of America." In Jacobson, ed., op. cit., p. 81. Paul Nyden, *Black Coal Miners in the United States* (NY, 1974). All information on the UMW, unless otherwise noted, is from this CPUSA paper.

3. Gutman, op. cit., pp. 53–55.

4. President's Coal Commission, *The American Coal Miner* (Washington DC, 1980), p. 20; Eileen Whalen & Ken Lawrence, *Liberation for the Oppressed Nations and Peoples of Southern Africa* (Jackson, 1975), p. 7.

5. Gutman, op. cit., pp. 57–58.

6. Whalen & Lawrence, op. cit., pp. 7–9.

7. *All Africa Is Standing Up*. Vol. 2, No.4, May 1978, p. 4.

8. Foner, *Organized Labor and the Black Worker* op. cit., p. 418.

9. Ibid., p. 418.

10. Interview.

War Prison, U. S. A.

Interned Japanese Believe Their Homes On The West Coast Are Now Gone Forever

By ROBERT GEIGER
AP Feature Writer

AMACHE, Colo. — Two years after Pearl Harbor many younger residents of Granada Japanese relocation center are convinced they never will be permitted, to return to their former west coast homes.

Some older Japanese, even after 19 months in relocation camps,

Third Of A Series

believe—or at least hope—they will get back there "some day, when war ends."

But many Japanese parents are urging their children to leave Amache and establish themselves in other parts of the nation, away from the west coast, which is an area in which resettlement has been restricted, says Walter Higuchi, chairman of the Amache Japanese council and spokesman for 7,500 Japanese who live in camp.

These Japanese, theoretically, are free to leave and take jobs. They are part of the Japanese moved from military areas in Washington, Oregon, California and Arizona to relocation centers in California, Arizona, Utah, Idaho, Wyoming, Colorado and Arkansas.

In the sifting process to segregate loyal U. S. Japanese from those who wanted to return to Japan, there have been 9,077 persons of all ages registered in Amache, in 16 months.

About 125 were sent to the Tulelake, Calif., camp where recent disorders have occurred. All of these indicated their desire to restore their Japanese citizenship.

One hundred seventy-four young men joined the U. S. army; 1,441 persons were approved by the FBI and investigating boards and were granted indefinite leave from camp to obtain jobs outside.

Amache, a temporary camp, is a wind-tormented little village of temporary type army barracks in the old dust bowl country. There are 30 blocks of tarpaper-covered

MRS. GEORGE MATSUURA, with three children, finds life in relocation camp is not too bad.

barracks with 12 barracks in each block.

The barracks are divided into rooms of three sizes, 16 by 20 feet; 20 by 20 feet and 24 by 20 feet for families of various sizes.

W. J. Hanson, the leave officer, says most of its citizens could obtain indefinite leave, to work in many parts of the nation.

"Applications for leave are being approved rather swiftly," he says. "Each Japanese is investigated thoroughly and is given a hearing before he leaves."

If the Japanese care to work in camp, they are paid from $12 to $19 a month. In addition they get their food, lodging and coal, and

a clothing allowance of $3.50 a month.

Mrs. George Matsuura, young, native born, half Eurasian, half Caucasian, is an eloquent spokesman for the Japanese. Her husband is in the U. S. Army. They have a son, 12, and Mrs. Matsuura and the boys live with her father, former importer-exporter of fine art goods, in one of the barracks rooms.

"Most Japanese are not complaining," says Mrs. Matsuura. "Our treatment and our life here has been better than some expected."

Tomorrow: Tip To U. S. Women: Don't Trust Axis Prisons.

APPENDIX I

CASH & GENOCIDE

The True Story of
Japanese-American Reparations

*This article was hastily written for the New Afrikan revolutionary move-
ment in the late 1980s, at a time when there were confused discussions
going on about the surprising Japanese-American reparations legislation
then in Congress. The overall story can still stand as correct, but there
are small factual inaccuracies of the moment. The individual dollar
amounts for the u.s. reparations for Aleut peoples were changed after this
article was written (upped to $16,000). We received reparations in one
lump sum payment, not dragged out over ten years as first proposed in
Congress (although the payouts were only slowly dispersed well into the
Clinton administration years). In the 25 years since then, the freer Aleut
communities have grown economically, both from their commercial fishing and from the islands' role as a regional fishing industry supply base.*

*What wasn't clear enough to us when this article was put together was
how the u.s. government intended to use these reparations as a cover for
quietly maintaining its "legal" right under u.s. law to carry out ethnic
targeting, ethnic removal, and ethnic cleansing anytime in the future. We
decided to leave the original article unchanged, though, as evidence of
the earlier movement discussion. This article was originally circulated as
a discussion paper in the Winter of 1988, and later published in the New
Afrikan revolutionary nationalist journal, **Crossroad**, in April 1989.*

How did Japanese-Americans get over $3 billion in reparations from the USA? What's behind this surprising act "to right a grave wrong," as none other than Ronald Reagan called it last August?[1]

Japanese-American reparations is as much about New Afrika and the indigenous nations—particularly the Pribilof Aleuts, as shown extensively below—as it is about Japanese. Even more so. When right-wing president Reagan signed the reparations act into law on August 10, 1988, many New Afrikans saw it as a precedent that morally must be extended to them. But what the U.S. Empire is doing now is more about preparations than reparations, i.e., preparing their Empire to do New Afrikan genocide, covering up and legitimizing the genocide they've already done to the Native Nations.

> "'The Japanese people were just awarded $20,000 each for
> America's mistreatment of them, for putting them in camps
> during world War II,' Queen Mother Audley Moore reminded
> the gathering at her 90th birthday celebration in Harlem last
> summer. She raised the obvious question: 'When will our
> elected officials, our people in Congress, begin to demand
> reparations for the almost irreparable damage that slavery did
> to our people? When will We get paid for the 18 hours a day,
> 7 days a week labor that We were forced to do for free during
> slavery?'"[2]

Some people are naturally expressing resentment at Japanese-Americans for somehow getting preferential treatment. Writing for *The Final Call*, Sept. 16, 1988, J. Wayne Tukes asks: "Why should African-American tax dollars be used to compensate others?" Tukes sees a conspiracy, with Japan behind it all: "What kind of pressure is Japan placing on the American government/business to extract a public and financial apology at this time? Is it because of the position Japan holds in the current world economy?"

Two African-American reporters for *The Sun*, Sandra Crockett and Jerry Bemby, put forward another theory: That reparations is due to Japanese Americans' superior political power. In their column "$1.7 Million and a Mule," the two reporters incorrectly calculate that the Japanese-Americans will get "restitution that amounts to $6,666.00 for each year of suffering ... At the going government rate of $6,666.00 per year, and calculating it from the arrival of the first slaves in the early 1600s to the signing of the Emancipation Proclamation in 1863 ... black Americans are due $1.7 million each."[3]

After telling their readers that "a lot of black Americans were probably appalled" at the U.S. giving reparations to Japanese-Americans, Crockett and Bemby say that Japanese-Americans' apparent power should be an example to black politicians: "Japanese American lobbyists pushed hard to get the bill passed and did an admirable job. So it's time that the members of the Congressional Black Caucus begin pushing..."

These kind of theories sound plausible, but they aren't even close to true. To sum up what really happened:

Japanese-American politicians didn't fight for us to get reparations. Nor was there any mass movement or struggle or lobbying for it until the U.S. government gave the go-ahead. Japanese-American reparations first came into legislation as part of a bill by a white congressman to compensate for the genocide of the Pribilof Aleut indigenous people. Japan, which doesn't consider Japanese-Americans to be Japanese ... couldn't care less and wasn't involved at all.

Japanese-American congressmen were **against** cash reparations at first, until the U.S. ruling class decided that **it** needed this and told them to jump in and take the credit for it. That's a matter of record. The bill **covers up** U.S. genocide against the Aleut peoples, and U.S. plans for new genocide against New Afrika. It's about nothing but genocide, coming and going.

Just to clear away some fantasies: This bill doesn't mean that every Japanese-American won the lottery or that our community is being compensated for suffering and loss of human rights. What it means is simply that those survivors of the WWII concentration camps still alive today (about ten percent of our people) will be repaid for our property losses back then.

In 1942 we were ordered to sell all our land, businesses, farms, houses, and household goods before we boarded the trains to the camps. White settler vultures, knowing we had no bargaining position, bought up everything we had for nickels and dimes. A new car was worth maybe $50 that day, a home maybe $300 or $500. Many whites just went down to the courthouse and said that a Japanese had sold them their farm, and were given title as new owners. All legal to this day.

Our going to concentration camps was a big holiday to nearby white settlers, a close-out sale. After the War the U.S. government itself assessed our direct property losses at $400 million in 1940 dollars (many billions in today's inflated dollars). The Evacuation Claims Act after the War only compensated us for those losses at 8 percent or 8¢ for every dollar we lost. So, in effect, this reparations act only repays the property losses of 48 years ago, and only for those 60,000 individuals still alive on the day Ronald Reagan signed the bill. And by the terms of the act, repayment will be stretched out over a ten year period or more, with the dying getting theirs first.[4] *

THE FULL STORY

Played down in the news about Japanese-American reparations was the section of the act giving an estimated 400 Pribilof Aleuts $12,500 each. The reparations act established that the Pribilof Aleuts deserve less compensation than Japanese-Americans because their WWII imprisonment was supposedly **justified**. This is where the real story begins.[5]

Most people never heard of the Pribilof Aleuts before this, and if the U.S. has its way never will know about them. They are an indigenous people (who do not like being called "Indians"), living on a desolate chain of islands in the Bering Sea between the USSR and Alaska. Until the year 1966 they were the last remaining slaves in the USA.

---

* This article was written before the reparations act was finalized into administrative form. In the finished act, the u.s. government gave up on all its penny-pinching hopes. Everyone got one-time reparations payment in full, not in annual payments stretched out over years. In a surprise, the number of Japanese-American camp survivors still alive when the bill was signed turned out to be many more than the government planners had counted on having to pay.

When the expansionist USA purchased Alaska from the Russian Empire right after the U.S. Civil War, in 1867, the Pribilof Aleuts were just considered part of the property being sold. For the Pribilof Islands, uninhabited by humans before their "discovery" by the Russian explorer Gerasim Pribilof in 1786, are home to 1.5 million seals. The great seal colony, valuable because of their fur, became an imperial business owned by the Russian Czars.

To get the workers needed to hunt the seals and process their pelts, the Czars forced hundreds of indigenous families from the larger Aleutian Islands to move to the Pribilofs to be imperial serfs. Serfs were the bottom class in pre-socialist Russian society. While they could not be bought and sold as chattel slaves were in the U.S., serfs were still a class of slaves. The property of wealthy masters to whom they owed life-long obedience and labor, serfs lived without wages or rights. On the Pribilofs, the Aleut slaves were given Russian names and converted to the Russian Orthodox faith. The islands became slave plantations.

To the Pribilof Aleuts, the change of Euro-capitalist owners in 1867 changed nothing in their own lives. For their seal hunt became a profitable U.S. government monopoly, and they became slaves of the USA. From 1867 to 1966, everything and everyone on the Pribilof Islands was owned by the U.S. government. Although the Bering Sea is rich in fish, the Pribilof Aleuts were **forbidden to fish or work for themselves!**

Their food and housing was doled out or withheld as punishment by the white slave-owners from the U.S. Fish and Wildlife Service. Their only work was the annual seal harvest, while they survived the rest of the year by running up their debt at the U.S. government-owned store. Federal agents tightly controlled travel to and from the islands. Outsiders who might raise political questions were kept out.[6]

In 1942 this tight little slave colony was interrupted by World War II. Japanese military forces captured the Aleutian Islands of Attu and Kiska in June 1942. Hundreds of Aleuts fled to the mainland. U.S. military authorities decided to remove the remaining slaves, since their communities were needed as military camps and the fur trade was suspended anyway. Then, too, the U.S. didn't entirely trust their slaves.[7]

Ordered by soldiers to board military transports with only what they could carry in their arms, 881 Pribilof Aleuts were relocated to old, unused buildings at abandoned Alaskan mines and canneries. Survivors remember that they were dumped without blankets or even food, forced to live in derelict wooden barracks that had only gaping holes where windows and doors used to be. After two Alaskan winters, one out of every four Pribilof Aleuts had died from malnutrition and exposure.[8]

Another surprise gift from America awaited them in 1945 when they were returned to the Pribilofs. Everything was gone. GIs had burglarized their communities, stealing all the religious icons from the churches and taking "souvenirs" from the homes. Everything that the GIs didn't want or couldn't take—native boats, homes, churches, clothing, and dishes—had been smashed. Appeals to the U.S. for emergency compensation brought a response from the U.S. President Franklin Roosevelt, who authorized $10,000 compensation—not $10,000 for each person or each family, but for the entire community—about $12 each. Labor and life with the seal harvest began again on Amerika's arctic slave plantation.

The first change came only in the 1960s, as the world anti-colonial revolution was pressing the U.S. Empire to reform. A political candidate for the Alaskan State legislature tried to visit the Pribilofs, but was denied permission to speak with the Pribilof Aleut slaves by their white overseers. It was a local scandal, since America always pats itself on the back for allegedly abolishing slavery before in 1863.

So in the 1966 Fur Seal Act, a U.S. Senate amendment gave the Pribilof Aleuts the right to travel freely and speak to whomever they wished for the first time in their colonial history. The U.S. government was still their only employer, and still owned the islands and all the physical property on them, however. It wasn't until 1978 that the Pribilof Aleuts were finally given the right to vote, to have their own local government, and to own their own homes. Finally, they have reached the level of New Afrikans and Puerto Ricans.[9]

The 1988 reparations act, in addition to paying Aleut survivors $12,500 each, gives the Pribilof Aleut communities $5 million as tardy reimbursement for the WWII burglary by U.S. troops as well as $1.4 million as compensation for destruction of religious property. The Aleut people get another $15 million to finally settle and make permanent their involuntary exclusion from Attu Island in the Aleutians. Attu was taken for a U.S. naval base and is now forbidden to native people as a U.S. government "wildlife sanctuary."[10]

This reparations act is serving genocide, both coming and going. The act gives Aleuts money in return for finalizing U.S. ownership of their islands and natural resources. It even justifies their WWII removal and internment. It is important to America right now to make everything look nice, to pay small amounts of cash to supposedly settle all the old human rights injustices. Because the U.S. is quietly wiping out the Aleut people. They don't want Aleut labor anymore and, in fact, the possibility of Aleut claims to control their islands and the rich seabed around them is seen as a problem for America, a problem for which America has a "Final Solution."

U.S. military planners have always seen the Pribilofs and Aleutians as the stepping stones for invaders to the "soft underbelly" of the South Alaskan coast. Their doctrine calls for maintaining strategic control of these colonial islands as a military barrier against the Russians. That is why they've never permitted the Aleuts to return to Attu Island. Their worst-case nightmare would be for native people to demand sovereignty and kick the U.S. military out.

Pribilof Aleut poverty (there is 80 percent unemployment) is "Made in the USA." With one of the world's richest fishing areas, with large seal herds for food, oil, and fur, the Pribilofs can easily support an Aleut population of only 750. But being U.S. citizens, being part of the U.S., means that all those resources are owned by the U.S. Empire. The reparations act, in appearing to right old injustices, in setting the seal on U.S. ownership of the fur seal trade and fishing rights, is legalizing the decline of Aleut population.

To help break up Pribilof Aleut communities, the U.S. government has even suggested ending the fur seal hunt, supposedly out of respect for animal rights. The seal hunt isn't so profitable anymore, anyway. Once the Aleuts gained certain rights in the 1960s and 1970s, and started demanding things like electricity, medical care, and wages, the profits went away. It wasn't seals that were the origin of profits, it turns out, but owning whole villages of slave women, children, and men.

GROUP OF ALEUT CHILDREN IN FRONT OF A SCHOOL, 1938.

U.S. TROOPS IN ALEUT ISLANDS, WORLD WAR II.

Aleuts are still forbidden by U.S. law from hunting seals for themselves, since the government says that its treaty with Japan and Canada forces it to own the fur seal trade (Canada and Japan are 15% each minority partners). To the Aleuts this is the final irony. In 1911 there were 300,000 seals on the Pribilofs, but now there are 1.5 million (25,000 are killed each year). While Aleuts go hungry and their numbers shrink. One Aleut leader said: "If we didn't have the fur harvest, we on the Pribilofs wouldn't have anything. Once there were 15,000 Aleuts. Now there are 3,000 to 1.5 million seals. It's the Aleut people who are the endangered species."[11]

THE NEW AFRIKAN EQUATION

It isn't that Japanese-Americans don't justly deserve reparations. We do, and this $20,000 is tiny in terms of what we suffered, but that has nothing to do with why the U.S. ruling class is doing this. In 1979 the first congressional bill was introduced to give cash reparations to U.S. civilian internment survivors. Its sponsor, Rep. Mike Lowry (D-Wash.), proposed giving each Aleut and Japanese-American survivor $15,000 plus $15 for each day imprisoned. His bill was instantly unpopular with the white nation. There was the usual moaning from the brain-dead white majority (Lowry got calls demanding "Why are we paying the people who attacked us at Pearl Harbor?"), from candidate Ron Reagan and the GOP.

Japanese-American congressmen, like Norman Mineta (D-Calif.), who are put into congress to represent white interests, were the loudest in their opposition to the Lowry bill. We watched the strange sight of the biggest Japanese-American politicians, such as U.S. senator Daniel Inouye (D-Hawaii), attacking the idea of Japanese-American reparations while New Afrikan congressmen like Ron Dellums (D-Calif.) were fighting for it.[12]

U.S. senator Inouye, who was never imprisoned himself, argued that giving the rest of us money would dishonor the memory of our noble suffering: "You can't put a price tag on it. Putting a price tag on it would cheapen the whole thing."[13]

Intelligent settler opposition to reparations wasn't really concerned about Japanese-Americans one way or the other, but was
afraid that a bad example was being set for New Afrikans! Samuel
Rabinove, the director of anti-discrimination programs for the
American Jewish Committee, warned against Japanese-American
reparations in this way: "If $25,000 restitution were to be paid
for each of the 120,000 Japanese-Americans incarcerated, what
would be a fair and reasonable sum for each of the 25 million black
Americans who are descended from slaves and who have suffered the
most grievous injustice since Emancipation? What would be a fair
and reasonable sum for each of the one million American Indians
living today for the virtual genocide perpetrated on their peoples?
Any attempts to quantify appropriate reparations for blacks and
Indians simply boggle the mind and quickly become political im-
possibilities. A special reparations payment for one group but not
for the others is difficult to rationalize."[14]

Within that settler debate on Japanese-American reparations
loomed the much larger issue of America's unresolved war with its
New Afrikan colony. It was for this reason that the U.S. ruling class
decided on not merely Japanese-American reparations, but for a **final round** of public settlements of "all other" human rights and territorial claims against the Empire. If need be, the ruling class was going to shove reparations and cash settlements of treaty claims down
the throats of its racist white citizenry.

This policy was advanced, step by step, even during the reactionary Reagan years, precisely because **"human rights" is a ruling
class strategy!** When reparations finally came up for a vote in 1988,
the way had been arranged behind the scenes. Rep. Lowry had with-
drawn his name, so that the bill could be reintroduced as the work
of the Japanese-American congressmen who had at first opposed
it. The Republican Party joined the Democrats on this. While a
fogged-in Ronald Reagan kept wondering why people wanted reparations, and threatened to veto the bill, his White House Chief of
Staff, Howard Baker, and vice-president Bush supported reparations.
It sailed through the Senate by 69 votes for to 27 against, and Reagan
obediently signed it into law.

America needs to look like it has clean hands on colonialism, has to have final settlements on territorial claims. Because human rights is a world issue now. People around the world already know that the USA is a center of injustice and violence-for-profit.

Look at how the U.S. government has been unable to kill the rumors that Americans are adopting Latin American infants to use as organ donors for their white children. This charge was first made by the wife of the president of Honduras, a pro-U.S. death squad pretending to be a nation. Since then it has appeared, despite U.S. protests, in hundreds of newspapers in Asia, Afrika, and all over the world.

Last October, the European Parliament passed a French motion to condemn the U.S. for this inhuman practice. That's a special embarrassment for America, since among the 12 nations of the European Parliament are America's closest NATO allies. Even after the U.S. State Department got the UN Secretary-General Javier Perez de Cuellar to confirm their denial, that this rumor was without any factual basis, the story still spreads and spreads. Washington cannot stop it, because the people of the world believe that this is exactly what "J.R. Ewing" would do.[15]

The U.S. ruling class needs human rights settlements to help America keep its stolen territory. The world balance of power is shifting. Large empires like the USA and USSR are declining faster and faster, and small oppressed nations within them are kicking to be independent. If that's obviously true for Estonia and Armenia and Tibet and Northern Ireland, why isn't it going to be true for Hawaii and Aztlán and New Afrika, too?

Now the U.S. ruling class wants its government to spread some cash around. They want to get people's voluntary-looking consent to U.S. government ownership of Third World land and natural resources. This policy led to the historic 1971 Alaska Native Claims Settlement Act. Without voluntary agreement by the 80,000 Inuit, Aleut, and other natives of Alaska, who are the true owners, the U.S. couldn't safely invest billions to develop the huge Alaskan oil fields.

Just imagine what a small Inuit (whites call them "Eskimos" but that isn't their name) liberation army, with sticks of dynamite, could do to the lonely crude oil pipelines snaking their unguarded way across the arctic tundra. In return for recognizing U.S. sovereignty over their lands and resources, the 80,000 native people got $1 billion, got to set up 13 regional economic development corporations, and got back 44 million acres of arctic territory for themselves (until white people discover something else valuable there).

"Let's Make A Deal!" is the hottest neocolonial operation going in the U.S. Every year there are more cash settlements. Last August, the 1,400 member Puyallup "tribe" whose 1873 reservation included what later became the city of Tacoma, Washington, accepted $162 million and 900 acres of forest and waterfront land to settle their claim to the city.[16] Ironically, when the U.S. army first rounded up the Japanese-Americans in Seattle in 1942, it named its temporary internment camp after the Native peoples—"Puyallup Assembly Center."[17]

There are cases now where the U.S. government is forcing cash on reluctant Native Nations ("Indians"). In California, the U.S. government is urging Yurok peoples to accept $15,000 each in return for renouncing all rights to their reservation. In the Black Hills of South Dakota, a sacred Sioux religious and cultural area that U.S. corporations want to rip up for uranium and other minerals, the U.S. congress has voted the Lakota Nation $1.5 billion as a final settlement. But the struggle goes on, because the Lakota have officially refused the money—they want their land and sovereignty, instead. Did you ever think you'd see the day when white people were trying to force an indigenous nation to take $1.5 billion?

This is why the U.S. ruling class didn't blink an eyelash at the $3–4 billion that Japanese-American reparations will eventually cost. (To save face for Republicans, the Act appropriates only $1.25 billion. That sum is put in a trust and invested, with the interest paid out each year for ten years or more, **limited to** $500 million in any one year. Total payout will be well over $3 billion.) Billy Joe Blob, white neanderthal, scratches his head and can't believe that "colored people" are getting all this money. But the U.S. ruling class knows what it's doing.

WHAT ABOUT NEW AFRIKA?

The struggle for New Afrikan reparations is coming. In fact, last November 25, people watching the Morton Downey, Jr. television talk show saw a free-for-all on the topic of New Afrikan reparations, with guests including reparations organizers and New Afrikan independent presidential candidate Lenora Fulani. The ruling class is stalling for now, saying that Civil Rights has settled all New Afrikan human rights claims. Japanese-Americans get $3 billion-plus, the Puyallup get $162 million, and New Afrikans get Jesse—a low-calorie substitute.

Don't forget: reparations are part of the **preparations**. All these settlements recognizing U.S. sovereignty, all these cash deals showing good-hearted Uncle Sam trying to right old human rights abuses, are setting a scene. They are encircling New Afrika, trying to isolate New Afrika internationally. Why, even former presidents Ford and Carter have said that the U.S. might have to offer Puerto Ricans a showdown "statehood or independence" plebiscite. America ain't offering New Afrika any choices or plebiscites, though, because the Empire has a different solution on the way.

Until 1988, committing genocide wasn't a felony, not even a misdemeanor, in the U.S. It's no coincidence that after stalling for 40 years, the U.S. Senate finally completed ratifying the international genocide treaty at the same session that approved Pribilof Aleut and Japanese-American reparations. For the first time genocide is a Federal crime. We know why the white nation never wanted genocide to be illegal. They put Nazis and Japanese warlords on trial for doing genocide, but were very careful never to make it a crime inside the U.S.—until now, when they feel safely shielded by their human rights and reparations offensive.

On December 9, 1948, the UN General Assembly had passed the pact outlawing genocide, and 97 nations had ratified the treaty. Not the U.S. however, where the genocide treaty was frozen in the U.S. Senate for 40 years. Why? New Afrika, of course!! After the treaty was finally enacted into U.S. law last summer, the *New York Times* admitted: "Senate racists fought it out of fear that Blacks might use it." Behind the story of Japanese-American reparations and settlements of human rights claims, is the unresolved war between America and New Afrika: Independence or Genocide.[18]

ENDNOTES

1. *Chicago Tribune*, August 11, 1988.

2. *NY Amsterdam News*, August 6, 1988.

3. *The Sun*, August 16, 1988.

4. Michi Weglyn, *Years of Infamy* (New York, 1976), p. 274.

5. *Alaska Daily News*, August 5, 1988.

6. *New York Times*, June 27, 1981.

7. *Christian Science Monitor*, September 22, 1981.

8. Ibid.

9. *New York Times*, June 27, 1981.

10. *Los Angeles Times*, August 5, 1988.

11. *New York Times*, June 27, 1981.

12. Full description of how Japanese-American congressmen opposed the Lowry Bill can be found in the *Newsletter* of the National Council for Japanese-American Redress (Chicago).

13. Liz Nakahara, "Shadows of War." *Washington Post*, July 14, 1981.

14. *New York Times*, November 12, 1979.

15. *New York Times*, October 20, 1988.

16. *New York Times*, August 29, 1988.

17. Weglyn, p. 79.

18. *New York Times*, October 18, 1988.

APPENDIX II

STOLEN AT GUNPOINT

Interview with J. Sakai
by Ernesto Aguilar

Ernesto Aguilar: In the early 1980s you wrote *Settlers: Mythology of the White Proletariat,* a book that took a deep historical look at the role of white workers in the lives and histories of oppressed people. Can you break down for listeners what inspired you to write *Settlers* and the most important ideas that you put forward in it?

J. Sakai: Well, I wrote it because at that time—and we're talking about the mid-'70s when I started working on it—it seemed to me that every time there was a struggle or an outbreak of something, or an act of injustice happened, racism, there were always more and more calls to study people of color. More books piling up about us, we're getting funded to do things, but actually, we're not the problem. The problem is white people. So I said "What about them?"

The other thing, of course, is, at the time, I was working in an auto parts plant. As a revolutionary, I had been taught all this stuff about class unity and how white workers and workers of color were going to unite. Except in real life I didn't actually see that. What I saw was there were some good guys who were white, to be sure, but

This interview was conducted on June 17, 2003, and originally aired on the Latino-culture program *Sexto Sol* on KPFT radio in Houston, Texas.

basically the white guys were pretty reactionary and they were always selling us out. So I was trying to figure out where did racism in
the white working class actually begin? Was there a point where they
started selling out or got misled or something?

EA: And where did that lead you?

JS: That led me all the way back to Plymouth Rock! I'm not a historian, or wasn't then. I started reading and figured "Maybe it happened
in the 1930s, before we were born." Or "Maybe it was the 1920s," going back and back. It was like treading water. I never found ground.

I figured out that actually there wasn't any time when the white
working class wasn't white supremacist and racist and essentially
pro-Empire. Yet I couldn't figure, "How did this happen?"

That's when this whole idea came to me, which isn't my idea.
But at the time I knew a lot of African revolutionaries in exile from
Zimbabwe and South Africa, whose people were waging guerilla
wars against the colonial powers. They were always talking about
white people, but they didn't really mean race. They kept using
the term "settlers" and they kept talking about "settler colonialism."
Then I ran into some Palestinians and they talked about the Israelis
that way. It was "settler colonialism," i.e., that European populations
had been imported into these countries to act as the agents for capitalism and for the ruling classes. And at that point, of course, the
light bulb went on over my head and I said, "My god, that describes
Amerika." That's the central idea in *Settlers*—that the U.S. really
isn't a society in which there's different races and we're trying to get
along. That may be true on the surface, but, in its actual history, it's
an Empire of imported European settlers who always were given
special privileges to be the occupation army over all the rest of us.

I can't say that made my book popular, but it certainly raised a
lot of controversy at the time.

EA: Do you think some of the historical points you brought out
were the most important points of the book? Especially when you
look at revolutionary literature, particularly anti-imperialist literature over the past 30 years, 40 years, 50 years even, you don't see

that point brought out as clearly as it was in *Settlers*, which put it in a way that really crystallized it for a lot of people.

JS: In part because it was written at a juncture in history where we were going through all these intense struggles, in the '60s and '70s, and my feeling and I think a lot of people's feeling was, we've waited 400 years for the unity, so if it can't come in 400 years, then how long are we supposed to wait for this stuff? How real is it? Why don't we take a look at this idea instead of just taking it as a given?

And I've gotta tell you that, even in integrated stuff, the difference between different peoples really meant a lot back then. One of the things I tell young people I know who are starting to learn about stuff, is not to believe what's in the history books and television because a lot of it is not true.

EA: Indeed it isn't. To put this in a context for the *gente*, what was Mexican land was settled in the early 1800s and resulted in the U.S. seizing over half of Mexico's land in 1848 with the Treaty of Guadalupe Hidalgo. The places we know as Texas, Califas, Arizona, and many of the other States in the Southwest were ancestrally held by Mexicans, and became part of the United States as part of a forcible campaign to take the land. It isn't taught that way in history books. How was the Amerikan West settled, and how does that differ from popular conceptions you were just mentioning? I can think of, off the top of my head, cowboys and rugged individualism, people coming and settling the land that was just here with buffalo just dancing around and ready for the taking…

JS: The mythology of the West and Southwest is that all this land was empty, and the Europeans came and filled the land because there was hardly anyone there before. And, if they were there, they weren't important because it was a few people, they didn't know what they were doing, or were just wandering around in the sun and so on. No idea is given to the fact that these are whole other nations, whole other societies. The settler invasion, powered by immigration from Europe, and the development of capitalist armies, mechanization and industrialization, over the course of centuries, completely overwhelmed all these other societies on the continent.

The United States is a unique nation because it's always been an Empire. It's never been just a nation of ordinary people. From its very beginnings, it has been an illegitimate nation in the sense that, in order to become a nation, it had to conquer other people, take their land, and enslave them. There literally has been no point in Amerikan history where that wasn't true, because that's the basis of what being Amerikan is—which is, of course, the whole problem in the social character of the question of justice here.

EA: Certainly.

JS: So you see these struggles going on. I remember in the '60s when Reies Tijerina and the Alliance were fighting on the Spanish land grant question in the Southwest. A lot of people had no idea that these grants had ever even existed, or that legal title to much of the land in the Southwest was held, and still is held, by Mexican families and Chicano families. Or that this land was never, ever legally part of the United States in terms of being owned by white business interests. This land was all stolen at gunpoint. Time after time, Reies and his people would hold meetings and produce documents, records from Mexico City, proving all these things. So this whole illusion that the Southwest, for example, was not populated and they just expanded into it, filling the empty space with shopping malls, factories, and whatever they did, is just nonsense. This is just conquest. It's no different than Japan invading China in the 1930s, or any other conquest of Empire. That produces a peculiar dynamic inside Amerika because this is a country where the various citizens, the various parts of the population, their fundamental relationship was formed by war, not by peace. And that still echoes into our lives today.

EA: One of the important things about Reies Tijerina's work around land grants, was that it exposed to a lot of Mexicanos that a lot of the grants and treaties were violated. Not that it's much of a revolutionary concept to a student of history to see that the United States violates land grants and treaties. But it exposed to a lot of young Chicanos and Chicanas that the U.S. doesn't have a good track record at all. I know we're getting into topics of settler colonialism and its implications. Just so we're clear, how does settlerism differ from racism and white supremacy?

JS: That's a good question. Certainly racism is a phenomenon that's worldwide; you have it in Japan and France and Russia and so forth. But what's different here, and in countries like Canada, Israel, South Africa, and other places, is that the European population is not indigenous. The European population actually was imported as part of the process of colonization, to be an army of occupation over the conquered territories and peoples. And that's formed the essential character of the United States as a settler country, so that the question isn't just racism. The question is national divisions between people. For example, the question of self-determination for all colonized peoples always is at the heart of political matters.

During the '60s, there was a lot of revolutionary nationalism. People talked about liberating Aztlán, the whole Southwest. Black revolutionary nationalists talked about liberating a Black nation in the historically Black-majority South, the five States of the Black Belt. And, of course, Indian activists talked about their Native lands.

A lot of people didn't understand what this was about, and viewed this almost as legal questions of "Are you entitled to this territory or that territory." But this isn't a legal question, it's a question of self-determination.

The essence of decolonization is really simple: the oppressor can't decide for the oppressed. In Amerika, that means the white majority has no right to decide for the oppressed. How could that ever be just? It's true they could have the majority of votes—under their system—but I think only Mexican people, indigenous people, Chicanos, various Native American peoples have the right to decide the destiny of the Southwest, because that's theirs. I don't think white people have any vote in it at all. Not because I think there is something wrong with them as a race, but frankly the oppressors have no vote in deciding what the oppressed do with their society and their lives. That's the simplest kind of understanding of decolonization one can have, but it's essential. The revolutionary nationalism that a lot of people in the '60s talked about gets confused when

people look at it today, but it's really all about self-determination for
oppressed people.

EA: I think it is critical what you were saying about the growth of
the Chicano movement in the '60s, and the growth of consciousness
about Aztlán and nationalism itself. Particularly as it relates to Raza,
one of the criticisms I have heard from white theorists is this: although Chicanos identify as opposing the miseducation and genocide unleashed by the colonizing society, our identification—as
Latinos, Chicanos—with historical or cultural icons such as the
Aztec warriors is no better. Of course, this is from academic theorists or whatever else. You've analyzed a lot of these counterinsur-
gencies directed at oppressed people. How should young Chicanos,
in your view, look at this criticism?

JS: Well, all I can say is, as an Asian guy, Bruce Lee was an enormous
cultural divide to us, because, before Bruce Lee, we had no role models. I guess it sounds funny to people today. We had no images. We
weren't on TV or movies. We just weren't there. Although we were
the cooks in the Westerns, where there were almost no Mexicans because I guess they'd been killed. And the Indians were being killed,
but there'd always be one Chinese guy who'd be cooking because
the goddamned cowboys couldn't cook for themselves, I guess. We
had no image of ourselves that was strong.

    Bruce Lee was fantastic, in terms of that. It just made an in-
credible difference, even though there was nothing radical about his
ideas, per se, but culturally it doesn't work like that. A lot of the political correctness theory about who you should identify with or not
is pretty artificial, and a lot of it is worse than artificial.

    This is a long explanation, but if you read *Occupied America* by
Rodolfo Acuña—

EA: Great book!

JS: Great book. It's heavy. Incredibly detailed. Rich. Fantastic. He
talks about Reies Tijerina, and he mentions in a line, "In May and
June 1968, Tijerina participated in the Poor People's Campaign.

There he proved to be an independent leader, threatening to pull the Chicano contingent out unless Black organizers did not treat them better." That's only one sentence. But to somebody who was there, for a lot of us who were there, Reies Tijerina was like a stroke of lightning falling on us. It was just tremendous; meeting him and watching him and the other people from the Alliance, although I think at that time they were calling themselves the Confederation of Free City States.

EA: José Angel Gutiérrez, one of the founders of La Raza Unida Party, calls Reies "the Chicano Malcolm X" for the way he approached his politics and the way he was out front about it.

JS: He was an incredibly strong guy. I heard there's been criticism of him later because he got more conservative or tactical, but back then, it wasn't just that he'd led his men and women to occupy Kit Carson National Park, took over land, and arrested sheriff's deputies and things like that. Their illegal acts are tremendously just. It's just wonderful! And this is the kind of thing you don't get out of these history books.

We're talking around 1968, and those of us who had been through the Civil Rights movement that had brought us into politics, a lot of us were pretty cynical and pretty disillusioned. Things had changed. There was a lot of money to be made in the Civil Rights movement if you wanted to sell out, cater to various interests—political interests and businesses and such. A lot of corruption was starting to take place at the top. Lots of bureaucracy. The Poor People's Campaign is what got Martin Luther King killed because he got out of the straight Civil Rights thing and said "We need to unite all the poor people in Amerika, and I'm calling on everyone to come to Washington, DC and we're just going to take over the DC Mall. We're going to pitch tents and live there until our demands are met. We want an end to the Vietnam War, we want all these things."

King had always very consciously had a policy, which he was public about. He fought local white Southern racists. He did not fight the Federal government. He kept saying he wouldn't fight the Federal government. This is when he decided he had to fight the

Federal government, and he was proposing that all poor people unite in one movement against the government. In my opinion, that's why they killed him. That was too much. He was supposed to be the safe alternative to Malcolm X, but he was turning radical himself.

So even though he'd been assassinated during the preparations, his group went ahead and held a Poor People's Convention. Just imagine a sea of tents taking over the Mall in Washington, which, with the rain and everything else in the middle of the summer, was a sea of mud. Thousands of people were living there and trampling there. And, frankly, conditions were miserable—there was no food. I remember a lot of mornings for adults, there was no food, because the inside Civil Rights bureaucracy had stolen all the money that had been donated for food. Some of the kids would get little boxes of dry cereal, no milk and no fruit. So when we met Reies and he heard about this, he just invited us all, "Bring your kids, come to our place for lunch." He had taken his people out, totally out, he took the Alliance out of the mud. He said we don't have to live like this to make our point. He demanded that they find some place better, and, in fact, they found a private school that was unoccupied during the summer, and got permission for the Chicanos to use it. So hundreds of Chicanos moved in, fired up the kitchen, it was just a tremendous place. It was like a carnival and school. Reies invited us and our kids to come eat lunch. He was an incredible guy.

We were used to these top-down leaders. I don't want to mention any names, but the big leader would appear. He wasn't staying with us, of course. He was staying at a luxury hotel in DC, and literally, I'm not fooling you, a limousine would pull up, and this guy would get out. This guy would get out and have his overalls, but they were brand-new, starched, just taken out of the bag. Brand-new starched white t-shirt. Lead us in a few chants, pop back into his limousine and drive off.

EA: That's messed up!

JS: Y'know, and Tijerina was a one-man leadership type guy, but he interpreted that as meaning, if he wanted everybody to get up for a demonstration at 8, he'd be up at 7. If there wasn't enough food, he'd eat less. And it was just really impressive. Actually one of the things that impressed me about him most is he had this phenomenal memory. You'd talk to him for two minutes. And a week later, you'd meet him. He'd remember your name; he'd remember every word you said, because he was really listening to you. The Crusade for Justice people from Denver, Corky Gonzáles's people?

EA: Yeah?

JS: They were really impressive. There were about 400 of them. They were about half-Chicano, half-Black. I could be wrong, but it seemed to me very much Black, and very shoulder-to-shoulder, very tough group of people.

EA: I've spoken with Jesús Salvador Treviño, a writer who documented a lot of Corky's work, and the Raza Youth Liberation conferences in Denver, and I think one thing he mentioned as he came to consciousness is key to that. He said as he grew up that it was a given that there were Chicanos and oppressed people who were working lawns, going to jail and such, but something he learned from people involved in movements and who talked about history was that they put these things in context. They made sure people understood there is a systemic reason why oppressed people are at lower economic rungs in this society. The reason they're there is not because they're lazy or shiftless or whatever else the education system puts on you. Jesús said Corky brought a lot of these ideas out to so many young people to understand that oppression does not occur in a vacuum, but is deep and historical, and there's a reason for it.

JS: The other thing is—and I really remember this about the Chicano movement of the 1960s and '70s—people really practiced solidarity between oppressed peoples that you hear some people talk about, but sometimes it is more lip service than real. When AIM did the takeover at Wounded Knee, and got surrounded by the U.S. Army and had the siege and got shot up and everything? The largest demonstration in the U.S. was in Denver supporting them. The only large one, and it was the Crusade for Justice, it was mostly Chicano.

When Affirmative Action first started getting attacked in California in the early '80s—the law school I think it was at Berkeley ended the quota for Asian Americans, and the Chicanos offered to give part of their slots to Asians to fight for the principle of representation. And a lot of that spirit has been lost.

There's this thing that's happening; what used to be militant politics against systemic injustice, against capitalism as a system, has turned into ethnic politics for a lot of people, with the veneer of seeming to be militant, protesting about this and that, but underneath it is an attitude of "we should just look out for ourselves. We really shouldn't care about anybody but ourselves. And as for everyone else, we should say nice things, but potentially they could be an enemy, so we really should only think of us." I know that Asians are told that by conservative forces in our communities, and certainly Black people are told this, because it's the Amerikan way to subvert militant consciousness in people's movements by trying to make them more capitalist.

Jefferson tried to do that with the Indians in the Iroquois Confederacy. He sent them messages saying, "You should join the United States. You're good people, we want to get together with you, but your laws aren't any good. That's why we need to bring you into our country instead of just leaving you in your country, because your laws don't protect private property. You share everything in common." And although he didn't say it, of course, he knew in the Iroquois Confederacy that women had tremendous legal powers under their laws and government. You couldn't have a war unless three-quarters of the mothers, women who had borne children, voted for the war, for example, under their laws. No men could vote for war. This was the indigenous way of having a society that Jefferson thought was really crazy. "You really need to join us, have our laws, which protect private property, you can get rich, and you'll like it much better." Of course, what he really meant was, "we want to take you over and, if you don't have private property, you can't sell us everything you have, which we want you to do. So we're going to get you to do this or we're going to shoot you, one or the other." Which is their standard approach to these things, as we can see in Afghanistan and Iraq.

EA: I was about to mention that!

JS: They're bringing democracy to Iraq, only they don't seem to be doing a good job of it right now.

EA: You see a lot of mounting resistance.

JS: The thing is, they're invading the whole world essentially, and it's true they can conquer any part of it they want to, but that doesn't mean people are going to like them, or put up with it, or not resist. Of course people are going to resist, from all kinds of points of view. I don't think this is ever going to end until they leave. That's actually what I think. And I think the same thing is true for Amerika. I don't think there is any solution to any of these problems until Amerika is desettlerized.

EA: One question from a listener is: How do we "desettlerize" a country like the U.S. or Israel? Especially in a place like the U.S. where many righteous national liberation movements, such as the Black/New Afrikan and the Chicano movements especially, overlap and may contradict Native land claims and national liberation?

JS: I don't think any of us are going to have problems solving our relations with each other as long as we get the U.S. Empire and capitalist rip-offs out of the way. There is plenty of land in Amerika. Everyone could live here who lives here, quite well, with a lot of autonomy, a lot of justice, a lot of room for expression and development. But the obstacle isn't each other, in that sense.

As for desettlerization, it's already happening, because settlerism is a phenomenon of the past, really. All over the world, settler societies, as we saw in Africa, are going out of business. In Algeria, which was officially a province of France until the 1950s revolution, you had a million French settlers living there, and virtually the whole of the French army occupying it. Finally they all had to leave. Yeah, Algeria has a lot of problems, but it is Algerian.

I don't think that's going to happen here, obviously, because there's no place for that kind of migration to happen. But desettlerization isn't happening that way. Like in Israel, the problem is not that Jewish people live in Palestine. The problem is there are special laws, unjust laws, that deny land to Palestinians who live there while, of course, giving land to Zionists, even though they may have no connection whatsoever to Palestine that anybody can prove, except they say they follow the Jewish religion. They come from Russia, they come from Brooklyn, they come from wherever.

People look at Amerika and they don't see how Amerika could be desettlerized, but it's being desettlerized right now.

It's funny. The place where I work, the other guys who work there are Mexican. They're not Chicano, they're Mexican. First-generation. This is not their home—their home is back in Mexico. Very conservative family people in a social way. More conservative than I am, for sure. They're exactly the kind of Mexicans that the Republican Party and Bush are aiming at as the ideal minority. In fact, some of the guys voted for Bush, because he sounded like a better leader or something. So they're not radical in any political sense whatsoever.

But it's interesting when you talk to them about Amerika. They don't believe in the United States. At all. What they think is that the United States and Mexico are really just one country. To them it isn't just Aztlán. It isn't just the Southwest. It's that, there's Mexico, which is, to them, a special place, a really good place. Too poor, but a good place. As they say, "It has everything but money." And then there's Amerika. Lots of different people live here. They think that's great, and just how it should be. But, they've noticed this funny thing. And I don't want to insult anybody, but the way they look at it, Amerikans don't like to work. We're in the wealthy suburbs, and there are Mexicans all over the place, of course. All the landscaping, porters, guys unloading trucks, people laying masonry for the patios, all the workers are Mexican. So their view is they don't quite understand Amerika, but they've figured out one thing: real Amerikans aren't into working. They don't understand it, but okay, fine by them. To them, there's this huge land, which frankly needs them, because they're the people who are going to do the work. They actually don't believe in a separate United States in any real sense of the word—immigration laws, borders. They think that's nonsense.

It isn't just because of the legal history, but really, to them, it's their country as much as it is anyone else's. And they're not nationalistic in any narrow sense about it. They talk about the fact that, "Yeah, Mexican guys live here." One guy knows a guy who married a Polish woman, who immigrated from Poland, and he thinks that's great. But to them, Amerika doesn't belong to the people who call themselves Amerikans. That's where they differ from the Republicans and George Bush. They're part of the actual reversal of the Treaty of Guadalupe Hidalgo that's going on, only it's happening in a very postmodern way. It isn't simply reversal in terms of the Southwest. Clearly the whole character of the Southwest is changing year by year.

I'm in the Midwest, and when the Mexican Consulate said it was going to issue ID cards so that people could get bank accounts and everything else, we literally had a traffic jam. There were 10,000 people lined up on the main business street. Completely bizarre. And all the right-wingers are having fits! They're writing letters to the newspaper saying, "This Mexican ID card is as good as an Amerikan birth certificate. How can we let this happen?" But the logic of modern globalized life is that they have to. The banks want bank accounts with this money in it, so they want these people to have consular IDs, which aren't Amerikan in any way whatsoever. You can just see, year by year, the whole shift starting to happen socially, culturally. It has to happen in a political sense, of course, and it hasn't yet. But you certainly can see the underlying migration that is a migration not just geographically, but is changing politics just as surely as when Black people left the South and immigrated to the Northern industrial cities, or when we Asians came to Hawaii and the West Coast in the nineteenth century.

EA: Is that how you see desettlerization working, where you see this migration of peoples? It sounds like that is how it is working in practice in the Midwest, and historically how it has worked in the South as well as the Northeast—would you say that is how desettlerization will happen in the United States over the next few years?

JS: That's the underlying historical thing that will happen, but it isn't going to deal with the whole political struggle, which we're now engaged in, because, of course, the white settler population has essentially had a historic 400-year pact with capitalism, which is that they will get the best of everything. Maybe that won't be a lot, but it will be the best of the little. They will get the best of everything that is available in return for supporting capitalism and the U.S. Empire and its conquest over other people, as well as its exploitation. Well, frankly, globalization and the desettlerization of North America is threatening that. How long can you have a population in which more and more people don't actually work? I mean, you say the word "welfare" in Amerika and everybody's supposed to picture a Black woman in a housing project. But the real welfare is for white middle-class people. You have entire office buildings and cities full of people who don't actually produce anything. They move paper around, they bill people, they do things, but they don't actually produce anything. Everything that is produced is produced somewhere else by somebody else. And the question is how long can that be maintained?

I would say it's breaking down even now. It certainly is in Europe, and that's why there are fascist movements and all this right-wing stuff happening in Europe. Because the social compact is breaking down, and it's going to happen here too. And the political struggle is not going to happen peacefully, in the sense that it's not going to be some gradual social process. The underlying economics are one thing. The political struggle over who gets what out of that and whether there will be a just society or not is a whole other question.

EA: Another question from the audience: What are some of the biggest misconceptions about your writing, and how do you respond to some of the critics who have written about your writing?

JS: Actually, although I've heard a lot of criticism, there hasn't been a lot of writing criticizing it. I always tell people I don't have a problem with criticism, just write down factually where the mistakes are and we can argue about that. At that point, people disappear, because they can't seem to locate those things.

I'd say the biggest misconception, though, is that people think I'm talking about race alone, that everything in Amerika is determined by race, and that's not really what I'm saying. What I'm saying is that race in Amerika has been used as an identifier for capitalism to form and control classes, that race is not just a metaphor for class, but an identifier of class in real terms. So that everything is upside-down—things that are racial are really about class. Like Affirmative Action. The real Affirmative Action is the enormous built-in advantages that white middle-class people, particularly from the suburban school systems have, that get them into universities, and getting corporate jobs and networking. Everybody knows this. It's not a big deal. It's just a fact, right? So that's the actual Affirmative Action. These other programs are really to compensate for that, and are just the warped forms that the Civil Rights victories of the 1960s forced upon the society. I mean, I don't personally view them as significant. The fight over them really is, in a funny way, a fight within settler society, within imperialism itself, over how it's going to manage itself.

In the University of Michigan case, where Bush—supposedly on the advice of Condoleezza Rice, his African American advisor—weighed in on the side opposing the university's Affirmative Action policy. All of a sudden, the three former Joint Chiefs of Staff, former heads of West Point and the Naval Academy, as well as General Motors, Microsoft, and dozens of other major corporations all filed briefs supporting Affirmative Action. So we're not in this fight actually. This is a pure ruling class fight, having it out with each other. That's what's interesting about it—it's their problem.

Since it originally arose over law school—not something I would ever myself want to do, nor would I urge any sane person to do—I really couldn't care less.

EA: Another question from the audience: To what extent does this analysis depart from traditional Marxism that reduces everything to class? Where does your analysis relate to or differ from anti-racist feminism as presented by people like Gloria Anzaldúa, who argue that all systems of oppression are connected in some way?

JS: To the last, I really agree. All systems of oppression are connected. The difficulty is in figuring out what these connections are.

Part of the problem I have with anti-racist feminism is that a lot of it is very middle class, and it's used to actually muddy the question of oppression, i.e., suddenly everybody's oppression is equal. Well, actually, everybody's oppression isn't equal, and I tend to be very concrete about those things myself.

EA: Thank you!

JS: Growing up in a Japanese American family, you've been to camp. When I was a little kid, people talked about camp, "going to camp," "this happened at camp." When I was a kid, I didn't know that—and this happened in everyone's family—it was a way of talking about being in the concentration camps without being blunt and saying it, so if you were overheard by the kids, then they won't know what you were talking about. I didn't actually find out about concentration camps until white people started stopping me on the street and giving me various explanations of why I shouldn't blame them for it. When I was a young kid. I can't count the number of people who told me, "That wasn't a real concentration camp you and your family were in. That was the Jews in Germany. They got killed. That was the real concentration camp. You weren't really in a concentration camp." Oh, thanks.

Actually, I would never say—I've never met a Japanese-American who said—what we went through was anything like what the Jews in Europe went through under Nazism. Literally never heard anybody even hint that that could be true, because that would be crazy. You'd have to be a nut to think that. But it doesn't mean what we went through wasn't real. It doesn't mean that there weren't terrible human losses out of it. It doesn't mean that the reparations program that Ronald Reagan and Bill Clinton did isn't just a piece of junk, in my opinion, compared to what happened. And is not any actual reparations or justice.

There's this funny thing where middle-class people are always inventing trendy ways to be oppressed, in which their oppression is somehow just as real as yours. I don't think so, but it's not my appointed task in life to argue with them.

I do think, and this is true, that because the interconnection of oppressions is something we still don't understand real well. Like a lot of people were having this political fight over Oliver Stone's movie *JFK*? It was supposed to be so radical because it says he was killed by a conspiracy? Well, it's this complete piece of junk. Who were the conspirators? I was sitting in this movie and couldn't believe what I was seeing. The conspirators were this group of gay, stereotyped, mincing kind of queens, who, at one point, even wore dresses. So, gay people were the conspiracy that killed JFK?! This is the progressive, radical, threatening movie? Gimme a break. It's nothing but homophobic junk. If you really wanted to have a movie in which you really showed the people who killed JFK, they'd be white guys wearing three-piece suits, sitting in corporate boardrooms and hanging out at the Pentagon. They wouldn't be gay people from Latin America. The fact that that could go over in Amerika without people burning down movie theaters shows how deeply ingrained the homophobia in this society is, for real.

EA: Can you give people an idea of some of the things you're up to?

JS: Well, along with some other comrades, I've been working on trying to better understand the whole new popular wave of far right-wing politics and fascism in the world, because, to us, that's the new threatening phenomenon happening. Not just in Europe, but here, in India, etc. You've always got to watch the new semi trailer coming up in your rearview mirror, threatening to drive you off the road.

PHOTO CREDITS

Cover. Top: "Detroit, Michigan. Riot at the Sojourner Truth homes, a new U.S. federal housing project, caused by white neighbors' attempt to prevent Negro tenants from moving in. Sign with American flag 'We want white tenants in our white community,' directly opposite the housing project." Arthur S. Sigel, 1942. Library of Congress (LOC) LC-USW3-016549-C. Bottom: Kids in west side lot toss a few bricks. Ed Ford, 1962. LOC LC-USZ62-122639.

6. "Plymouth in 1622." W.L. Williams, 1901? LOC LC-USZC4-4992.

11. "Massacre of the St. Francis Indians." 1883. LOC LC-USZ62-55118.

31. Illustration captioned "Bacon Demanding His Commission," subcaptioned "from the painting by Kelley" from page 104 of J.A.C. Chandler's Makers of Virginia History (New York: Silver, Burdett & Co., 1904). Wikimedia Commons.

48 Left: Detail, "Le Gal. Toussaint-L'Ouverture remettant au Gal anglais..." LOC LC-USZ62-7860. Right: "[Haiti - Revolution, 1791-1804] Revenge taken by the Black Army for the cruelties practised...by the French." 1805. LOC LC-USZ62-49048.

61. "The Trail of Tears," painted by Robert Lindneux in 1942. (Woolaroc Museum, Bartlesville, Oklahoma)

69. Detail, "The riots at New York." 1863. LOC LC-USZ62-89865.

77. "Chinese fishing village—Monterey." ca. 1907. LOC LC-USZ62-90223.

83. "Colorado—the anti-Chinese riot in Denver, on October 31st..." 1880. LOC LC-USZC2-760.

97. "Scenes in Memphis, Tennessee, during the riot—burning down a freedmen's school-house; Shooting down negroes on the morning of May 2, 1866." Creator: Alfred R. Waud. Tennessee State Library and Archives.

99. Illustration of newspaper article "Louisiana and the rule of terror: portr. of Julia Hayden..." 1874. LOC LC-USZ62-55606.

105. "Leaders of the Knights of Labor." Kurz & Allison, ca. 1886. LOC LC-DIG-pga-01926.

112. "The U.S. Hotel badly needs a 'bouncer.'" Joseph Ferdinand Keppler, 1883. LOC LC-DIG-ppmsca-28375.

118. "Suffragettes parading with banner 'President Wilson favors votes for women.'" ca.1916. LOC LC-USZ62-38965.

119. "Georgia convicts working on a road in Oglethorpe County." Jack Delano, 1941. LOC LC-USF33-020862-M1.

130. "Katipuneros." 1898. Wikimedia Commons.

131. Detail, "Three dead 'insurgents' lying on battlefield during the Philippine insurrection." ca. 1899. LOC LC-USZ62-100490.

142. Top: "Factory workers assembling engines at Leland & Faulconer Manufacturing Co., Detroit, Mich." 1903? LOC LC-DIG-det-4a26764. Bottom: "Some, but only a small part, of the workers who pick shrimp in the Biloxi Canning Factory..." Lewis Wickes Hine, 1911. LOC LC-USZ6-1154.

151. "Many peoples—one nation. Let us unite to Americanize America." Ray Greenleaf, 1917. LOC LC-USZC4-7389.

168. "Family leaving damaged home after 1919 Chicago race riot." New York Public library, Schomburg Center for Research in Black Culture. Digital ID: 1217208.

180. "Strikers guarding window entrance to Fisher body plant number three. Flint, Michigan." Sheldon Dick, 1937. LOC LC-USF34-040028-D.

192. "Ponce Massacre." Carlos Torres Morales, a photo journalist for the newspaper El Imparcial, 1937. Wikimedia Commons.

193. "Relatives of Nationalists killed in the Ponce massacre in front of Nationalist Party headquarters. Machine gun bullet holes in the wall." Edwin Rosskam, 1937. LOC LC-USF34-012572-E.

197. "Street corner, Black Belt, Chicago, Illinois." Edwin Rosskam, 1941. LOC LC-DIG-ppmsca-01595.

224. "San Francisco (Calif.) evacuation—a family starts for the bus that will take them from the control station to the train depot." Signal Corps U.S. Army, 1942. LOC LC-USZ62-133825.

226. "Zoot suiters lined up outside Los Angeles jail en route to court after feud with sailors." 1943. LOC LC-USZ62-113319.

228. "United States Department of the Interior advertisement offering 'Indian Land for Sale'. The man pictured is a Yankton Sioux named Not Afraid Of Pawnee." 1911. Wikimedia Commons.

235. "Turpentine worker's family near Cordele, Alabama..." Dorothea Lange, 1936. LOC LC-USF34-T01-009425-E.

246. "Parkin (vicinity), Arkansas. The families of evicted sharecroppers from the Dibble plantation..." John Vachon, 1936. LOC LC-USF34-014007-E.

254. "Evicted sharecroppers along Highway 60, New Madrid County, Missouri" Arthur Rothstein, 1939. LOC LC-DIG-fsa-8a10602.

259. "Parkin (vicinity), Arkansas. The families of evicted sharecroppers of the Dibble plantation. They were legally evicted the week of January 12, 1936..." John Vachon, 1936. LOC LC-DIG-fsa-8b30944.

260. "Booker T. Washington..." Between 1890 and 1910. LOC LC-USZ62-119898.

263. "Marcus Garvey, 1887–1940." 1924. LC-USZ61-1854.

268. "Washington, D.C. Portrait of A. Philip Randolph, labor leader." 1942. LOC LC-USW3- 011696-C.

274. BSCP strike notice, Detroit, June 7, 1928. Original in Chicago Historical Society.

275. BSCP strike cancellation notice, Detroit, June 8, 1928. Original in Chicago Historical Society.

277. "Mrs. Eleanor Roosevelt and others at the opening of Midway Hall..." 1939. Wikimedia Commons.

286. "Production. Willow Run bomber plant..." Ann Rosener, 1942. LOC LC-DIG-fsa-8e11160.

287. "A good job in the air cleaner of an army truck, Fort Knox, Ky..." Alfred T. Palmer, 1942. LOC LC-DIG-fsac-1a35222.

302. "Robert Thompson and Benjamin Davis surrounded by pickets as they leave the Federal Courthouse in New York City." C.M. Stieglitz, 1949. LOC LC-USZ62-111434.

305. "Residential section, middle income class, Dubuque, Iowa." John Vachon, 1940. LOC LC-USF33-T01-001712-M3.

324. "297 of 366" by mjtmail (tiggy), 2012. Flickr. CC by 2.0.

326. "3rd world factory." Ironchefbalara, 2009. Flickr. CC by 2.0.

331. "Farm in Chimaltenango, Guatemala." World Bank Photo Collection, 2009. Flickr. CC BY-NC-ND 2.0.

332. "Seagate's Clean Room." Robert Scoble, 2008. Flickr. CC by 2.0.

336. "Sweatshops across the world." Marissaorton, 2008. Flickr. CC BY-SA 2.0.

338. Top: Apollo 11 moon landing. NASA, 1969. Bottom: "Boy at La Chureca, the community of people who live and work at the Managua city garbage dump." eren {sea+prairie}, 2008. Flickr. CC BY-SA 2.0.

342. "Steel workers forming a rebar cage." Washington State Department of Transportation, 2011. CC BY-NC-ND 2.0.

343. "Day 84—West Midlands Police—Archived photo of Resource Allocator and Despatchers." West Midland Police, 2012. Flickr. CC BY-SA 2.0.

345. "Building Trades Unemployment Insurance Rally." Bernard Pollack, 2009. Flickr. CC by 2.0.

355. "Guns and Sheets South Eastern Ohio, KKK." Paul M. Walsh, 1987. Flickr. CC BY-SA 2.0.

365. Detail, "Batman anti-racism." From DC publication "A Date With Judy" 1949. Uploaded to Flickr by Luis Daniel Carbia Cabeza, 2011. CC BY 2.0.

414. Top: "The population of the Aleutians..." V.B. Scheffer, 1938. LOC LC-USW33-029785-C. Bottom: "WWII Aleutians Campaign, circa 1945." Uploaded to Flickr by somethingsally. CC BY-SA 2.0.

418. "17.EasterMonday.Street.WDC.17apr06." Elvert Barnes, 2006. Flickr. CC by 2.0.

PM Press was founded at the end of 2007 by a small collection of folks with decades of publishing, media, and organizing experience. PM Press co-conspirators have published and distributed hundreds of books, pamphlets, CDs, and DVDs.

Members of PM have founded enduring book fairs, spearheaded victorious tenant organizing campaigns, and worked closely with bookstores, academic conferences, and even rock bands to deliver political and challenging ideas to all walks of life. We're old enough to know what we're doing and young enough to know what's at stake.

PM Press is always on the lookout for talented and skilled volunteers, artists, activists, and writers to work with. If you have a great idea for a project or can contribute in some way, please get in touch.

PM Press
P.O. Box 23912
Oakland, CA 94623

www.pmpress.org

FRIENDS OF PM PRESS

These are indisputably momentous times—the financial system is melting down globally and the Empire is stumbling. Now more than ever there is a vital need for radical ideas. Friends of PM allows you to directly help impact, amplify, and revitalize the discourse and actions of radical writers, filmmakers, and artists. It provides us with a stable foundation from which we can build upon our early successes and provides a much-needed subsidy for the materials that can't necessarily pay their own way. You can help make that happen—and receive every new title automatically delivered to your door once a month—by joining as a Friend of PM Press. And, we'll throw in a free T-shirt when you sign up.

Here are your options:

- **$30 a month** Get all books and pamphlets plus 50% discount on all webstore purchases
- **$40 a month** Get all PM Press releases (including CDs and DVDs) plus 50% discount on all webstore purchases
- **$100 a month** Superstar—Everything plus PM merchandise, free downloads, and 50% discount on all webstore purchases

For those who can't afford $30 or more a month, we're introducing Sustainer Rates at $15, $10, and $5. Sustainers get a free PM Press T-shirt and a 50% discount on all purchases from our website.

Your Visa or Mastercard will be billed once a month, until you tell us to stop. Or until our efforts succeed in bringing the revolution around. Or the financial meltdown of Capital makes plastic redundant. Whichever comes first.

PUBLISHED BY PM PRESS

Modern Politics
by C.L.R. James • Edited by Noel Ignatiev
PM Press/Charles H. Kerr 2013
978-1-60486-311-6
176 Pages • $16.95

A History of Pan-African Revolt
by C.L.R. James
Introduction by Robin D.G. Kelley
PM Press/Charles H. Kerr 2012
978-1-60486-095-5
160 Pages • $16.95

State Capitalism and World Revolution
by C.L.R. James, Raya Dunayevskaya, and
Grace Lee Boggs
Introduction by Paul Buhle
Preface by Martin Glaberman
PM Press/Charles H. Kerr 2013
978-1-60486-092-4
160 Pages • $16.95

**A New Notion: Two Works by
C.L.R. James: "Every Cook Can Govern"
and "The Invading Socialist Society"**
by C.L.R. James • Edited by Noel Ignatiev
PM Press/Charles H. Kerr 2010
978-1-60486-047-4
160 Pages • $16.95

PUBLISHED BY PM PRESS

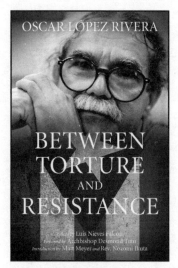

Oscar Lopez Rivera:
Between Torture and Resistance
by Oscar López Rivera
PM Press 2013
978-1-60486-685-8
160 Pages • $15.95

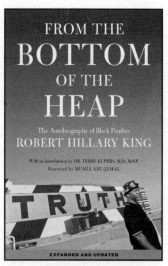

From the Bottom of the Heap:
The Autobiography of Black Panther
Robert Hillary King
by Robert Hillary King
PM Press 2012
978-1-60486-575-2
272 Pages • $17.95

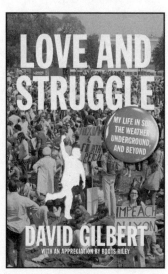

Love and Struggle: My Life in SDS,
the Weather Underground, and Beyond
by David Gilbert
PM Press 2012
978-1-60486-319-2
352 Pages • $22.00

Maroon the Implacable: The Collected
Writings of Russell Maroon Shoatz
by Russell Maroon Shoatz
PM Press 2013
978-1-60486-059-7
312 Pages • $20.00

Turning Money into Rebellion: The Unlikely Story of Denmark's Revolutionary Bank Robbers

Edited by Gabriel Kuhn

Foreword by Klaus Viehmann

ISBN: 9781604863161

240 pages • paperback • $19.95

Blekingegade is a quiet street in Copenhagen. It is also where, in May 1989, the police discovered an apartment that had served Denmark's most notorious twentieth-century bank robbers as a hideaway for years.

One of the most captivating chapters from the European anti-imperialist milieu of the 1970s and '80s; the Blekingegade Group had emerged from a communist organization whose analysis of the metropolitan labor aristocracy led them to develop an illegal Third Worldist practice. While members lived modest lives, over a period of almost two decades they sent millions of dollars acquired in spectacular heists to Third World liberation movements.

Turning Money into Rebellion *includes historical documents, illustrations, and an exclusive interview with Torkil Lauesen and Jan Weimann, two of the group's longest-standing members. It is a compelling tale of turning radical theory into action and concerns analysis and strategy as much as morality and political practice. Perhaps most importantly, it revolves around the cardinal question of revolutionary politics: What to do, and how to do it?*

> "This book is a fascinating and bracing account of how a group of communists in Denmark sought to aid the peoples of the Third World in their struggles against imperialism and the dire poverty that comes with it. The book contains many valuable lessons as to the practicalities of effective international solidarity, but just as importantly, it is a testament to the intellectual courage of the Blekingegade Group."
>
> —Zak Cope, author of *Divided World Divided Class: Global Political Economy and the Stratification of Labour Under Capitalism*

ANTI-COLONIAL WRITINGS & ARTWORK BY GORD HILL

500 YEARS OF INDIGENOUS RESISTANCE	500 YEARS OF RESISTANCE COMIC BOOK	THE ANTI-CAPITALIST RESISTANCE COMIC BOOK
PM PRESS 2010	ARSENAL PULP PRESS 2010	ARSENAL PULP PRESS 2013
ISBN 9781604861068	ISBN 9781551523606	ISBN 9781551524443
96 PAGES • $10.00	87 PAGES • $12.95	96 PAGES • $12.95

WARRIORPUBLICATIONS.WORDPRESS.COM

Warrior Publications is published in occupied Coast Salish territory (Vancouver, Canada). Its purpose is to promote warrior culture, fighting spirit, and resistance movements.

In addition, this website seeks to function as an historical archive of Indigenous anti-colonial struggles and resistance, and to provide analysis of these struggles.

Warrior Publications is maintained by Gord Hill (Kwakwaka'wakw nation), who frequently writes under the pseudonym Zig Zag.

To contact Warrior Publications, you can email: zig_zag48@hotmail.com

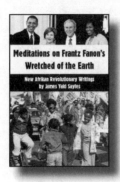

Meditations on Frantz Fanon's Wretched of the Earth: New Afrikan Revolutionary Writings

by James Yaki Sayles

ISBN: 978-1-894946-32-2 • 399 pages • $20.00

One of those who eagerly picked up Fanon in the '60s, who carried out armed expropriations and violence against white settlers, Sayles reveals how, behind the image of Fanon as race thinker, there is an underlying reality of antiracist communist thought.

Stand Up Struggle Forward: New Afrikan Revolutionary Writings On Nation, Class And Patriarchy

by Sanyika Shakur

ISBN: 978-1-894946-46-9 • 208 pages • $13.95

A collection of writings by Sanyika Shakur, formerly known as Monster Kody Scott, including several essays written from within the infamous Pelican Bay Security Housing Unit in the period around the historic 2011 California prisoners' hunger strike, as well as two interviews conducted just before and after his release in Black August 2012.

Divided World Divided Class: Global Political Economy and the Stratification of Labour Under Capitalism

by Zak Cope

ISBN: 978-1-894946-41-4 • 385 pages • $20.00

*Demonstrating not only how redistribution of income derived from super-exploitation has allowed for the amelioration of class conflict in the wealthy capitalist countries, **Divided World Divided Class** also shows that the exorbitant "super-wage" paid to workers there has meant the disappearance of a domestic vehicle for socialism, an exploited working class. Rather, in its place is a deeply conservative metropolitan workforce committed to maintaining, and even extending, its privileged position through imperialism.*

Basic Politics of Movement Security
"A Talk on Security" by J. Sakai &
"G20 Repression & Infiltration in Toronto:
An Interview with Mandy Hiscocks"
ISBN: 978-1-894946-52-0 • 2014 • 72 pages • $7.00

There are many books and articles reporting state repression, but not on that subject's more intimate relative, movement security. It is general practice to only pass along knowledge about movement security privately, in closed group lectures or by personal word-of-mouth. Adding to the confusion, the handful of available left security texts are usually about underground or illegal groups, not the far larger public movements that work on a more or less legal level. Based on their own personal experiences on this terrain, these two "live" discussions by radical activists provide a partial remedy to this situation.

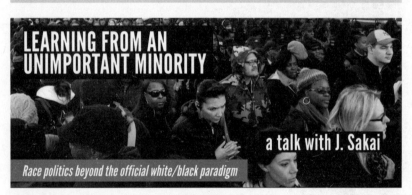

Learning from an Unimportant Minority:
Race Politics Beyond the Black/White Paradigm
ISBN: 978-1-894946-60-5 • due out in early 2015

Race is all around us, as one of the main structures of capitalist society. Yet, how we talk about it and even how we think about it is tightly policed. Everything about race is artificially distorted as a White/Black paradigm. Instead, we need to understand the imposed racial reality from many different angles of radical vision. In this talk given at the 2014 Montreal Anarchist Bookfair, J. Sakai shares experiences from his own life as a revolutionary in the united states, exploring what it means to belong to an "unimportant minority."